PSYCHOLOGY LIBRARY EDITIONS: COGNITIVE SCIENCE

Volume 9

NEO-PIAGETIAN THEORIES OF COGNITIVE DEVELOPMENT

NEO-PIAGETIAN THEORIES OF COGNITIVE DEVELOPMENT

Implications and applications for education

Edited by
ANDREAS DEMETRIOU, MICHAEL SHAYER
AND ANASTASIA EFKLIDES

LONDON AND NEW YORK

First published in 1992 by Routledge

This edition first published in 2017
by Routledge
2 Park Square, Milton Park, Abingdon, Oxon OX14 4RN

and by Routledge
711 Third Avenue, New York, NY 10017

Routledge is an imprint of the Taylor & Francis Group, an informa business

© 1992 Andreas Demetriou, Michael Shayer and Anastasia Efklides: the collection as a whole; individual chapters; the contributors.

All rights reserved. No part of this book may be reprinted or reproduced or utilised in any form or by any electronic, mechanical, or other means, now known or hereafter invented, including photocopying and recording, or in any information storage or retrieval system, without permission in writing from the publishers.

Trademark notice: Product or corporate names may be trademarks or registered trademarks, and are used only for identification and explanation without intent to infringe.

British Library Cataloguing in Publication Data
A catalogue record for this book is available from the British Library

ISBN: 978-1-138-19163-1 (Set)
ISBN: 978-1-315-54401-4 (Set) (ebk)
ISBN: 978-1-138-19159-4 (Volume 9) (hbk)
ISBN: 978-1-138-19162-4 (Volume 9) (pbk)
ISBN: 978-1-315-64037-2 (Volume 9) (ebk)

Publisher's Note
The publisher has gone to great lengths to ensure the quality of this reprint but points out that some imperfections in the original copies may be apparent.

Disclaimer
The publisher has made every effort to trace copyright holders and would welcome correspondence from those they have been unable to trace.

Neo-Piagetian theories of cognitive development

Piagetian theory was once considered able to describe the structure and development of human thought. As a result, it generated an enthusiasm that it could direct education to develop new teaching methods, particularly in science and mathematics. However, disillusionment with Piagetian theory came rather quickly because many of its structural and developmental assumptions appeared incongruent with empirical evidence.

In recent years several neo-Piagetian theories have been proposed which try to preserve the strengths of Piaget's theory, while eliminating its weaknesses. At the same time several other models have been advanced originating from different epistemological traditions, such as cognitive/differential psychology or socio-historical approaches.

Neo-Piagetian Theories of Cognitive Development is unique in representing most of these theories and traditions. Specifically, the authors focus their work on the educational implications of their research. The chapters are organized in three parts: the first part presents some widely known models of cognitive development and discusses their implications for different aspects of education; the second part is devoted to learning and cognitive acceleration; while part three highlights teaching methods that would improve the acquisition of particular skills in specific areas.

Written by an eminent group of truly international contributors, *Neo-Piagetian Theories of Cognitive Development* will be invaluable to students and researchers in cognitive development and education, as well as educational policy makers.

Andreas Demetriou is Professor of Developmental Psychology at the Aristotelian University of Thessaloniki; **Michael Shayer** is Lecturer in Psychology at King's College, University of London; **Anastasia Efklides** is Professor of Psychology at the Aristotelian University of Thessaloniki.

Neo-Piagetian theories of cognitive development

Implications and applications for education

Edited by Andreas Demetriou,
Michael Shayer, and Anastasia Efklides

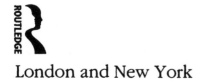

London and New York

First published in 1992 by
Routledge
11 New Fetter Lane, London EC4P 4EE

Simultaneously published in the USA and Canada by
Routledge
a division of Routledge, Chapman and Hall Inc.
29 West 35th Street, New York, NY 10001

© 1992 Andreas Demetriou, Michael Shayer, and
Anastasia Efklides: the collection as a whole;
individual chapters: the contributors.

Typeset in Garamond by LaserScript Limited, Mitcham, Surrey
Printed and bound in Great Britain by
Mackays of Chatham PLC, Chatham, Kent

All rights reserved. No part of this book may be reprinted or
reproduced or utilized in any form or by any electronic,
mechanical, or other means, now known or hereafter invented,
including photocopying and recording, or in any information
storage or retrieval system, without permission in writing
from the publishers.

British Library Cataloguing in Publication Data
A catalogue record for this book is available from the
British Library.

Library of Congress Cataloging in Publication Data
Neo-Piagetian theories of cognitive development/
  edited by Andreas Demetriou, Michael Shayer, and Anastasia Efklides.
  p. cm. – (International library of psychology)
Chiefly papers presented at three symposia held
at the 3rd European Conference for Research on Learning and Instruction,
held in Madrid, in September 1989.
Includes bibliographical references and index.
1. Cognition in children – Congresses. 2. Constructivism
(Education) – Congresses. 3. Piaget, Jean, 1896– – Congresses.
I. Demetriou, Andreas. II. Shayer, Michael. III. Efklides,
Anastasia. IV. Series.
BF723.C5N44 1992
155.4'13 – dc20   92-12220
                                                                  CIP

ISBN 0–415–05471–0

Contents

List of figures and tables vii
List of contributors x
Foreword xii
Introduction 1

Part I General principles of cognitive organization and change and implications for education

1 Cognitive development in educational contexts: implications of skill theory 11
  Thomas R. Bidell and Kurt W. Fischer

2 Modes of learning, forms of knowing, and ways of schooling 31
  John B. Biggs

3 The role of central conceptual structures in the development of children's scientific and mathematical thought 52
  Robbie Case

4 Social organization of cognitive development: internalization and externalization of constraint systems 65
  Jaan Valsiner

5 Structural systems in developing cognition, science, and education 79
  Andreas Demetriou, Jan-Eric Gustafsson, Anastasia Efklides, and Maria Platsidou

Part II Inducing cognitive change

6 Problems and issues in intervention studies 107
  Michael Shayer

Contents

7 Training, cognitive change, and individual differences 122
Anastasia Efklides, Andreas Demetriou, and Jan-Eric Gustafsson

8 Improving operational abilities in children: results of a large-scale experiment 144
Benö Csapó

9 Training scientific reasoning in children and adolescents: a critical commentary and quantitative integration 160
Luc Goossens

Part III Applications in specific domains

10 Value and limitations of analogues in teaching mathematics 183
Graeme S. Halford and Gillian M. Boulton-Lewis

11 Developing thinking abilities in arithmetic class 210
Lauren B. Resnick, Victoria Bill, and Sharon Lesgold

12 Causal theories, reasoning strategies, and conflict resolution by experts and novices in Newtonian mechanics 231
J. Ignacio Pozo and Mario Carretero

13 Cognitive prerequisites of reading and spelling: a longitudinal approach 256
Wolfgang Schneider and Jan Carol Näslund

Concluding chapter

14 Returning to school: review and discussion 277
John B. Biggs

Name index 295
Subject index 300

Figures and tables

FIGURES

1.1 The developmental ladder (1A) and the developmental web
metaphor (1B) for conceptualizing developmental pathways   13
2.1 Modes, learning cycles, and forms of knowledge   39
2.2 An ordered outcome mathematics item   47
3.1 Hypothesized control structures underlying children's balance
beam performance at different ages   56
3.2 Conceptual progression across a variety of quantitative tasks   58
5.1 The structure of abilities according to the longitudinal study   88
5.2 The structure of abilities according to the metacognitive study   97
6.1 Growth curves for height   108
6.2 The effects of a medical intervention   109
6.3 Curves of cognitive development for different percentiles of the
child population   112
7.1 Mean post-test level scores of the quantitative-relational SSS as
a function of the pre-test level score of the respective SSS,
treatment group, and age   137
7.2 Mean post-test level scores of the causal-experimental SSS as
a function of the pre-test level score of the respective SSS,
treatment group, and age   138
8.1 The effect of training on the combinative ability, the logical
ability, and the systematizing ability   153
10.1 A structure-mapping analysis of a simple analogy   184
10.2 Four levels of structure mapping   186
10.3 Structure-mapping analysis of some concrete aids   191
10.4 Structure-mapping analysis of a place-value analogue   194
10.5 Structure-mapping analysis of a decomposition analogue   196
10.6 Structure-mapping analysis of a subtraction analogue   197
10.7 Structure-mapping analysis of acquisition of the distributive law   201
10.8 Correspondence between base-10 and base-2   205
11.1 The protoquantitative schemas   215

11.2 Topic coverage planned for a single month in second grade 220
11.3 A second-grade problem and several solutions 222
11.4 Change in achievement test scores for the first grade 223
11.5 Change in achievement test scores for the second grade 224
11.6 Change in achievement test scores for the third grade 225
12.1 Tasks 236
12.2 Correct answers to the problems involved in task II 236
12.3 The arrangements used in tasks II and III 238
12.4 Typical answers at each level of the inertia and the free fall tasks 242
13.1 Relative contributions of the three phonological processing components, verbal intelligence, and early literacy to the prediction of reading comprehension in second grade 267
13.2 Best-fitting structural equation model for the reading comprehension construct 268
13.3 Best-fitting structural equation model for the spelling construct 270

TABLES

1.1 A developmental sequence of skills for arithmetic relations 22
2.1 Modes and levels in the SOLO taxonomy 39
3.1 Cross-task variability in passing rates as a function of task 61
3.2 Pattern of transfer after teaching the dimensional structure 61
4.1 A formalized example of the range of possible internalization consequences, following child's and 'social other's' (caregiver's) actions 69
5.1 Regressions of the school-achievement variables on the cognitive variables 94
6.1 Changes in class means for 12+ boys expressed as percentiles in relation to the CSMS survey data 113
7.1 Loadings of the pre-test variables on the latent variables 130
7.2 Correlations among the latent pre-test factors 131
7.3 Correlations between pre- and post-test factors 132
7.4 Mean pre- and post-test quantitative-relational and causal-experimental SSS level scores of subjects having the same pre-test level scores in the two SSSs as a function of treatment group and age 134
7.5 Frequency of subjects per age and cognitive level who succeeded in the training tasks of the causal-experimental and quantitative-relational SSS 135
8.1 The system of the experimental groups 147
8.2 Results of ability tests at the beginning of the experiment (% of the maximum test score) 151

8.3 The effects of training on the operational abilities: the size and significance of the effects	152
9.1 Number of studies in each of the three categories of three moderator variables for different types of training effectiveness	169
9.2 Summary of effect-size statistics	170
9.3 Mean effect sizes as a function of three moderator variables	171
10.1 Examples of concepts at each level of structure mapping	189
12.1 Frequency of subjects per response category in the case of the five concepts investigated	243
12.2 Cognitive conflict resolution	250
13.1 Means, standard deviations, and range for the predictors and criterion variables included in the analyses	264
13.2 Zero-order and partial correlations of predictor variables with reading and spelling measures	265
13.3 Intercorrelations among latent variables	268

Contributors

Thomas R. Bidell, Harvard University, Graduate School of Education, Roy E. Larsen Hall, Appian Way, Cambridge, Massachusetts 02138, USA.

John B. Biggs, Department of Education, University of Hong Kong, Pokfulam Rd, Hong Kong.

Victoria Bill, 634 LRDC, 3939 O'Hara Street, University of Pittsburgh, Pittsburgh, PA 15260, USA.

Gillian M. Boulton-Lewis, Brisbane College of Advanced Education, St Lucia 4067, Australia.

Mario Carretero, Faculty of Psychology, Universitad Autonoma Cantoblanco, 28049 Madrid, Spain.

Robbie Case, School of Education, Stanford University, Stanford, California 94305-2384, USA.

Benö Csapó, Department of Education, Attila Jozsef University, H-6722 Szeged, Petofi sgt. 30-34, Hungary.

Andreas Demetriou, Department of Psychology, Aristotelian University of Thessaloniki, Thessaloniki 540 06, Greece.

Anastasia Efklides, Department of Psychology, Aristotelian University of Thessaloniki, Thessaloniki 540 06, Greece.

Kurt W. Fischer, Harvard University, Graduate School of Education, Roy E. Larsen Hall, Appian Way, Cambridge, Massachusetts 02138, USA.

Luc Goossens, Department of Psychology, Catholic University of Leuven, Tiensesraat 102, Leuven B-3000, Belgium.

Jan-Eric Gustafsson, Department of Education and Educational Research, Gothenburg University, Box 1010, S-431 26, Molndal, Sweden.

Graeme S. Halford, Department of Psychology, The University of Queensland, St Lucia 4067, Australia.

Sharon Lesgold, 634 LRDC, 3939 O'Hara Street, University of Pittsburgh, Pittsburgh, PA 15260, USA.

Jan Carol Näslund, Max-Planck-Institute für Psychologische Forschung, Leopoldstrasse 24, Postfach 440109, D-8000 Munchen 40, Germany.

Maria Platsidou, Department of Psychology, Aristotelian University of Thessaloniki, Thessaloniki 540 06, Greece.

J. Ignacio Pozo, Faculty of Psychology, Universitad Autonoma Cantoblanco, 28049 Madrid, Spain.

Lauren B. Resnick, 634 LRDC, 3939 O'Hara Street, University of Pittsburgh, Pittsburgh, PA 15260, USA.

Wolfgang Schneider, Max-Planck-Institute für Psychologische Forschung, Leopoldstrasse 24, Postfach 440109, D-8000 Munchen 40, Germany.

Michael Shayer, King's College London, Centre for Educational Studies, University of London, Cornwall House Annex, Waterloo Rd, London SE1 8TX, UK.

Jaan Valsiner, Department of Psychology, The University of North Carolina, Chapel Hill, NC 27599-3270, USA.

Foreword

An important development during the past decades in research on learning, development, and instruction has been the increasing tendency towards integration of different subfields of psychology as well as between theory-oriented inquiry and research aiming at the improvement of practice. The present volume, which mainly brings together in a coherent way the papers presented in three symposia organized at the Third European Conference for Research on Learning and Instruction (Madrid, September 1989), reflects both trends.

Echoing in some way the title of an article by Gardner and Hatch (1989) on 'Multiple intelligences go to school' which illustrates the rapprochement between differential psychology and education, this volume is symptomatic of the interest of developmental psychology in the improvement of education. But this publication also endorses Weinert's (1989) observation that 'the artificial frontiers erected between developmental psychology, learning research, studies of individual differences, and educational psychology are gradually losing their traditional importance' (p. 6). This blurring of the boundaries between those sub-disciplines of psychology is certainly a typical feature of European research (see also Shuell 1987), and is, for example, well illustrated in the collaborative work of Demetriou, Efklides, and Gustafsson reported in the present volume.

Bridging the gap between theory building, on the one hand, and contributing to the improvement of educational practice, on the other, has become more and more prominent in research on learning, development, and teaching. This book contributes to this bridging in two different ways. First of all, by the set of papers presented in the last part, that focuses on domain-related developmental aspects that are relevant for instruction in different subject-matter fields. Second, by presenting, in Part II, a series of intervention studies on inducing cognitive change. This also illustrates a powerful characteristic of European research on the acquisition of knowledge and skills, namely, the use of teaching experiments in ecologically valid settings as a research strategy.

It seems to me that the present volume shows that we are facing an exciting future in research on cognition, learning, development, and instruction, in which the growing interaction and co-operation between scholars representing different domains of expertise will contribute to the elaboration, enrichment, and validation of an empirically underpinned theory of knowledge and skill acquisition that constitutes a solid basis for the design of powerful teaching-learning environments.

Erik De Corte
First President of EARLI

REFERENCES

Gardner, H. and Hatch, T. (1989) 'Multiple intelligences go to school: educational implications of the theory of multiple intelligences', *Educational Researcher* 18 (8): 4–10.

Shuell, T.J. (1987) 'The European connection: book review of *Learning and Instruction: European Research in an International Context*, Volume 1', *Educational Researcher* 16 (6): 45–6.

Weinert, F. (1989) 'The impact of schooling on cognitive development: one hypothetical assumption, some empirical results, and many theoretical implications', *EARLI News* 8: 3–7.

Introduction

THE STATE OF THE ART

School is the place of disciplined and directed thinking *par excellence*. One of the major aims of school is to deepen and enhance the student's understanding of the world, herself included. Towards this aim, school functions are organized around three goals: the transmission of culture-valued knowledge, the development of learning skills, and the cultivation of creative thinking that would make the student a prospective inventor of new knowledge about the world. This is precisely the object of study of the psychology of cognitive development. Since the early days of Piaget, this field has focused on understanding the structure and the dynamics of change of the person's understanding of the world. In fact, *Genetic Epistemology*, Piaget's own academic offspring, intended to enlighten the phylogenesis of knowledge by studying its ontogenesis and vice versa. It is natural, then, that Piagetian theory has appealed to people in education since the 1960s, when it dominated the field of developmental psychology.

There was an enthusiasm at that time founded on the belief that, at last, we had found the means to send thinking to school, to paraphrase the title of the Furth and Wachs's (1975) book. Piagetian theory has been considered particularly appropriate to direct education in two important respects: (a) the development of new teaching methods that would capitalize on the exploratory and inventive activities of the child himself; (b) the strengthening of the teaching of specific school courses, particularly in science and mathematics, by cultivating and consolidating the basic thought structures of scientific and mathematical thinking.

Optimism in science, especially in new fields of inquiry, does not usually last for a long time. The present case is no exception. Disillusionment with Piagetian theory came rather quickly and scepticism about its educational applications grew at a proportionate pace. It was already evident by the early 1970s that Piagetian theory could not fulfil the promise that many of the pro-Piagetians thought it held out for education. However, this is not equivalent to saying that thinking has not gone to school at all, because it has.

Although, to our knowledge, there has as yet been no systematic evaluation of the impact exerted by Piagetian theory on the different facets of education, one conclusion can unhesitatingly be stated. Piaget has altered the way we view our children. Thanks to his genius, children are not viewed as little and imperfect adults any more. Instead, they are viewed as constructive cognitive beings who have theories about the world as well as about their own minds, theories which colour the way the world is represented and understood at different ages. Thus, it is now commonly accepted that education should respect children's theories and competencies if it is to keep the children self-engaged in the construction of understanding, which in our culture is a process that may lasts for decades.

Piagetian theory was shown to be problematic in its flexibility to accommodate evidence regarding some important aspects of cognitive organization and growth. Prominent among these are the following: (1) the organization of concepts and mental operations into adaptive systems able to represent accurately the different domains of the environment and direct the acquisition of efficient action patterns; (2) the possible role of processing limitations that may set the upper limits of the structures the mind may construct and operate upon at a given moment in its development; (3) the mechanisms and the nature of learning; (4) the involvement of the social environment in the process of the construction of meaning about the world as well as the construction of means for learning; (5) intra- and interindividual differences in regard to all four preceding aspects.

In recent years several neo-Piagetian theories have been proposed which try to preserve the strengths of Piaget's theory while eliminating its weaknesses. The theories of Case, Demetriou, Fischer, Halford, and Pascual-Leone are probably the most systematic attempts to advance a comprehensive model of cognitive development that would cope with the problems noted above better than Piagetian theory (for all these theories, see Demetriou 1988). At the same period a number of other models have been advanced which originate from different epistemological traditions, such as the socio-historical tradition or the tradition of cognitive or differential psychology.

Most of these theories and traditions are represented in this volume. Specifically, this volume may be seen as complementary to another volume recently edited by Demetriou (1988). That volume explored the theoretical implications of the integration of the theories into a unified system. The contributors to this volume have been asked to focus their contributions on the educational implications and applications of their theories. To a greater or lesser extent each of the contributions is organized around the five points noted above.

OVERVIEW OF THE VOLUME

The first part comprises five chapters. Each of these chapters presents a general model of cognitive development and the implications that this model may have for different aspects of education.

In the first chapter, *Thomas Bidell* and *Kurt Fischer* first discuss the epistemological reasons for the limited educational applicability of classical theories such as Piagetian or learning theory. They then present the general premises of Fischer's skill theory and argue that, because of its very nature, it can help overcome the limitations of traditional theories. The key construct of Fischer's theory is the notion of skill. A skill is defined as 'an attribute of a person-in-a-context, not the person alone nor the environment alone'. This orientation enables Bidell and Fischer to discuss how school activities must be organized if they are to be conducive to the development of specific skills for particular subject-matter areas, such as mathematics or reading. Also, it provides a frame for understanding intra- and inter-individual developmental variability and the existence of alternative developmental pathways as a necessary characteristic of development.

John Biggs presents his theory in the second chapter. This theory also represents developing intellect as a multimodal and multidimensional entity. However, this theory is unique in at least two of its basic assumptions: first, that the different modes of representation which are associated with the major developmental stages (i.e., the sensori-motor, the ikonic, the concrete-symbolic, the formal, and the postformal) do not supplant each other with growth but remain active, each facilitating and broadening the functioning of the others; second, that each of these modes is associated with one of several different forms of knowing: tacit, intuitive, declarative, theoretical, and meta-theoretical. These views suggest that learning may be very different from how it is represented by traditional theories. Biggs also relates his well-known SOLO taxonomy for evaluating the outcomes of learning to the theory of development proposed in this chapter.

In his chapter, *Robbie Case* discusses the theoretical and empirical problems faced by the classic structuralist position and he proceeds to propose his own alternative to the Piagetian notion of structure. This is what he calls 'central conceptual structures' (CCS). CCSs are networks of concepts that organize knowledge and processing in different domains. He also outlines the points at which this notion is relevant to education: it can direct the development of better curricula and better teaching methods, especially in relation to mathematics and science; it can also be of use to the education of disadvantaged learners.

Jaan Valsiner's chapter is a unique complement to the volume. It is the only chapter to represent directly and explicitly the recent developments in the socio-historical approach to cognitive development. According to Valsiner, cognitive development is the result of constant internalization and externalization of culturally valued constraint systems. This process is thought to transform the experiences stemming from the child–environment interactions into systems of signs which govern the adaptation of the child by canalizing action towards permissible, and away from non-permissible, action patterns. The role of schooling in this internalization–externalization process is discussed.

The last chapter of the first part is contributed by *Andreas Demetriou, Jan-Eric Gustafsson, Anastasia Efklides*, and *Maria Platsidou*. This chapter explores the educational implications of the theory of cognitive development proposed by two of the present editors. This theory claims that the products of person–environment interactions are organized in specialized structural systems (SSSs) which preserve the peculiarities of different reality domains. The SSSs identified so far are concerned with qualitative, quantifiable, causal, spatial, and formal reality. Changes in the specialized structural systems are conditioned by two domain-free systems, a hypercognitive general self-monitoring-and-self-government system and a processing-potentials system. The chapter discusses the relations between the organization of individual mind and the structure of knowledge in science and education. Based on these general premises, a number of predictions are tested regarding the relations between cognitive structures and school achievement. The three studies presented show how achievement in different school subjects is related to the various structures described by the theory.

The second part is devoted to learning in general and cognitive acceleration in particular. The papers in this part are mainly concerned with the training of scientific reasoning skills, such as the design of experiments and logical or mathematical reasoning.

In his chapter, *Michael Shayer* crystallizes his long experience in cognitive acceleration. In so doing, he formulates a general scheme about the general and specific goals that an acceleration study should try to attain. He also proposes a general scheme that would direct the evaluation of the short- and long-term effects of training as well as their possible impact on school achievement.

The chapter by *Anastasia Efklides, Andreas Demetriou*, and *Jan-Eric Gustafsson* presents a rather complex cognitive acceleration study. This study was designed with the aim of testing the learning implications of the theory presented in the chapter by Demetriou *et al*. It shows, in line with the basic postulates of this theory, that cognitive acceleration is possible but inscribed within the limits of the SSSs identified by the theory. Moreover, the various SSSs are differentially amenable to training.

The results of the study presented in the chapter by *Benő Csapó* point in the same direction. In his study, Csapó attempted to train three types of mental operations: in his terms, systematizing, combinative, and logical. These in fact correspond to the qualitative-analytic, the verbal-propositional, and the causal-experimental SSS described in the chapter by Demetriou *et al*.

Like Efklides *et al.*, Csapó found that some operations (the combinative) are more amenable to training than others (the systematizing) and that each type of operation is amenable to training at different ages.

The final chapter of the second part is contributed by *Luc Goossens*. Goossens has applied a relatively new statistical approach, known as meta-analysis, to investigate the effectiveness of training as this is suggested by cognitive acceleration studies. Goossens meta-analysed thirty-eight studies concerned with the training of scientific reasoning published in the literature over a period of fifteen years. He found substantial effects of training but these did not generalize to non-trained abilities such as proportional reasoning. This finding is in agreement with those of Efklides *et al.* and Csapó and provides strong support to the notion of domain-specific structures advocated by all the theories presented in the first part of this volume.

The chapters in the third part are more specialized than those presented in the two first parts. That is, these papers make use of general principles with the aim of highlighting the understanding of either specific knowledge domains, such as mathematics or physics, or skills, such as reading, and of developing methods that would improve their teaching.

Graeme Halford and *Gillian Boulton-Lewis*, in particular, show how Halford's structure-mapping theory can be used to analyse the processing load required for understanding the analogues used in the teaching of mathematics. Such an analysis reveals that the use of analogues might facilitate or inhibit comprehension depending on the way they are used and the processing load they pose.

The paper by *Lauren Resnick*, *Victoria Bill*, and *Sharon Lesgold* offers a fresh approach to the teaching of mathematics. It is based on the assumption that cognition is not 'sets of competencies-in-the-head but forms of cultural practice'. In this respect, the critical element of teaching is an 'apprenticeship environment' in which mathematical concepts can be scaffolded. School could serve this purpose provided it does not 'teach' but 'does' maths. Clearly, these ideas are closed to the models advanced by Bidell and Fisher and Valsiner.

The paper by *Ignacio Pozo* and *Mario Carretero* addresses the problem of cognitive change in the domain of physics in general and Newtonian mechanics in particular. They compare three different approaches to cognitive change, namely the Piagetian paradigm that emphasizes general cognitive reorganizations, the conceptual change model that stresses the role of misconceptions in science, and the novice-expert approach that attributes change to the acquisition of specialized knowledge. Their results come out in favour of the conceptual change and the novice-expert models of learning.

Finally, *Wolfgang Schneider* and *Jan Carol Näslund* deal with the prerequisites of reading ability. Drawing upon theoretical constructs elaborated by other authors in this volume, they provide detailed results regarding the relationships between reading comprehension and spelling, on the one hand, and general abilities, such as verbal intelligence and working memory, and more specific ones, such as phonological awareness, recoding in lexical access, and early literacy, on the other hand.

CONCLUSIONS

In the concluding chapter, *John Biggs* provides a synthesis of the whole volume. Let us then summarize the general conclusions as suggested by Biggs's and our reading of the work presented in this volume. First, we know better than a few years ago how the mind is organized and how these organizations are related to mental activities occurring in the school. If properly used, this knowledge may lead to better curricula and better evaluation methods. However, we still do not understand very well how cognitive structures interact with each other and how their formation is affected by the structure of knowledge as it exists in our present educational and broader cultural environment. The role of symbolism in this process is also not satisfactorily understood. Second, we also know that both mental and school-specific knowledge structures are constrained by both internal and social constraint systems. Thus, we have to take these limitations into account if what we transmit in our schools is to be fully and permanently assimilated. However, our knowledge is still very limited about how we can planfully use the social constraint systems to circumvent the internal constraint systems, to the extent that this is possible. Third, we have already gathered firm knowledge about the developmental and cognitive preconditions under which learning may occur. However, we still need to learn a lot more about how learning situations work in the mind and/or the brain to alter its present state into a more advanced one. Thus, we are not yet very knowledgeable about how to engineer specific learning environments aimed at quickly and efficiently imparting specific knowledge structures useful to a particular individual of a particular age for a particular purpose. Finally, we now know a lot more than before about the dimensions of individual differences in cognitive functioning and about how these are related to dimensions of school achievement. However, we are still far away from an educational system that would be organized in such a way that would make each individual at one and the same time able to expand his talents fully and to ameliorate his weaknesses. We hope that this volume will be a step forward in our long way towards the grasp of the knowledge and understanding we need in order to elevate our education to the level which would provide the conditions for our civilization, and certainly for each unique individual, to put the happiest moments of their history at the service of their present and future.

The physical origin of the contributors to this volume is worth mentioning because it is a sign of the vigour of the field and it justifies an optimism that the field may be able to fulfil these hopes. They come from four continents and from twelve countries. This indicates, on the one hand, that the present volume literally represents the universal state of the art in the field. On the other hand, it also indicates that the field can profit from and fertilize ideas which grow all over the world. One must note in this regard that the *European Association for Research on Learning and Instruction* has been very instrumental in this regard since it started in 1985. The contributions to this volume were first presented at the Third Conference of EARLI which was held in Madrid in September 1989.

REFERENCES

Demetriou, A. (ed.) (1988) *The Neo-Piagetian Theories of Cognitive Development: Toward an Integration*, Amsterdam: North-Holland.

Furth, H. G. and Wachs, H. (1975) *Thinking Goes to School: Piaget's Theory in Practice*, New York: Oxford University Press.

Part I

General principles of cognitive organization and change and implications for education

Chapter 1

Cognitive development in educational contexts
Implications of skill theory
Thomas R. Bidell and Kurt W. Fischer

As interest in cognitive developmental theory grew under the influence of Piaget's work, the potential for a cognitive developmental approach to education seemed great. Behaviouristic approaches were largely retreating from classrooms in the face of a rising concern with children's intellectual growth and autonomous activity in learning. Yet, despite the apparent promise, attempts to apply cognitive developmental theory have not met with widespread success, and there has remained a sizeable gap between developmental theory and educational practice. One major cause of this continuing gap has been the fundamentally context-neutral conceptions of cognitive abilities found in traditional theories of cognitive development.

The purpose of the present chapter is to advance an alternative view of cognitive abilities as context-embedded skills (Fischer 1980) and to discuss some of the implications of that viewpoint for educational research and practice. The argument begins with a critique of context-neutral conceptions of human abilities and a brief review of some of the educational problems associated with these conceptions. We then go on to define a new conception of cognitive abilities as context-embedded skills which moves beyond these problems, providing theoretical and methodological tools that can be used to understand the process of cognitive development as it takes place in different contexts and especially in educational settings.

CONTEXT-NEUTRAL CONCEPTIONS OF COGNITION

The conception of cognitive development that has influenced education the most has been the Piagetian theory of stage structure. Discussion of context-neutral conceptions of cognition will therefore concentrate mainly on stage structure, touching upon psychometric and competency conceptions only enough to indicate the ways that they share the context-neutral focus.

Piagetian stage structures

There has always been a tension in Piagetian theory between its constructivist framework and its structuralist stage model. Constructivism characterizes the acquisition of knowledge as a product of the individual's creative self-organizing activity in particular environments. The structural stage model, on the other hand, depicts knowledge in terms of abstract universal structures independent of specific contexts. Indeed, the constructivist framework portrays an active human agent who knows the world by transforming it and actively adapting to its constraints. That view seems antithetical to the idea of abstract universal structures of knowledge virtually unaffected by vast individual differences in the sociocultural contexts and life histories of the people constructing the knowledge. If knowledge is in fact constructed in interaction with specific environments, then the nature of those environments should affect both the process of construction and the organization of the resulting knowledge.

For example, children solve arithmetic problems through a wide range of strategies constructed in a variety of specific contexts (Charbonneau and John-Steiner 1988; Saxe 1990). For young children, finger-counting strategies are prevalent, but in many schools contexts finger-counting is discouraged and children invent more subtle strategies including counting of marks on papers or counting without verbalizing. In some situations children are taught to make use of features on the numerals, like corners or curves, as 'counters'. Each of these strategies involves some kind of organization of the thinking involved, and each situation calls for a different set of organized activities. One is hard pressed to understand the relation between the organization of each of these specific activities and the abstract concept of stage structure. Knowledge of an individual child's stage of number conservation provides virtually no information about the organization of these specific skills or the ways in which a teacher might engage them in an educational interaction.

Yet, ironically, while educators have been attracted to Piagetian theory largely by its constructivist framework, it has been the structuralist stage theory that has received the most attention in educational research and applications (but, for constructivist approaches, see Duckworth 1989; Kamii 1985; Kamii and DeVries 1980). Piagetian constructivism has been attractive to educators because it emphasizes precisely those humanistic aspects of cognitive acquisition that behaviourism has denied – the creative activity of the human agent organizing herself and her environment (Bidell and Fischer 1992). Unfortunately, Piaget seldom drew a sharp distinction between his constructivist framework and his structuralist stage theory, and his descriptions of constructive mechanisms were couched in extremely general, even elusive terms (Piaget 1970). As a result, the emerging fields of cognitive development and developmental education adopted the stage theory as a testable, tangible point of departure for applying Piagetian theory to the classroom.

A corollary of this stage framework is a unilinear conception of the developmental pathway. Because each individual passes through the same sequence of universal stages, all individuals must share the same pathway of development and the same developmental outcome. Each person climbs essentially the same ladder from start to finish (Figure 1.1A). From this perspective it is difficult to understand how differing contexts and forms of social activity might influence the direction and outcome of development. Yet evidence from studies of cultural and gender differences suggests that developmental pathways and outcomes may differ considerably according to the systems of social expectations and cultural values within which individuals construct their knowledge (Gilligan and Attanucci 1988; Rogoff 1990; Saxe 1990; Whiting and Edwards 1988).

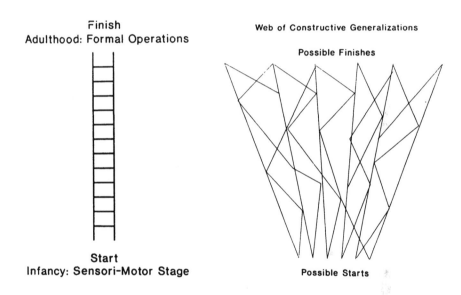

Figure 1.1 The developmental ladder (1A) and the developmental web metaphor (1B) for conceptualizing developmental pathways

Domain specificity and competence

Because of widespread recognition that the conception of universal stage structure does not account for the variability found in real people, the principle of domain specificity has been accepted by most contemporary cognitive developmental theorists (Carey 1985; Case 1985; Feldman 1980; Fischer 1980; Gardner 1983). According to these domain-specificity theories, knowledge is not organized in unitary structures that cut across all types of tasks and situations. Instead, knowledge is organized within specific domains defined by particular contents or tasks, such as arithmetic, spatial properties, social interactions, or music.

The recognition that knowledge does not have to be organized in single unitary structures is an important step away from context-neutral conceptions of cognition. Nevertheless, the principle of domain specificity alone is not sufficient for a context-embedded conception of cognition. Domain specificity theories often foster an organism/environment split by maintaining conceptions of cognitive abilities that focus mainly on the organism, the individual person free of contextual influences.

An extreme example of this split is the Chomskian conception of cognitive competence (Chomsky 1986). This framework portrays cognitive abilities as highly specific to particular domains such as language, spatial relations, or mathematics, and it locates these abilities almost entirely within the organisms, typically as innate endowments or modules (Fodor 1983; Spelke 1988). This strategy has the effect of conceptually separating the organism from the environment and reducing the role of the environment to little more than a trigger activating a specific form of a module.

Thus, despite the recognition of domain specificity, cognitive abilities continue to be portrayed in ways that separate context-specific performance from organismic cognitive structure. This conception therefore shares the problems of Piagetian stage structures with regard to education. With organism and environment radically separated, it is difficult to analyse how educational interventions in everyday performance might affect knowledge acquisition. Furthermore, even though different developmental pathways are prescribed for different domains, the pathways remain unilinear within those domains. The endpoint is determined biologically, and it is difficult to see how the person's autonomous exchanges with the social environment might affect the course of this pre-established pathway to knowledge.

Psychometric intelligence

The most pervasive domain-specificity approach in education is probably the psychometric theory of intelligence, which is embodied in most educational tests. Psychometric conceptions do not make such a strong theoretical division between organism and environment as the Chomskian perspective, but they still focus the majority of attention on the role of the person rather than the environment. They thus perpetuate the organism/environment split by default, as it were.

Contemporary psychometric theories have partly addressed this problem by differentiating conceptions of cognition into differing domains or types of intelligence, such as verbal, spatial, musical intelligences (Demetriou this volume; Gardner 1983; Horn 1976; Sternberg 1985). Abilities are assessed separately for specific domains (classes of tasks or contents), still with the goal of characterizing the individual's ability independent of the wealth of environmental factors that influence behaviour within that domain.

Individuals can thus have strengths and weaknesses in different domains, but the abilities continue to be placed primarily in the individual. The person is still cast as the main character, with the environment treated as something to be controlled or minimized. There are no specific provisions for understanding the role of context in the construction of knowledge or in the channelling of developmental pathways within each domain.

PROBLEMS OF CONTEXT-NEUTRAL THEORIES IN EDUCATION

Because context-neutral theories of cognitive development split the organization of knowledge from practice in context, they pose a fundamental contradiction for educators who wish to use them as tools for analysing specific educational processes. If the organization of thought and knowledge is primarily a property of the person (whether organized within or across domains) and therefore relatively impervious to contextual variation, then how can specific educational interventions affect it? Two particularly troublesome problems are an emphasis on an abstract concept of readiness and an inflexibility with regard to social and cultural diversity in development.

The readiness dilemma

Because of the split between organism and environment, context-neutral theories engender artificial divisions between development and learning and between cognitive structure and educational content. Cognitive structures are seen as the product of a developmental process that is somehow independent of learning. Development supplies general structures of knowledge, which have the educational role of *readiness*, preparing children's minds for the experience of learning. Learning, on the other hand, has the role of *filling up* these preformed structures with educational content.

This artificial division of structure from content creates what might be called the readiness dilemma. Educators are forced to choose between the false alternatives of concentrating either on children's cognitive structural development or on their learning. Either one must work to stimulate the development of cognitive structures to get children ready to learn (which is problematic since development is presumed to be mostly spontaneous) or one must wait patiently until the developmental process yields readiness on its own.

The first horn of this dilemma has led some educators to reduce the goals of education to those of development itself (Kohlberg and Mayer 1972). Then education requires methods of *inducing structural development*, such as teaching logic directly to children (Furth and Wachs 1974) or presenting materials just beyond a current stage in hopes of inducing children to stretch their cognitive structures upward (Turiel 1969). On the other hand, the second horn of the dilemma has led many proponents of stage theory to advocate a strategy of *wait and pounce:* observe children's developmental progress and wait for just the right opportunity to introduce some stage-appropriate content.

Both of these alternatives disregard and devalue the everyday ongoing teacher–child and peer interactions that constitute the vast bulk of educational activities, and so both approaches have proven consistently futile. Because both alternatives ignore the everyday constructive activity through which children organize their knowledge, it is impossible for teachers to track the developmental process. Teachers are placed in the position of chasing after each child, attempting first to assess her stage of development and then trying to devise educational activities with just the right degree of cognitive challenge. The consistent experience of teachers in this position has been characterized best by Eleanor Duckworth (1979): 'Either we're too early and they can't learn it or we're too late and they know it already.'

Social and cultural diversity in development

A second problem with context-neutral theories for educational intervention lies in their implications about the pathways and outcomes of development. Context-neutral conceptions suggest a unilinear pathway of development (either within or across domains), abstracting a single sequence of acquisitions from the diversity of real children's encounters with the environment. A major goal of education then becomes a matter of seeing all children through this unilinear sequence to a particular form of understanding at the end (Kohlberg and Mayer 1972).

Portraying educational objectives in terms of a single universal sequence and outcome poses two related problems for educating children from diverse social and cultural backgrounds. First, it restricts the flexibility of educational practice in adapting to differences in styles of thinking and learning. A single standard of development tends to rule out a priori the possibility of adapting developmentally based educational approaches to the needs of specific cultural, class, or gender groupings. Selecting a single developmental pathway – generally that which typifies white, middle-class, male development – as the standard of educational achievement risks alienating children who bring diverse backgrounds to the school culture.

Second, when the adoption of a single developmental standard is combined with the readiness perspective described above, it can lead to an inadvertently discriminatory *laissez-faire* approach to teaching in which children who do not belong to the dominant sociocultural tradition fail to receive training in academic skills presumed to develop in everyone (Delpit 1988). The readiness approach functions adequately for the majority of white middle-class children who, when left to their own devices, can be counted upon to develop, for example, mainstream literacy skills. On the other hand, children whose cultural contexts support different kinds of skills may be losing vital instructional time while teachers are waiting for them to become ready for literacy training.

Instead of separating the organization of children's knowledge from the everyday activities and interactions in which they must create that organization, cognitive developmental theory should describe the ways that cognitive organization is constructed in the context of everyday activity. Such descriptions call for new conceptions of cognitive abilities – not as abstract organismic structures but as context-specific organizations of thought and action.

COGNITION IN CONTEXT: THE NATURE OF SKILLS

One approach that offers a context-embedded conception of cognition is skill theory (Fischer 1980). The neo-Piagetian concept of skill[1] shares the constructivist approach in Piaget's theory, which originally attracted educational interest: knowledge acquisition as an action-based, self-regulating, constructive process. But skill theory describes that process in terms of the construction of specific, context-embedded skills rather than the general equilibrium of cross-contextual logical structures.

A skill is defined as a control structure governing a specific class of actions that a person can perform in a specific context. A skill is therefore defined mutually by the activity of the person and the nature of the context where the activity is carried out. A skill is an attribute of a person-in-a-context, not of the person alone nor the environment alone (Fischer and Farrar 1987). The person and environment collaborate to produce the skill; the collaboration is especially obvious for the social environment, where people collaborate in producing skills, but the physical environment also collaborates in the production of skills.

An example of a skill may be drawn from the development of arithmetic knowledge. When a young child can help set the table by counting out four forks and placing each by a plate, the child exhibits a skill governing a counting activity that controls the variation presented by the quantity of forks in the drawer and plates on the table. This is a specific numerical skill that the child has constructed for an express purpose in a particular context. This skill will undoubtedly eventually contribute to a more general and abstract set of mathematical skills, but it does not, in itself, imply a generalized structure of quantitative knowledge independent of the context of helping to set the table. Indeed, the 3- or 4-year-old child who counts the forks competently in this familiar context will often be lost when confronted with an unfamiliar numerical correspondence task involving counting materials in a preschool setting. While the fork-counting skill represents enduring quantitative knowledge on the part of the child, it is a knowledge that is equally defined by the child's activities and the context in which those activities are organized and used.

Of course, knowledge is not forever stuck in narrow contexts. Skill theory specifies how broader forms of cognitive organization emerge from a process of *constructive generalization* (Bidell 1990; Fischer and Farrar 1987), not from the application of ready-made general structures. Constructive generalization involves the co-ordination of specific skills from particular contexts to form new skills capable of functioning across the original contexts. To extend the above example, when a child has developed counting skills for setting the table at home and also for matching count words to numerals in preschool, she may co-ordinate the two skills to form a new, more general skill for using numerals to represent the results of a count in these contexts. This generalization process occurs naturally, but it also takes work on the part of the child.

The concept of skill, then, does not separate children's constructive activity in context from the structural organization of their knowledge. Instead, skills are constructed during everyday activity in specific contexts, and they are affected by those contexts, including importantly the actions of other people. This framework holds a number of implications for understanding how particular educational contexts may affect learning and how educational professionals might better intervene in the learning process.

THE SKILL APPROACH AND EDUCATION

Because skill theory connects organism and environment instead of separating them, it transforms much traditional wisdom about the application of cognitive developmental theory to education. Instead of starting from abstract descriptions of stage structures and attempting to apply them across contexts, skill theory starts with the actions of the person-in-a-context, examining the process of development as it occurs in everyday settings. Analysis of skill structures is important, but they are always tied to actions in context.

Moreover, within a skill theory approach, the aims of education go far beyond promoting a purely cognitive progression through stages. Cognitive theory is explicitly viewed as one among many tools through which to gain an understanding of the educational process (Fischer and Bullock 1984). Education is a broadly social endeavour involving cognitive development, emotional development, social interaction, and a range of cultural factors including ethnicity, race, class, and gender. The nature of this endeavour cannot be reduced to any one of these factors but instead needs to be linked to the participants' own activities and goals and those of the social system of which it is a part. In this sense, the goals of education are self-determined by its participants at many levels.

Yet cognitive development is a central part of education, cognitive developmental theory can provide crucial insights into educational processes. Skill theory offers both conceptual and methodological tools that are useful in understanding and guiding educational interventions in the everyday construction of skills. The remainder of this chapter presents some of the main educational implications of these tools for analysing cognitive development in school contexts.

Merging cognitive structure and academic content

One important implication of the skill concept is that cognitive structure and academic content should not be rigidly separated. Children do not apply pre-existing general cognitive structures to the tasks and materials encountered in schools, but they construct context-specific cognitive structures to organize their activities in each type of task or learning situation in which they participate.

For instance, in learning an algorithm for two-place addition, a child must construct a cognitive structure (or structures) to organize the various components of the task. These components will include some procedure for addition, such as counting fingers, counting marks on the paper, or recalling number facts. Other components may include information about the meaning of numerals, the meaning of place values, and the procedures for adding, such as placing the answer at the bottom of columns of figures. All these specific features of the arithmetic algorithm must be organized by a cognitive structure that constitutes a skill for two-place arithmetic algorithms.

A related implication is that development and learning should be integrated in educational thinking. In context-neutral theories which split learning from development, the process of development must first produce a presumed general competence at mathematics so that the process of learning specifics, like arithmetic algorithms, becomes possible. In the skill perspective, on the other hand, the construction of the cognitive structure for the arithmetic algorithm *is* the process of cognitive development in this specific context. The processes of development and learning converge in the processes of construction and generalization of skills.

In this way the skill approach places central developmental and educational value on the everyday activities of teaching and learning that have been lost in the gulf between context-neutral structures and academic content. Context-neutral theories have implied a devaluation of these everyday interactions, either disregarding them to concentrate on inducing structural development or treating them as a secondary mechanism for filling pre-established structures with content. The skill approach places the everyday activities of teaching and learning at the heart of the process of cognitive development as it occurs in schools. The focus is on understanding how knowledge is constructed in everyday activities of educational contexts, including how the organization of the contexts contributes to the knowledge constructed.

Evaluating cognitive development in context

The merger of cognitive structure with academic content holds important consequences for assessing cognitive development in school settings. Instead of attempting to predict people's performance in context from assessments based on abstract conceptions of stage structures, skill theory analyses and predicts development in context for individual people within each content domain.

With context-neutral perspectives, educational evaluation has involved establishing a set of privileged tasks which were presumed to tap underlying universal capacities – and which therefore were used to define the standard for development, supposedly independent of context. Conservation of number, for instance, has been widely supposed to predict the ability to reason logically about number (Gelman and Gallistel 1978). In this task children must understand that changing the length of a row of objects, such as ten pebbles, does not affect the number of objects. Performance on this task (as well as other privileged tasks) has been shown to be highly variable and to show little if any correlation with educational achievement (Fischer and Bullock 1984; Gelman and Baillargeon 1983). Nevertheless, the belief that such tasks somehow reveal an individual's true cognitive level remains remarkably tenacious in many educational circles.

Skill theory takes the opposite approach. Instead of trying to find ways of making children's performances adapt to a pre-established norm, skill theory adapts the developmental measure to the child's context, typically using tasks closely related to what children do in school and other everyday situations. Key for constructing such measures is the technique of task analysis in terms of skill hierarchies. With the task-analysis procedures, one can determine the cognitive-structural demands of a given task in relation to a hierarchy of potential skill complexity (Fischer 1980). By applying these procedures to the tasks and contents children encounter in schools, educators can analyse and predict *developmental sequences* for important skills and use those sequences to evaluate developmental progress in the relevant school contexts.

An important strength of this context-sensitive approach to measurement is that small cognitive reorganizations can be detected (Bidell and Fischer 1992). In contrast, Piagetian theory and most neo-Piagetian theories (for example, Biggs and Collis 1982; Case 1985; Halford 1982) provide only a few major divisions for the course of development over a period of several school years. Skill sequences not only account for such long-term changes but also describe much smaller steps, which reflect the construction of specific skills needed to organize a specific task or situation. In this way, skill sequences typically describe a finely graded series of many developmental steps. For example, for the years when children move from concrete to formal operations according to Piagetian theory, skill sequences easily differentiate eight to twelve steps, with the number varying with task, child, and age period (Fischer 1980).

A study of the development of arithmetic knowledge in white, middle-class students in Denver, Colorado, illustrates how developmental sequences can be produced for a content area that is important in schools (Fischer and Kenny 1986). The focus was development of understanding of relations among everyday arithmetic operations, a topic that bears directly on an important issue in mathematics education. Educators frequently want to know whether children understand the principles involved in computational problems or are merely learning rote procedures. Traditional Piagetian concrete and formal operations tasks do not address such a question because performance on these tasks, such as conservation of number, does not obviously relate to children's understanding of specific academic content, such as the relations between addition and subtraction.

Instead of attempting to use Piagetian tasks to predict children's level of arithmetic understanding, Fischer and Kenny (1986) used skill theory procedures to analyse a developmental sequence for understanding relations among arithmetic operations. The tasks were expressed in terms close to those that children use in everyday discourse about arithmetic, and they dealt only with positive whole numbers, which is common in most early arithmetic education. The sequence was tested with students ranging in age from the third grade to early college, and it was found to be highly reliable.

Table 1.1 shows the skill sequence for arithmetic relations, including both broad developmental levels and more detailed steps within levels. The first two levels involve a transition from representational to abstract knowledge. At the earliest level analysed, Level Rp3, children used systems of concrete representations to understand how to accomplish correctly and consistently the specific procedures of addition, multiplication, subtraction, and division. But they explained what they had done only in the concrete terms of the specific computations. Next, at Level Rp4/A1, children went beyond concrete procedures to conceptualize the operations themselves. These children have general definitions of each of the arithmetic operations, such as 'Addition is putting two numbers together to get a larger number' or 'Multiplication is taking one number and combining it a specific number of times to get a larger number'.

The operations can be partially ordered in developmental steps within each level, based on both task complexity and the standard order of teaching the operations in Denver schools (see Table 1.1). Addition is taught first, and subtraction and multiplication are taught later, often in terms of their relation to addition. Division is by far the most complex operation, and it is taught last and mastered late. Within these limits, different children and different contexts produce different orderings.

Table 1.1 A developmental sequence of skills for arithmetic relations

Step*	Level	Skills for arithmetic operations
	Rp3	Concrete explanations of specific calculations in arithmetic operations:
1		Addition as a specific number problem
2		Subtraction as a specific number problem
3		Multiplication as a specific number problem (Division is usually taught after the first abstractions develop)
	Rp4/A1	Abstract definitions of arithmetic operations:
4		Addition as a type of numerical operation
5		Subtraction as a type of numerical operation OR multiplication as a type of numerical operation
6		Either subtraction or multiplication as a numerical operation (whichever was not done in step 5)
7		Division as a type of numerical operation
	A2	Abstract relations of closely related arithmetic operations:
8		Relation of addition and subtraction as opposite operations OR of addition and multiplication as similar ones
9		Relation not understood in step 8 is understood
10		Relation of multiplication and division as opposite operations OR of subtraction and division as similar ones
11		Relation not understood in step 10 is understood
	A3	Abstract relations of distantly related arithmetic operations:*
12		Relation of subtraction and multiplication as double opposite operations OR of addition and division as double opposites
13		Relation not understood in step 12 is understood
	A4	Principle unifying four arithmetic operations
14		Relations of addition, subtraction, multiplication, and division in terms of directionality of change and partitioning into single numbers or groups

*More steps occur at every level than are shown here, so that the sequence becomes complex, with many, potentially predictable individual differences in the exact steps. For brevity, very few steps are shown beyond Level A2.

The last three levels depict the extension of the children's knowledge to increasingly complex relations among operations through the co-ordination of abstract skills. With Level A2 skills adolescents co-ordinated two operations, such as addition and subtraction or addition and multiplication, to specify the general relation between them. They understood that 'Addition and multiplication are similar because they both involve combining numbers to get a larger number, but they are different because addition uses single numbers while multiplication works with groups of numbers.' The ordering of steps within the level is affected strongly by the difficulty students have with division. With Level A3 skills teenagers understood even more complicated relations, involving connections between more dissimilar operations, such as addition and division or subtraction and multiplication. Addition and division both involve manipulating numbers together, but they are different in two ways: addition works with single numbers and combines them to get a bigger number, whereas division works with groups of numbers and separates them to get a smaller number. Finally, at Level A4, young adults are capable of forming an understanding of arithmetic based on an abstract principle that simultaneously co-ordinates all the operations. This co-ordination involves two dimensions – directionality in quantity (increase or decrease) and partitioning of quantity (single numbers or groups).

Using these sorts of sequences for school-based content, teachers and educational researchers can begin to examine the specific developmental sequences of a whole range of essential academic skills and social understandings in the context of schools. They can also use these sequences to gauge developmental relations between different aspects of students' performances, such as calculation of mathematical problems and grasp of mathematical concepts.

A fundamental strength of such skill sequences is that they capture the diversity of development along with the commonalities: developmental patterns are not the same for all children, even within a relatively homogeneous group such as white, middle-class schoolchildren in Denver, as shown in Table 1.1. Developmental patterns typically vary with context, task, and person, reflecting the diversity that real people show in skill development. For example, some children understood the abstract concept of subtraction before that of multiplication (Level Rp4/A1), and some understood multiplication before subtraction. Thus, skill analysis can show development can be similar in meaningful ways in most children in a particular social group, while at the same time it is importantly different across children and contexts.

Developmental range

Another important feature of the skill approach is that it provides tools for analysing some of the mechanisms by which social interactions influence the processes of learning and direction of development. An especially important kind of contextual influence is the change in cognitive level that occurs with differences in a person's environmental context. Contrary to the context-neutral perspective, an individual's level of cognitive ability in a given task or situation is not rigidly determined by a pre-established logical system, but is highly flexible, and differs according to the degree of social support afforded by a given situational context. The *developmental range* (Fischer *et al.* in press; Kitchener and Fischer 1990) describes the range of developmental levels an individual can exhibit on a given task across a variety of contexts.

Teachers encounter the developmental range daily in the variations in cognitive ability children exhibit in different classroom situations. A child shows a high-level understanding when she is closely following an argument led by the teacher; she can effectively restate and explain the argument in her own terms. Then a few hours later, when she encounters the topic again, she seems to have lost the understanding, falling back to a much less sophisticated way of thinking.

Vygotsky (1978) first called attention to this phenomenon with his concept of the zone of proximal development (Newman, Griffin, and Cole 1989; Rogoff 1990). Vygotsky's concept referred to a range of levels of ability that an individual could achieve under differing conditions of social support. According to Vygotsky, development taking place in the near term (proximal) comprises the formation of new cognitive abilities with the support of the social environment. When that social support varies, the level of children's performance varies through a zone or range. Skill theory thus shares with Vygotskian theory the idea that the level of skill is context-dependent, with social support playing a central role in variations in level.

Skill theory describes the developmental range in terms of the level of cognitive performance a child can achieve under differing social support conditions. When a child performs a task independently, with no special help either from other people or from the structure of the situation, the child performs at his or her *functional* level, which is typically modest. The same child's level of performance on the same task improves to her *optimal* level when environmental influences converge to support sophisticated behaviour. When the material is familiar and someone or something has just primed the key elements of the task (for example, through modelling them or giving instruction about them), the child can sustain high-level performance. With the convergence of all these environmental factors and motivation to perform well, the child can truly produce her highest level of skill. But behaviour falls right back down to the functional level as soon as the contextual support of priming key elements is removed. That is what happens when a student produces a high-level understanding with the support of the teacher's argument but a low-level one on her own. Both functional and optimal levels are real indexes of the child's understanding, because that understanding truly varies with contextual support.

Besides optimal and functional levels, children can function at a still higher, *scaffolded* (Bruner 1982; Wood 1980) level. Scaffolding involves co-participation in the task by another person with a higher level of skill than the child, such as an adult or older child. With the scaffolding that this other person provides, the child and adult together can successfully perform a task that the child could not do independently even with the support of modelling or instruction. In development the child eventually appropriates the scaffolded level, first making it her optimal level and then eventually her functional level.

The social aspect of collaboration between person and environment is especially clear in the phenomena of developmental range. Most of the contextual supports for optimal and scaffolded levels come from other people, either directly through modelling, instruction, or co-participation, or indirectly through texts, diagrams, or other materials that support high-level skills.

The developmental range gives educational practitioners a tool for conceptualizing and measuring the effects of the social context of classroom interventions. Teachers need not wait for the emergence of readiness to begin teaching content. With this tool, they can learn to analyse ongoing interactions to understand how their activities support and steer the construction of specific context-related skills.

For example, consider the addition of small numbers, a skill that young children typically construct by co-ordinating previously acquired counting skills. This skill commonly develops in a sequence of (at least) three major steps (Resnick and Ford 1981; Gelman and Gallistel 1978). The first step is simply the ability to count small quantities. The second step is a strategy called counting-all, in which children solving a problem like 4 + 3 first count out four items (fingers, blocks, marks on paper), then count out three more, and finally, pooling the two groups, count all of them to arrive at the sum of seven. In the third step, known as counting-on, children recognize that only the second count is necessary since the result of the first count will be the same as the first term of the problem – in this case, 4. Thus children using this strategy select only three items and proceed by saying '4' and then counting on from that point '5, 6, 7'.

Consider a 6-year-old boy who on his own can count small quantities, putting him at the functional level of step 1. When a teacher demonstrates the counting-all strategy (step 2), this same child can immediately perform the addition by counting out each of the terms and then counting the whole – his optimal level. Of course, a bit later, after the contextual support of the demonstration has dissipated, he can no longer do counting-all. Next, a teacher participates in the task with the child, counting out the first term and asking the child to count the second term only. Now the child and the teacher show a scaffolded level of counting-on (step 3). Without the scaffolding, the boy falls back again to step 1.

Developmental range provides a tool for examining how environmental support affects cognitive development, but it should not be taken as a method of artificially speeding up development. The skill approach assumes that both the person's constructive activity and the support for that activity contribute to the construction of new skills. Consideration of developmental range may facilitate formulation of specific teaching strategies by helping practitioners to gauge the impact of their activities on the construction of particular knowledge. But it is not helpful, for example, always to give contextual support or scaffolding to induce the highest possible level of performance. For many purposes in the real world, children need to maintain control over their own constructive processes and to be able to perform at a high functional level, without much contextual support.

Constructive generalization

One of the most difficult problems for education has been generalization, how people take a concept or behaviour from one context and transfer it to another context. One reason for these persistent difficulties has been the failure of models of learning to incorporate the contributions of both person and environment. Stage models have predicted immediate transfer through the application of universal organismic structures, or they have mostly ignored the difficulties of transfer (Piaget 1970). Behaviourist models have emphasized the difficulties of transfer across contexts and not explained the powerful generalizations that do sometimes occur (Skinner 1969).

The concept of skills as properties of persons-in-contexts solves this problem. Skills are neither applied in blanket form across contexts nor imposed on the person by experience in particular contexts. They are constructed in one context and then must be generalized through reconstruction to other contexts (Fischer and Farrar 1987). Skill theory provides guidelines for understanding and working with the process of constructive generalization as it operates in educational settings.

Since skills are context-specific they naturally follow a movement from familiar to new, so that near generalization is much easier than far generalization. Skills generalize most readily to those contexts most similar to the one where the skill was constructed. This means, among other things, that skills transfer more readily to tasks that share similar content or materials and are in the same general area or domain.

One of the characteristics of skill sequences is that they specify an order of generalization, and so they can give educators a window on constructive generalization and a guide to intervention to promote and guide generalization. Skill sequences can be constructed for virtually any relevant content, providing a fine-grained analysis of generalization in any domain of educational interest. They can serve as tools to gauge a student's relative levels of performance in differing situations, guide educational intervention, and monitor generalization.

The concept of developmental range adds power to the sequence, providing educators with a tool that specifies ways of intervening to guide constructive generalization. Since skills vary in level as a function of contextual support and scaffolding, generalization can be influenced by manipulating support in the form of modelling, prompting, or scaffolding; and the student can gradually move towards using the generalized skill independently without support.

In this way, developmental range provides guidelines for understanding when and how to offer differing types of support to individuals attempting constructive generalization in new situations or domains. Children attempting to work in situations where their functional level is very low relative to task demands may need to be scaffolded, co-participating with a teacher, older child, or peer. Others may need only to have the skill modelled or to encounter the task in a more familiar setting. Still others may need simply to work at their functional level, with no particular support, to generalize skills to already familiar settings.

Alternative developmental pathways

Related to the concept of constructive generalization is the notion of alternative developmental pathways (Fischer 1980; Bidell and Fischer 1992). The context-neutral concept of a universal pathway up a developmental ladder ignores the reality of alternative developmental sequences among culturally diverse groups and risks alienating or discriminating against members of those groups. The skill theory concept of constructive generalization implies alternative developmental pathways both for individuals and for different social or educational groups. If skill construction is context-related and depends partly on available contextual support, then in different contexts people will construct different sets of skills and follow different pathways.

For this reason, the course of cognitive development is better represented by a web than a ladder. In contrast to the developmental ladder with its single beginning and ending points (Figure 1.1A), the developmental web (Figure 1.1B) suggests a variety of potential starting points with multiple developmental pathways leading to a variety of outcomes, together with commonalities among pathways. Furthermore, the web suggests a constructive process in which both organism and environment contribute to the shape and direction of the developmental pathway: each strand in a web is determined jointly by the current position of the web builder and the available environmental support on which the strand is built.

Within the web of potential developmental pathways, it is possible for different individuals to exhibit either *convergent* or *divergent* development relative to one another. For instance, children may enter school with greatly differing literacy skills, but through constructive generalization in the same school environment they may arrive at similar literacy skills. On the other hand, children who start with essentially the same literacy skills may construct importantly different skills because of different learning environments or different capacities they have for analysing language.

CONCLUSION: BEYOND READINESS IN DEVELOPMENTAL EDUCATION

The traditional separation of cognitive structure from context-embedded activity creates a readiness dilemma, placing educators in a helpless position – either waiting for cognitive structures to develop and then leaping in to fill them with knowledge or ignoring the day-to-day business of schooling in an attempt to stimulate cognitive development.

The skill approach points to a way beyond the readiness dilemma because it unites cognitive structure with the person's constructive activity in context. In the skill approach, there is no need to wait for development to teach content, because the construction of an understanding about any single situation or task *is* development. Similarly, there is no requirement to replace everyday teaching and learning with special instruction in logic or other privileged tasks because development is already taking place *in* these everyday interactions.

From the skill-theory perspective, every child is ready to learn, indeed, is learning and developing in daily social interactions in educational contexts. The educator's task is to understand and participate effectively in that process. This perspective removes the helplessness of the wait-and-leap strategy that stems from the context-neutral approach to cognitive structure and affirms the developmental value of the everyday activities of both teachers and learners. The conceptual and methodological tools derived from the context-embedded framework of skill theory can provide educators with options for understanding and intervention in place of the helpless prescriptions of the context-neutral perspectives on developmental education.

ACKNOWLEDGEMENTS

This work was supported in part by grants from the Spencer Foundation, NIMH, NICHD, the MacArthur Foundation Network on Early Childhood, Boston College, and Harvard University. We thank Daniel Bullock, Catherine Knight, and Walter Kuleck for their contributions to the arguments and methods presented in this paper.

NOTE

1 Skill theory has no historical or conceptual relationship with the educational strategies grouped under the heading of so-called 'skills' approaches. These approaches generally disregard cognitive structure and seek to break up edu-

cational content into atomistic units. The skill theory conception of skills is precisely the opposite, emphasizing the holistic organization of human thought and action in context.

REFERENCES

Bidell, T. R. (1990) 'Mechanisms of cognitive development during problem-solving: a structural integration approach', unpublished doctoral thesis, Harvard University, Cambridge, MA.
Bidell, T. R. and Fischer, K. W. (1992) 'Beyond the stage debate: action, structure and variability in Piagetian theory and research', in R.J. Sternberg and C.A. Berg (eds) *Intellectual Development*, New York: Cambridge University Press.
Biggs, J. and Collis, K. (1982) *Evaluating the Quality of Learning: The SOLO Taxonomy (Structure of the Observed Learning Outcome)*, New York: Academic Press.
Bruner, J. S. (1982) 'The organization of action and the nature of adult–infant transaction', in M. Cranach and R. Harre (eds) *The Analysis of Action*, New York: Cambridge University Press.
Carey, S. (1985) *Conceptual Change in Childhood*, Cambridge, MA: MIT Press.
Case, R. (1985) *Intellectual Development: A Systematic Reinterpretation*, New York: Academic Press.
Charbonneau, M. P. and John-Steiner, V. (1988) 'Patterns of experience and the language of mathematics', in R. R. Cocking and J. P. Mestre (eds) *Linguistic and Cultural Influences on Learning Mathematics*, Hillsdale, NJ: Erlbaum.
Chomsky, N. (1986) *Knowledge of Language: Its Nature, Origin, and Use*, Westport, CN: Praeger.
Delpit, L. D. (1988) 'The silenced dialogue: power and pedagogy in educating other people's children', *Harvard Educational Review* 58: 280–98.
Duckworth, E. (1979) 'Either we're too early, and they can't learn it or we're too late and they know it already: the dilemma of "applying Piaget"', *Harvard Educational Review* 49: 297–312.
—— (1989) *The Having of Wonderful Ideas and Other Essays on Teaching and Learning*, New York: Teachers College Press.
Feldman, D. (1980) *Beyond Universals in Cognitive Development*, Norwood, NJ: Ablex.
Fischer, K. W. (1980) 'A theory of cognitive development: the control and construction of hierarchies of skills', *Psychological Review* 87: 477–531.
Fischer, K. W. and Bullock, D. (1984) 'Cognitive development in school-age children: conclusions and new directions', in W. A. Collins (ed.) *The Years from Six to Twelve: Cognitive Development during Middle Childhood*, Washington, DC: National Academy Press, pp. 70–146.
Fischer, K.W., Bullock, D., Rotenberg, E.J., and Raya, P. (in press) 'The dynamics of competence: how context contributes directly to skill', in R. Wozniak and K. Fischer (eds) *Development in Context: Acting and Thinking in Specific Environments*, JPS Series on Knowledge and Development, Hillsdale, NJ: Erlbaum.
Fischer, K. W. and Farrar, M. J. (1987) 'Generalizations about generalization: how a theory of skill development explains both generality and specificity', *International Journal of Psychology* 22: 643–77.
Fischer, K. W. and Kenny, S. L. (1986) 'The environmental conditions for discontinuities in the development of abstractions', in R. Mines and K. Kitchener (eds) *Adult Cognitive Development: Methods and Models*, New York: Praeger, pp. 57–75.

Fodor, J. (1983) *The Modularity of Mind: An Essay on Faculty Psychology*, Cambridge, MA: MIT Press.
Furth, H. G. and Wachs, H. (1974) *Thinking Goes to School: Piaget's Theory in Practice*, New York: Oxford University Press.
Gardner, H. (1983) *Frames of Mind: The Theory of Multiple Intelligences*, New York: Basic Books.
Gelman, R. and Baillargeon, R. (1983) 'A review of some Piagetian concepts', in P. H. Mussen (ed.) *Handbook of Child Psychology*, Vol. 3: *Cognitive Development*, J. H. Flavell and E. M. Markman (eds), New York: Wiley, pp. 167–230.
Gelman, R. and Gallistel, C. R. (1978) *The Child's Understanding of Number*, Cambridge, MA: Harvard University Press.
Gilligan, C. and Attanucci, J. (1988) 'Two moral orientations: gender differences and similarities', *Merrill-Palmer Quarterly* 34: 223–37.
Halford, G. S. (1982) *The Development of Thought*, Hillsdale, NJ: Erlbaum.
Horn, J. L. (1976) 'Human abilities', *Annual Review of Psychology* 27: 437–86.
Kamii, C. (1985) *Young Children Reinvent Arithmetic: Implications of Piaget's Theory*, New York: Teachers College Press.
Kamii, C. and DeVries, R. (1980) *Group Games in Early Education*, Washington, DC: NAEYC.
Kitchener, K. S. and Fischer, K. W. (1990) 'A skill approach to the development of reflective thinking', in D. Kuhn (ed.) *Developmental Perspectives on Teaching and Learning Thinking Skills, Contributions to Human Development*, Basel, Switzerland: Karger.
Kohlberg, L. and Mayer, K. (1972) 'Development as the aim of education', *Harvard Educational Review* 42: 449–96.
Newman, D., Griffin, P., and Cole, M. (1989) *The Construction Zone: Working for Change in School*, Cambridge: Cambridge University Press.
Piaget, J. (1970) 'Piaget's theory', in P. H. Mussen (ed.) *Carmichael's Manual of Child Psychology*, Vol. 1, New York: Wiley.
Resnick, L. B. and Ford, W. (1981) *The Psychology of Mathematics for Instruction*, Hillsdale, NJ: Erlbaum.
Rogoff, B. (1990) *Apprenticeship in Thinking: Cognitive Development in Social Context*, New York: Oxford University Press.
Saxe, G. B. (1990) *Culture and Cognitive Development: Studies in Mathematical Understanding*, Hillsdale, NJ: Erlbaum.
Skinner, B. F. (1969) *Contingencies of Reinforcement: A Theoretical Analysis*, New York: Appleton-Century-Crofts.
Spelke, E. S. (1988) 'Where perceiving ends and thinking begins: the apprehension of objects in infancy', in A. Yonas (ed.) *Perceptual Development in Infants: The Minnesota Symposia in Child Psychology*, Vol. 20. Hillsdale, NJ: Erlbaum.
Sternberg, R. J. (1985) *Beyond IQ: A Triarchic Theory of Intelligence*, New York: Cambridge University Press.
Turiel, E. (1969) 'Developmental processes in the child's moral thinking', in P. Mussen, J. Langer, and M. Covington (eds) *New Directions in Developmental Psychology*, New York: Holt, Rinehart & Winston.
Vygotsky, L. S. (1978) *Mind in Society: The Development of Higher Psychological Processes*, Cambridge, MA: Harvard University Press.
Whiting, B. B. and Edwards, C. P. (1988) *Children of Different Worlds: The Formation of Social Behavior*, Cambridge, MA: Harvard University Press.
Wood, D. J. (1980) 'Teaching the young child: some relationships between social interaction, language, and thought', in D. R. Olson (ed.) *The Social Foundations of Language and Thought*, New York: Norton.

Chapter 2

Modes of learning, forms of knowing, and ways of schooling

John B. Biggs

SCHOOLING, FORMS OF KNOWLEDGE, AND DEVELOPMENTAL THEORY

Schooling and knowledge

Seligman (1970) tells us that he once ate some sauce béarnaise in a restaurant and shortly afterwards was violently ill. He could not eat sauce béarnaise for some considerable time afterwards, although he knew that the culprit was not the sauce but gastro-enteritis. Seligman's vomit was as Newton's bruised scalp; it suggested a seminal idea, in this case that we are 'prepared' biologically to acquire some learnings, in particular those with survival value, much more easily than others. To learn instantly to avoid foods associated with illness is to display phylogenetic wisdom.

So too is to learn with hair-trigger sensitivity such acts as walking, talking, recognizing the emotional states of others, and those skills likely to be taught in a family or small-group context. Such learnings are ancient, being displayed by *homo habilis* three million years ago, but are important today, particularly in the lives of preschool children. The kind of knowledge thereby acquired enables us to engage the world directly, and belongs to the category of what Ryle (1949) called 'knowing-how'.

These biologically prepared learnings provide a sharp contrast to those required by contemporary society of its children but which are not so readily acquired. Unprepared learnings are disembedded from familiar teachers and contexts; they are concerned not with immediate action upon objects but with action upon symbols which stand for real objects (Donaldson 1978). The distinction is clear in Donaldson's discussion of the use of language. Informal language is 'embedded' in a known personal context. Gesture and intonation disarm anaphoric reference; a nudge and a wink identify 'what's 'is name', but an outsider is baffled.

Formal language is deliberately structured to be independent of the narrator and disembedded from context because its message is usually not within the receiver's direct experience. The knowledge it conveys is 'knowing-that' (Ryle 1949), consisting of propositions about the world, often organized into subject disciplines (mathematics, biology, history, psychology, and so on). That such knowledge is independent of the receiver's experience may be alienating; there is no felt need to learn it (Resnick 1987). Its acquisition requires a teacher, persuasion, and a formal structure such as a school, thereby creating problems of an iatrogenic kind. In more reckless times, these problems led some to advocate 'deschooling', the functional knowledge of school being learned more joyfully in the market-place (Illich 1971). Now, some would handle the iatrogeny with reschooling; instead of taking school to the market-place, they would bring market-place to school, to 'situate' students' cognition (Brown, Collins, and Duguid 1989; Resnick, Bill, and Lesgold this volume).

The problem is that our cultural heritage is necessarily comprised of unprepared learnings, which need to be preserved in sender-proof form – via a symbol system and minus the body language – so they do not have to be learned afresh by each new generation. These learnings need to be taught by subject specialists, in designated institutions. Schools are there to help people to master those things they would not otherwise learn and which it is believed to be important that they should learn; a minor role of schools is to assist also in the acquisition of other forms of knowledge. Whether disembedded content has to be taught in a disembedded fashion is one issue; another is whether disembedded content is in fact worth teaching at all (Brown, Collins, and Duguid 1989).

Forms of knowledge

Ryle's distinction between knowing-how and knowing-that is useful, but they are not the only forms of knowledge. There are others, which bring out more clearly their relationship both with cognitive development and with the role of school.

(a) *Tacit* knowledge is manifested by doing and is usually not verbally accessible; some forms of tacit knowledge may be verbalized, others may not (Wagner and Sternberg 1986). A gymnast, for example, may be quite unable to express how she performs a particular act; the important thing is that she can do it perfectly at will, and that is the evidence for her knowledge.

(b) *Intuitive* knowledge is directly perceived or felt, and may include aesthetic knowledge and the kind of knowledge displayed when mathematicians or scientists apprehend an idea or solution before they are able to elucidate it symbolically.

(c) *Declarative* knowledge is expressed through the medium of a symbol system in a way that is publicly understandable, and is identifiable with Ryle's knowing-that. Declarative knowledge for present purposes is considered as a level of abstraction corresponding to first order description within the given system.

(d) *Theoretical* knowledge is at a higher level of abstraction than that declared within the given system, and is mappable on to, and often subsumed under, a more abstract statement of knowledge.

(e) *Metatheoretical* knowledge refers to that at the cutting edge of research activity, going beyond the bounds of conventional theory to that point where paradigm may be shifted.

(f) *Procedural* knowledge refers to knowing-how to go about a task or operation, as in tacit knowledge, but, unlike tacit knowledge, is not necessarily unverbalized, and may be linked to declarative and theoretical knowledge.

(g) *Conditional* knowledge provides the metacognitive support for procedural knowledge (Paris, Lipson, and Wixson 1983): knowing-how-and-why. Such knowledge may operate with children learning comprehension strategies in reading, the context, referred to by Paris *et al.*, but it is also often required in professional practice (see below).

As we have noted, schools have deliberately aimed at levels (c) and (d), downplaying the procedural aspects of (a) and (b) as 'optional extras' (physical education); where they are taught, it is with a declarative emphasis (learning about art and music). The tertiary system has aimed at levels (d) and (e); all systems have found difficulty with handling procedural (f) and conditional (g) knowledge.

It will be argued here that the forms of knowledge (a) to (e) are hierarchical and developmental, so that declarative knowledge, for example, has its roots in tacit and intuitive knowledge. Bruner (1960/77) made this point in his notion of the spiral curriculum, but unfortunately it has been ignored, most particularly in its implications for developmental theory. On the contrary, developmental theory has mainly focused on a type of stage theory wherein each succeeding stage replaces or subsumes its predecessor, the effect of which has been bleakly cognitive; the acquisition of non-logical components in the construction of knowledge then becomes an aberration, not part of the framework of construction. The student is thus forced to focus on the logical and declarative ('what I can say' and 'what follows from what'), rather than on the intuitive and procedural ('what I feel' and 'what I can do, and know that it works').

Theories that are meant to 'go to school' should be at least in part derived from classroom data (Biggs 1976; Desforges and McNamara 1977). If everyday learning has its context, by the same token so does classroom learning. How does developmental theory pick up this challenge?

PIAGETIAN THEORY: PROBLEMS AND POSSIBILITIES

Piagetian theory saw cognitive development as proceeding in discrete stages, a logical structure (*structure d'ensemble*) defining each stage and governing all performances carried out within it: an example *par excellence* of the Deterministic State Model or DSM (Valsiner this volume).

Decalages

Exceptions to stage-typical performance (*décalages*) are regarded in this version of the DSM as atypical and infrequent: a position which raises both theoretical and empirical problems, as has been pointed out by many writers, including contributors to this volume (see Case 1985; Demetriou and Efklides 1988; Fischer and Silvern 1985).

The demonstration that context plays a major role in correct responding to several of the standard Piagetian tasks (Borke 1978; Donaldson 1978) was important. In the context of school, decalage is extremely common; a student can appear to be giving 'early formal' responses in mathematics and 'early concrete' in history, or formal in mathematics one day and concrete the next (Biggs and Collis 1982). Such observations clearly indicate shifts in learning, performance, or motivation rather than in cognitive development (Biggs 1980).

The nature of a stage

The apparent frequency of *décalage* must mean that stages ought not to be defined structurally (Fischer and Bullock 1984). How then should they be defined?

Let us look first at the evidence for stage-like phenomena:

1 There are age periods when all but exceptional children (in Western society) learn key tasks:
- infancy: all children learn to co-ordinate their actions with the environment;
- early childhood: all learn to speak;
- childhood (around 6 years to adolescence): all learn to use second-order symbol systems;
- adolescence: most (not all) learn to form theories about their world and how it might be ordered otherwise.

2 During such key periods, when learning is optimally complex, the performances of different children on particular tasks resemble each other more than the performances of the same child at earlier or later periods.

3 Optimally complex learning becomes increasingly abstract at each succeeding stage.

4 The way the same task is handled at various periods reveals qualitative differences, or discontinuities, between stages.

What varies here is evidently not structure but the *mode of representing* the contents learned, which range from the most concrete (sensori-motor) acts in infancy, through mental images in early childhood and symbolic representations in later childhood, to formal theories by late adolescence.

Further, as Bruner (1960/77) originally implied, these modes *accrue* from birth to maturity. The later developing, more abstract modes do not replace earlier ones but coexist with them. The latest to develop simply represent a current ceiling to abstraction, not a standard to which all current performances must conform.

Sub-stages

Several theorists postulate sub-stages that recycle during successively higher stages (Biggs and Collis 1982; Case 1985; Fischer 1980). Fischer and Pipp (1984) distinguish between *optimal level* and *skill acquisition*, the former referring to the highest level of abstraction available for representing a problem, indexed by developmental stage, the latter to the way skills or competencies grow until they reach that optimal level which indexes learning. That is a useful distinction and, to maintain it, the first is referred to here as 'stage' and the second, or sub-stage within a stage, as 'level'. Four such levels are commonly observed, as outlined below; each subsumes the preceding one, the topmost becoming the lowest unit at the next stage (Case 1985; Fischer 1980). Disagreement exists, however, on the nature of the organization of the levels, their content specificity, and on the mechanism of generalizing to the next stage.

MODES OF REPRESENTING REALITY

The basis of the present theory is that the modes of representing reality form the basis of the developmental stages, with four stages postulated up to late adolescence, and a fifth, postformal, stage sometimes appearing towards adulthood (Fischer and Silvern 1985). Later modes are suggested not to replace their predecessors in the ontogeny of the individual, as do Piagetian stages, but to coexist with them, thereby greatly expanding the cognitive repertoire of the mature adult as compared to that of the young child.

The following modes, and the age at which each typically emerges, may be distinguished:

1. *Sensori-motor* (from birth). The neonate interacts with the world in the most concrete way possible: by giving a fixed motor reflex to a sensory stimulus. During the development of the primary, secondary, and tertiary circular reactions (Piaget 1950), sensori-motor learning becomes highly

organized and complex, and, during infancy, remains the major mode available for learning, although, from one year or so, beginnings of the next mode (ikonic representation) becomes available, as when Grandpa is recognized in a black-and-white photograph.

Sensori-motor learning itself does not fade after infancy, but becomes increasingly efficient (see below). The knowledge gained by such learning is tacit, exemplified by skilled gymnasts or sportspeople. The criterion of their knowledge is performative, but they can't necessarily explain how they do it. Declaring their knowledge is simply a different issue. The course of their performance is monitored and adjusted by kinaesthetic feedback; the ongoing 'feel' tells them when and how to adjust their performance.

2. *Ikonic* (from around 18 months). Piaget (1950) defined thought as the 'internalization of action'; the simplest way of doing that is to imagine the action, by forming what Bruner (1964a) referred to as an internal picture or 'ikon'. The stage following the sensori-motor is therefore called *ikonic*, beginning after the first year of life and generalizing, with the help of language (for which it is a necessary prerequisite), after 18 months. Ikonic thought draws heavily on visual imagery and affect.

With such a mode as their most powerful tool for encoding reality, young children explain the mysteries of human interaction in terms of stories with clear stereotypical characters and obvious plots, in what Egan (1984) calls the 'mythic' stage. Adult versions of ikonic thought can be on a level with this, as in fantasy films and the razzamatazz of professional wrestling, but adult ikonicizing rises beyond myth making, as is evident in the intuitive knowledge displayed in aesthetics, and even by mathematicians and scientists. For example, Gardner (1985) relates the story of Kekulé's realization of the structure of the organic ring compounds, a realization preceded by a hypnagogic dream of six snakes chasing each others' tails. The 'truth' thus revealed had then to be established to the satisfaction of the scientific community by evidence and argument.

The ikonic mode is thus not a presymbolic mode of information processing restricted to early childhood; it continues to grow in power and complexity well beyond childhood. Whether that increase occurs solely within the ikonic mode, or in interaction with other modes, is an important question considered later. Another of Gardner's stories illustrates such interaction: Isadora Duncan, on being asked to explain what a particular dance 'meant', replied: 'If I could tell you what it is, I would not have danced it' (Gardner 1985: 225). The calisthenics weren't the point either; their ikonic software was.

3. *Concrete-symbolic* (from around 6 years). Surely the most interesting and profound change occurring throughout the childhood years – and which corresponds to the years of compulsory schooling in most countries, as it happens – is that which permits the acquisition and instrumental use of the skills of text processing (Mason and Allen 1986). The symbol systems of

written language and signs give us one of the most powerful tools for acting on the environment, and they include writing itself, mathematical symbol systems, maps, and musical notation.

The point of this stage, reflected in the suggested name, is the ability to process symbols in a disembedded context, cold, with little paralinguistic support (Donaldson 1978): to outgrow the warm fuzzies of ikonicism, to be sure, but not necessarily in order to work within a structural system of logical operations. The task is defined existentially rather than logically, so that mastery of these systems, and of their application to real world problems, is the major task in primary and secondary schooling. Learning to read in order to read to learn, and learning to write in order to learn more effectively, may sound catchy things to do, but they capture the principal aims of schooling: to help the individual handle a world in which symbol systems are a major tool.

4. *Formal* (from around 14 years). If the concrete-symbolic mode is to symbolize reality, the formal mode is that by which we theorize about reality. Formal thinking thus refers to a superordinate abstract system in which any given topic is embedded, and which can be used to generate hypotheses about alternative ways of conceptualizing the world. Thinking in the formal mode transcends the particular, beginning to appear, in some individuals with respect to their particular specializations, from around 14 years of age. It does not however generalize to all thinking, and in some individuals may not develop at all.

This superordinate system becomes identifiable with the body of knowledge that currently prevails in a discipline. Professional, as opposed to technical, competence requires an understanding of first principles, so that the practitioner can generate viable alternatives when rule-of-thumb prescriptions prove inadequate to the particular case. The formal mode is the level of abstraction usually required in undergraduate study; admission to university should require some evidence of formal thought in the proposed area of study (Collis and Biggs 1983).

5. *Postformal* (from about 20 years). Qualitative improvements in cognition occur well into adulthood: in the affective and social domains (e.g. Erikson 1959; Levinson *et al.* 1978), in cognitive processes (Schaie 1979), and in metacognitive aspects of thinking (Volet, Lawrence, and Dodds 1986; Demetriou and Efklides 1985).

What might then best characterize postformal thought? If formal thought is the level of abstraction optimal at undergraduate level and in professional practice, questioning the conventional bounds of theory and practice, and establishing new ones, presumably constitutes postformal thinking. Postformal thought may be seen in high-level innovations in many fields, such as the prodigious performances in music, mathematics, literature, and the arts noted by Gardner (1985). Demetriou and Efklides (1985) define postformal thought operationally with tests requiring the respondent to operate in novel

38　General principles of cognitive organization and change

systems and, in a metacognition test, to report on their processing while solving novel problems; few could do so (see also Commons, Richards and Kuhn 1982). Such a deficit may explain the difficulty some hitherto high-achieving undergraduates have in coming to terms with the requirements of research, as opposed to coursework, higher degrees (Collis and Biggs 1983).

LEARNING CYCLES: THE SOLO TAXONOMY

The next question involves learning itself, the growth of response complexity within a stage. In studying the growth of topic competence in school subjects, Biggs and Collis (1982) found a consistent, hierarchical sequence that they called a *learning cycle*. The same pattern of learning cycle was found to be applicable to a variety of tasks and in several modes: to the learning of geography in the concrete-symbolic mode (see below) and to the learning of motor skills.

Thus, knowing at what point an individual may be in the learning cycle gives an indication of how far learning has progressed within a given mode. Such information may be used to evaluate learning outcomes: hence the SOLO taxonomy, SOLO being an acronym for 'structure of the observed learning outcome'. The taxonomy may be used to evaluate learning quality or to set curriculum objectives (Biggs and Collis 1989), but the present point is to conceptualize the model within the broad framework of cognitive theory.

Five basic levels in the learning cycle can be distinguished: prestructural, unistructural, multistructural, relational, and extended abstract. Unistructural, multistructural, and relational responses fall within a given mode. Prestructural responses belong in the previous mode, indicating that learning is at too low a level of abstraction for the task in question, while extended abstract responses are at a level of abstraction that extends into the next mode and become the unistructural level of that next mode. Table 2.1 describes these levels in relation to a given mode, here called the 'target' mode.

The focus of learning is within the target mode, and its progress denoted by levels 2, 3, or 4, thus describing the point in the learning cycle already reached by the learner.

DEVELOPMENTAL GROWTH, LEARNING, AND SCHOOLING

The present model provides a macrostructure for viewing learning and development, and, as the main database for the model originated in the classroom, it is particularly relevant to learning in the context of school. The modes provide the representational media for the contents of learning; these contents then become progressively organized within the learning cycle. However, learning may be not necessarily remain intramodal; as will be detailed below, much learning is cross-modal, as is the case with extended

Modes of learning, forms of knowing, and ways of schooling   39

Table 2.1 Modes and levels in the SOLO taxonomy

Mode		Structural level (SOLO)
Next	5.	*Extended abstract.* The learner now generalizes the structure to take in new and more abstract features, representing a new and higher mode of operation.
Target	4.	*Relational.* The learner now integrates the parts with each other, so that the whole has a coherent structure and meaning.
	3.	*Multistructural.* The learner picks up more and more relevant or correct features, but does not integrate them.
	2.	*Unistructural.* The learner focuses on the relevant domain and picks up one aspect to work with.
Previous	1.	*Prestructural.* The task is engaged, but the learner is distracted or misled by an irrelevant aspect belonging to a previous stage or mode.

abstract responses themselves. There are other, educationally significant, tasks which involve cross- or multi-modal learning. The essentials of the model are given in Figure 2.1.

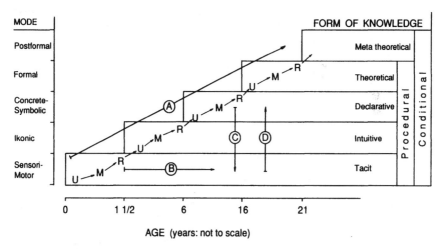

Figure 2.1 Modes, learning cycles, and forms of knowledge

Modes typically appear at the ages indicated on the abscissa, and accumulate as indicated on the ordinate, remaining as potential media for learning throughout life. The learning cycle progresses from unistructural (U), through multistructural (M), to relational (R) within each mode, the extension from relational to extended abstract involving a cross-modal transfer to unistructural in the next mode. Each of the four lines, (a), (b), (c), and (d), represents a qualitatively different kind of cognitive performance:

(a) the course of optimal development;
(b) the course of learning within a mode (intramodal), which in each case deals with a particular kind of content, leading to a particular form of knowledge, as indicated in the right of Figure 2.1;
(c) top-down facilitation of lower-order learning (multimodal);
(d) bottom-up facilitation of higher-order learning (multimodal).

(a) The course of optimal development

The diagonal line (a) represents the course of development as studied by developmental psychologists. Part of the course runs within a stage, through levels or sub-stages, but the main interest is across stages, on the maximum degree of abstraction that can successfully be handled at any given age, both within and across tasks. This optimal growth is slow and spontaneous, appearing to involve the following factors:

(i) *Physical maturation.* A necessary if not sufficient condition for the development of higher order thinking is almost certainly physiological (Fischer and Bullock 1984). Case (1985) suggests that the mechanisms may be the progressive mylenization of the nervous system.

(ii) *Relational level responding in the previous mode.* Piaget never once reported the emergence of a new stage from the 'middle' of the previous one; his frequent reporting of vacillatory or transitional responses emphasizes the importance of immediate prior competence. The novice-expert studies likewise invoke high competence with the given before generalization to new domains occurs (Chipman, Segal, and Glaser 1984). A prerequisite to a cross-modal shift, via the extended abstract response, is thus likely to involve relational-level responding in that same topic in the previous mode.

(iii) *Availability of working memory.* Several writers have emphasized the role of working memory in development (for example, Case 1985; Demetriou *et al.* this volume; Halford 1982), the information-to-noise ratio improving from unistructural to relational, thus allowing 'room' for radical restructuring at the extended abstract level.

(iv) *Social support.* Several writers refer to social support as a factor in hastening development (Bidell and Fischer this volume; Valsiner this volume; Vygotsky 1978/1934). When a child is within the zone of proximal development, appropriate social support from parent or teacher may enable the child to operate at a higher level than without such support.

(v) *Confrontation with a problem.* When an individual is presented with a problem that creates an 'optimal' mismatch between what is known and what is needed to be known, that person becomes involved in a cognitively complex way that is motivated intrinsically (Hunt 1961). Such motivated mismatches frequently occur at times of developmental significance (White 1959).

Progression along line (a) thus appears to involve maturation, prior knowledge base, social support and associated expertise, and confrontation with particular problems that are cognitively involving.

When performance is suboptimal

Suboptimal performance, which is of course extremely common, occurs below the diagonal, being mapped on to earlier modes than the optimal. Two such instances are: (i) children's alternative frameworks and (ii) adults' everyday learning.

Children explain phenomena in ways that are alternative to the official 'accepted' frameworks taught in the science curriculum (e.g., Driver 1983). They may learn a concrete-symbolic, or a formal, statement of a physical principle, but for explanatory purposes rely on their primary experiences; cold is seen as a property of objects as much as is heat. Marton and Ramsden (1988) cite examples of students who correctly describe, with detailed diagrams, what 'photosynthesis' is, but who are unable to see the difference between how plants and animals obtain food.

Another example of suboptimal behaviour is everyday performance by adults. The study by Ceci and Liker (1986) of compulsive racetrack gamblers, who predicted the winning horse in 93 per cent of races, is startling. In arriving at their predictions, gamblers took account of up to fourteen independent variables (referring to horses' past performances, including jockey ability, racetrack conditions, lifetime's earnings of horse, and so on) to predict the outcome. The gamblers, to cast the problem in a formal mode algorithm, 'calculated' the main effects and major interactions between these variables as if in a multiple regression equation, often taking eight hours of intensive study without the aid of calculating devices. It was however quite unclear – both to the author and to the subjects – how these enormous 'regression equations' were in fact calculated. It is likely that their knowledge was derived intuitively, from the ikonic mode.

(b) The course of learning within a mode

Line (b) represents the simplest case of learning, the learning cycle that occurs from U to M to R within a mode. The purest case of such learning is in infancy, where the sensori-motor mode is the only one available. Tacit knowledge of sensori-motor skills, however, may be of an extremely high order of complexity; in adults, it is far beyond the highest relational level at which infants respond. Is this just a 'better' relational response than an infant's, or is it qualitatively different? It is suggested that the latter is the case: such qualitative differences in performance, apparently homogeneous modally speaking, do not utilize just one mode; adults draw upon higher-order modes in order to augment their performance in lower-order modes (see next section).

Applying (b)-type lines to each mode, optimal competence leads to a particular form of knowledge: sensori-motor to tacit, ikonic to intuitive, concrete-symbolic to declarative, formal to theoretical, and postformal to metatheoretical. Procedural knowledge may occur within all modes, except possibly metatheoretical. A formal operation involves knowing-how at a theoretical level, but taking that to a metatheoretical level must involve conditional knowledge. Conditional knowledge itself, then, may potentially operate across all modes, linking action with theory at different levels.

At adult levels of competence in these forms of knowledge, the question of whether intuitive is 'higher' than sensori-motor, or lower than theoretical, is meaningless: is a champion gymnast cleverer than a hack poet? It may well be that these forms of knowledge evolve in a developmental sequence, but, at the highest levels of expression, they operate, as Gardner (1985) puts it, as 'autonomous' intelligences.

Schooling centres on the concrete-symbolic mode. The original work with the SOLO taxonomy (Biggs and Collis 1982) described the course of such learning in particular topics within the secondary-school curriculum with the concrete-symbolic as the target mode, prestructural responses being located in the ikonic and extended abstract in the formal mode.

However, as may be seen from Figure 2.1, the concrete-symbolic mode evolves from sensori-motor and ikonic foundations, so that any topic raised at the concrete-symbolic stage has an ancestry in the earlier modes. It is possible that direct instruction may short-circuit this existing experiential hierarchy, substituting a network of concepts and propositions that are self-referential and that coexist within the concrete-symbolic mode itself. This would then leave the task of *explaining* experience to knowledge embedded in sensori-motor and ikonic modes, as noted in the case of children's alternative frameworks.

In other words, learning within concrete-symbolic and formal modes leads to declarative knowledge comprising propositions that may link (more or less richly) to each other, but which do not integrate with personal experience or generate action. There are aspects of this kind of learning, such as its detachment from affect and experience, that recall descriptions of 'surface', as opposed to 'deep', learning (Biggs 1987).

(c) 'Top-down' facilitation of lower-order learning (multimodal)

The sensori-motor learning of adolescents and adults is vastly superior to that of infants. Not only are the brains and nervous systems of adults more highly developed than those of infants, adults use higher-order modes to facilitate lower-order learning. For example, motor skills can be considerably enhanced by mental rehearsal alone (Paivio 1986). A mechanism allowing for this is represented by line (c) (Figure 2.1).

Fitts (1962) postulates three stages in motor-skill learning: *cognitive* analysis of the task and verbalization of what is involved, so that the learner understands what to do; *fixative*, involving practice to the point of competent performance; and *autonomous*, involving further practice to the point of automaticity. Presumably the target in motor-skill learning is sensori-motor, but the first stage does not even involve the target mode; the kind of knowledge aimed at here is declarative (to verbalize and to understand what is involved). The fixative stage focuses primarily on the sensori-motor (target) mode, and the final goal of autonomous skill involves tacit, procedural knowledge.

Several modes are thus likely to be engaged in performing the skill, although its main realization is in the sensori-motor mode. Individuals with different purposes, however, would variously utilize different modes in the service of skill learning. Performing artists will naturally focus on the skill itself, perhaps to the point of unimodality in the case of Olympic athletes. Other prodigious performers are multimodal. Isadora Duncan's dancing, for example, requires immense sensori-motor skill, but the ikonic mode defines her performance as a dance, rather than as callisthenics. Coaches would be more orientated towards the higher-order modes, involving declarative and theoretical knowledge of physiology, nutrition, and mechanics, in order to derive the conditional knowledge leading to better strategies for training and performance.

While professionalism certainly has its basis in the formal mode, the form of knowledge aimed at in professional practice is conditional, which implies multimodality, linking procedural with declarative or theoretical knowledge. A professional person is one whose role in the community requires informed action, skill in carrying out the role, and a theory guiding its deployment. One of the most difficult tasks of professional training is the integration of the practicum, or clinical experience, with theory. In teacher education, practice teaching tends to be one thing (the important thing, in students' eyes) and the psychology of learning very much another, student teachers all too often seeing the latter as a time-wasting irrelevance in their education. Teacher educators are wearily familiar with the perennial attempts at linking the two; such attempts are doomed to failure if conceived within a multi-structural framework, such that the problem is seen as selling the idea that both components, practicum *and* theory courses, have to be slotted in somehow.

Such a multistructural conception of professional training is now disappearing; problem-based learning in the professions is one increasingly popular alternative. Here, the content learned – of a medical, paramedical, agricultural, or other degree (see Boud 1985) – is presented in context; anatomy is taught in so far as it is required for the treatment of (very carefully selected) patients, so that the content itself has a relation both to the body of knowledge of which it is part and to a palpable problem, in which particular skills need to be developed.

(d) 'Bottom-up' facilitation of higher-order learning (multimodal)

The second form of multimodal learning is where the target is a high-level mode, and lower levels are invoked to achieve learning, as indicated by line (d) (Figure 2.1). Bruner (1964a) has given this version of multimodal learning its most straightforward formulation. In tracing the developmental sequence he described as enactive-ikonic-symbolic, Bruner concluded that even to learn at the symbolic level, it was better to retrace through enactive (sensori-motor) and ikonic levels; to stay within the symbolic level, he thought, produced learning that was shallow and narrow in its range of application or, as we would now say, was more surface than deep in quality.

Bottom-up learning has long been advocated in progressive educational circles. Inductive, experiential, workshop, constructivist, and discovery classroom methods all assume the bottom-up principle, but it has been comparatively neglected in psychological theory.

EDUCATIONAL IMPLICATIONS

The present model is broad in its implications for education, and some of the more obvious ones can be considered under the headings of curriculum, method, and assessment.

Curriculum

SOLO provides a means by which curriculum objectives can be stated in which qualitative levels of performance may be stipulated; this is something of a breakthrough, as criterion-referencing tends to have been limited to cases where the criterion level of performance is defined quantitatively (e.g., 90 per cent of items correct), which tends to be either arbitrary or trivial. Defining the criterion performance in terms of a SOLO level, on the other hand, indexes performance at a specified grade level to a point in the learning cycle of that topic. Some implications of the model have been spelled out: for setting curriculum objectives at a systemic level, and with reference to school-based curriculum development, in Biggs and Collis (1989), and for science education in Collis and Biggs (1989).

The multimodal case is more complex, not least because the role of the school is commonly to teach declarative knowledge within the concrete-symbolic mode, ikonic and sensori-motor modes being only for structuring non-academic subjects such as art, music, and physical education (Collis and Biggs 1991). It would follow from the present discussion, however, that lower-order enabling objectives could be expressed in ikonic and perhaps sensori-motor modes, even though the target mode is ultimately concrete-symbolic or even formal, as likewise argued in Bruner's (1960/77) notion of the spiral curriculum.

Apart from the expression of curriculum objectives, there is the question of curriculum design, particularly relevant to 'top-down' multimodal learning. Where procedural and conditional knowledge are concerned, the theoretical and performative aspects need to be integrated, not simply placed in the curriculum side by side.

Method

Egan describes an interesting attempt in the elementary school to 'use the power of the story form in order to teach any content more engagingly and meaningfully' (1988: 2). The story form has been well learned in the ikonic mode prior to school, and Egan proposes that it can be used to draw students into any academic content: a clear example of a bottom-up approach, attacking a concrete-symbolic target from an ikonic baseline. He uses a technique of abstracting conflicting concepts that are intrinsic to a topic and working through the conflict in such diverse areas as social science, mathematics, English, and science. Obviously, the technique does not cover the whole curriculum of each, but it provides a structure, motivation, and imaginative challenge that offer a useful framework for the less interesting concrete-symbolic content to follow.

The memory models proposed by Tulving (1985) and Neisser (1967), whereby an event is 'dismembered' along several dimensions, have clear implications for teaching method, which become sharper when the dimension can be identified with modes of representation, as these provide a level of abstraction and a target for selecting different dimensions for emphasis. The analogy is to a library referencing system; the more cross-references there are, the more likely it is that the material will be easily accessed, given also that some dimensions are more powerful than others: title and author, for instance, are usually more powerful than date of publication or publisher. Activity in a variety of dimensions reinforces learning and subsequent recall and, in the case of declarative and theoretical knowledge, those dimensions should include the most abstract the learner can handle. Good teaching in turn should then invoke a variety of means of encoding content, instead of simply teaching within the concrete-symbolic mode. The more an activity links the content to sensori-motor, ikonic, and higher modes – or to procedural, episodic, and semantic memories if you like – the more likely it is that learning will be remembered and used.

The multimodal model would further specify in what medium those activities might be, in proportion to the target mode. For example, in using the Dienes blocks, symbolic activity would need to be carefully highlighted and integrated with manipulating the blocks, otherwise the 'play' would become the point of the activity, not the conceptual understanding (Bruner 1964b; Dienes 1963).

MacKenzie and White (1982) criticize the usual school excursion as merely a 'conducted tour', the conceptual material it is supposed to enrich having already been taught and not being seen as part of the excursion activity. In their 'process' version of a coastal geography excursion, they carefully linked each activity to a corresponding curriculum objective, of which there were thirty-five in all. The activities themselves were also selected to be 'memorable', such as chewing mangrove leaves, leaping from rock platforms, and wading through a mangrove swamp. Recall on an ordinary factual test later was several times higher than that from either an ordinary excursion plus lesson or lesson only.

There is actually little new about teaching through the use of many modes; as noted above, progressive educators have long been inventive in this direction. What may be surprising is that this kind of approach has not been used more widely; or perhaps, in the dynamics of educational innovation, it may not be so surprising (Reid 1987). What is new, perhaps, is that cognitive developmental theory provides a clear rationale for this kind of teaching. While progressive educators thought that they had found the rationale for what they were already doing in traditional Piagetian theory (e.g., McNally 1975), they were mistaken; ironically, because it is in fact quite hard to derive practices from genetic epistemology, and Piaget never intended for a moment that they should be.

Assessment

The present model has quite important implications for assessment; it was in that context that the SOLO taxonomy was first applied (Biggs and Collis 1982). The theory has two elements in common with recent research into the nature of student learning: (i) learners' comprehension of taught content is gradual and cumulative, and (ii) qualitative changes take place in the nature both of what is learned and how it is structured (Chi, Glaser, and Rees 1982; Ramsden 1988). Both elements are recognized in curriculum development, but they have not been systematically addressed in assessment technology (Masters 1987). Attainment testing should reflect this orderly progression. If it did, with respect to particular concepts, skills, or other curriculum content, teachers would be able to see how far along the path towards expertise given students, or a whole class, may be.

Classifying responses in terms of the point in the learning cycle at which a student can optimally perform can be done either in an open-ended

Modes of learning, forms of knowing, and ways of schooling   47

format, as in the geography example, or in an objective-type format (Collis and Davey 1986; Wilson 1989). In the latter, the test format is similar to a multiple-choice item, but instead of opting for the one correct alternative out of the four or so provided, the student is required to attempt all alternatives (sub-items), which are ordered into a hierarchy of complexity that reflects successive stages of learning that concept or skill. The students respond to the sequence as far as they can go. The information so derived tells the teacher what stage towards competence in that topic either an individual or a whole class has reached. In constructing such items, the aim is to ask a series of questions about a stem in such a way that satisfactory responses require a more and more sophisticated use of the information in the stem.

To illustrate the possibilities of the model, consider a finding from a pilot study, in which an ordered-outcome mathematics test was given to several hundred seventh-grade students in two Hong Kong schools (Biggs *et al.* 1988). Responses to one item were as seen in Figure 2.2.

Toothpicks are used to make the above patterns. Four are used to make one box, seven to make two boxes, etc.

		FORM 1	
		School A	School B
UNISTRUCTURAL	a. How many toothpicks are used to make three boxes ?	96%	99%
MULTISTRUCTURAL	b. How many more toothpicks are used to make 5 boxes than used to make 3 boxes ?	74%	76%
RELATIONAL	c. Calculate how many boxes can be made with 31 toothpicks ?	57%	70%
EXTENDED ABSTRACT	d. If I have made y boxes, how many toothpicks have I used ?	6%	48%

(from Biggs, Lam, Balla & Ki, 1988)

Figure 2.2 An ordered outcome mathematics item
Source: Biggs *et al.* 1988

It can be seen that the two schools perform almost identically up to multistructural level, but they diverge sharply thereafter, with School B performing at eight times the level of School A in the extended abstract sub-item: 48 per cent compared to 6 per cent. Differences between the students in Schools A and B are thus manifested only in the most cognitively complex processes. A conventional test, comprising an aggregate of mixed items scored correct or incorrect, would be unlikely to pick up this probably important qualitative difference in the students' mathematical thinking.

So far, all these applications of the model have been unimodal within the concrete-symbolic mode; the full thrust of the model would be realized when assessing multimodally. Although there may be only one (usually concrete-symbolic) target mode, its sensori-motor and ikonic back-up is invariably not assessed at present. Given the appropriate technology, one might then envisage a profile: assessment of competence within the target mode and support assessments of competence within the back-up modes. That is, however, to look well beyond developments so far.

CONCLUSIONS

We return to our original question: what does cognitive developmental theory have to offer education? The answer depends on the nature of the theory and its relation to its contexts of application.

Most developmental theorists do not derive their theories from the context of school, which as we have seen is a peculiar one, requiring of students performances of a cognitive purity that fits ill with their everyday life. Knowledge has many forms, which evolve from representational modes, which provide each with a special validity at various developmental periods in life.

The present theory is a schematic one that owes much to other neo-Piagetian models, but differs in two main ways: in its use of school learning data and in its assumption that new stages do not supplant previous ones. It is similar particularly in the feature that a within-stage cycle of structuring the contents of learning repeats across stages (in this case, across modes).

In this modes × levels model, four different kinds of competence can be represented: the course of optimal development, the course of learning within a mode (unimodal), 'top-down' facilitation of lower-order learning (multimodal) and 'bottom-up' facilitation of higher-order learning (multimodal). The first two kinds of competence have been studied extensively: the last two, multimodal, kinds rather less so. Five forms of knowledge emerge directly from each of the five modes – tacit, intuitive, declarative, theoretical and metatheoretical – with a sixth, procedural, operating within modes, and a seventh, conditional, across modes. Each of these forms of knowledge (except metatheoretical) may be a target in school learning.

Educational implications in the areas of curriculum, instructional method, and assessment are suggested. In essence, unimodal and multimodal statements of curriculum objectives can be made, which provide a way of criterion-referencing school performance in terms of learning quality, instead of, as more usually, in terms of the amount learned. Moreover, taking into account the developmental 'history' of an item of learning suggests that enabling objectives, expressed in lower-order modes than the target mode, might be effective.

In fact, several teaching methods do exactly that, from Egan's (1988) attempt to base the elementary-school curriculum on the story form to discovery methods that have a long educational history. There are two major features to these methods: (i) they require learner activity in lower-order modes, but (ii) they focus activity on the target mode, this usually being the most abstract mode available. To focus exclusively on the latter may result in surface rather than deep learning.

Implications for assessment are particularly important, as they require one to rethink the model of assessment that is most often used in schools. Several writers (Masters 1987) have pointed out that the assumptions emerging out of recent research about the nature of learning are quite different from those underpinning most current evaluation technology. Likewise, the major assumption here is that learning grows longitudinally, changing qualitatively along the way. Evaluation technology, on the other hand, assumes that learning is discrete, binary (right/wrong), and with each operationally defined 'unit' of learning being algebraically interchangeable with any other unit. Each such assumption is inappropriate, but an elaborate technology has been able to make them 'work' actuarially, thus developing an alternative framework concerning the nature of learning that has been detrimental to our thinking about curriculum, teaching method, and assessment itself.

REFERENCES

Biggs, J. B. (1976) 'Educology: the theory of educational practice', *Contemporary Educational Psychology* 1: 274–84.
—— (1980) 'Developmental processes and learning outcomes', in J. R. Kirby and J. B. Biggs (eds) *Cognition, Development and Instruction*, New York: Academic Press.
—— (1987) *Student Approaches to Learning and Studying*, Hawthorn, Vic.: Australian Council for Educational Research.
Biggs, J. B. and Collis, K. F. (1982) *Evaluating the Quality of Learning: The SOLO Taxonomy*, New York: Academic Press.
—— (1989) 'Towards a model of school-based curriculum development and assessment: using the SOLO Taxonomy', *Australian Journal of Education* 33: 151–63.
Biggs, J. B., Lam, R. Y. L., Balla, J. R., and Ki, W. W. (1988) 'Assessing learning over the long term: the "Ordered Outcomes" model', paper given to Annual Conference, Hong Kong Educational Research Association, 26–27 November.
Borke, H. (1978) 'Piaget's view of social interaction and the theoretical construct of empathy', in L. S. Siegel and C. J. Brainerd (eds) *Alternatives to Piaget*, New York: Academic Press.
Boud, D. (ed.) (1985) *Problem-Based Learning in Education for the Professions*, Sydney: Higher Education Research and Development Society of Australasia.
Brown, J. S., Collins, A., and Duguid, P. (1989) 'Situated cognition and the culture of learning', *Educational Researcher* 18 (1): 32–42.
Bruner, J. S. (1960/77) *The Process of Education*, Cambridge, MA: Harvard University Press.
—— (1964a) 'The course of cognitive growth', *American Psychologist* 19: 1–15.
—— (1964b) 'Some theorems on instruction illustrated with reference to mathematics', in E. R. Hilgard (ed.) *Theories of Learning and Instruction*, 63rd Yearbook of the

National Society for the Study of Education, Chicago: University of Chicago Press.
Case, R. (1985) *Cognitive Development*, New York: Academic Press.
Ceci, S. J. and Liker, J. (1986) 'Academic and nonacademic intelligence: an experimental separation', in R. J. Sternberg and R. K. Wagner (eds) *Practical Intelligence*, Cambridge: Cambridge University Press.
Chi, M. T. H., Glaser, R., and Rees, E. (1982) 'Expertise in problem solving', in R. Sternberg (ed.) *Advances in the Psychology of Human Intelligence*, Vol. 1, Hillsdale, NJ: Erlbaum.
Chipman, S., Segal, J., and Glaser, R. (eds) (1984) *Thinking and Learning Skills*. Hillsdale, NJ: Erlbaum.
Collis, K. F. and Biggs, J. B. (1983) 'Matriculation, degree requirements, and cognitive demands in universities and CAEs', *Australian Journal of Education* 27: 41–51.
—— (1989) 'A school-based approach to setting and evaluating science curriculum objectives: SOLO and school science', *Australian Journal of Science Teachers* 35 (4): 15–25.
—— (1991) 'Developmental determinants of qualitative aspects of school learning', in G. Evans (ed.) *Learning and Teaching Cognitive Skills*, Hawthorn, Vic.: Australian Council for Educational Research.
Collis, K. F. and Davey, H. A. (1986) 'A technique for evaluating skills in high school science', *Journal of Research in Science Teaching* 23: 651–63.
Commons, M. C., Richards, F. A., and Kuhn, D. (1982) 'Systematic and metasystematic reasoning: a case for levels of reasoning beyond Piaget's stage of formal operations', *Child Development* 53: 1058–69.
Demetriou, A. and Efklides, A. (1985) 'Structure and sequence of formal and postformal thought: general patterns and individual differences', *Child Development* 56: 1062–91.
—— (1988) 'Experiential structuralism and neo-Piagetian theories: towards an integrated model', in A. Demetriou (ed.) *The Neo-Piagetian Theories of Cognitive Development*, Amsterdam: North-Holland.
Desforges, C. and McNamara, D. (1977) 'One man's heuristic is another man's blindfold: some comments applying social science to educational practice', *British Journal of Teacher Education* 3: 27–39.
Dienes, Z. P. (1963) *An Experimental Study of Mathematics Learning*, London: Hutchinson.
Donaldson, M. (1978) *Children's Minds*, Glasgow: Fontana.
Driver, R. (1983) *The Pupil as Scientist*, Milton Keynes: Open University Press.
Egan, K. (1984) *Educational Development*, Oxford: Oxford University Press.
—— (1988) *Teaching as Storytelling: An Alternative Approach to Teaching and the Curriculum*, London: Routledge.
Erikson, E. (1959) *Identity and the Life Cycle*, New York: International Universities Press.
Fischer, K. (1980) 'A theory of cognitive development: the control and construction of hierarchies of skills', *Psychological Review* 57: 477–531.
Fischer, K. and Bullock, D. (1984) 'Cognitive development in school-age children: conclusions and new directions', in W. Collins (ed.) *Development during Middle Childhood: The Years from Six to Twelve*, Washington, DC: National Academy of Sciences Press.
Fischer, K. and Pipp, S. (1984) 'Process of cognitive development: optimal level and skill acquisition', in R. Sternberg (ed.) *Mechanisms of Cognitive Development*, New York: W. H. Freeman.
Fischer, K. and Silvern, L. (1985) 'Stages and individual differences in cognitive development', *Annual Review of Psychology* 36: 613–48.

Fitts, P. (1962) 'Factors in complex skill training', in R. Glaser (ed.) *Training Research and Education*, Pittsburgh: University of Pittsburgh Press.
Gardner, H. (1985) *Frames of Mind*, London: Paladin.
Halford, G. S. (1982) *The Development of Thought*, Hillsdale, NJ: Erlbaum.
Hunt, J. McV. (1961) *Intelligence and Experience*, New York: Ronald.
Illich, I. (1971) *Deschooling Society*, London: Penguin.
Levinson, D., Darrow, C., Klein, E., Levinson, H., and McKee, B. (1978) *The Seasons of a Man's Life*, New York: Knopf.
MacKenzie, A. and White, R. T. (1982) 'Fieldwork in geography and long-term memory structures', *American Educational Research Journal* 19: 623–32.
McNally, D. W. (1975) *Piaget, Education and Training*, Sydney: Hodder & Stoughton.
Marton, F. and Ramsden, P. (1988) 'What does it take to improve learning?', in P. Ramsden (ed.) *Improving Learning: New Perspectives*, London: Kogan Page.
Mason, J. M. and Allen, J. B. (1986) 'A review of emergent literacy with implications for research and practice in reading', in E. Z. Rothkopf (ed.) *Review of Research in Education*, Washington, DC: American Educational Research Association, pp. 3–48.
Masters, G. (1987) 'New views of student learning: implications for educational measurement', *Research Working Paper 87.11*, University of Melbourne: Centre for the Study of Higher Education.
Neisser, U. (1967) *Cognitive Psychology*, New York: Appleton-Century-Crofts.
Paivio, A. (1986) *Mental Representations: A Dual Coding Approach*, New York: Oxford University Press.
Paris, S., Lipson, M., and Wixson, K. (1983) 'Becoming a strategic reader', *Contemporary Educational Psychology* 8: 293–316.
Piaget, J. (1950) *The Psychology of Intelligence*, London: Routledge & Kegan Paul.
Ramsden, P. (ed.) (1988) *Improving Learning: New Perspectives*, London: Kogan Page.
Reid, W. A. (1987) 'Institutions and practices: professional education reports and the language of reform', *Educational Researcher* 16 (8): 10–15.
Resnick, L. B. (1987) 'Learning in school and out', *Educational Researcher* 16 (9): 13–20.
Ryle, G. (1949) *The Problem of Mind*, New York: Barnes & Noble.
Schaie, K. W. (1979) 'The primary mental abilities in adulthood: an exploration in the development of psychometric intelligence', in P. Baltes and O. Brim (eds) *Life Span Development and Behavior*, New York: Academic Press.
Scribner, S. (1986) 'Thinking in action: some characteristics of practical thought', in R. J. Sternberg and R. K. Wagner (eds) *Practical Intelligence*, Cambridge: Cambridge University Press.
Seligman, M. E. P. (1970) 'On the generality of the laws of learning', *Psychological Review* 77: 406–18.
Tulving, E. (1985) 'How many memory systems are there?', *American Psychologist* 40: 385–98.
Volet, S., Lawrence, J. A., and Dodds, A. E. (1986) 'Adolescents' organizational strategies for planning errands', in C. Pratt, A. Garton, W. E. Tunmer, and A. R. Nesdaile (eds) *Research in Child Development*, Sydney: Allen & Unwin.
Vygotsky, L. (1978/34) *Mind and Society*, Cambridge, MA: Harvard University Press.
Wagner, R. K. and Sternberg, R. J. (1986) 'Tacit knowledge and intelligence in the world', in R. J. Sternberg and R. K. Wagner (eds) *Practical Intelligence*, Cambridge: Cambridge University Press.
White, R. W. (1959) 'Motivation reconsidered: the concept of competence', *Psychological Review* 66: 297–333.
Wilson, M. (1989) 'A comparison of deterministic and probabilistic approaches to measuring learning structures', *Australian Journal of Education* 33: 127–40.

Chapter 3

The role of central conceptual structures in the development of children's scientific and mathematical thought

Robbie Case

THE CLASSIC STRUCTURALIST POSITION AND ITS DILEMMAS

An issue that has played a central and controversial role in the field of intellectual development, virtually since its inception, is the question of whether or not children pass through a set of general stages in their intellectual growth. Baldwin (1894) was probably the first to postulate a set of general cognitive-developmental stages. However, it was Piaget's (1954, 1962) re-working of Baldwin's theory that had the greatest impact on the field, for what Piaget added to Baldwin's account was the notion of a 'logical structure': that is, a coherent set of internal operations that were domain-independent, and whose gradual evolution and transformation were responsible for propelling children through the observed sequence of cognitive-developmental changes.

As Piaget's theory became widely known, a reaction eventually set in against it. Particularly in North America, investigators began to see children's development as more domain-, task-, and context-specific than Piaget's theory implied. Moreover, the data that they gathered appeared to provide much stronger support for this view than for the Piagetian one (Brainerd 1978; Gelman 1969; Flavell 1982). Among the most important data were those that showed (i) insignificant correlations between developmental tests that Piaget had claimed tapped the same underlying logical structure, (ii) substantial asynchrony in the rate of development of concepts that Piaget had claimed depend on the same underlying logical structure, and (iii) strong concept-specific training effects on logical tasks such as conservation: that is, training that showed transfer to other tasks having the same conceptual content (e.g., different forms of conservation), but no transfer to other concepts whose acquisition Piaget had claimed depends on the same logical structure (e.g., classification or class inclusion).

During the early 1980s, two different directions were taken by investigators who remained interested in the original Piagetian claim, yet who wished to re-work that claim in response to the new empirical data that had been gathered. The first direction, which became known as the 'neo-Piagetian' one and which is well represented in the present volume, was to retain a general-systems perspective, but to introduce a stronger set of assumptions concerning the specificity of children's conceptual learning and its environmental dependence (Case 1978, 1985; Biggs and Collis 1982; Fischer 1980; Fischer and Canfield 1986; Halford 1982). According to this view, the development of children's concepts, control structures, and skills takes place in a fashion that is quite specific. However, (i) a common structural sequence can also be identified across different content domains, tasks, and contexts, and (ii) a common structural ceiling is also reached at any age, under optimal environmental conditions, due to the existence of age-related organismic constraints. The way in which these ceilings have been characterized varies considerably from theorist to theorist, as does the way in which the underlying organismic changes are construed. What remains common, however, is a commitment to the notion that intellectual development includes processes that are general and stage-like, as well as those that are domain-, task-, and content-specific.

A second direction that was taken in response to the dilemma of the 1970s owed its basic assumptions more directly to Chomsky than to Piaget. According to this view, the mind is essentially modular. Nevertheless, within any one of these modules, there is a great deal of internal structure. Some of this structure is present at birth. Thus, for any given module, children begin their life pre-tuned to pay attention to certain particular features of their environment and to relate these features in particular ways (Spelke 1988). Then, as they grew older and come into contact with certain types of physical and cultural experience, their original naive or 'pre-wired' structures become re-worked into more sophisticated systems or 'theories' (Carey 1985, 1988). This results in a general and stage-like change, but only in the domain to which the theory is applicable. Stage-like change is thus possible *within* any given domain, but unlikely *across* domains. Since each theory is 'informationally encapsulated', it is most likely to follow its own unique developmental trajectory, and to develop at its own unique rate (Carey 1985; Gardner 1983; Gelman 1986; Kharmiloff-Smith 1989; Keil 1986; Spelke 1988).

A similar conclusion was reached by a third group of investigators who were working in the tradition of learning theory. This group was not particularly interested in module-specific theories or general-systemic constraints. However, they *were* interested in what they referred to as the transition from 'novice' to 'expert' theories (Simon and Simon 1978), and they regarded the child, in effect, as a 'universal novice' (Chi and Rees 1983). Although their epistemological position was different, then, they were in agreement with the neo-innatist theorists in suggesting that cognitive structures are domain-specific (Chi and Rees 1983; Chi 1988).

For the past five years or so, my students and I have been operating within the first (neo-Piagetian) tradition. However, as we have accumulated an increasing amount of data across different domains, we have begun to discern a pattern which is similar to that postulated by those operating within the second and third (i.e., modular or domain-specific) frameworks. In attempting to explore and conceptualize these data, we have been led to postulate the existence of a new construct, one that we think may have an important role to play in bridging the gap between the modular and general-system perspectives and perhaps be of interest to those in the learning tradition as well. In this chapter, I shall give a brief account of this concept and the data from which it has been derived. I shall then return to the data that were problematic for the classic structuralist position and indicate the form of solution which this new construct offers. Finally, I shall consider the relevance of this problem for some of the classic problems of schooling, to which the present volume is devoted.

THE NOTION OF A CENTRAL CONCEPTUAL STRUCTURE

I call the construct in which we have become interested a *central conceptual structure*. A central conceptual structure is defined in our lexicon as a system of semantic nodes and relations that has a very broad domain of application and that plays a pivotal role in children's intellectual growth (Case and Griffin 1990; Case 1992). Like the encapsulated theories postulated by modular theorists, such structures are not applicable to the entire range of children's experience, merely to experience within some particular domain. The sorts of domains we have examined are extremely broad ones, however, and transcend what are normally termed 'disciplines' or 'subject-matter areas' by educators or learning theorists. In addition, they conform to the general forms specified by neo-Piagetian theorists, and are subject to the central systemic constraints they have specified. As a consequence – at least under optimal environmental circumstances – we believe that they develop at approximately the same rate, across the full range of domains that are of relevance in children's daily life.

The conceptual structure on which we have focused most intensively is the one by which children conceptualize number, and it is this structure on which I shall concentrate in the next section.

CENTRAL CONCEPTUAL STRUCTURES IN THE DOMAIN OF NUMBER

My interest in children's conceptual central structures emerged from a series of studies that were conducted using Siegler's (1978) version of Inhelder and Piaget's (1958) balance beam. On this task, children go through the following developmental progression. At 4 years of age, they can predict which side of a beam will go down when one side is piled high with weights and the other has almost none (Marini in press). At 6, they can predict which side of a beam will go down when all strong visual cues are removed and a stack of washers is placed on one side that differs by only one unit from that on the other (Siegler 1978). At 8, they can predict which side will go down when two stacks of washers are identical, but placed at slightly different distances from the fulcrum (Siegler 1978). Finally, at 10, they can predict which side will go down when the weight and distance variables are set in conflict, and the only visible cue as to which side will go down is which variable has the greater numerical contrast (Marini 1992).

In our own work with this task, we had suggested that the control structures underlying children's success were those illustrated in Figure 3.1. What we did in our first study, then, was simply to vary the content of the problems with which children were presented and to design a set of problems that could be solved by a formally identical set of control structures. On one such task, for example, we asked our experimental subjects which of two children would be happier at a birthday party, a child who was hoping for X marbles and received Y marbles, or a child who was hoping for P marbles and received Q marbles (Marini 1992). We then presented the children with a sequence of four tasks that were formally identical to those that had already been created for the balance beam. In the first task, the number of marbles wished for by each child (X and P) were equal, and the number received by one child (Y) was much greater than the number received by the other (Q). In the second task, the numbers wished for were again equal, but the number received by the two children (Y and Q) differed by one unit. In the third task, a difference was introduced in the number of marbles wished for, while the number of marbles received by the two children was made identical. Finally, in the fourth task, a difference was introduced in both variables: i.e., the number of marbles wished for and the number received. Moreover, the direction of these two differences was set in conflict, such that both children got slightly more than they had originally hoped for. Thus, in order to succeed, children had to notice the exact number of 'extra' marbles each child received, over and above what s/he had originally wanted.

Under these circumstances, what we found was as follows. (1) The sequence of control structures that emerged on the birthday party task was identical to the sequence that emerged on the balance beam task. (2) The age at which the different structures emerged was also identical (Marini 1992).

In our second set of studies, we presented children with problems that varied more widely in format, and that involved questions about time (Case, Sandieson, and Dennis 1986) or money (Case and Sandieson 1983; Griffin, Case, and Sandieson 1992). What we found here was a bit more surprising, and is best illustrated, again, with a concrete example. When 6-year-olds were asked to answer a question that involved placing three clocks in order from earliest to latest, they were able to perform the task correctly, even though the strategy that this task requires is quite complex, and more like the one that 8-year-olds employ on other problems. Recall that, on the balance

8 YRS:

    COUNT WTS ON SIDE A Q_{WT} (A)
    COUNT WTS ON SIDE B Q_{WT} (B)

    COMPARE MAG ●STORE●
    COUNT DIST ON SIDE A Q_{DIST} (A)
    COUNT DIST ON SIDE B Q_{DIST} (B)
    IF Q_{WT} (A) ≈ Q_{WT} (B)
    AND Q_{DIST} (A) > Q_{DIST} (B) (or vice versa)
        PICK (A) DOWN (or vice versa)
            (*otherwise proceed as at 6*)

6 YRS:

    COUNT WTS ON SIDE A Q_{WT} (A)
    COUNT WTS ON SIDE B Q_{WT} (B)
    COMPARE MAG
    IF Q_{WT} (A) > Q_{WT} (B) (or vice versa)
        PICK (A) DOWN (or vice versa)
            (*otherwise =*)

4 YRS:

    CLASSIFY SIDE A   w/r WT
    CLASSIFY SIDE B   w/r WT
    IF   A (or B) BIG   w/r WT
    AND OTHER SIDE NOT, PICK A (or B) DOWN
            (*otherwise GUESS*)

Figure 3.1 Hypothesized control structures underlying children's balance beam performance at different ages

beam, 8-year-olds' first step is to compare the magnitude of the weights by counting each stack, then store their answer to this sub-problem, and compare the magnitude of the distances from the fulcrum, by counting the number of pegs between each stack of weights and the fulcrum. What 6-year-olds do on the above clock-ordering task is very similar. First they compare the time on the first two clocks, by counting the hash marks on the clock face; then they store their answer to this sub-problem, and compare the time on the second two clocks in a similar manner. At an abstract level one could say that they employ a very similar set of procedures to 8-year-olds'; namely (1) count, count, compare; (2) count, count, compare; (3) apply simple seriation rule to determine answer.

Thus far, then, one could say that we were simply rediscovering the well-known phenomenon that was mentioned in the introductory section, namely the high degree of task-specificity that children's intellectual competence exhibits during the course of its development. When two sets of tasks are designed so as to be completely equivalent in their question format, stimulus array, degree of familiarity, etc. (as in the birthday party task and balance beam task comparison), then their development appears to proceed at a constant rate. However, when task factors are allowed to vary more widely across two tasks (as in the comparison between the balance beam task and the clock-ordering task) major developmental asynchronies become apparent.

What we found to be most interesting about the foregoing findings was not simply that they reproduced the well-known pattern of task specificity or decalages, however. Rather, it was that, on closer inspection, there was one respect in which they did not reproduce this finding. Across the full range of eighty or so tasks in our battery, the *general level of conceptual understanding* that children appeared to display appeared to remain more or less constant within each of the four age groups that were studied.

As Figure 3.2 suggests, 4-year-olds were able to solve most tasks that required them to classify some variable in a polar fashion, and to notice its relationship to some other polar variable, regardless of the strategic complexity that this entailed. Similarly, 6-year-olds were able to solve most tasks that required them to order a set of objects along a single quantitative dimension. Again, this appeared to be true regardless of the strategic complexity that was involved, as the contrast between the clock-ordering task and the balance beam task actually demonstrates. (Although the *strategies* that the children use at 6 and 8 on this task are equivalent, the conceptions are not. The 6-year-old 'double counting' strategy – i.e., the strategy that is observed on the clock task at the age of 6 – requires children to think in terms of only a single quantitative dimension. By contrast, the 8-year-old 'double counting strategy' – i.e., the strategy that is observed on the balance beam or birthday party tasks at the age of 8 – requires them to think in terms of two quantitative dimensions.) Eight-year-olds were able to solve most tasks that required them to realize that two variables were of potential relevance. Finally, 10-year-olds were able to solve most tasks that required them to understand the nature of the relationship between two quantitative variables, in additive or subtractive terms.

To summarize: it seemed that, while there was a modest amount of developmental variability from task to task as a function of the *specific* knowledge that the task required, or the complexity of the strategy that had to be deployed, the really major developmental differences, as well as the cross-task consistency within any age level, were a function of the more general conceptual structures that the tasks required.

COMPARISON BETWEEN THE NOTION OF A CENTRAL CONCEPTUAL STRUCTURE AND THE PIAGETIAN NOTION OF A 'STRUCTURE OF THE WHOLE'

As was mentioned in the introduction, the central conceptual structures we have studied are like those that have been proposed by modular theorists of the neo-innatist and learning schools, in that they apply only to one specific

58 General principles of cognitive organization and change

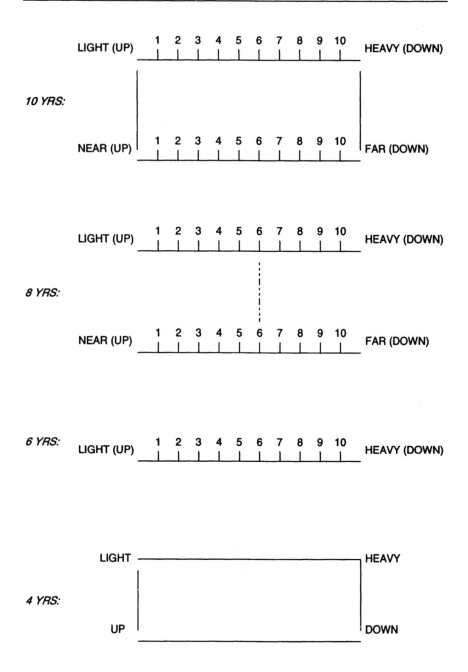

Figure 3.2 Conceptual progression across a variety of quantitative tasks

domain. They are also like the entities that have been postulated by neo-Piagetian theorists, both in their general form and in the organismic constraints to which they are subject. As a consequence, we believe they have the potential to bridge the gap between the 'general-systems' approach of neo-Piagetian theory and more modular approaches of the neo-innatist and learning schools.

What may be less obvious is the relationship of central conceptual structures to the 'structures of the whole' that were postulated by Piaget in his classic structural theory. This relationship is of obvious importance, for if the structures we are postulating are identical to Piaget's they will fall prey to the same criticisms. Before concluding, therefore, it is worthwhile to consider both the similarities and the differences.

Like Piaget's 'structures of the whole', the central conceptual structures we have hypothesized:

- are internalized sets of operations
- are arranged into coherent systems
- change only gradually in their constituent make-up
- have different characteristic forms
- define different major stages and sub-stages of development
- are used to make sense of, or learn new things about, the external world.

There are also many similarities between the classic Piagetian suggestions concerning the *origins* of such structures and those that we would endorse. Each higher-order structure, we would agree

- is assembled out of lower-order structures
- which become differentiated and co-ordinated
- via autoregulative processes (e.g., equilibrium, reflexive abstraction)
- which are activated by the universal human experience of trying to make sense of, or abstract invariants from, the normal flux of human experience.

Although there are many similarities between the two constructs, the following set of properties do not appear to be ones which are the same as – or even necessarily compatible with – the classic Piagetian notion. The structures we have proposed

- are organized sets of concepts and conceptual relations, not logical ones
- are universal with regard to sequence but potentially specific with regard to their form and incidence of occurrence
- are applicable to a broad range of content, but only within a specific domain

- are acquired via socially facilitated processes, i.e., processes which call the subject's attention to certain factors, and encourage certain kinds of constructions rather than others.
- are potentially teachable, in a rather direct fashion.

In summary, the structures which we have illustrated for the domain of number are semantic, not syntactic ones. Although they may well have certain logical characteristics (e.g., reciprocity) at certain ages, they are not developmentally constrained by these properties. Moreover, the underlying acquisition processes on which they depend, while they may well have certain universal autoregulative features, are nevertheless also ones with a strong social component. The result is that children are seen as reconstructing the conceptual inventions of prior generations, rather than abstracting universal logic invariants from their own epistemic activity.

THE DILEMMAS OF THE CLASSIC STRUCTURALIST POSITION REVISITED

At the beginning of this chapter, I suggested that three of the major empirical 'anomalies' for which the classic structuralist position offered no solution were as follows. (i) Insignificant correlations were often found among developmental tests that Piaget had claimed tap the same underlying logical structure. (ii) Substantial asynchrony was often found in the rate of development of concepts that Piaget had claimed depend on the same underlying logical structure. (iii) Strong concept-specific training effects were often found on logical tasks such as conservation: i.e., training that showed transfer to other tasks having the same conceptual consent, but no transfer to other concepts whose acquisition Piaget had claimed depends on the same logical structure.

How does the notion of a central conceptual structure fare in dealing with these three problems?

1. *Inter-task correlations.* With regard to the correlational problem, we have found high inter-task correlations before age is partialled out (e.g., circa .8: Marini 1984) and substantial and significant correlations even afterwards (e.g., circa .4), within test batteries that tap the same conceptual structure.

2. *Decalages.* With regard to the decalages problem, we have found that some cross-task variability remains, but that it is contained to the limits suggested by the theory. A set of illustrative data is presented in Table 3.1.

3. *Instruction.* Finally, with regard to the instructional problem, we have found that the pattern of transfer is the one that would be predicted by our theory. There *is* broad transfer across tasks that are structurally equivalent but which have widely different surface content. Table 3.2 presents an illustration of the pattern of transfer after teaching the 6-year-old structure indicated in Figure 3.2 to a group of lower-class 4.6-year-olds, whose initial performance indicated they did not already possess it.

Table 3.1 Cross-task variability in passing rates as a function of task

		Task 1	Task 2	Task 3	Task 4
Age	Level				
	2	10%	20%	10%	15%
	1	71%	71%	90%	85%
6.5 years	0	100%	100%	100%	100%
	2	0%	0%	0%	0%
	1	9%	16%	5%	16%
5.4 years	0	91%	84%	75%	60%

Table 3.2 Pattern of transfer after teaching the dimensional structure

	Treatment Pre–Post	Control Pre–Post
Balance	0% 36 (57)*	0% 7%
Birthday	0% 64 (86)	0% 7%
Money	0% 43 (78)	0% 29%
Time	0% 79 (100)	11% 29%

*Figures in brackets indicate percentage passing post-test, from among groups who succeeded on the training items.

Although the classic structural position ran into serious difficulties, then, and has in general been abandoned, it would appear that there is a closely analogous 'neo-structural' position which defines its underlying terms slightly differently and remains viable. This position also appears to be one that offers a possible solution to the conflict between general-system and modular theorists of the post-Piagetian era. The conclusion I draw is that we may be in danger of 'throwing out the baby with the bath water' if we abandon the classic structuralist position altogether, or even if we endorse too completely one of the various 'functionalist' or 'neo-Piagetian' views of cognitive development. It would appear, rather, that the notion of a central conceptual structure should be further developed and explored, and related to similar emergent concepts being proposed by other theorists (e.g., Demetriou's notion of a 'structural' system).

RELEVANCE FOR EDUCATIONAL PRACTICE AND THEORY

Since the theme of the present volume is an educational one, I would like to conclude by suggesting several broad areas of educational theory and practice to which the notion of a central conceptual structure might be relevant.

1. The first general area is curriculum theory. At present, methods of curriculum planning include the rational analysis of the content domain to be taught and the sequential programming of this material according to rules of logical dependence. If A is a component of AB, then it must precede it in the curriculum, etc. (Gagne 1968). As yet, however, there has been relatively little work on how to identify the 'conceptual core' of different subject areas. Attempts to use expert definitions of such conceptual cores (as in the New Maths, PSSC Physics, etc.) have often floundered because they have not been rooted in an understanding of children's thought or understanding. There has been a good deal of excellent recent work on how to identify and deal with children's 'naive theories' (Chi 1988; Carey 1988) that is relevant to such a specification. What the present construct might possibly contribute to this ongoing work is (i) a set of concrete suggestions concerning core conceptual understandings in the areas of mathematics, (ii) a methodology for identifying such core understanding in other areas, and (iii) a general system (though of course not the only one) within which to conceptualize the entire enterprise of planning curricula that are developmentally sensitive yet content-based.

2. The second area of educational relevance is instructional theory. Here again, a good deal of work has already been done on how to teach children particular skills or concepts in a developmentally sensitive fashion. Some of the early work focused on children's information processing limitations and how to teach complex strategies in a fashion that takes these into account (Case 1978). More recent work has focused on children's limited conceptual representations and how to take these into account as well (Case, Sandieson, and Dennis 1986). What the present notion offers is the potential of combining these techniques with a model of children's central conceptual representations. And this in turn offers the potential of combining a set of criteria for how to teach with a set of criteria for determining *what* to teach.

3. The third general area to which the notion of a central conceptual structure might have relevance is that of early education for disadvantaged learners. By most political criteria, the American Project Headstart can be considered an outstanding success. However, from an intellectual point of view, it did not completely fulfil its promise, for it never really identified the hidden intellectual competencies disadvantaged preschoolers lacked that other children did not. While one could expose children to the same sorts of preschool experiences that middle-class children often received, and while the children appeared to enjoy such programmes and benefit from them, it was never really made clear (i) what forms of experience such students

needed which middle-class children did not, and (ii) what parts of the traditional middle-class curriculum could be dispensed with without leading to serious subsequent problems. There is a good deal of work presently being conducted on precisely these problems. However, the notion of a central conceptual structure offers the potential for situating future research thrusts on this problem within a more systematic and secure developmental framework. Essentially, the notion is that, if a small set of central preschool structures can be identified and taught to disadvantaged preschoolers (as in the study reported in the previous section), then these children may be in a far stronger position to begin their first formal instruction in most school subjects, and thus be on a more equal footing with other learners.

4. A fourth and final area to which the present construct might be of long-term relevance would be improving education in science and mathematics, in order to increase the pool of individuals who can benefit from, and actively participate in, a society in which 'high technology' plays a crucial role. If it should turn out that there are certain central conceptual structures at high levels which many economically *advantaged* students lack (or have insufficiently consolidated), then the specification of some of these might permit these structures to be taught directly as prerequisites to instruction in whatever subject matter the school deems relevant.

REFERENCES

Baldwin, J. M. (1894) *The Development of the Child and of the Race*, New York: Macmillan. (Reprinted by Augustus M. Kelley, 1968.)

Biggs, J. and Collis, K. (1982) *Evaluating the Quality of Learning; the Solo Taxonomy*, New York: Academic Press.

Brainerd, C. J. (1978) 'The stage question in cognitive-developmental theory', *The Behavioral and Brain Sciences* 1: 173–82.

Carey, S. (1985) *Conceptual Change in Childhood*, Cambridge, MA: MIT Press.

—— (1988) 'Reorganization of knowledge in the course of acquisition', in S. Strauss (ed.) *Ontogeny, Phylogeny, and Historical Development*, New York: Ablex.

Case, R. (1978) 'A developmentally based theory and technology of instruction', *Review of Educational Research* 48 (3): 439–63.

—— (1985) *Intellectual Development: Birth to Adulthood*, New York: Academic Press.

—— (1992) *The Mind's Staircase: Exploring the Conceptual Underpinnings of Human Thought and Knowledge*, Hillsdale, NJ: Erlbaum.

Case, R. and Griffin, S. (1990) 'Child cognitive development: the role of central conceptual structure in the development of scientific and social thought', in C. A. Hauert (ed.) *Advances in Psychology: Developmental Psychology*, North Holland: Elsevier.

Case, R. and Sandieson, R. (1983) 'A developmental approach to the identification and teaching of central conceptual structures in the middle grades', in J. Hiebert and M. Behr (eds) *Research Agenda in Mathematics Education: Number Concepts and Operations in the Middle Grades*, Hillsdale, NJ: Lea, 1988, pp. 236–70.

Case, R., Sandieson, R., and Dennis, S. (1986) 'Two cognitive developmental approaches to the design of remedial instruction', *Cognitive Development* 1: 293–333.

Chi, M. T. H. (1988) 'Children's lack of access and knowledge reorganization: an example from the concept of animism', in M. Perlmutter and F. E. Weinert (eds) *Memory Development: Universal Changes and Individual Differences*, Hillsdale, NJ: Erlbaum.
Chi, M. T. H. and Rees, E. T. (1983) 'A learning framework for development', in M. T. H. Chi (ed.) *Trends in Memory Development*, New York: Karger.
Fischer, K. W. (1980) 'A theory of cognitive development: the control and construction of hierarchies of skills', *Psychological Review* 87: 477–531.
Fischer, K. W. and Canfield, R. L. (1986) 'The ambiguity of stage and structure in behavior: person and environment in the development of psychological structures', in I. Levin (ed.) *Stage and Structure: Reopening the Debate*, Norwood, NJ: Ablex.
Flavell, J. H. (1982) 'On cognitive development', *Child Development* 53: 1–11.
Gagne, R. M. (1968) 'Contributions of learning to human development', *Psychological Review* 75: 177–91.
Gardner, H. (1983) *Frames of Mind: The Theory of Multiple Intelligences*, New York: Basic Books.
Gelman, R. (1969) 'Conservation acquisition: a problem of learning to attend to relevant attributes', *Journal of Experimental Child Psychology* 7: 167–87.
—— (1986) 'First principles for structuring acquisition', Division Presidential Address, American Psychological Association, New York.
Griffin, S., Case, R., and Sandieson, R. (1992) 'Synchrony and asynchrony in the acquisition of everyday mathematical knowledge: toward a representation theory of children's intellectual growth', in R. Case (ed.) *The Mind's Staircase: Exploring the Conceptual Underpinnings of Human Thought and Knowledge*, Hillsdale, NJ: Erlbaum.
Halford, G. S. (1982) *The Development of Thought*, Hillsdale, NJ: Erlbaum.
Inhelder, B. and Piaget, J. (1958) *The Growth of Logical Thinking from Childhood to Adolescence*, New York: Basic Books.
Keil, F. C. (1986) 'On the structure-dependent nature of stages of cognitive development', in I. Levin (ed.) *Stage and Structure: Reopening the Debate*, Norwood, NJ: Ablex.
Kharmiloff-Smith, A. (1989) 'Commentary', *Human Development* 32: 272–5.
Marini, Z. A. (1984) *The Development of Social and Physical Cognition in Childhood and Adolescence*, unpublished doctoral dissertation, University of Toronto (OISE), Toronto.
—— (1992) 'Synchrony and asynchrony in the development of children's scientific reasoning: re-analyzing the problem of decalages from a neo-structural perspective', in R. Case (ed.) *The Mind's Staircase: Exploring the Conceptual Underpinnings of Human Thought and Knowledge*, Hillsdale, NJ: Erlbaum.
Piaget, J. (1954) *The Construction of Reality in the Child*, New York: Basic Books.
—— (1962) *The Origin of Intelligence in the Child*, New York: Norton.
Siegler, R. S. (1978) 'The origins of scientific reasoning', in R. S. Siegler (ed.) *Children's Thinking: What Develops?*, Hillsdale, NJ: Erlbaum.
Simon, D. P. and Simon, H. A. (1978) 'Individual differences in solving physics problems', in R. S. Siegler (ed.) *Children's Thinking: What Develops?*, Hillsdale, NJ: Erlbaum, pp. 324–48.
Spelke, E. S. (1988) 'Where perceiving ends and thinking begins: the apprehension of objects in infancy', in A. Yonas (ed.) *Perceptual Development in Infancy: Minnesota Symposia in Child Psychology*, Hillsdale, NJ: Erlbaum, pp. 197–234.
Strauss, S. and Ephron-Wertheim, T. (1986) 'Structure and process: developmental psychology as looking in the mirror', in I. Levin (ed.) *Stage and Structure: Reopening the Debate*, Norwood, NJ: Ablex, pp. 59–76.

Chapter 4

Social organization of cognitive development

Internalization and externalization of constraint systems

Jaan Valsiner

Building a theory of development is a difficult epistemological task that requires clarity in its basic assumptions before any empirical data can guide psychologists' thinking further in productive ways. In our contemporary empiricism-dominated psychology, theoretical efforts are rare, which has serious consequences for the science (see Toulmin and Leary 1985). Before we can learn anything about the empirical side of development, we need to clarify what development is and how we conceptualize its organization. It is only then that we can begin to address the issue of applicability of the basic theoretical knowledge to any area of application, such as schooling. Such applications are particularly complicated as the area of application is embedded in the ideological texture of the given society at a given time.

If we start from an axiom that development constitutes a temporal transformation of structures, we have entered the mode of reasoning that perhaps can be labelled 'dynamic structuralism' or 'structural dynamism', or (in a more familiar vein) 'genetic epistemology'. This axiomatic beginning is not yet a theory of development, of course; it only demarcates the basic perspective upon what development is and not *how* it takes place. It is that latter issue that we need to deal with, alongside specifying what kinds of 'structures' we have in mind and by what rules their 'transformations' take place over time.

TWO METATHEORETICAL PERSPECTIVES ON THE ORGANIZATION OF DEVELOPMENT

We can trace two basic kinds of views on how development is organized. The more familiar of the two – let us call it the Deterministic State Model (DSM) – is embedded in those accounts of development that expect an orderly deterministic transition from clearly definable 'less mature' states of the developing organism to 'more mature' or 'adult' states. These 'states' (or, more familiarly, 'stages') are conceptualized to be relatively stable, homogeneous entities that do not require any further explanation. In fact, theoretical systems based on this perspective try to *explain* development on the basis of that metatheoretic view of transitions from one homogeneous, entified state to another. This model leads the investigator to the phenotypic analysis of development, to use Kurt Lewin's terminology here: development is made equivalent to a series of intermediary forms (phenotypes) that can be found in the movement from immature to the adult status of the organism. The deterministic ethos of this approach is given by its retrospective look at the known courses of already accomplished developmental cases. It axiomatically eliminates the possibility of unexpected events ('developmental surprises') in the course of development.

The line of reasoning used in turning the basically descriptive approach into a causative one is interesting in itself, as it can be characterized as a sequence that co-ordinates deductive and inductive inference processes. First, the beginning and 'adult' states are defined (by inductive evidence), after which it is assumed that N different intermediate steps *must* be present in either a unilinear (the usually assumed case) or multilinear 'trajectory' from the beginning to the adult state. This deductively constructed model is subsequently inductively confirmed by empirical evidence about the discriminability of homogeneous classes (states) of phenomena over developmental time. Since phenomena of development are sufficiently heterogeneous to 'fit' with a number of theoretical models that are mapped upon them, and periods of rapid change are interspersed with periods of relative stability, it is not difficult to 'discover' the 'stages' in the description of development. The 'empirical support' (descriptive adequacy) gained for the deterministic state model is subsequently used as the proof for its adequacy as *the* explanation of development as well. For instance, Piaget's stage account of development often becomes explanatory in its use in psychological discourse, despite the fact that Piaget's own explanation of development is present elsewhere – in his equilibrium theory.

It should be obvious that the family of DSM models constitutes a metatheoretical perspective that is neither provable nor disprovable by empirical evidence or theoretical argumentation. It is a constructed 'picture' of developmental issues that is predicated upon a general world-view void of uncertainty as a substantive concept. In contrast, the second metatheoretical model that we will examine here starts from accepting the notion of uncertainty in developmental phenomena, and tries to integrate it into the theoretical discourse.

This second general approach to development could be called the Indeterministic Constraints Model (ICM). Its presence in psychology has been relatively rare (with some notable exceptions: Fishbein 1976; Gollin 1981; Gottlieb 1976). This model treats developmental process as partially indeterministic (hence unpredictable to a large extent), depending upon the limiting conditions in organism–environment relations (hence the emphasis on 'constraints'), and does not assume predetermined unilinear progression (unilinearity) in development. From that perspective Baldwin's (1906: 21) two postulates of the 'genetic science' constitute the foundation of the model. First, the logic of development is expressed in *nonconvertible propositions* (i.e., if A becomes B, it does not necessarily follow that B becomes A). Second, development entails sequences of events that cannot be exactly predicted *before* the development takes place (by foresight) and cannot be fully explained *after* it has occurred (hindsight). This (seemingly agnostic) perspective on development captures the *time-boundedness* of developmental processes, and the impossibility of an investigator of development having full knowledge about the set of possibilities for further development at each time moment. In our contemporary terminology (see Simon 1957), the class of problems which researchers of development handle is necessarily 'ill-defined', since the phenomenology of development is bound to irreversible time and organism–environment transaction. In short, the class of ICM models can be described as open-systemic and interactionistic. This model leads investigators to the 'conditional-genetic' (genetic = developmental) investigation, to use Kurt Lewin's terminology again.

It is quite obvious that I have used the ICM model in my efforts to build a theory of development (see Valsiner 1987). In the interesting discussions and elaborations that have taken place around this effort (see Elbers 1988; Goudena 1988; Oppenheimer 1988; Van der Veer, Miedema, and Wardekker 1988; Van Oers 1988; Valsiner 1988a, 1989a; Winegar 1988; Winegar, Renninger, and Valsiner 1989), a number of unexplored issues have emerged. First and foremost, the difficulty with the constraints-based perspective on human development is in the asymmetry between the child's relationships with the external environment and with the internal (psychological) one, for defining 'constraints' (and accessing the process of development as that of 'constraining'). In the child–environment relationships, the constraining process can be quite easily observable in the divergence of actions of the child and the caregiver. Not so in the child's relationship with his own self, however – here we cannot trace the child's constraining of his own psychological development in any direct way.

Thus, a rather interesting paradox emerges: the ICM models can be quite appropriately applicable when we are interested in the realm of organism–environment relations (or in the so-called field of 'social development'). However, their usability is far from clear if we are interested in the intra-organismic psychological processes which in our contemporary psychology are often labelled 'cognitive development'. The use of the DSM metatheoretical model has largely been associated with the new version of psychology ('cognitive psychology') that carries on the time-honoured tradition of studying mental phenomena *in* the minds of persons. While putting a strong emphasis on the psychological phenomena 'in the mind', contemporary cognitive psychology has artificially separated its domain of investigation from the phenomenology that is observable 'in-between the minds'. In other terms, the linkage of intra-personal cognitive functions has become separated from the interpersonal psychological world, very much along the lines of the DSM metatheoretical model explained above. The goal of this chapter is to chart out some ways in which the ICM metatheoretical model can be used in the study of cognitive development. This model – given its open-systemic nature – makes it a necessary condition that intrapersonal psychological phenomena be studied in co-ordination with interpersonal phenomenology.

INTERNATIONALIZATION–EXTERNALIZATION AS A CONSTRAINING PROCESS

The concept of 'internalization' has for long been used by those developmental psychologists who have followed the idea of the primacy of children's social experience in their mental development (see Valsiner and Van der Veer 1988; Van der Veer and Valsiner 1988). However, it is only rarely that the organization of the internalization process has been explicitly talked about (Goldstein 1933; Vygotsky 1934: ch. 7). The main feature of the internalization process that has been established in these previous analyses is the transformational nature of this process: external (social) experiences which are structured in specific ways are gradually 'taken in' to the intrapsychological cognitive-affective system of the self and modified (restructured) according to the previous structure of that self. The transformational nature of the internalization process guarantees that the internalized version of external (social) experiences is *not* an 'internal replica' of the latter, but a transformation of it into a novel form.

The transformational nature of internalization fits well into the co-constructivist perspective on development (see Valsiner 1988b, 1989a: ch. 3). The child is an active co-constructor of knowledge in the internalization process, by way of selectively transforming the 'given cultural message' from the interpersonal sphere into a different intra-individual psychological form. Thus, from the perspective of the 'social others' (parents, teachers, etc.) of a developing child, the expected 'effects' of their efforts at guiding the child towards acceptance of a particular moral value may 'backfire'. Because of the active role of the 'recipient' (child) in transforming a social expectation into a form that may (sometimes) be the opposite to 'social input', purposive efforts towards 'social control' over children are likely to fail in their explicit form. It is through the transformation of social experience into intra-personally novel form that cognitive development becomes an open-ended process capable of adaptation to new external demand conditions (see Luria 1976).

OPEN-ENDEDNESS OF THE INTERNALIZATION OF CONSTRAINING

It is the 'social others' of developing children who participate in the construction of constraining frameworks that guide the internalization process.

Social organization of cognitive development 69

Importantly, no particular action strategy of these 'social others', nor their combination, needs to provide a full guarantee for child's internalization result, since the child takes a co-constructor role in the internalization process. Let us work through a formal example that should illustrate that.

Table 4.1 A formalized example of the range of possible internalization consequences, following child's and 'social other's' (caregiver's) actions

Caregiver	no action	A	B	C	new action
Child: no action	— or ?	X or Y or ?	Y or Z or ?	X or Z or ?	?
a	X or (Y&W) or ?	X or Y or ?	Z or Y or ?	(Z&Y) or (Z&X) or ?	?
b	(W&Z) or X or ?	Z or (X&Y) or ?	(Y&Z) or (W&Z) or ?	(W&Y) or W or ?	?
c	Y or Z or ?	X or (W&Z) or ?	(Z&X) or Y or ?	(Z&X) or (Y&W) or ?	?
new action	?	?	?	?	?

Table 4.1 represents a highly simplified and abstract case of the ways in which a child's internalization outcomes (depicted as symbols in the cells) depend upon the child's previous actions (rows: 'no action', a, b, c, and 'new action') and upon the actions of the 'social other' in conjunction with those of the child (columns: 'no action', A, B, C, and 'new action'). The intersection of rows and columns gives us a particular constraining condition that occurs in child's interaction with another person. It can lead to different possible internalization consequences as presented in the matrix in the form of combinations of symbols W, X, Y, Z, and ?.

A number of features in Table 4.1 are interesting in connection with the present discussion. First, the sets both of the child and of the 'social other' are *open-ended* – new action strategies can be added, by both the child and the other, and with often indeterminate consequences for internalization (denoted by ?-s in all cells of the table). Second, *all* consequences depicted in the table (except for cell #1, and the last row and column) are disjunctive (in the exclusive sense of the term). Thus, if the 'other' 'responds' to child's 'no action' (i.e., *de facto* the caregiver initiates the interaction episode) by the strategy denoted by B, then the outcome (consequent) state of affairs is *either* Y *or* Z, *or* some new, previously unknown version (denoted by ?). It is easy to see how this nature of the consequence is a simplification of real-life conditions. In the latter, invariably for every cell, the 'no outcome' option should be added alongside the '?' outcome, since many child–caregiver interaction bouts lead to no specific results in the domain of internalization. More importantly, however, the disjunctive nature of consequences illustrates the small (only partially known) set of possible outcomes. It is assumed that the caregiver, responding in way A to child's action a, arrives at the result of either X or Y, or at some new outcome (cell 2.2 in Table 4.1). At the moment of the interactive encounter, however, the caregiver has no way of knowing (predicting) which of the outcome ends up being the case in the internalization sphere of the child (if any).

Third, nine of the fifteen cells with outcomes in Table 4.1 include *complex* consequences. For instance, cell 3.3 includes either a combination of Y & Z, or a combination of W & Z (or some novel indeterminate outcome –?). Whichever of the two determinate versions ends up occurring as a result of child's action b, followed by the caregiver's B, it includes Z with absolute certainty.

Now, of course, the 'social other' of the developing child is not a neutral 'calculator' of possible outcomes in internalization, given the conjunction of actions in the child–other interaction process. Instead, the 'social other' has his or her own goals in the effort to guide the child's internalization process, which entails the valuation of different possible outcomes. Let us attribute 'positive' and 'negative' values to different outcome conditions in Table 4.1. For example, let X be the 'negative' outcome and W the 'positive' outcome in the child's internalization results, as the caregiver perceives it. If we analyse Table 4.1 now from that value-laden perspective, we can see that some cells (2.1, 3.1, 3.4, 4.2, and 4.4) inevitably lead to either one or the other determinate outcome. Other cells include possible 'negative' or neutral (1.2, 1.4, 2.2, 2.4, 3.2, and 4.3); 'positive' or neutral (3.3); and neutral or neutral (1.3, 2.3, and 4.1) outcomes.

The caregiver, given the present situation, can act in different ways on the child's actions, with *particularly* indeterminate sets of consequences. For example, if the caregiver wants to initiate interaction with the child (the case of child's 'no action' row), two (A and C) out of the three determined strategies lead to the *possibility* of reaching a 'negative' consequence. Only strategy B leads to neutral outcome of either Y or Z. Contrast this with the caregiver's response to child's action c (row 4 in Table 4.1). Whatever the caregiver decides to do, its possible consequences are rather complicated. Caregiver's actions A, B, or C may end with the 'negative' consequence X. 'No action' on caregiver's part, however, leads to guaranteed neutral outcome of either Y or Z. A particular parent, when faced with such a situation, can decide to act in accordance with different action plans. She (or he) can take the risk of facing a negative outcome while hoping for a positive one.

In this case, actions A and C may be decided upon. Or, he (or she) may introduce a novel action ('new action'), the internalization consequences of which (given child's action c) are not known. Or, the caregiver may indeed elect the course of no intervention ('no action'), thus resulting in neither 'positive' nor 'negative' consequences.

This abstract example leads to analysis of structurally complex conditions of real-life social negotiation of the children's internalization processes. The majority of internalization consequences of child–'other' social interaction episodes may lead to unexpected results, due to the child's co-constructor's role in determining which of the possible internalization outcomes of external experiences emerges. The child may construct a version of the self-constraining structure that the 'social other' wishes, in the mind; but it is equally possible that the internalized self-constraining structure is constructed exactly in order to *overcome* the structure of the external constraining system in the realm of psychological functioning. It is the function of our cognitive-affective system to be capable of coping with a variety of conditions of external experience, in ways that go beyond that experience in our thinking, feeling, and imagination. Accounts of adults' coping with severely constrained external life conditions indicate that well, like the following description of a 'counteractive' role of internalization, given by a former Soviet political prisoner's description of psychological survival:

> I set myself the task of constructing a castle in every detail, from the foundations, floors, walls, staircases, and secret passages right up to the pointed roofs and turrets. I carefully cut each individual stone, covered the floor with parquet or stone flags, filled the apartments with furniture, decorated the walls with tapestries and paintings, lit candles in the chandeliers and smoking torches in the endless corridors. I decked the tables and invited guests, listened to music with them, drank wine from crystal goblets, and lit up a pipe to accompany coffee. We climbed the stairs together, walked from chamber to chamber, gazed at the lake from the open veranda, went down to the stables to examine the horses, walked around the garden – which also had to be laid out and painted. We returned to the library by way of the outside staircase, and there I kindled a fire in the open hearth before settling back in a cozy armchair. . . .
>
> . . . I lived for hundreds of years in that castle and shaped every stone with my own hands. I built it in between interrogations in Lefortovo, in the camp lockup, and in the Vladimir punishment cells. It saved me from apathy, from indifference to living. It saved my life. Because one must not let oneself be paralyzed; one cannot afford to be apathetic – this is precisely when they put you to the test.
>
> (Bukovsky 1978: 21–2)

Bukovsky's account indicates the possibilities of an individual's constructive imagination to counteract efforts of the 'social others' to force the person to accept the external expectations in his internal psychological sphere. Internalization involves an active construction role on behalf of the internalizing person – a role that includes the building of 'defences' against some enforced internalization suggestions.

Of course, researchers who have put a strong explanatory emphasis on the internalization process have overlooked the other side of the same coin – how is it ever possible to know anything about the transformation involved in internationalization? If internalization were the sole process by which cognitive development took place, then it would be in principle impossible to study it since most of the process takes place 'within' the mind, hence in ways that cannot be studied by any external procedure. Since 'direct access' to the cognitive processes 'in the mind' is not possible, any cognitive research would turn out to be impossible in principle. Fortunately, we need not view internalization as a process which does not have its opposite counterpart. Instead, it is feasible to posit (following the open-systemic ideology of the ICM) that, in parallel with transformation of the external experience into the internal sphere, the opposite process of transformation of the internal experience into the external sphere takes place. That process of *externalization* makes it in principle possible to study cognitive development at all (Oerter 1990). The child externalizes the internal experience in play, the adults externalize theirs in different ways of constructing their man-made environments (Heidmets 1985). If we consider the classic experiments of Piaget from the 1920s onwards, then it becomes obvious that these experiments tap into the child's externalization of internal knowledge which had previously become internalized and is made explicit by the careful instruction and experimental set-up that trigger the externalization process. Likewise, the use of 'thinking aloud protocols' in contemporary cognitive psychology (Ericsson and Simon 1980, 1984) constitutes a use of the subjects' capability of externalization of their internal(ized or -ing) experiences in the course of the problem-solving task. And, of course, all the rich history of the use of the introspective method in psychology relies fully on the externalization process. In short, if the externalization process were absent, all psychological research beyond observation of external behaviour for the sake of that behaviour would be impossible. Or, in the realm of everyday life, the mere fact that human beings take turns (change between 'speaker' and 'listener' roles) in their interaction with others indicates the intertwined nature of the two processes.

EXTERNALIZATION AS A CONSTRUCTIVE PROCESS

Now, we reach a critical junction in our construction of the unity of internalization and externalization process. Namely, we have to decide what assumptions about the nature of the externalization process we make, given the transformational nature of the internalization process. The easiest (and the least realistic) option would be either to view externalization as giving us the 'replica' of the internalized knowledge as it is or to view it as a step-by-step retracing of the internalization (i.e., externalization = reverse process to that of internalization) that reproduces the original external experience that was internalized in the first place. If either of these assumptions could be taken as the starting point for understanding externalization, psychologists' methodological problems would become relatively easily soluble: our subjects' personal introspections or retrospections could be viewed as valid representations of the internal psychological phenomena, and the process of internalization could be studied *post factum* through experimentally triggered externalization processes. Likewise, Freudian reconstructions of the psychological past of the psychoanalytic clients would have to be accepted as true, if we considered externalization as a mere 'reverse tracing' of the transformations that were involved in internalization. This would violate Baldwin's 'first postulate' of developmental logic, as it assumes that development can be studied in terms of convertible propositions (if A becomes B in internalization, then B becomes A in externalization).

Indeed, it would be rather unrealistic to assume that externalization differs from internalization as a mere 'passive' process that 'reveals the truth'. Recollecting Baldwin's postulate of development taking place in convertible propositions, that would be the case of A becoming B by internalization, and B (internal) staying B while externalized. Instead, similarly to the internalization process, externalization involves *constructive* transformation of the internalized psychological phenomena into the interpersonal domain (i.e., A becomes B in internalization, B becomes C in externalization). The implications of accepting this assumption are fundamental. First, no direct access to the 'true inside' of the 'individual mind' is in principle possible (since any instruction given to the subject to trigger externalization leads to constructive transformation of the internal phenomenon into a novel form that becomes externally available). Thus, all empirical research on cognitive development that looks only at the *outcomes* of the externalization process is unable to infer anything about the 'true' underlying processes that govern the sphere of cognition. Second, it is the study of the externalization process itself – the ways in which whatever-is-inside becomes transformed into the externally available product – that may replace the impasse of inferring 'mental representations' from the outcomes of externalization. Instead of 'revealing' what exists 'inside', our experimental triggering of the externalization leads to the possibility of progressive study of how the cognitive system is self-pre-adapting to the handling of experiences that lead to further internalization.

CO-ORDINATION OF INTERNALIZATION AND EXTERNALIZATION

It is possible to consider two forms of temporal organization of the co-ordination of internalization/externalization processes – the parallel functioning of the two and delayed functioning of the externalization relative to internalization. Which of these two forms happens to be used in the given task situation depends directly on the ways in which the task situation is set up. Educational practices from different cultures or historic epochs provide ample evidence for cases where the child's active participation in the learning situation is either suppressed (e.g., teacher-dominated religious schools with a strong emphasis on rote learning) or enhanced (e.g., learning in dialogue with the teacher). If the child's active externalization is suppressed in the learning process, it is delayed until the opportune time arrives; if it is enhanced then internalization and externalization may proceed simultaneously. In this latter case, any externalized aspect of knowledge can feed back into the internalization process by way of an internal feedback loop. The best example of the functioning of such feedback loops is in the effect of mnemotechnics in taking in information to be memorized – the effort of 'taking in' that information is paralleled by the process of producing artificial means that, if they become linked with the memorization process, can guide the latter to higher efficiency.

The external social experiences of the developing child are structurally organized by way of systems of constraints upon their actions (Valsiner 1987). This can be observed in both formal and informal education settings, where the child's learning is canalized in specifiable directions by setting up and reorganizing the constraint systems. What has remained underdeveloped in this perspective on child development is the internalization and externalization of the constraint structures by the developing child.

Obviously, the developing child is not re-creating in his mind the exact structure of the constraints that is being experienced in interaction with the environment. Instead, the child constructs a system of personal senses (to use the Paulhan/Vygotsky distinction of 'sense' from 'meaning', cf. Paulhan 1928; Vygotsky 1934) that serves as the psychological mediating device in organizing his actions, affect, and reasoning. Thus, internalization of constraint systems operating in child–environment interaction takes the form of a semiotic process, in which signs are constructed as vehicles for both self- and action-control. The central argument here is that *the constructed signs act in the mind of the person as self-constraining mechanisms.* By constructing a sign to help oneself to 'make sense' of an undifferentiated problem situation, we clarify that situation while eliminating many aspects of it which do not 'make sense' from the perspective to which the newly constructed sign has taken us. Human beings are constantly constructing (and reconstructing) signs they use in their cognitive functioning so as to delimit the excessive uncertainty and reduce it to a manageable state. The latter state, however, is not strictly defined by the use of signs. Instead of being representations of 'prototypical' examples of objects or events, signs define the set of all possible examples of the given kinds of phenomena, and differentiate those from the rest. Thus, the constructed sign 'rules in' a non-homogeneous (fuzzy) set of 'targets', at the same time 'ruling out' the rest of the experience (internal or external) from consideration. Once the given sign is constructed to delineate the given set, it provides a 'surplus sense' to all the phenomena that are 'ruled in' by the sign, and allows us to set up contrasts with what is 'ruled out' by the sign.

The constructed signs do not constitute a homogeneous 'layer' of cognitive organizing devices, but become differentiated and hierarchically integrated (cf. Heinz Werner's 'orthogenetic principle'). Thus, meta-level sign construction leads to the development of signs that organize other signs, and so on. At the top of this (human) cognitive activity we find abstract, widely used but in principle undefinable concepts, like 'love', 'patriotism', 'intelligence' (see Valsiner 1984a, 1984b), 'cognition', and many others. These concepts are used simultaneously in the interpersonal communication ('collective culture'; see Valsiner 1988b) and in the intra-personal, cognitive-affective organization of individuals' psychological worlds. These high-level abstract concepts provide individuals with constantly adjustable organizing devices for lower-level signs and (eventually) the most concrete level acting and thinking. By being flexibly linkable to different concrete domains of sense of actions, these permanently 'ill-defined' general concepts are more adaptive for the cognitive processes of the person than if they were strictly definable. Or, in other terms, the open-endedness of human cognitive functioning is guaranteed by the flexibility of applying general concepts to constrain new domains of experience, thus enabling further cognitive development. The relationships of concepts within their (non-strict) hierarchical structure constitute the framework within which the deductive reasoning process proceeds – to be linked at some level of the hierarchical structure with the inductive reasoning process.

The fuzzy-set nature of the domains demarcated by constructed signs makes the 'landscape' set up for reasoning similar to that of constraining in child–environment relationships. Certain subsets of the phenomena to which the given sign is linked at the given time are 'better representatives' of the sign than others (hence the possibility that any 'prototypes' can be found within these sets). Furthermore, different subsets of the phenomena subsumed under the given sign can be organized differently, eg., some may constitute a 'taxonomic classification' while others are organized as a 'functional classification', and still others may mix these two kinds of classificatory principles. Thus, the signs designate 'complexes' used in reasoning, parts of which guide the reasoning process in specifiable directions while blocking other possible directions. In development, these 'complexes' are constantly in the process of being restructured – in co-ordination with the person's social experiences.

The dynamic nature of the internalization/externalization processes sets up clearly specifiable conditions that must be met by empirical research methodologies that are used for the study of these processes. It is clear that the usual confusion of levels analysis – inductive generalization from samples to populations, followed by deductive construction of generic models on the basis of populations (see Valsiner 1986, 1989b, 1989c) – is an invalid epistemological strategy for the study of dynamic constructive phenomena. This rules out any sample-based aggregational analysis of a statistical kind, and replaces it with in-depth microgenetic analysis of individual cases. The analysis of inter-individual differences is of relevance only for the documentation of variability of different forms of internalization/externalization, but has no consequence for the analysis of how each of those forms functions in the case of particular individuals.

GENERAL DISCUSSION: HOW CAN THIS THEORY 'GO TO SCHOOL'?

The school world constitutes one of the many environmental settings the structure of which is set up to assist children in the internalization and externalization of cultural messages (see Valsiner 1989a; ch. 8). The present theoretical system 'goes to school' through its 'back door' – instead of its being applicable to the study of children by themselves, we are emphasizing the role of child–school environment interaction in the process of cognitive development. Thus, the structure of school environment – the semiotic organization of constraint systems that the 'collective culture' sets up on the basis of the physical environment of the school – is the basis on which all of the teaching/learning process takes place. The constraint systems of the school environment define the meaningful context within which children internalize *and* externalize their psychological constructions, which constitutes the process of cognitive development. Thus, it is not only (or mainly) the teacher's purposeful constraining of pupils' actions in the classroom setting, but the ways in which this constraining (and the taught/learned material) is transformed by pupils into externalized versions of self-constraining, mostly outside the activities in the classroom. That emphasis on the transfer of internalized constraint systems to other domains to be externalized allows the perspective described in this chapter to be used in educational research. It is the collective-cultural context of educational events at school (see Smollett 1975; Wolcott 1974 for particular examples) that determines the general direction of 'effects' of schooling. The active role of the internalizing/externalizing pupils may enhance, maintain, neutralize, or block the achievement of primary educational targets, as 'boundary negotiation' effort that demonstrates pupils' co-constructivist role in their cognitive development in the school setting.

This chapter was written with the aim of extending the 'bounded indeterminacy' perspective (Valsiner 1987) to the study of cognitive development. Cognitive development is a result of constant ('on-line') internalization and externalization processes that transform experiences from child–

environment relationships into a semiotically coded form of internal senses. The latter are organized as complexes of signs that canalize the child's thinking and acting in directions marked by constructed positive connotations, and away from negative-connotational domains of reasoning. In sum, cognitive development is a means to the end of adaptation to life conditions by an active individual who constructs his own self under the directed guidance of the 'collective culture'.

REFERENCES

Allport, G. W. (1942) *The Use of Personal Documents in Psychological Science*, New York: Social Science Research Council.
Baldwin, J. M. (1906) *Thought and Things: A Study of the Development and Meaning of Thought*, Vol. 1, London: Swan Sonnenschein.
Bukovsky, V. (1978) *To Build a Castle: My Life as a Dissenter*, New York: Viking Press.
Elbers, E. (1988) 'Freedom and determinism in child development', *Comenius* 32: 389–97.
Ericsson, K. A. and Simon, H. (1980) 'Verbal reports as data', *Psychological Review* 87 (3): 215–51.
—— (1984) *Protocol Analysis: Verbal Reports as Data*, Cambridge, MA: MIT Press.
Fishbein, H. D. (1976) *Evolution, Development, and Children's Learning*, Pacific Palisades, CA: Goodyear Publishing.
Goldstein, K. (1933) 'L'analyse de l'aphasie et l'étude de l'essence du langage', *Journal de Psychologie* 30: 430–96.
Gollin, E. (1981) 'Development and plasticity', in E. S. Gollin (ed.) *Developmental Plasticity: Behavioral and Biological Aspects of Variations in Development*, New York: Academic Press, pp. 231–51.
Gottlieb, G. (1976) 'The roles of experience in the development of behavior and the nervous system', in G. Gottlieb (ed.) *Neural and Behavioral Specificity*, New York: Academic Press, pp. 25–54.
Goudena, P. P. (1988) 'How does it feel to be a child?', *Comenius* 32: 407–12.
Heidmets, M. (1985) 'Environment as the mediator of human relationships', in T. Garling and J. Valsiner (eds) *Children within Environments: Toward a Psychology of Accident Prevention*, New York: Plenum, pp. 217–27.
Luria, A. R. (1976) *Cognitive Development*, Cambridge, MA: Harvard University Press.
Oerter, R. (1990 in press) 'Self-object relations as the basis of human development', in L. Oppenheimer and J. Valsiner (eds) *The Origins of Action*, New York: Springer.
Oppenheimer, L. (1988) 'Culture and history, but what about theory? Valsiner's cultural-historical theory of development', *Comenius* 32: 413–26.
Paulhan, F. (1928) 'Qu'est-ce que le sens des mots?', *Journal de Psychologie* 25: 289–329.
Simon, H. (1957) *Models of Man*, New York: Wiley.
Smollett, E. (1975) 'Differential enculturation and social class in Canadian schools', in T. R. Williams (ed.) *Socialization and Communication in Primary Groups*, The Hague: Mouton, pp. 221–31.
Toulmin, S. and Leary, D. E. (1985) 'The cult of empiricism in psychology, and beyond', in S. Koch and D. E. Leary (eds) *A Century of Psychology as Science*, New York: McGraw-Hill, pp. 594–617.

Valsiner, J. (1984a) 'Conceptualizing intelligence: from an internal static attribution to the study of the process structure of organism–environment relationships', *International Journal of Psychology* 19: 363–89.
—— (1984b) '"Intelligence" as person–environment relationship in structured action contexts', paper presented at the 23rd International Congress of Psychology, Acapulco, September.
—— (1986) 'Between groups and individuals: psychologists' and laypersons' interpretations of correlational findings', in J. Valsiner (ed.) *The Individual Subject and Scientific Psychology*, New York: Plenum, pp. 113–51.
—— (1987) *Culture and the Development of Children's Action*, Chichester: Wiley.
—— (1988a) 'A constraints-based theory and its interpretations: a reply', *Comenius* 32: 427–41.
—— (1988b) 'Ontogeny of co-construction of culture within socially organized environmental settings', in J. Valsiner (ed.) *Child Development within Culturally Structured Environments*, Vol. 2, *Social Co-construction and Environmental Guidance of Development*, Norwood, NJ: Ablex, pp. 283–97.
—— (1989a)_ *Human Development and Culture*, Lexington, MA: D.C. Heath.
—— (1989b) 'Persevering habits: on the limits of usefulness of statistics in psychologists' reasoning', in J. A. Keats, R. Taft, R. A. Heath, and S. H. Lovibond (eds) *Mathematical and Theoretical Systems*, Amsterdam: North-Holland, pp. 59–67.
—— (1989c) 'From group comparisons to knowledge: a lesson from cross-cultural psychology', in J. P. Forgas and J. M. Innes (eds) *Recent Advances in Social Psychology: An International Perspective*, Amsterdam: North-Holland, pp. 501–10.
Valsiner, J. and Van der Veer, R. (1988) 'On the social nature of human cognition: an analysis of the shared intellectual roots of George Herbert Mead and Lev Vygotsky', *Journal for the Theory of Social Behaviour* 18 (1): 117–36.
Van Oers, B. (1988) 'Activity, semiotics and the development of children', *Comenius* 32: 398–406.
Van der Veer, R. and Valsiner, J. (1988) 'Lev Vygotsky and Pierre Janet: on the origin of the concept of sociogenesis', *Developmental Review* 8: 52–65.
Van der Veer, R., Miedema, S., and Wardekker, W. (1988) 'Vrijheid in gebondenheid: Valsiners visie op de ontwikkeling van het kind', *Comenius* 32: 379–88.
Vygotsky, L. S. (1934) *Myshlenie i rech*, Moscow-Leningrad: Gossochekgiz.
Winegar, L. T. (1988) 'Children's emerging understanding of social events: co-construction and social process', in J. Valsiner (ed.) *Child Development within Culturally Structured Environments*, Vol. 2, *Social Co-construction and Environmental Guidance of Development*, Norwood, NJ: Ablex, pp. 3–27.
Winegar, L. T., Renninger, K. A., and Valsiner, J. (1989) 'Dependence–independence in adult–child relationships', in D. A. Kramer and M. J. Bopp (eds) *Transformation in Clinical and Developmental Psychology*, New York: Springer.
Wolcott, H. F. (1974) 'The teacher as an enemy', in G. D. Spindler (ed.) *Education and Cultural Process: Toward an Anthropology of Education*, New York: Holt, Rinehart & Winston, pp. 411–25.

Chapter 5

Structural systems in developing cognition, science, and education

Andreas Demetriou, Jan-Eric Gustafsson, Anastasia Efklides, and Maria Platsidou

Cognitive developmental theory has always been of interest to people in education. This is not unnatural given that the theory of cognitive development and the process of education converge on three important issues.

First, the cognitive developmental theorist attempts to specify the cognitive competence of the person at the successive phases of her development. The educator attempts to organize the curriculum in such a way that it is maximally assimilable by the person *at the age at which it is taught*. Therefore, the knowledge offered by the cognitive developmentalist can direct the curriculum designer to develop teaching materials matching the assimilatory capabilities of the learner. This would evidently maximize the efficiency of the transmission of knowledge to the student by the educational system.

The second major focus of the cognitive developmentalist is the understanding of cognitive change as such. That is, the mechanisms and processes which cause the transformation of a given level of competence L into a higher level of competence $L+1$. In a similar vein, education capitalizes on cognitive change. The transmission of knowledge presupposes effective teaching methods. To be effective, teaching methods have to be able to make the student move from a lower to a higher level of understanding. Therefore, understanding the dynamics of cognitive development might be able to assist people in education in their attempt to develop effective teaching methods.

Finally, cognitive developmental theory focuses on the description and explanation of individual differences in the structure, rate, and mechanisms of cognitive development. Correspondingly, education deals with intra- and inter-individual variation. If it is going to achieve its aims, education has to be able to meet the special needs and proclivities of different individuals as well as to provide them with the opportunity to cultivate their particular talent. Towards this aim, education would be better able to be geared to the needs of the learner if it could be guided by an accurate map of the structures developing intellect is composed of and the mechanisms propelling its growth.

Needless to say, the results of educational practice speak directly to the adequacy of cognitive developmental theory. Specifically, succeeding or failing to transmit a given body of knowledge or develop a certain skill in the student might be informative about the student's level of competence. Having one method of teaching succeeding and another failing might reveal how cognitive change takes place during macrodevelopment. Finally, the pattern of successes and failures in relation to blocks of subject matter forming the curriculum might point out the boundaries between cognitive structures, which function as the basis of intra- and inter-individual differentiation along with cognitive growth.

Therefore, a general metatheory is needed that would be able to integrate cognitive development proper and education in a common frame. This is a necessary step if the theory of cognitive development is going to be of systematic use to educational practice and if educational practice is going to be able to inform cognitive developmental theory. Basically, this frame would involve propositions about the three sets of bi-directional relations outlined above. This chapter is intended as a contribution to the formation of this frame. To this end, we will attempt to show how our theory of cognitive development can be used to derive predictions regarding school achievement.

Specifically, we will first give an outline of the structure and development of cognition as described by our theory. Then an analysis will be attempted of the structure of science, mainly as it is represented in the organization of educational institutions. Based on the theory and the analysis of the educational system, we will then state predictions regarding the possible pattern of relations between cognitive development and school achievement and present empirical evidence related to the validity of these predictions. This evidence is drawn from three large research projects undertaken in direct relation to our present purposes. Finally, we will outline the general metatheory referred to above.

THE THEORY

Our theory postulates that cognition develops across three fronts. These are briefly described below.

The Specialized Structural Systems (SSSs)

The first front involves a set of SSSs that enable the person to represent, mentally manipulate, and understand specific domains of reality and knowledge. Five SSS were identified: (1) the qualitative-analytic; (2) the quantitative-relational; (3) the causal-experimental; (4) the verbal-propositional; and (5) the spatial-imaginal.

Each of the SSSs differs from the others in three important respects: namely, (a) the reality domain it interacts with, (b) the modular operations it employs to solve the problems presented by the SSS-specific domain, and (c) the symbolic systems and sub-systems to which it is biased. Because of these differences, the SSSs are felt or cognized by the person herself as distinct from each other. As a result, the development of each SSS may to a large extent be autonomous of the development of the other SSSs. Of course, it is assumed that developmental variation between SSSs is not unlimited. The limits are defined by the condition of the two domain-general systems to be described below. It can only be mentioned here that a number of studies have provided ample empirical evidence in support of the functional autonomy of the five SSSs (Demetriou and Efklides 1985; Demetriou, Efklides, and Platsidou in press; Shayer, Demetriou, and Prevez 1988; Efklides, Demetriou, and Gustafsson this volume).

The *qualitative-analytic* SSS is applied on categorical, matrix, and serial structures. This system is primarily analytical in that its functioning is based on the disentangling of the 'pure' properties of objects (e.g., the 'greenness' or 'redness' or the 'squareness' or 'circularness' of objects). It is only on the basis of this analyticity that one can build hierarchies of classes or relational structures that organize these properties into representational systems able to guide the understanding of the qualitative world (for instance, geometrical figures which involve green squares, red squares, etc.).

The *quantitative-relational* SSS is concerned with the quantifiable aspects of reality. As such, it is relational in nature because any quantity Q exists in relation to other quantities Q±1. Thus, this system involves abilities that enable the thinker to specify the relations between quantities so as to grasp their intra- and inter-dimensional relations.

The *causal-experimental* SSS is applied on causal reality structures. It is directed at disembodying cause–effect relations out of broader networks of phenomenally relevant but essentially irrelevant relations in regard to a phenomenon, and at building models representing these networks of relations. Combinatorial, hypothesis formation, experimentation, and model construction abilities are involved in this SSS.

The *verbal-propositional* SSS is concerned with the formal relations between mental operations rather than the relations between the objects denoted by the propositions involved in a propositional argument. Although it involves deductive or inductive reasoning, it is now well known that this type of reasoning, when embedded in a propositional structure, requires a kind of decontextualized approach to problems. As a result, efficiency in this SSS is not closely related to other domains of cognitive activity which may also involve deductive or inductive reasoning (cf. Demetriou and Efklides 1988).

The *spatial-imaginal* SSS is directed to those aspects of reality which can be visualized by the mind as integral wholes and processed as such. This system involves abilities such as mental rotation, image integration, and image reconstruction.

The domain-general software

The second front refers to a domain-general system that involves models, rules, and strategies underlying self- and task-monitoring, -understanding, and -management. This system is regarded as the interface between (a) cognition as a whole and reality and (b) any of the SSSs. This system is involved in making decisions of three different kinds.

First, decisions as to the SSS-task affiliation. This is a family of decisions aiming to ensure that (a) the right SSS and (b) the most relevant task-specific schemes will be brought to bear on the task at hand. Second, decisions about the relations between the SSSs, their possible interplay, and the ways in which one can be transformed into any of the others. Third, decisions regarding the efficient use of the processing resources to be discussed below. Therefore, this system may be regarded as the domain-general software of cognition (DGS).

The domain-general hardware

The third front refers to the domain-general hardware of cognition (DGH). At the functional level, the DGH may be considered to be a construct that constrains the complexity and quality of the information structures the intellect can represent and process at a given moment in its development. It is assumed that this construct involves three components: speed of processing, control of processing, and storage. Speed of processing basically refers to the minimum speed at which a given mental act may be efficiently executed. Control of processing refers to a mechanism which functions under the guidance of the task-goal like a filter permitting only goal-relevant schemes to enter processing space. Storage refers to the maximum number of schemes that the person can process at the same time. Particular combinations of the three components are involved in the functioning of all SSSs at all developmental phases (Demetriou *et al.* in press).

In our theory, the development of the systems involved in any of the three fronts is by and large a self-propelled process. However, the *initiation* of changes in a system may be *triggered* by changes in any of the other systems. In fact, it is assumed that the co-occurrence of changes in systems of all three fronts may be the cause of the massive intellectual reorganizations that have been associated with the major stages of cognitive development. Moreover, the theory assumes that the functional status of the systems in one front may condition the way the systems in the other fronts are used. Overall, the theory postulates that reality and knowledge structures are represented and processed by the SSSs. These make use of processing resources (DGH) under the guidance of the person's meaning-making super executives (DGS) (Demetriou *et al.* in press).

It needs to be mentioned that many other cognitive developmental or psychometric theories have been concerned with the various abilities and functions referred to above (e.g., see Case; Bidell and Fisher this volume). However, this is the only theory which attempts to integrate the constructs regarding the domain specificity, the self-awareness and directedness, and the structural limitations of intelligence into a unified developmental model. This integration provides the basis for a better explanation of phenomena already known and the discovery of new ones. Clearly, this model may have important implications for education.

COGNITIVE STRUCTURES IN SCIENCE AND EDUCATION

We have theorized that the SSSs represent in the individual the general fields of science that are cultivated in some degree of autonomy from each other. Specifically, it was assumed that the qualitative-analytic SSS corresponds to what might generally be called taxonomic science. In this category one would include fields such as natural history, palaeontology, and the like: that is, those fields which increase our understanding of the world primarily by categorizing and interrelating things. The quantitative-relational SSS is clearly related to mathematics: that is, to the field that builds on, models, and perfects our understanding of the quantifiable aspects of our actions on the world and/or the world itself. The causal-experimental SSS obviously corresponds to experimental science in general: that is, to that branch of intellectual activity that enables humans to grasp the real by transcending the apparent. The spatial-imaginal SSS is clearly related to those aspects of scientific or artistic activity that presuppose or result in the visualization of the reality concerned. One may refer here to arts such as architecture, painting, and sculpture. The verbal-propositional SSS seems more related to canonical science than to anything else. Logic or grammar are the most telling examples one might invoke in this regard. Finally, the DGS seems more related to the sciences of consciousness than to sciences concerned with external reality: one may refer here to fields such as psychology or philosophy. It goes without saying that these fields are represented as such in the school curriculum or in the structure of tertiary institutions.

One might object to the validity of the structure of intellect–structure of science correspondences drawn above on the basis of three admittedly strong arguments. First, one might argue that science at the social-cultural level is organized on the basis of material availability and/or general efficiency. In contrast, individual structures may indeed reflect the constructional and functional peculiarities of our biological endowment. Second, the boundaries between academic fields are not fixed and this is made all the more evident today when new fields are created out of the combination of fields regarded in the past as separate. The third reason is related to the first two. Specifically, even when two fields appear resistant to integration, such as the theory of literature and mathematics, the one may still be very useful to the needs of the other. It is quite common nowadays among students of literature to use statistical estimations in their attempt to decipher and decode the structure of literary products.

One can accept these arguments without rejecting the structure of intellect–structure of science correspondence proposed above. Specifically, one might argue, in response to the first objection, that general efficiency at the level of social institutions presupposes that these institutions are organized in a way that builds on and extends rather than competes with the structural and functional peculiarities of the human mind. The creation of new scientific fields that go beyond traditional boundaries is not a problem to a theory of mind (collective or individual) that favours the existence of structurally and functionally autonomous systems. For example, the present theory is based on the assumption that a given object, by itself, does not constrain the SSS which can be brought to bear on it. An object can be classified, enumerated, subjected to experimental manipulations, imagined, or 'denoted' in a propositional argument. Therefore, any SSS could be applied, depending on the needs or the intentions of the thinker. This implies that two or more SSSs may be applied on the same object, if required. As a result, the systems applied may be interrelated and mapped on to each other without losing their autonomy. Therefore, the coactivation of different SSSs and/or scientific fields raises the problem of understanding how the one is translated into, or subordinated to, the others, rather than indicating that their autonomy is abolished. Having drawn the cognition–science–education relations as specified by our theory, we will now state the alternative predictions that can be tested by the studies to be presented below. These predictions are concerned with the structural boundaries and functional relations that may be found between cognitive and school-achievement abilities.

ALTERNATIVE PREDICTIONS ABOUT COGNITIVE DEVELOPMENT–SCHOOL-ACHIEVEMENT RELATIONS

With respect to the structure of abilities, a literal interpretation of the views advanced above would lead to the prediction that there is a one-to-one correspondence between cognitive structures as revealed by performance on cognitive tests and the structures underlying school-achievement abilities. In terms of our theory, this prediction leads to the hypothesis that one should find one constellation of school-achievement abilities for each of the SSSs described by the theory. Alternatively, however, one might assume that cognitive and school-achievement ability structures may not exactly coincide. The argument has been mentioned above that the two kinds of structures may to a certain extent obey different rules of organization because they are collectively elaborated over historical rather than individual time. Therefore, collective cognitive structures might be more general than individual ones.

The postulation of both domain-general and domain-specific factors as organizing forces of any intellectual activity justifies the assumption that neither the general systems alone nor the SSSs would suffice to account for performance on any one of the courses offered at school. For such an account to be possible, one needs to have a good estimate of the functioning both of the general systems and of the SSS primarily related to the course concerned. The abilities involved in the general systems are needed to boost the person's attempts to organize her overt and covert cognitive activity so as to meet the demands posed by requirements which are complex and new for her. The abilities involved in the SSSs are needed as the representational channels through which this or that type of knowledge is received and fixed into the cognitive system.

STUDY 1: COGNITIVE AND SCHOOL-ACHIEVEMENT STRUCTURES: LONGITUDINAL EVIDENCE

Rationale and design

In this investigation, a series of two- and three-year studies were co-ordinated in order to study cognitive development from 10 to 17 years of age. The main purposes of the investigation were as follows. First, to find out whether the SSSs already referred to tend to preserve their functional autonomy over time or whether they tend to merge into a single system. Were it true that the SSSs do preserve their identity, it would be of interest to find out how the SSSs interact during development. Thus, the second aim was to specify the relations between the SSSs the study focused on. Finally, the study aimed to produce evidence concerning the relations between school performances, on the one hand, and the cognitive phenomena referred to above, on the other.

Method

Subjects

Of the various groups involved in this study only two are relevant to the purposes of the present chapter. Specifically, a group of ninety-seven subjects was first tested at seventh grade (mean age 13 years and 4 months). A second testing took place twelve months after the first testing. A second group of ninety-two subjects was first tested at eighth grade (mean age 14 years and 5 months) and also retested twelve months afterwards. All subjects came from upper-middle-class families. Males and females were about equally represented in each age group. Therefore, when co-ordinated, the results from the two groups can shed light on the structure and relations of abilities for the age span 13 to 15 years.

Task batteries

The study was addressed to three SSSs: namely, the qualitative-analytic, the causal-experimental, and the verbal-propositional. Therefore, the following three task batteries were used.

The qualitative-analytic SSS battery. This battery involved twelve Raven-like matrices. The geometrical figures appearing in the matrices varied systematically in regard to the number (2, 3, 6, 10, and 16) and the type of attributes to be integrated. Specifically, the attributes were either continuous (e.g., the size of a figure) or discontinuous (e.g., the shape of a figure), rotated (e.g., the orientation of the diagonal of a figure) or unrotated. In two of the simplest matrices, the relevant attributes were intermingled with irrelevant patterns. Therefore, dissociation of relevant from irrelevant information was required before the application of qualitative-analytic operations. Two of the nine cells of each matrix (the middle and the lower right cell) were empty. The task of the subject was to fill in the empty cells correctly by choosing the figure appropriate to each from a set of eight figures depicted below the matrix. A score of 0, 1, and 2 was given to no, one, and two correct choices respectively. Overall, this battery was addressed to abilities attained between 7–8 and 13–14 years of age.

The verbal-propositional SSS battery involved twenty items. This set of items made it possible to manipulate systematically three main factors: (a) the type of logical operation involved (e.g., *modus ponens* and *modus tolens*); (b) the verbal-logical form of the argument given to the subject (affirmation or denial); and (c) the definition of the parameters of the logical argument (i.e., ill- or well-defined arguments). Responses to the items were scored as 0 (logically invalid responses), 1 (valid responses with no justification), and 2 (valid and fully justified responses).

The causal-experimental SSS battery involved seventeen items. These items were addressed to the ability to draw conclusions from data, isolate variables, evaluate the validity of ready-made experiments, and design experiments in order to test hypotheses. As before, each of these abilities was tested at different degrees of complexity and familiarity. The logical form of the tasks was also manipulated. Overall, this and the verbal-propositional battery were addressed to abilities acquired between about 9 and 18–20 years of age.

Scoring

Performance on each task in each battery was scored according to a rather complex set of scoring criteria which cannot be presented here due to space limitations (see Demetriou *et al.* in press). For the purposes of the present chapter two scores were created to represent performance on each battery. Each was the average of the scores attained on half of the scores involved in a battery. All conceptual, content, and developmental variations were represented in each of these 'half scores'. This manipulation was deemed necessary for technical as well as substantial reasons (see Gustafsson 1988).

Measures of school performance

School performance was not measured by special measures designed for the purposes of the present study. Instead, the regular school grades were used. Specifically, the school grades obtained by each student on a number of subjects at the period when each testing took place were recorded. The following courses were involved: ancient Greek, modern Greek, composition, history, mathematics, physics, and chemistry.

The evaluation of school performance in Greek secondary education ranges from 0 to 20. In practice, however, grades below 7 are extremely rare. It also has to be noted that, as in any other country, the specific grade given to a student may be affected by factors actually unrelated to her performance, such as the personality of the student and the teacher, the expectations of the teacher and so on. To cope with these problems, the 0 to 20 school scale was reduced to a five-point scale. Specifically, the school grades 0–9, 10–12, 13–15, 16–18, and 19–20 were reduced to 0, 1, 2, 3, and 4, respectively.

In the end, four school-achievement scores were used in the analyses to be presented below: (a) the language score (this is the average of the scores attained on ancient Greek, modern Greek, and composition); (b) the history score; (c) the mathematics score (this is the average of the scores attained on algebra and geometry); and (d) the natural science score (the average of the scores attained on physics and chemistry). This manipulation was suggested by the results of traditional factor analysis applied to the data for exploratory purposes.

Results and discussion

The evidence generated by this study can be used to shed light on three general issues: namely, (a) the structural organization of school-achievement and cognitive abilities, (b) the direction and degree of causal relations between these abilities, and (c) the possible differentiation of structural and causal relations as a result of development. The attempt was made to shed light on these issues through a sequence of confirmatory factor analyses and structural equation models fitted with the latest version of the EQS program (Bentler 1989).

A model that would be consistent with our theory would have to involve two sets of assumptions. The first set is concerned with the structure of performance *within each testing wave*. The second is concerned with *the causal relations between the factors of the first and the second wave*.

In regard to the first type of relations, it has been assumed that two kinds of latent factors are needed to account for the variance on the two observed

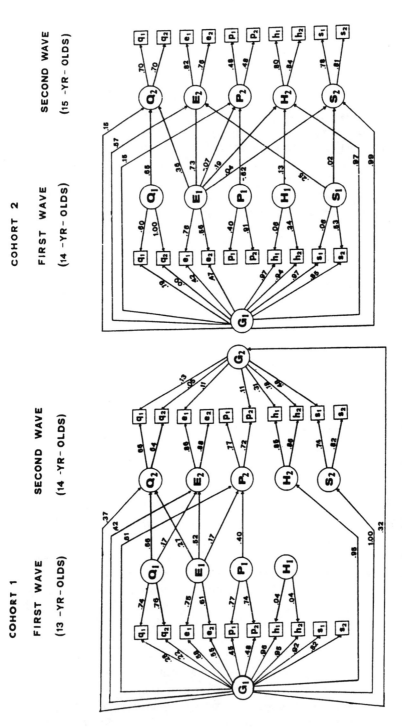

Figure 5.1 The structure of abilities according to the longitudinal study

Note The symbols q, e, p, h, s, and G refer to the qualitative-analytic, the causal-experimental, the quantitative-relational, the verbal-propositional SSS, humanities, science, and the general factor, respectively. Lower-case and upper-case letters denote observed and latent variables, respectively. Subscripts to observed variables simply enumerate them. Subscripts to latent variables denote testing waves.

scores representing an SSS or a school-achievement ability: namely, a general factor and a series of ability-specific factors. If found, this general factor might be regarded as a gross representation of the involvement of the two DG systems in the performance on each task. The ability-specific factors would signify the autonomy of the SSSs as organizational forces of cognitive activity. Regarding the school-achievement scores, it has been assumed that the language and the history scores would load on a factor of humanities and the mathematics and natural science scores on a general science factor.

Three main assumptions were tested regarding causal relations from the first to the second testing wave. First, the major part of the variance of each SSS, or each school-subject-specific factor, at the second wave must be accounted for by the corresponding factor of the first wave. Second, a weaker but still significant part of the specific factors' variance at the second wave would have to be accounted for by the general factor at the first wave. A direct causal path would directly run from the general factor of the first to the general factor of the second wave. Third, a minor part of the variance of the specific factors at the second wave would have to be accounted for by other specific factors at the first wave. Such a model would suggest that the systems represented by the factors are autonomous and self-regulated constructs. It would also suggest, however, that they draw upon a general underlying pool of potentials and strategies and upon each other as they move from one developmental level to the next.

Figure 5.1 shows the models best fitting to the performance attained by the first ($x^2(148) = 135.209$, p = .766; comparative fit index = 1.000) and second cohort ($x^2(138) = 142.632$, p = .376, comparative fit index = 1.000). It can be seen that these models are very close approximations to the general model postulated above.

Regarding the first cohort, the three SSS-specific factors and the general factor emerged clearly at the first testing wave. However, the school-achievement-specific factors did not show up. Interestingly enough, the loadings of all four school-achievement scores on the general factor was almost unity. The SSS-specific factors preserved their status at the second testing wave. However, the general factor became very weak and the school-achievement-specific factors emerged clearly at the second testing wave. The causal paths running from the factors of the first to the factors of the second wave came out almost entirely as predicted. Specifically, with the exception of the propositional SSS, autoregression coefficients were always higher than regression coefficients on other factors. Moreover, the regressions of the SSS-specific factors on the first wave general factor, although lower, were significant. Due to the absence of school-specific factors at the first wave, their loadings on the first-wave general factor was almost unity. A reciprocal but low exchange of loadings between SSSs was also evident. However, no path was found running from a first-wave SSS-specific factor to a second-wave school-achievement-specific factor.

The results from the second cohort validated and extended those obtained from the first cohort. Specifically, at the first testing wave (the reader is reminded that the age of the second cohort subjects at the first wave was the same as that of the first cohort at the second testing) all five specific factors and a rather weak general factor were present. This factor pattern greatly resembles the factor pattern of the first cohort at the second testing. However, at the second testing wave the general factor vanished. The causal relations between the SSS-specific factors from the first to the second wave were similar to those described above. The school-achievement-specific factors were still mediated by the general rather than by any of the specific factors. However, some reciprocal exchange of causal influences, although weak, between the school-achievement-specific factors and the causal-experimental SSS did emerge in the case of this cohort.

Three main conclusions are suggested by the results shown in Figure 5.1. First, performance on a task is stably determined by both the task-related SSS and a general component that surpasses the SSS. This is perfectly in line with the basic assumptions of our theory.

Second, school achievement cannot be identified with the abilities involved in the SSSs represented by the three task batteries used in the study. Evidently, school achievement involves something more than plain cognitive abilities. This 'more' is very often equivalent to the general factor. Thus, the interaction between the refined cognitive abilities represented by the three batteries and school achievement is *mediated* by the general components of developing intellect.

Third, development appears to result in the strengthening of the role of the specialized factors and the corresponding weakening of the role of the general factor. This is particularly true in relation to school achievement. The result of this tendency is the emergence of direct interactions between cognitive and school-achievement factors in the later phases of development. The studies to be described below will shed more light on these phenomena.

STUDY 2: FLUID INTELLIGENCE, SSSs, AND SCHOOL ACHIEVEMENT

Rationale and design

One problem with the study reported above is that it does not allow a simple and clear-cut separation of general and domain-specific dimensions of performance. This is due to the fact that it included no direct measures of the abilities supposed to be directly associated with the general components of intelligence. The purpose of the second study is to make this distinction empirically. Thus, this study involved two types of tasks. First, tasks shown by earlier psychometric research to be directly associated with fluid intelligence. Second, tasks addressed to two SSSs, specifically, the causal-experimental SSS, which was involved in the first study, and the quantitative-relational SSS. In the paragraphs below, a brief introduction to the basic concerns and findings of modern psychometric psychology will be attempted. The relations between this line of research and our theory will also be outlined.

In the course of the twentieth century, several competing models of the structure of intelligence have been suggested. Some of these models focus upon a general factor of intelligence (e.g., Spearman 1904; Vernon 1950). Other models describe the structure of intelligence in terms of a large set of dimensions, all of which are ascribed equal generality (e.g., Guilford 1967; Thurstone 1938). As is well known, both types of models have received considerable empirical support over the years. This suggests that a model of the structure of intelligence should encompass both a general factor and more narrow or specialized dimensions.

Starting from the hierarchical models of Vernon (1950) and Cattell-Horn (e.g., Cattell 1971; Horn 1986), and using confirmatory factor-analytic techniques, Gustafsson (1984) showed that it is possible to construct a hierarchical model of intelligence which simultaneously includes general and specific dimensions of ability. Most previous models of intelligence may be regarded as special cases of this model. In a very brief and schematic outline, the model has the following components. At the lowest level, the model includes a number of 'primary' mental abilities such as induction, verbal comprehension, space, and flexibility of closure. At an intermediate level, the two dimensions of most central importance to the model are fluid intelligence (Gf), which is mostly related to induction, and crystallized intelligence (Gc), which is mostly related to verbal abilities. A general visualization factor has also been identified. At the highest level, the model includes a factor of general intelligence, on which all the broad abilities have loadings. A rather striking result, however, is that this factor has been consistently found to be perfectly correlated with the Gf-factor. This indicates that the g-factor is equivalent to fluid intelligence.

It has already been mentioned that this study aimed to investigate the relations between general intelligence as defined by psychometric theory and the SSSs as described by our theory. Therefore, in regard to the aims of the present chapter, this study provides the ground for obtaining answers to questions such as the following. The first question concerns the dimensionality of the SSSs, and particularly to what extent they overlap with psychometrically identified factors. In other words, do the SSS-specific factors persist as constructs needed to account for performance on cognitive tasks even when the construct representing the psychometrically defined general intelligence is directly involved? If this is the case, the SSSs capture aspects of cognitive functioning that evaded previous research. The second question is concerned with the relative contribution of the general and the SSS-specific factors to the variance of different school subjects and the possible variations of this contribution at different phases of development. For instance, does the decrease of the importance of the general factor and the increase of the importance of the SSS-specific factors hold, as suggested by the first study, even when the general factor is measured in a more direct and powerful way?

Method

This study is described in detail by Efklides, Demetriou, and Gustafsson (this volume). Therefore, the reader is referred to that chapter for details regarding the method of the study. Below, a brief summary will be provided with an emphasis on the points where there were differences between the aspects of the study concerned with school achievement and those that were of primary interest to Efklides *et al.*

Subjects

The school grades were not available for all of the subjects described by Efklides *et al.* Specifically, there were no grades for the primary-school subjects. In addition, the school records for a few of the subjects were not complete. These subjects were excluded from the analyses to be described below. Thus, the results to be presented below are based on a total of 783 subjects. Of these subjects, 271, 250, and 262 were drawn from grades seven (12-year-olds), nine (14-year-olds), and eleven (16-year-olds), respectively. The genders were about equally represented in each age group, as were low SES subjects of rural and urban residence and upper-middle-class subjects of urban residence.

Tasks

Each of the quantitative-relational and the causal-experimental SSSs was examined by the batteries with four tasks each (QR1-QR4 and CE1-CE4) described in Efklides *et al.* A set of four tests was used to measure fluid intelligence (Gf). Three of these tasks were selected from the Kit of Factor-Referenced Cognitive Tests (Ekstrom, French, and Harman 1976): namely, the *letter sets test* (LS), the *figure classification test* (FC), and the *hidden figures test* (HF). A *number series test* (NS) devised by Gustafsson, Lindstrom, and Bjorck-Akesson (1980) has also been used. All tests require the systematic organization of items of information so that the rule governing their organization can be induced and applied in order to organize further items of information (see Efklides *et al.* this volume). Only the tasks administered as pre-tests will be analysed here, so any effects of the treatments investigated in the training study do not enter into the present study.

The school grades were the same as those described in the first study. In all, therefore, eight SSS-specific (two SSSs by four tasks each), four g-specific, and five school-achievement-specific scores (those used in the first study plus biology – a science score was not available for the 12-year-olds) were included in the analyses to be described below.

Results and discussion

The approach to data analysis adopted in this study was similar to that adopted in study 1. That is, the attempt was made to demarcate structural boundaries and structural relations by means of confirmatory factor analysis and structural equation models. Regarding the issue of structure identification, the general model tested was very similar to that tested on the results of the longitudinal study (see Figure 5.1). This model was tested separately for each age group. It assumes that there is a general factor which is primarily represented by the four Gf-tests. At the same time, it is assumed that this factor accounts for a significant portion of the variance on each of the other eight tests addressed to the two SSSs. The model also assumes that the four tests selected to measure the quantitative-relational SSS are related to a second factor and the four tests selected to measure the causal-experimental SSS are related to a third factor. The fit of the model to the performance of each of the three age groups was excellent. Therefore, it is to be concluded that our SSSs do capture structures of ability that go beyond general intelligence. The model confirmed by the results of Efklides *et al.* and shown in Table 7.2 of their chapter is a close approximation to the model specified here.

Therefore, we may now turn to the second main concern of this study. How are the two SSSs and Gf related to school achievement? This question has been investigated by extending the model described above to include as dependent variables grades in different subject matter areas: (a) language; (b) history; (c) mathematics; (d) science; and (e) biology. No measurement model has been imposed on the dependent variables so the grades have been entered as observed variables. Independent variables are the Gf, the quantitative-relational, and the causal-experimental factors.

Table 5.1 presents the standardized regression coefficients for each of the dependent variables on the three independent variables in each of the three age groups. These suggest the following conclusions.

First, Gf appears to be the strongest predictor at all age levels. However, its relative importance diminishes from one level to the next. Gf accounts for between (a) 25 and 52 per cent of the variances among 12-year-olds, (b) 16 and 32 per cent among 14-year-olds, and (c) 2 and 26 per cent among the 16-year-olds, respectively.

Second, the contribution of the SSSs to the variance of school-achievement scores, although lower, is generally significant. It goes up to 6 per cent, 19 per cent and 16 per cent among the 12-, the 14-, and the 16-year-olds. It needs to be recognized, however, that the increase in the contribution of the SSSs to the variance of school-achievement scores does not fully compensate for the corresponding decrease in the contribution of the general factor. The total amount of school-achievement variance accounted for (i.e., the sum of the variance accounted for by the general and the two SSS-specific factors averaged across school subjects) at the age of 12, 14, and 16 years was 39 per cent, 36 per cent, and 25 per cent, respectively. This clearly implies that control is gradually passed over to factors not represented in the study. These factors might be cognitive or non-cognitive.

The third conclusion is concerned with the relative contribution of the SSS-specific factors with increasing age. Specifically, the contribution of the quantitative-relational factor increased from 12 to 14 years of age in all school subjects, and decreased from 14 to 16 years of age in all subjects but biology. The contribution of the causal-experimental factor was virtually nil at 12 and became significant at 14. At the age of 16, this contribution remained stable or increased in all subjects but biology. This finding implies that the functional status of a system at a given developmental phase is a crucial factor of this system's involvement in the intellectual activity of the person. For instance, at the age of 12 years, the causal-experimental SSS is practically unformed. Therefore, it could not be a predictor of other parameters at this age.

Table 5.1 Regressions of the school-achievement variables on the cognitive variables

	Gf			*QR*			*CE*		
Var/age	12	14	16	12	14	16	12	14	16
Language	60*	42*	34*	25*	26*	19	04	25*	24*
History	55*	40*	24*	19*	44*	21	00	05	28*
Maths	72*	56*	51*	17*	25*	16	01	28*	33*
Science	–	46*	35*	–	24*	22	–	30*	28*
Biology	50*	48*	16	17*	25*	40*	02	22*	07

Notes: The symbols Gf, QR, and CE stand for fluid intelligence, the quantitative-relational, and the causal-experimental SSS, respectively. The decimal point was omitted.
* The asterisks indicate that a loading is statistically significant.

The fourth conclusion is concerned with the relative accountability of the variance of different school subjects. From the most to the less accountable, the different school subjects are as follows: mathematics (a mean of 46 per cent of variance accounted for if the three age groups are pulled together), language (32 per cent), science (30 per cent), history (29 per cent), and biology (27 per cent). It should also be mentioned that the weakening effect of age on the accountability of school subjects was less profound in the case of mathematics as compared to the rest of the school subjects. These results are very interesting in their implication that the possible effects of development on the engagement of cognitive factors in school performance interact systematically with the nature of the school subject concerned. We will return to this issue later on in the discussion.

STUDY 3: SCHOOL ACHIEVEMENT AND METACOGNITION

Rationale and design

The main purpose of this study was to investigate the person's awareness regarding several parameters of cognitive functioning. Specifically, the study aimed to investigate the ability of the person to (a) decipher the similarities and differences between the operations belonging to the various SSSs described by our theory; (b) evaluate the relative processing load of tasks associated with different developmental levels; (c) evaluate the success of the solution given to the tasks processed. Therefore, the study aimed to test the assumption that the *subjective* structure of developing intellect mirrors its objective structure. This would imply that there is a general functional system enabling the person to both monitor and regulate her own cognitive functioning. Evidently, this would be consistent with the idea put forward in the introduction about the presence of a DGS. The results obtained supported this assumption strongly. Specifically, it was found that the same SSS-specific factors are needed to account for performance itself as for metacognitive evaluations regarding perceived difficulty and success of performance on the same tasks (Demetriou and Efklides 1989).

The present study provides an advantage, in as far as school achievement is concerned, relative to the studies already presented. Specifically, it involved five of the seven major constructs which, according to the theory, compose developing intellect: that is, four SSSs (the causal-experimental, the quantitative-relational, the imaginal-spatial, and the verbal-propositional) and domain-general software. Therefore, on the one hand, this study provides the ground for directly specifying the relations between different school subjects and DGS, that is, one of the main components of general intelligence. These relations could only be indirectly inferred from the results of the first two studies. In those studies, general intelligence was represented by general reasoning tasks rather than by tasks representing its monitoring and regulatory components. On the other hand, by having involved more SSSs, this study is more appropriate than the studies presented before for disentangling the direct relations between specific SSSs and specific school subjects.

Method

Subjects

A total of 435 subjects were tested. Specifically, 91, 82, 93, 61, 55, and 53 were tested from each of the secondary school grades seven through twelve. The corresponding ages were 12 through 17, respectively. Different socioeconomic classes (SES) and the sexes were about equally represented in each age group.

Cognitive tasks

Eight paper-and-pencil tasks were given to each subject. A pair of tasks was addressed to each of the causal-experimental, quantitative-relational, imaginal-spatial, and verbal-propositional SSSs. One of the tasks of each pair was addressed to the first (L1) and the other to the third (L3) formal-like level of each SSS. In general, the abilities tapped by the sets of L1 and L3 tasks are acquired at 11 to 13 and 16 to 18 years of age, respectively.

Metacognitive evaluation

To obtain a measure of the various aspects of metacognitive awareness, the subjects were asked to evaluate (a) the *difficulty* of each task by focusing on the complexity of the operations they applied when processing the task and (b) their *success* on each task. That is, they were asked to judge how correct they considered the solution they had produced. Finally, the subjects were asked to evaluate (c) the *similarity* between pairs of tasks belonging to the same or a different SSS and to explain their similarity ratings. In general, these ratings may be regarded as indicative of the person's sensitivity to the characteristics of the operations applied on the tasks associated with the SSSs represented in the study.

Results and discussion

Because of space considerations, only the most general model tested will be presented here. In its generality, however, this model goes well beyond those validated by the first two studies because it presents a more comprehensive picture of the organization of cognitive and metacognitive skills and of their relations with school achievement. This model was tested on the following scores.

  a) *The SSS scores.* Eight scores representing performance on each of the eight tasks addressed to the four SSSs.

  b) *The metacognitive analysis scores.* The three scores attained on each of the metacognitive analysis items.

  c) *The cognitive-metacognitive (COMET) and the metacognitive-metacognitive (METMET) consistency score.* Each of the difficulty evaluations was subtracted from its corresponding performance or success-

evaluation score to give an index of consistency between cognitive performance and metacognitive evaluation or between different aspects of metacognitive evaluation, respectively. In each case, the eight scores were first averaged and then squared to give a general COMET and a general METMET score.

e) *The school-achievement scores.* The five school-achievement scores used in the second study: namely, a language, a history, a mathematics, a science, and a biology score.

The model best fitting to the structure of these scores is shown in Figure 5.2 ($x^2(79)$ = 80.720, p = .364, comparative fit index = .999). It can be seen that this model involves five first-order factors: one for each of the four SSSs, and one for the three metacognitive analysis scores. There is also a second-order factor which has loadings on all four SSS-specific factors. Therefore, this is the *cognitive performance* factor. Finally, a third-order factor accounted for the variance of the cognitive performance factor (the loading of 1.00 should be noted) and the metacognitive-analysis factor. Therefore, this is a truly general factor surpassing cognitive performance and a component of domain-general software.

The school-achievement scores were entered as dependent variables in the

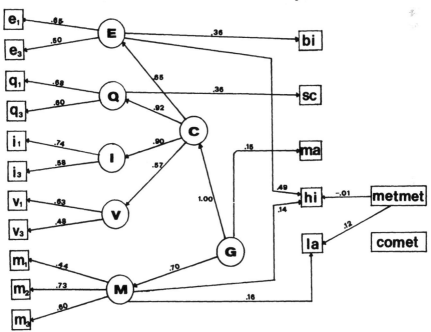

Figure 5.2 The structure of abilities according to the metacognitive study
Note: The symbols e, q, i, v, m, C, G, bi, sc, ma, hi, and la refer to the causal-experimental, the quantitative-relational, the spatial-imaginal, the verbal-propositional SSS, metacognitive analysis, cognitive performance, the general factor, biology, science, mathematics, history, and language, respectively. The subscripts 1 and 3 in the case of the four SSSs denote the developmental level of the tasks.

model to be accounted for by the latent variables specified above. This strategy was adopted because the intention was to build a unified model to represent the structural and causal relations between cognitive and school-achievement scores. In this model, each of the school-achievement scores would be allowed to connect to its 'preferred' cognitive system, specialized or general. Given the completeness of the measures of the present study, this strategy allows one to test directly the basic prediction stated in the introduction. That is, that the minimum number of paths from cognitive factors to school-achievement scores that would saturate the model would connect school-achievement scores to those cognitive factors which, according to our theory, are the most closely related to them. Finally, it should be noted that the two metacognitive-consistency indexes were treated as independent variables.

It can be seen that the relations obtained are in general agreement with this prediction: that is, language proved to be dependent on the metacognitive analysis and the METMET index. History was dependent on the metacognitive analysis and the causal-experimental factor. Mathematics was dependent on the general factor. Biology was dependent on the causal-experimental factor. It is to be noted, however, that science was dependent on the quantitative-relational and not on the causal-experimental factor. It is also to be noted that the verbal-propositional and the imaginal-spatial factors appeared totally unconnected to school achievement. The findings will be integrated with those obtained from the other two studies in the discussion below.

GENERAL DISCUSSION

The discussion below will summarize the main results and conclusions of the three studies. The aim is first to outline a general model that might be able to show how cognitive development and school achievement may be interrelated. The practical implications of this model will then be stated.

Cognitive and school-achievement structures during growth

First, school-achievement scores load on different factors than cognitive scores. In a way, the school-achievement factors are broader and more inclusive constructs than the cognitive factors. For instance, the science school-achievement factor involves our causal-experimental and the quantitative-relational SSS. The humanities factor, which involves school achievement in language and history, does not directly correspond to any of the systems described by our theory. We must therefore conclude that the abilities underlying school achievement and cognitive tests are not identical.

Second, a general factor always seems to be needed to account for a part of the variance of cognitive performance. However, school achievement is much more closely dependent upon the general factor than cognitive performance. In fact, the general factor is enough to account for the total of school-achievement variance in early adolescence. Therefore, when no direct relations seem to exist between specialized cognitive abilities and school achievement, the general components of intellect appear to function as the mediators which connect the demands placed upon the person by the educational system to the specialized representational and processing systems that he possesses. This pattern of results is in agreement with that anticipated on the basis of the first of the predictions stated in the introduction.

There are two reasons able to account for this state of affairs. First, individual and social cognitive constructions are worked out in the context of different kinds of interaction networks and on different planes of abstraction. Individual constructions are by definition always closer to the direct object–subject interactions because they reflect the person's attempt to assimilate the world on a particular occasion and for a particular purpose. In contrast, collective constructions, especially the products of science, are, and should by definition be, more remote from the particulars of objects and personal interaction networks, because otherwise they would not be able to generalize across occasions and individuals. That is, they could not be general and collective.

In addition, collective cognitive constructions are made by mature cognitive beings on the basis of earlier collective constructions. Therefore, they are at a higher level of abstraction than individual constructions because of their very origin as products of cognitive beings functioning at the latest stages of their own intellectual development. As such, they are more likely than individual constructions to involve higher-order relations between lower-order structural systems. It is a matter of fact, however, that social institutions, such as education, attempt to impart to the individual the socially rather than the individually defined cognitive structures. That is, the general and abstract rather than the personal and object-centred structures. This orientation seems to have two main implications.

On the one hand, it forces school achievement to be patterned according to the social rather than the individual demarcation of knowledge structures. As a result, the structures able to express school performance appear more general than the structures that reflect the organization of cognitive abilities. This does not imply that the two kinds of structures are incompatible. It might be the case that the socially demarcated structures show the ultimate end towards which the individual structures tend.

On the other hand, this very same reason biases functioning in the context of the school towards the general rather than the more specialized components of cognition. Evidently, to grasp abstract and disembedded concepts one needs to use one's general task- and self-monitoring skills and strategies more systematically than in the case in which there are assimilatory schemes directly applicable to the concept or the problem encountered.

Moreover, the fact that they are less readily assimilable implies that knowledge structures taught in school require high levels of motivation to be deciphered. This assumption implies that school grades reflect not only the cognitive aspects of the learner but also general motivational aspects which are biased to a holistic rather than a differentiated picture of cognitive functioning.

Third, increasing age causes the shift in the balance from the general to the more specific constructs of cognitive functioning. That is, the school-achievement factors gradually tend to become formulated as autonomous constructs needed to account for the variation of specific school grades. This is a highly interesting finding. It suggests that increasing *educational age*, whatever this term implies, results in the *crystallization of general or fluid abilities into systems of abilities representing different knowledge domains, however broad these domains might be*. Even more, these systems, once formulated, start to interact directly with the specialized cognitive systems. This interaction was usually significant and in the direction suggested by our theory. That is, humanities appeared more related to the factors representing the reflective components of developing intellect. Science appeared more related to what one may call the 'scientific SSSs', such as the causal-experimental and the quantitative-relational SSS. These results are clearly in line with the second of the predictions stated in the introduction in regard to the relative contributions of the general and specialized factors to school achievement.

Admittedly, however, the exact school subject–SSS correspondence did not always show up. For instance, science appeared related to the quantitative-relational SSS and not to the causal-experimental SSS as anticipated. There is one reason which seems a plausible interpretation of this finding: that is, school curricula for a given knowledge domain usually mix up concepts and operations pertaining to more than one SSS. In fact, it might even be the case that the concepts and operations dominating in the curriculum of a given school course may be associated to an SSS other than the one which would be considered as the most natural cognitive background for this school course. The school courses in science represent a good example of this case. Specifically, it is well known that the emphasis in these courses favours the *products* of scientific inquiry and their expression in exact mathematical formulations. The systematic teaching of the methods and processes leading to these products is usually a secondary aim of the teaching of science. Therefore, achievement in this course is associated more with the SSS favoured by the way teaching is organized than with the SSS which is ideally closer to this course.

The fourth conclusion is concerned with the dynamics of the shift from the general to the more specific constructs of cognitive functioning. Specifically, the timing of this shift appeared to be a function of factors such as the knowledge domain concerned and the developmental course of a given SSS. For instance, the contribution of Gf to the variance of mathematics, although steadily decreasing, was always very high. This might imply that the more abstract, demanding, and new a field of knowledge is *vis-à-vis* the person's earlier knowledge, the more it tends to rely on general abilities. Moreover, an SSS cannot be relied upon as an assimilatory system that can be used by the student as a means for understanding the knowledge transmitted by the school unless it has reached a certain threshold of functional sufficiency which meets the requirements of the transmitted knowledge. This assumption is suggested by findings such as the increasing contribution of the causal-experimental SSS to the variance of school achievement from the age of 12 to the age of 16 years.

Practical implications

Let us conclude by returning to our starting point. What practical implications are suggested by these findings in relation to the three issues of convergence between cognitive developmental theory and educational practice? The first issue was concerned with the need for a match between the student's capabilities and the demands placed upon her from the school subjects as represented in the curriculum addressed to her age. The finding that the lower the student's age, the more her school performance depends on general rather than specialized cognitive abilities has a very clear implication for the curriculum designer. It suggests that the subject matter addressed to the lower school grades has to involve concepts and must be organized in ways matching the students' developmental level of the general rather than of the specialized cognitive systems which are close to the subject matter concerned. This balance should gradually shift in favour of specialized knowledge along with increasing school age.

In so far as teaching methods are concerned, they should be more directly and systematically concerned with the enhancement of the efficiency of the general components of cognition. That is, our education should directly involve the students with activities that would raise their self-monitoring and -regulatory abilities. This would evidently back up their learning of skills and abilities. It should be stressed here that the present argument in no way implies that there should be courses especially devoted to the teaching of metacognition as such. This would run contrary to the basic premise of our theory about the domain specificity of cognitive functioning. What is suggested is that *the engagement with particular domains of knowledge should be structured in ways such that the assimilation of specialized knowledge and the construction of goal-directed skills would lead the student to acquire awareness and mastery of the mechanisms that he uses to assimilate knowledge and construct skills.* Space limitations do not allow a discussion of the possible means by which this can be done. However, the reader is referred to Efklides *et al.* (this volume) as their cognitive acceleration methods represent an attempt to implement these ideas in practice.

It should of course be noted that the differential strength of association between the general components of intellect and different subject matters suggests that the general-to-specialized systems ratio that one would use to organize different curricula and teaching methods should vary as a function of the subject matter concerned. The curricula and methods for the humanities should favour the general reflecting components of intellect. Science should lean more towards the 'scientific' SSS rather than the general components. Mathematics seems to depend more on the general hardware than the executive components of developing intellect (see Demetriou *et al.* in press). Finally, it must be noted that it might be profitable if education would consider introducing courses directly interacting with SSSs which are under-represented in the curriculum, such as the spatial-imaginal SSS. The attainment of this goal presupposes a thorough analysis of the way concepts produced by different SSSs are used to build the curriculum for a given school course. This would enable one to avoid the problems regarding the SSS–school-achievement relations that were encountered here.

The third point of convergence was concerned with individual differences. The studies presented so far revealed a rather strong association between the abilities described by our theory and school achievement. This implies that this theory and the diagnostic tools that may be devised on the basis of it would enable the teacher to identify the strong and weak points of his students with considerable accuracy. In turn, this would enable him, by drawing on the proposals advanced above in relation to the other two convergence points, to design his actions and curricula in a way that would maximize each student's strong points and remedy his weak points.

REFERENCES

Bentler, P. M. (1989) *EQS: Structural Equations Program Manual*, Los Angeles: BMDP Statistical Software.

Cattell, R. B. (1971) *Abilities: Their Structure, Growth, and Action*, Boston, MA: Houghton Mifflin.

Demetriou, A. and Efklides, A. (1985) 'Structure and sequence of formal and post-formal thought: general patterns and individual differences', *Child Development* 56: 1062–91.

—— (1988) 'Experiential structuralism and neo-Piagetian theories: toward an integrated model', in A. Demetriou (ed.) *The Neo-Piagetian Theories of Cognitive Development: Toward an Integration*, Amsterdam: North-Holland, pp. 173–222.

—— (1989) 'The person's conception of the structures of developing intellect: early adolescence to middle age', *Genetic, Social, and General Psychology Monographs* 115: 371–423.

Demetriou, A., Efklides, A., and Platsidou, M. (in press) 'Experiential structuralism: a frame for unifying cognitive developmental theories', *Monographs of the Society for Research in Child Development*.

Ekstrom, R. B., French, J. W., and Harman, H. H. (1976) *Kit of Factor-Referenced Cognitive Tests*, Princeton, NJ: Educational Testing Service.

Guildford, J. P. (1967) *The Nature of Human Intelligence*, New York: McGraw-Hill.

Gustafsson, J.-E. (1984) 'A unifying model for the structure of intellectual abilities', *Intelligence* 8: 179–203.

—— (1988) 'Hierarchical models of individual differences in cognitive abilities', in R. S. Sternberg (ed.) *Advances in the Psychology of Human Intelligence*, Vol. 4, Hillsdale, NJ: Erlbaum, pp. 35–71.

Gustafsson, J.-E., Lindstrom, B., and Bjorck-Akesson, E. (1981) 'A general model for the organization of cognitive abilities', report from the Department of Education, University of Goteborg.

Horn, J. L. (1986) 'Intellectual ability concepts', in R. J. Sternberg (ed.) *Advances in the Psychology of Human Intelligence*, Vol. 3, Hillsdale, NJ: Erlbaum, pp. 35–78.

Shayer, M., Demetriou, A., and Prevez, M. (1988) 'The structure and scaling of concrete operations: three studies in four countries', *Genetic, Social, and General Psychology Monographs* 114: 307–76.

Spearman, C. (1904) 'General intelligence objectively determined and measured', *American Journal of Psychology* 15: 210–93.

Sternberg, R. J. (1985) *Beyond IQ: A Triarchic Theory of Human Intelligence*, Cambridge: Cambridge University Press.

Sternberg, R. J. and Gardner, M. K. (1982) 'A componential interpretation of the general factor in human intelligence', in H. J. Eysenck (ed.) *A Model for Intelligence*, New York: Springer-Verlag.

Thurstone, L. L. (1938) 'Primary mental abilities', *Psychometric Monographs* 1.

Vernon, P. E. (1950) *The Structure of Human Abilities*, London: Methuen.

Part II
Inducing cognitive change

Chapter 6
Problems and issues in intervention studies

Michael Shayer

INTERVENTION AND NORMATIVE DATA

In educational research there is an important difference between intervention studies and the more usual studies of effects, which has been relatively unexamined. In comparison with medical studies it is clear that without a baseline of normative data which describes the growth of the child population with sufficient precision, it is not possible to gauge the meaning of an effect of a certain size which has been observed. Moreover, without such a body of normative data it would not be possible to follow the subsequent progress of a child so as to answer the question: has the intervention produced a permanent effect?

For example, Adey and Shayer (1990), Table III, reporting a two-year intervention study, cite for the boys in the experimental group, initially 12 years of age, a mean gain of 1.16 levels on Piagetian tests, compared with 0.27 levels for the controls over the same period (t = 5.0, df = 117, p<.01). Such information is usually the end of the data analysis in the psychological literature, yet it leaves unanswered three important questions. Quantitatively, where did the control and experimental groups range at pre-test in relation to the child population as a whole? What would the expected change have been over the two-year period for both groups, i.e. is the value of 0.27 levels gain for the controls typical of boys' development over this age range? Lastly, given that the difference between experimentals and controls is statistically significant, how important, quantitatively and qualitatively, might this gain be for the experimental students' learning?

For comparison, the work of Tanner (1978), Falkner and Tanner (1986) is used very widely in studies of child development in the international medical literature. In Figure 6.1 typical development curves are shown for boys' height for a representative British population sample. The heavy central curve is that for the average child, at the 50th percentile. In addition, curves for the 75th and 25th, the 90th and the 10th and the 97th and the 3rd percentiles are plotted to give an indication of the range to be expected in the population. Some of the data is cross-sectional and some is longitudinal,

108 Inducing cognitive change

and both are compatible. In addition, measurements on a single individual a little below the 25th percentile are superimposed to show the extent to which one can expect, under normal conditions, an individual's development to fit the population averages. In Figure 6.2 the way in which such normative data are used to assess the effect of a medical intervention is shown.

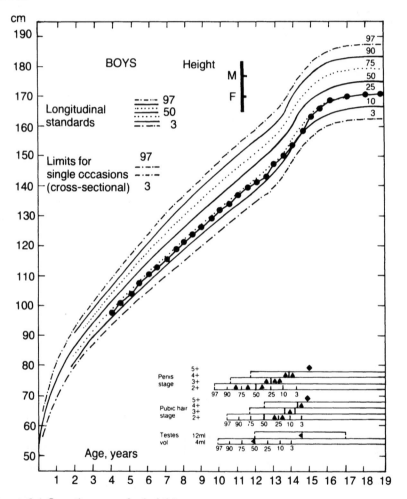

Figure 6.1 Growth curves for height
Source: Tanner 1978

So, over and above any data from schools which may show that an experimental group has achieved more than a control group, given a valid experimental design and statistical significance, to claim such an effect as an *intervention* study one needs evidence that a change in children's *development* has been achieved. For this there must also exist normative data against

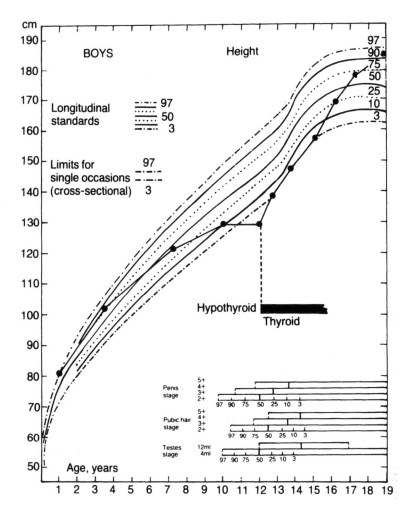

Figure 6.2 The effects of a medical intervention
Source: Tanner 1978

which the effect can be shown to stand out, and with which it can subsequently be compared. In the area of educational research, what kinds of data are comparable to Tanner's medical data?

Psychometric data, in which samples are large and representative enough to yield standardized scores, may appear to be the obvious analogy to medical data. Since most psychometric tests do not correspond in any obvious way to a possible teaching programme, they represent data at a sufficient level of abstraction from classroom intervention activity to distinguish specific learning from an effect of more general significance. However, I do not think that standardized test data are enough to justify the description 'intervention'. I believe that, unless there is a psychological model possessing both predictive and construct validity, the comparison with medical data cannot be sustained.

An example of the model having construct validity is the cognitive style, field independence (FI). This is sufficiently defined as a model (Witkin *et al.* 1962) and tested by, e.g., the Embedded Figures Test. However, in this case one does not have normative data so the effects of intervention have to be shown by pre/post-test comparisons between experimental and control groups (Collings 1987; Shayer 1987). There may be predictive correlation between FI and school achievement in, for example, science (Collings 1987), but, without normative predictive data on FI showing the relation between a given FI measure and, say, science learning, it is not possible to extrapolate from the effect-size of an FI intervention to the likely long-term effect on students' achievement.

NORM-REFERENCED VERSUS NORMATIVE DATA

A related problem occurs where normative data are in principle available, but are hidden in the standardization tables for, e.g., the Wechsler or other tests in which raw scores are converted to an IQ measure to remove the effect of age. This may have contributed to some of the doubts in the discussion of the Headstart data. It would easily be possible to reconvert the IQ measures, but in fact it hasn't been the custom to do so because of the confounding of the model itself with the process of norm-referencing. Elkind (1981) has discussed this as the form and traits problem: in addition to measures which compare children with others one needs also measures which tell what the children can actually do. What at present can be said about the difference there may be between a 12-year-old with a Wechsler score of 106 and a 15-year-old with the same score, in terms of their school achievement? Since the raw score the student has to achieve at the two different ages to be assessed at the same IQ level is different, the 'same' value would predict different things at different ages. The same objection can be made to any measure of *trait*, in Elkind's sense. The normative data needed are those of a population on a criterion-referenced test of *forms* of psychological performance. One of the strongest points in favour of Piagetian measures is that they do estimate a form of thinking, in Elkind's sense. Moreover, normative data from opinion-poll size samples for each year of age from 10 to 16 years are available from the literature (Shayer, Küchemann, and Wylam 1976; Shayer and Wylam 1978).

EFFECT SIZES

It seems desirable to have established a currency, an ECU for the effective comparison of intervention studies. Statistical significance will not do, because of its dependence on sample size. However small an effect difference is between experimental and control groups, if the sample numbers are large enough the difference will be statistically significant. Effect size as used in the meta-analysis literature seems a better candidate. Hyde (1981) has argued for the routine reporting of effect sizes as well as statistical significance in all experimental studies. But there are problems with the use of mean difference – the difference between experimental and control means in standard deviation units, either from the control only, or the root mean square value of experimental and control. Particularly with small samples, restriction of range of the control group in one study can mean that when two studies are compared the difference is not valid. Where school classes are the unit of sampling, and where internal selection within schools is practised, it will often be the case that the range within a class will be much lower than, say, even in a school year as a whole – thereby inflating the effect-size calculation. The other problem is that an effect size of, say, 0.8 SD may have a different meaning for a student initially average in ability/achievement and a student initially in the bottom 5 per cent range. *It would appear better to relate the effect size to normative data based on the child/student population as a whole, thereby making the analogy to the medical literature complete.*

This may be done by locating both control and experimental classes within Tanner curves of the psychological variable which is the subject of the intervention, and comparing their relevant percentile positions between pre- and post-tests. This is illustrated in the case of the CASE Project (Adey and Shayer 1990) by Figure 6.3. For the purposes of the comparison the nine control classes have been amalgamated, and then compared with individual experimental classes. The actual percentile points changes are shown in Table 6.1. In this way the effect sizes are calculated in terms of percentile shifts within the population as a whole, and in addition their range is located to alert the reader that a 25 percentile point change starting from the 5th percentile may have a different meaning from one starting at the 50th percentile. Note also in Figure 6.3 that, because the tests used are criterion-referenced, one can locate on the vertical axis a measure of what the changes are in behavioural terms. Those starting at the 5th percentile at 12 would change from middle concrete to mature concrete, whereas those starting at the 50th percentile would change from concrete generalization to mid-formal, both by the age of 14, for the same effect size in standard deviation terms.

THE ISSUES OF TESTING THE MODEL AND TESTING GENERALIZABILITY

I believe there is some confounding of these two issues, particularly when it comes to experimental design and testing for statistical significance. My own score after three bruising rounds with referees is 2–1 on publication of

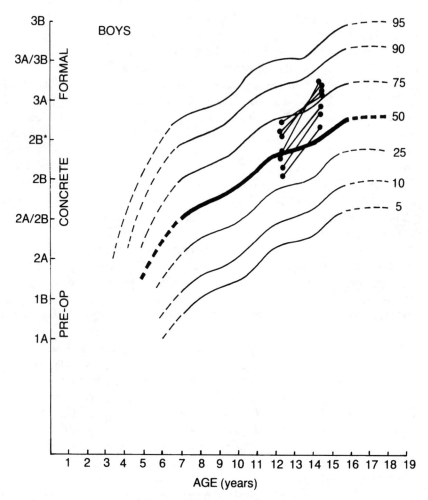

Figure 6.3 Curves of cognitive development for different percentiles of the child population
Source: Based on CSMS data and other sources

articles involving these issues. It is a problem common to intervention and curriculum development studies. Given that one has a promising model from which practice can be derived, then I believe there are two questions which need answering:

1. What effects and what size effects are achievable using this model? (*Primary effect study*)

2. To what extent can this model be internalized and successfully used by teachers other than those closely involved with its development? Actually question 2 breaks down into:

Table 6.1 Changes in class means for 12+ boys expressed as percentiles in relation to the CSMS survey data

Group	Pre-test at 12+	Post-test at 14+	Mean change
All Controls	52nd	49th	−3
Class			
0301	44th	68th	24
0302	33rd	55th	22
0701	62nd	77th	15
0801	37th	64th	27
0902	48th	83rd	35
1001	67th	75th	8
1101	58th	82nd	24
All Experimentals	51st	74th	23

Source: Adey and Shayer 1990

2a. Can the model be successfully used by certain other teachers, enthusiastic about its potentialities? (*Replication study*) And, given the answer, Yes, then:

2b. What types of inservice training programmes are most effective in inducting the nearest thing one can get to a random sample of teachers into the use of the model so as to produce effects on pupils comparable to those achieved under 1? (*Generalizability study*)

I know of three programmes concerned with the effects of Feuerstein Instrumental Enrichment (Haywood *et al.* 1982; Weller and Craft 1983; Blagg 1991) and one concerned with the effects of de Bono's CORT materials (Hunter-Grundin 1985) which ended up telling us almost nothing about either question 1 or question 2, because they made the mistake of confounding the two in a too ambitious programme of training teachers and then looking for the effects. If you try to train too many teachers, and under conditions where local support in schools may also be inadequate or nonexistent, then you end up having to take a view that the model was being used validly only in the classes where a substantial effect was obtained. It is then rather difficult to convince sceptics that the other seven or eighteen classes where no effect was obtained were due to the teachers not practising the model. In my own personal mythology of Awful Mistakes to Avoid by curriculum developers and educational researchers, the British Groundnuts scheme (OEEC 1953), where the pilot stage was dispensed with, bulks just as large as the Hawthorne experiment.

Another reason, other than that of confounding question 2 with question 1, is that I believe that the literature of models of inservice training of practising teachers is itself under-researched. Unless question 2 is broken down, and from a successful answer to 2a (replication) a suitable set of models described for question 2b, an adequate research design for 2b will not be achieved, and noise will obscure the signal. Generalizability itself requires alternative models of the variables which may affect the training: it is not enough just to test one approach and then report the results through a signal/noise model.

But this depends upon a satisfactory answer to question 1. Both curriculum developers and interventionists tend to show impatience based on optimism, and it is very difficult, I have found, to persuade them just to test the model in itself. In the medical literature a published primary effect study is the rule, rather than the exception. I think that the rules of the game are these: the sample of teachers (and students) should be small enough to ensure adequate control of the study in relation to use of the underlying model. The teachers need to be adequately supported: just how much support is probably impossible to foresee, so one should over-design, and withdraw support only when researchers and teachers are both satisfied that the support has served its purpose. One needs to ensure that the model/programme has been tested under near-optimum conditions. With modest resources and one researcher two teachers may be as many as one can control and support with confidence. Even with substantial resources, such as Feuerstein had in the Hadassah-Wiso-Canada research centre in Jerusalem, five teachers/schools is probably the upper limit for a study of this kind. Resnick (1989) reports a model primary effects study in the present symposium.

The research design should feature suitable control classes, as close to being a random sample from the same population as experimental classes as logistics allow and near-equality of number gives the greatest statistical efficiency. The larger the initial differences between control and experimental classes, the larger does the obtained effect size have to be before the statistical significance of the difference can be justified. In the testing I believe that it is important to separate the tests into those which test the model and those which test other effects which are also desired as a biproduct of the intervention. One wants to know whether the intervention has worked in terms of educational aims, but one also wants to know whether it has worked because of the model used.

The results of such a research design, if satisfactory, are then in principle dependent on the amount of training and support given, and the circumstances favouring success, which should both therefore be described adequately in the report. One may then proceed to question 2, preferably by the intermediate step 2a. The reason for this is that one may be uncertain of which of the conditions for the first study were necessary to success. One will necessarily not be able to offer as much support in a replication as in a primary effects study, so judgement will be needed, based on the experience of the initial study, of the minimum for a reasonable chance of transmitting the model to the new sample of teachers. One could, with a certain amount of risk, jump straight from a primary effect study to the design of a generalizability study, but it seems to me that by putting in the intermediate step of working with say, up to a dozen teachers, the feedback obtained will give much more information about the problems different teachers may have, first of understanding the model itself and then of putting it into practice in their teaching. Then this extra information should allow more valid theories to be put forward of those aspects of inservice training and support which are to be tested in the experimental test of generalizability. I can cite no example from the literature of such a study which is related to a clearly specified intervention model and tested by effects on pupils.

THE INADEQUACY OF PRE-TEST IMMEDIATE POST-TEST DESIGN

The scandal of the intervention study literature is the lack of good evidence showing improved school achievement as a result of intervention. There is no objection to immediate post-test for looking at the intervention in terms of its model. It is to be expected that the maximum effect will be present at the end of the intervention. But one problem arises if the post-test is only an indirect test of the model. One flaw in what was in all other respects a model replication study reported by Feuerstein *et al.* (1980) and Rand *et al.* (1981) was the use of the Thurstone Primary Mental Abilities test as one post-test for the effects of IE. Differential mental abilities are part of the model Feuerstein and his co-workers use for the designing of an adequate spectrum of learning experiences, so the choice was appropriate for testing the intervention model. But such a norm-referenced test, although valid for the different abilities, will only indirectly be related to the particular learning experiences the children have had. It seems to me that psychometric tests of this kind contain the hidden assumption that they are sampling in a representative way the different experiences which the child population can be expected to have had prior to testing in the total 24-hour-a-day combination of environments the children have been in. Items relating only to eccentric environments will have been eliminated as unreliable at the earlier stage of test development. So the children can now be compared in terms of how well they process the items, given the assumption that they have all been exposed equally to the environments to which the test items relate. But when such a test is now used to estimate the effects of an intervention, I believe a systematic underestimate will be obtained. This is because the effects of an intervention have important differences from 'natural' development. First, the training will have been experienced only in the specific learning contexts which relate to the different mental abilities. Second, the improved processing of that learning by the pupils will have occurred during a shorter period of their lives than 'normal' development would have taken. Both of these reasons suggest that, even if the effect of the intervention is valid and permanent, it will still take more times and occasions of life experience before as wide a range of environments as the test-items sample and relate to has been re-processed by the children.

The first conclusion from this line of argument is that if the maximum effect at post-test was to be estimated, then a new test of mental abilities (based on the Thurstone model) should have been designed which related to the IE learning contexts, but did not test the specific content of the IE lessons. Such a test has been labelled one of *near-transfer*. The second conclusion is that a different interpretation can be offered to the one given by Feuerstein to account for the fact that two years after the IE intervention the effect difference between experimentals and controls had gone up from 0.35 SD to about 0.9 SD as tested by a comparable test of mental abilities. Feuerstein argued that the experimental pupils had continued to develop faster than the controls even with no further IE. But it can be argued equally that the later result was simply a better estimate of the effect which was already there at post-test, and all that has happened is that the students have since re-processed more of their environments at the same level of processing.

The second inadequacy of the post-test design is more obvious: whereas a suitable post-test *can* be the best estimator of the effect of an intervention in terms of the intervention model(s) used, a test of achievement to estimate the secondary effects of the intervention – usually school achievement – is bound to yield an underestimate. The reason is closely related to the argument given above. If a standardized test of achievement is used, most of the questions are likely to relate to learning experiences prior to or outside the contexts of the intervention. The students will not have had the chance to process or re-process that learning at at a time when they have received the maximum effect of the intervention. In addition, if a school-based test of achievement is used, it is bound to be retrospective in what is examined. The questions may relate to any period in the previous two years of the students' learning. But if one postulates some kind of ogive learning curve for the effects of the intervention, it may not be until it is nearly two-thirds through that a substantial difference exists between experimentals and controls.

For both these reasons, then, standardized tests of achievement should not be used, and the right thing to do is to wait until the intervention is over, and then give both experimental and controls the same fresh learning experiences – preferably by being taught together in the same classes – and then design an achievement test which relates only to the content, skills, and context of that fresh learning. In this way the maximum secondary effect of the intervention can be estimated, undiluted by other earlier learning experiences. In Shayer and Adey (1992) the tests used were on the whole of the year's science learning in the year immediately following the CASE intervention. Whereas in Adey and Shayer (1990) immediate post-test of science achievement showed no difference between experimentals and controls, a year later experimentals outperformed controls by the same order of effect sizes that they had earlier shown on Piagetian tests (testing the model only) at immediate post-test.

'BRIDGING' AND TRANSFER

I believe that the last few years have shown a resurgence of ideas and methods which allow the old transfer-of-training issue to be re-examined and looked at in new lights. One approach was described by Salomon (1988, 1989) and Perkins and Salomon (1989) as the high road to transfer, as distinguished from the low road of context-specific generalization and automaticity. The high road involves, as well as practice, persuading the subjects to engage in their own mindful abstraction about the *principles* which lead to success in the tasks practised, and further to apply the same mindful abstraction to a new task context as a heuristic to spotting the principles which might apply. The neo-Piagetian model of Demetriou and Efklides which describes metacognition over and above differentiated mental capacities would seem to relate directly to this (Demetriou and Efklides 1989).

'Bridging' is a technical term much used in the practice of Feuerstein IE, and it may well be that when it is successful the teachers and students have intuitively hit on applications of the same principles as described by Salomon and Perkins. During and towards the end of every IE lesson students are urged to invent and talk through bridging examples where the same principles they have learnt and practised in the lesson are applied to other contexts within and without the school. The only problem is that this is the one part of the Feuerstein set of models which is left to intuition, or divergent thinking, and illustrated at best by lists of examples. More promising is a deductive/inductive use of Feuerstein's information-processing model of 'deficient cognitive functions'. Mehl (1985) and Froufe (1987) both analysed students' learning errors in the context of, respectively, undergraduate physics and high-school chemistry. By individual interview on typical problems, a list of typical cognitive functions responsible for failure on the problems was identified from Feuerstein's list of information gathering, processing, and communicating cognitive functions. From the list a set of algorithms was designed to assist the students to more efficient learning on those and related problems. In both studies impressively improved student learning in terms of experimental/control differences of 0.6 SD or more were reported for physics and chemistry. On the other hand, no improvements on any general tests or tests based on the intervention model were reported.

The paradox therefore exists that many interventions have been reported which showed gains in terms of the model used, but few if any gains on school achievement (and this includes Feuerstein's own reported research), but that when the same model is applied to the specifics of science learning, the learning is improved without any general improvement of intelligence.

One feels that in the paradox lies one line of solution to the problem of transfer, were the two procedures to be adopted simultaneously.

A PROBLEM IN THE DATA PROCESSING OF INTERVENTION STUDIES

Workers concerned with intervention studies may often have an overlap with those interested in the art of dynamic testing. Aspects of dynamic testing may capture better than static tests the intervention model used. Beasley (Beasley and Shayer 1990) succeeded in making part of Feuerstein's Learning Potential Assessment (LPA) battery yield a quantitative estimate of the processing level of students in terms of the deficient cognitive functions model, and was able to show that experimental students improved in their here-and-now performance on Matrix tasks relative to controls as a result of twenty months' IE. Embretson (1987) used a dynamic mode of testing for spatial abilities to test the effect of an intervention related to the same abilities. Both Embretson (1987) and Beasley and Shayer (1990) found that the gain-score part of the dynamic testing accounted for much more of the predictive validity than the initial static test. But when the data from such testing are analysed often problems arising from processing difference scores are encountered. Cronbach and Furby (1970) have given a mandatory warning to anyone working in this field, and also sketched a possible solution. Embretson (1988) in an excellent discussion has argued that item response theory (in particular, Rasch analysis) provides a way to conceptualize the analysis of difference scores which may be an alternative to the traditional psychometric approach.

More important still, she argues that research on the different facets of students' learning strategies can inform the design of a testing process in which students' ability to learn on task is tested in the dynamic test situation. The work on expert systems associated with, *inter alia*, Larkin and Rainard (1984) and Smith and Good (1984) has shown that quite small samples, well chosen, serve to identify the major learning behaviours on a class of tasks. Such a procedure adds to the work of Mehl and Froufe already mentioned in the design of a test which can be used as a valid predictor of the effect of an intervention programme on different students. Embretson argues that, with the present availability of computers, all the relevant facets of cues, learning prompts, etc., can be standardized in presentation, so that the information gathered during testing is (a) a better predictor of students' future or current learning and (b) relevant to the better design of instruction. The connection with this work and future intervention models and theory is clear.

A LAST WORD ON INTERVENTION VERSUS INSTRUCTION

Inspection of Figure 6.3 indicates that the spread of performance, in Piagetian terms, is far wider in 12-year-olds than could be predicted from the arguments of Jensen (1969). Were the heritability of intelligence as high as Jensen argued, the range of developmental curves would resemble those relating to height shown in Figure 6.1. The hereditability argument has itself been demonstrated to be untenable by Tizard (1983). There is therefore a question of whether improvement in school achievement can be brought about directly by improvement in instruction, or whether what is needed is a new set of professional teaching skills aimed at accelerating the cognitive development of children, from which improved learning would be a secondary consequence. It can be argued from Figure 6.3 (Shayer 1991) that improved instruction alone, as was attempted in the USA and Britain in the 1960s for science, is likely to affect the achievement only of the upper 30 per cent, on the grounds that only this range of children are realizing their genetic potential. This issue appears rather clearly in the primary effect study reported by Resnick (see Chapter 11). Are we dealing here with improved instruction in mathematics or are we dealing with an intervention strategy aimed at improving children's self-image as learners and with inducing metacognitive activity in which mathematics happens to be the major learning context which is addressed?

The reason for making this distinction is that when it comes to designing a generalizability study it may be important, in arranging teacher training, to have the underlying model which was responsible for the primary effect expressed in sufficient clarity and richness so that teachers can learn how to develop for themselves the new skills which are necessary for replication of what was achieved with direct assistance from the research team in the primary effect study. Only the real causation for the effects on mathematics achievement reported is likely to serve as an effective vehicle to communicate the teaching skills required to a fresh group of teachers.

REFERENCES

Adey, P. S. and Shayer, M. (1990) 'Accelerating the development of formal thinking in middle and high school pupils', *Journal of Research in Science Teaching* 27 (3): 267–85.

Beasley, F. and Shayer, M. (1990) 'Learning Potential Assessment through Feuerstein's LPAD: can quantitative results be achieved?', *International Journal of Dynamic Assessment and Instructions* 1 (2): 37–48.

Blagg, N. (1991) *Can We Teach Intelligence? A Comprehensive Evaluation of Feuerstein's Instrumental Enrichment Program*, London: Lawrence Erlbaum.

Collings, J. (1987) 'A study of the effects of field-independence training for early adolescents on science learning and cognitive development', unpublished PhD thesis, College of St Paul and St Mary, Cheltenham.

Cronbach, L. and Furby, L. (1970) 'How should we measure change – or should we?', *Psychological Bulletin* 74: 68–80.

Demetriou, A. and Efklides, A. (1989) 'The person's conception of the structures of developing intellect: early adolescence to middle age', *Genetic, Social and General Psychology Monographs* 115: 377–423.

Elkind, D. (1981) 'Form and traits in the conception and measurement of intelligence', *Intelligence* 5: 101–20.
Embretson, S. E. (1987) 'Improving the measurement of spatial aptitude by dynamic testing', *Intelligence* 11: 333–58.
—— (1988) 'Diagnostic testing by measuring learning processes: psychometric considerations for dynamic testing', in *Test Design: Developments in Psychology and Psychometrics*, New York: Academic Press.
Falkner, F. and Tanner, J. M. (1986) *Human Growth: A Comprehensive Treatise*, 3 volumes, New York and London: Plenum.
Feuerstein, R., Rand, Y., Hoffman, M., and Miller, R. (1980) *Instrumental Enrichment: An Intervention Programme for Cognitive Modifiability*, Baltimore: University Park Press.
Froufe, J. (1987) 'Feuerstein's theory applied to the school science curriculum', MA dissertation, King's College, University of London.
Haywood, H. C., Arbitman-Smith, R., *et al*. (1982) 'Cognitive education with adolescents: evaluation of Instrumental Enrichment', paper presented at symposium of 6th IASSMD, Toronto.
Hunter-Grundin, E. (1985) *Teaching Thinking: An Evaluation of Edward de Bono's Classroom Materials*, London: The Schools Council.
Hyde, J. S. (1981) 'How large are cognitive differences?', *American Psychologist* 36 (8): 892–901.
Jensen, A. R. (1969) 'How much can we boost IQ and scholastic achievement?', *Harvard Educational Review* 39: 1–123.
Larkin, J. and Rainard, B. (1984) 'A research methodology for studying how people think', *Journal of Research in Science Teaching* 21 (3): 235–54.
Mehl, M. (1985) 'The cognitive difficulties of first year physics students at the University of the Western Cape and various compensatory programmes', PhD thesis, University of Cape Town.
Organization for European Economic Cooperation (1953) *The Cultivation of Ground-Nuts in West Africa*, Paris: OEEC.
Perkins, D. M. and Salomon, G. (1989) 'Are cognitive skills context-bound?', *Educational Researcher* 18 (1): 16–25.
Rand, Y., Mintzker, R., Hoffman, M. B., and Friedlender, Y. (1981) 'The Instrumental Enrichment Programme: immediate and long-term effects', in P. Mittler (ed.) *Frontiers of Knowledge in Mental Retardation*, Vol. 1, Baltimore: University Park Press.
Resnick, L.B. (1989) 'Developing thinking abilities in arithmetic class', paper delivered at 3rd EARLI conference, Madrid.
Salomon, G. (1988) 'Two roads to transfer: two roads of transfer', paper delivered at the Annual Meeting of the AERA, New Orleans.
—— (1989) 'Why should a learner bother to transfer', paper delivered at AERA Annual Conference, San Francisco.
Shayer, M. (1987) 'Neo-Piagetian theories and educational practice', *International Journal of Psychology* 22 (5/6): 751–72.
Shayer, M. (1991) 'Improving standards and the National Curriculum', *School Science Review* 72 (260): 17–24.
Shayer, M. and Adey, P. S. (1992) 'Accelerating the development of formal thinking in middle and high school students, II: post-project effects on science achievement', *Journal of Research in Science Teaching* 29 (1): 81–92.
Shayer, M. and Wylam, H. (1978) 'The distribution of Piagetian stages of thinking in British middle and secondary school children, II: 14–16-year-olds and sex differentials', *British Journal of Educational Psychology* 948: 62–70.

Shayer, M., Küchemann, D. E., and Wylam, H. (1976) 'The distribution of Piagetian stages of thinking in British middle and secondary school children', *British Journal of Educational Psychology* 46: 164–73.

Smith, M. and Good, R. (1984) 'Problem solving and classical genetics: successful versus unsuccessful performance', *Journal of Research in Science Teaching* 21 (9): 895–912.

Tanner, J. M. (1978) *Foetus into Man: Physical Growth from Conception to Maturity*, London: Open Books.

Tizard, J. (1983) 'Race and IQ: the limits of probability', in A. D. B. Clarke and B. Tizard (eds) *Child Development and Social Policy: The Life and Work of Jack Tizard*, Leicester: British Psychological Society.

Weller, K. and Craft, A. (1983) *Making up our Minds: An Exploratory Study of Instrumental Enrichment*, Schools Council Publications.

Witkin, H.-A., Dyk, R. B., Paterson, H. F., Goodenough, D. R., and Karp, S. A. (1962) *Psychological Differentiation*, New York: Wiley.

Chapter 7

Training, cognitive change, and individual differences

Anastasia Efklides, Andreas Demetriou, and Jan-Eric Gustafsson

The training of cognitive abilities has been an object of study since the turn of the century, when learning phenomena started to be systematically investigated. The question posed then was how learning shapes current responses and how previous learning can affect subsequent behaviour. This is the problem of transfer of training, to which, despite a century's efforts at its conceptualization and measurement, a definitive answer has not yet been found (Cormier and Hagman 1987; de Corte 1987). The fact is, as Fleishman (1987) pointed out, we need to know more about the abilities used by the learner for both the training and the transfer tasks, and their interaction with training methods.

In developmental psychology, training of cognitive abilities has been mainly used in order to test assumptions about the origin and mechanism of cognitive change and the feasibility of cognitive acceleration. After about three decades of research in this direction, it has become clear that there are three issues that have not been resolved yet. These pertain to the method of intervention, the generalization of training effects, and individual differences. A factor that is particularly related to all of these issues is the abilities brought to bear by the individual when addressing the specific tasks. These abilities might be highly specialized skills or general abilities that are independent of the particular task addressed each time. Therefore, the first question to be answered in a developmental training study regards the role of broad and narrow abilities in the determination of training effects. The second question pertains to the effects of age and its interaction with the trained abilities. The third question involves the effects of the current developmental level of abilities in the acquisition of higher modes of thinking.

A theoretical framework that allows the investigation and possible answering of the above questions is that of neo-Piagetian theories. Neo-Piagetian theories claim that there is a general capacity factor, changes in which raise people's processing potential and enable them to acquire new concepts and operations (Case 1985; Halford 1988; Pascual-Leone 1988). However, Fischer's skill theory (1980; Fischer and Pipp 1984) and Demetriou and Efklides's theory of experiential structures (1988) postulate the existence of specialized abilities that account for performance in specialized knowledge domains. Thus cognitive development should be understood as a function of both the specialized and the general component of intelligence. From this point of view, one would expect limited generalization of training, because of the domain-specificity of cognitive structures, and a process of change that might be discontinuous or continuous depending upon the particular phase of development in which the person is. Specifically, it is assumed that there are abrupt changes associated with changes in processing potential and more gradual ones occurring within a stage of thinking (Demetriou and Efklides 1986; Fischer and Farrar 1988).

With regard to individual differences, experiential structuralism identifies two sources of variation: personal factors, such as age, sex, and socio-economic status, and cognitive factors, such as the level of development along the various specialized abilities. Thus, this theoretical framework allows the investigation of the dynamics of cognitive change as well as the interaction of the various abilities with individual-difference factors in the determination of training effects.

THE THEORY

Experiential structuralism distinguishes three levels of description of the cognitive system: a) the hardware or capacity characteristics of the system; b) metacognition or the personal theory of the mind; and c) the specialized structural systems (SSSs) that form the overt manifestation of the mind.

Five SSSs have been identified: the qualitative-analytic, the quantitative-relational, the causal-experimental, the imaginal-spatial, and the verbal-propositional. The modal characteristics of the various systems as well as their organizational principles are discussed in Chapter 5 of this volume.

The present study focused on two of the SSSs: the quantitative-relational (QR) and the causal-experimental (CE). The quantitative-relational SSS applies to quantifiable reality. It involves abilities enabling the thinker to quantify and measure reality elements, construct the dimensions that can capture their relations, and co-ordinate these dimensions into complex structures. Thus, this SSS can build quantitative models of reality. Measurement, number operations, ratio and proportion relations are typical tasks which require the application of the QR SSS. The causal-experimental SSS deals with interactive and causal structures which require a systematic way of disentangling the underlying causal relations. In such a case, application of the isolation-of-variables schema, hypothesis formation, experimentation, and building of explanatory models is needed.

A second postulate of experiential structuralism is the basically autonomous nature of the developmental trajectories of different SSSs. This is supposedly so because the abilities that constitute each SSS do not pose the same demands on cognitive resources. Thus, there may be differences in the level of development across SSSs. Nevertheless, there are some limitations to the independence of the development of different systems. This is suggested by the operation of domain-free factors, such as those to be described below. This is indicated by longitudinal findings revealing the presence of more or less general spurts at particular ages: that is, 2, 5, 11, and 15 years of age (Demetriou and Efklides 1986; Demetriou, Efklides, and Platsidou 1991). At these ages, the strategic orientation of thought seems to be changing and new forms of thinking to be acquired as a result. Smaller changes occur approximately every two years. Therefore, cognitive change is a function of the SSS involved and general constraints on cognitive functioning which are usually associated with age. The developmental level itself has also been shown to be a factor of change. That is, we found that the higher the level of a person, the more difficult it is to raise that level even further (Demetriou and Efklides 1986).

Metacognition is the second basic component of the cognitive system. It is considered to be the domain-general software that applies to the SSSs rather than to reality itself. It plays an important role in allocating mental resources and guiding the task-SSS affiliation, the selection of the SSS-appropriate procedures, solution monitoring, and feedback about the success of the solution produced. For this reason it is assumed to be an important component of the SSS acquisition process and it should be part of the training procedure.

The other component of the cognitive system is the domain-general hardware (DGH). This is a capacity factor at the core of the cognitive system, possibly constraining the effects of learning on development. Development is a function of changes in this capacity factor as well as in the SSSs. Up to now, a number of hypotheses have been advanced about the exact nature of this factor. Specifically, it is assumed that it involves speed and control of processing components of the cognitive system (Demetriou, Efklides, and Platsidou 1991).

Clearly, individual differences might be conceived in terms of both the SSSs and the DGH. Yet little is known about DGH that would allow any specific predictions. One hypothesis could be that it is related to g. In fact, the partitioning of the mind proposed by our theory bears many similarities to the structure of intelligence as described by modern psychometric theory. A model that is currently dominating psychometric theorizing is that proposed by Gustafsson (1984). This is a hierarchical model that involves both general and lower-order abilities. According to this model, at the lowest level there are factors similar to the 'primary mental abilities' identified by Thurstone, Guilford, and other researchers. Examples of such factors are: induction; verbal comprehension; space; and flexibility of closure. At an intermediate level the model identifies factors such as fluid intelligence (Gf), crystallized intelligence, and general visualization, each of them related to particular primary factors. At the highest level the model includes a factor of general intelligence, on which all the broad abilities have loadings. It is interesting to note, however, that this factor has been consistently found to be perfectly correlated with the Gf-factor. This means that the *g*-factor is equivalent to fluid intelligence.

There exists no generally accepted interpretation of the psychological nature of *g*, or Gf. However, there seems to be a relationship between the complexity of a task and its loading on Gf, and it also seems that a common denominator of tasks loading Gf is that they are 'content-free', i.e. they are relatively uninfluenced by previous acquisitions of knowledge structures or by experience in dealing with any particular system of symbols. Complexity and novelty thus seem to be important characteristics of tasks defining Gf (see Gustafsson 1988, for a further discussion about the interpretation of Gf). According to this definition, the *g* or Gf-factor of psychometric theories of intelligence is very close to DGH as defined by our theory.

Thus, SSS-specific tasks can be coupled with tasks tapping Gf, so that the exact contribution of broad and narrow factors in training effects at various age levels can be specified.

The specific predictions derived from experiential structuralism, and which concern the trainability of cognitive abilities, the generalizability of training, and the individual-differences factors that interact with training treatments, are the following:

1. Change of cognitive abilities through training is possible, because training provides learning experiences that specifically address SSSs and facilitate the grasp of their constitutional characteristics.

2. Training effects are a function of both general and specialized abilities. Thus, changes in the various SSSs are linked to both Gf and the particular SSS trained.

3. The various SSSs, due to their differential constitution, are differentially amenable to the effects of training. That is, there are aptitude–treatment interactions.

4. Training one SSS will not necessarily transfer to other SSSs. Training will lead to progression along the developmental sequence of the trained SSS but not that of the others.

5. Training interacts with age. Cognitive change, and consequently training effectiveness, is more probable at certain periods rather than others. For instance, training is expected to be least effective at the younger ages at which the SSS-related abilities of interest are not present and most effective at the ages at which they may be acquired.

6. Training interacts with the individual's developmental level. That is, lower developmental levels are more amenable to change than higher levels.

METHOD

Design

In order to test the hypotheses stated above, the following intervention study was designed. There were two experimental groups and one control group. The first group was trained on the quantitative-relational SSS (Quantitative-Relational Treatment Group, QRTG) and the second on the causal-experimental SSS (Causal-Experimental Treatment Group, CETG). The third received no training at all, and therefore it served as the control group (Control Treatment Group, CTG). The two genders and four age levels were about equally represented in each treatment group. All subjects were tested before and after training with the same battery of tasks. The battery consisted of four QR and four CE tasks. At the pre-test all subjects were also required to solve a set of four tasks addressed to Gf.

The cognitive level of subjects with respect to each SSS was also a factor in this study. Specifically, each subject was allocated to a level for each of the two developmental hierarchies represented in this study, that is, the QR and the CE hierarchy. In this way the effect of training in relation to the initial level of the subject can be specified. *Cognitive level* was estimated from performance on the pre-test tasks of both SSSs. Subjects were thus assigned to two levels, one for each SSS. Cognitive level ranged from 0 to 4. Assignment of level scores was deemed reasonable because the tasks of each SSS formed a 'perfect' scale in the Guttman sense. The subjects were given one of the level scores 1 through 4 that corresponded to the most difficult task they had solved. Level 0 was assigned to subjects who had failed all the tasks.

Training was group administered but individualized. Each subject was trained to solve tasks one level above his pre-test cognitive level. There was no training for subjects operating at level 4 in either SSS. Effort was made to have subjects of all cognitive levels of both SSSs in each training condition, so that the groups would not differ substantially in regard to each SSS's mean level score.

For each of the tasks used to assess the SSSs (see below), a detailed step-by-step demonstration of the solution of an equivalent problem was prepared in written form. An introduction informed the subject about the relevance of the problem to everyday life situations, so that the domain of application could be figured out. A second problem, structurally equivalent to the one used for demonstration, was given to the subject. The subject was instructed to apply the procedures involved in the demonstration task in order to solve this second task. Feedback with regard to the solution produced was given to the subject upon completion of the task. Specifically, the subject was given the correct answer to the problem. He was also instructed to compare step by step the solution he had produced with the model solution in order to check the adequacy of his own solution and to correct any mistakes made. The subjects were allowed to study the correct answer sheet for as long as they wished.

Subjects

One thousand and twenty-eight subjects were tested. Four age groups were represented in the sample: 10, 12, 14 and 16 years old. In all, 509 girls and 519 boys took part in the experiment. Regarding their socioeconomic origin, 313 came from high SES families of urban residence; 375 came from low SES families of urban residence; 340 came from low SES families and lived in rural areas.

Tasks

Experiential structuralism assumes that two tasks may be formally equivalent in regard to a hierarchy of levels of difficulty and still be different in regard to processing load. In order to test this assumption, the tasks used in this investigation were constructed in such a way that they retained their domain and procedural specificity but were matched in their underlying formal structure. Fischer's (1980; see also Chapter 1 of this volume) hierarchy of skill levels was used for that reason. Each of the four tasks addressed to each SSS corresponded to one of the four developmental levels of the tier of abstract thought: that is, the level of single abstract sets, abstract mappings, abstract systems, and systems of abstract systems.

Quantitative-relational SSS tasks

Four problems involving ratio and proportion relationships were addressed to the quantitative-relational SSS (QR1–QR4).

QR1: Subjects are presented with a two times two table showing a relationship between watering frequency (twice and four times/month) and yield (2 and 6 kgs/hectare for plant A and 3 and 6 kgs/hectare for plant B). The task is to find out which plant is more affected by watering and to explain why. Thus, two variations have to be co-ordinated into a single set that forms an abstraction.

QR2: Two tables like the one in QR1 (i.e., a double table) are presented, showing the effects of watering on plants A and B in two areas I and II. Thus, in this task two single sets/abstractions have to be combined.

QR3: Two double tables are presented showing the effects of watering on plants A and B in areas I and II, when fungi are and when fungi are not present. Thus four single (or two double) sets of data, representing a system of abstractions, have to be combined to solve the task.

QR4: Four double tables are presented showing the effects of watering on plants A and B in areas I and II, when fungi are present, with or without use of fungicide, and when fungi are not present, with or without use of fertilizer. Thus, four double or eight single sets of data have to be combined to solve the task. This task represents a system of abstract systems.

Causal-experimental SSS tasks

Four problems were constructed involving the design of experiments in order to test hypotheses (CE1–CE4). These tasks were structurally equivalent to the QR tasks in the sense that they also tapped the four skill levels of the tier of abstract thought.

CE1: A simple hypothesis is given ('The increase in watering frequency increases the productivity of plants') and the subject is asked to use plants A and/or B and two watering frequencies (twice a month or four times a month) to design an experiment to test the hypothesis (single abstraction).

CE2: A hypothesis is given about the interaction between two factors ('Watering increases the productivity of plant A, but does not affect the productivity of plant B'). An experiment, integrating two single ones, has to be designed to test the above hypothesis (abstractions mapping).

CE3: In this task, the experiment to be designed must test two interaction hypotheses, regarding the effects of watering on A in areas I and II and on B in areas I and II (abstract system). Thus a three-way design (plant x area x watering) has to be proposed.

CE4: In this task, yet another factor, fertilization, has to be taken into account. The solution of the task requires design of a four-way experiment (plant x area x fertilizer x watering). Such a design captures the interaction of two abstract systems, therefore it is a system of systems.

Fluid intelligence tests

A set of four tests was used to measure fluid intelligence (Gf), three of which were selected from the Kit of Factor-Referenced Cognitive Tests (Ekstrom *et al.* 1976):

The *Letter Sets* (LS) test contains fifteen items in which five sets of four letters are presented. The task is to find the rule which relates four of the sets to each other and to mark the one which does not fit the rule.

The *Figure Classification* (FC) test includes fourteen items presenting two or three groups, each containing three geometrical figures that are alike in accordance with some rule. The task is to discover these rules and to classify each of eight given test figures to one of the groups.

The *Hidden Figures* test (HF) presents sixteen items in which the task is to decide which of five geometrical figures is embedded in a complex pattern.

The HF test is constructed to measure field independence, or flexibility of closure, but is known to be a good indicator of *g* as well (Gustafsson 1984, 1988). The other two ETS tests are classified as measures of the inductive factor, which in turn more or less coincides with Gf (cf. Gustafsson 1984). Inductive ability was also tested with a number series test.

The *Number Series* test (NS) contains twenty items in which a series of five or six numbers is given, and the task is to add two more numbers to the series (Gustafsson, Lindstrom, and Bjorck-Akesson 1981).

Procedure

All subjects were tested before and after the training period with the same tasks on both occasions. All testing was carried out in groups in the pupils' regular classrooms. The pre-test session lasted for approximately two school hours, and comprised the eight SSS tasks, the HF test, and two of the inductive tasks. The training session was held about two weeks later, followed by administration of the eight SSS tasks as 'post-tests'. The training session lasted approximately half an hour. The training leaflets were personally addressed to each subject according to their assignment to the experimental groups and the level achieved at the pre-test. At the post-test session the third inductive test was also administered.

The presentation order of the three batteries was counterbalanced across subjects at both the pre- and post-test. At the training session, the experimental group subjects were instructed to study the problems, the solution, and the explanations provided so as to profit as much as possible from the opportunity to gain practice on the particular type of task. At the post-test, the control-treatment group subjects were instructed to do their best and to try to attend to the details of the tasks now that they were familiar with the requirements of the tasks. It was particularly stressed that they must try to improve their performance. No time limit was imposed at any of the three phases of the experiment.

RESULTS AND DISCUSSION

In order to test the first three hypotheses, which refer to the possibility of cognitive change and the role of general and specific factors in it, the data were analysed through a sequence of confirmatory factor analysis and structural equation models, fitted with the LISREL VI program (Jöreskog and Sörbom 1986). The aim of the analyses was to determine, first, the existence of Gf and QR and CE factors and, second, to specify their interaction with training. In these models it has been assumed that the four tests selected to measure Gf are related to one latent variable; that the QR1–QR4 tasks when administered as pre-test measure one factor

130 Inducing cognitive change

(PreQR), and when administered after training measure another factor (PostQR); and that, similarly, the CE1–CE4 tasks can be taken to measure the factors PreCE and PostCE. Separate models were estimated from the correlation matrices for each of the four age groups, but the three treatment groups at each age level were included in the same model for technical reasons.

Most of the results to be reported here were obtained in a model which included the full set of variables, but in order to make the presentation of results somewhat more easy to follow, different sub-sets of this model will be dealt with in steps.

Gf and SSS-specific factors

Table 7.1 presents the estimates of the loadings of the pre-test variables on the latent variables, with the estimates constrained to be equal for all the treatment groups within an age group. The estimates presented are the standardized loadings, which can be interpreted as correlations.

Table 7.1 Loadings of the pre-test variables on the latent variables

Var/age	Gf 10	Gf 12	Gf 14	Gf 16	PreQR 10	PreQR 12	PreQR 14	PreQR 16	PreCE 10	PreCE 12	PreCE 14	PreCE 16
HF	03	45	51	53								
NS	64	73	67	46								
LC	47	74	50	41								
FG	21	42	27	31								
QR1					49	61	49	36				
QR2					70	66	56	51				
QR3					22	46	66	66				
QR4					19	38	65	63				
CE1									20	24	44	34
CE2									15	38	47	42
CE3									58	74	63	70
CE4									50	54	60	68

The hypothesized Gf factor seems well supported by these data and with very few exceptions the estimated loadings are highly significant. The pattern of results obtained for PreQR also supports the existence of such a factor. The relations with PreCE also support identification of a latent variable, even though the factor is rather weak for the 10-year-olds. The results thus support identification of the hypothesized factors Gf, PreQR, and PreCE, and point out the existence of both general and specialized factors in cognitive organization.

Relations between Gf and the SSSs

The simplest way to study the relationship between Gf and the two SSSs is simply to estimate the correlations between the latent variables defined above. The correlations, estimated under the constraint that they should be equal in all treatment groups, are presented in Table 7.2.

Table 7.2 Correlations among the latent pre-test factors

Latent pre-test factors/age	10	12	14	16
Gf-PreQR	59	84	73	72
Gf-PreCE	44	63	46	41
PreQR-PreCE	24	47	66	63

Quite high correlations are obtained between PreQR and Gf. For the 12-year-olds the correlation is so high (.84) that PreQR virtually collapses into Gf. The correlations between PreCE and Gf tend to be lower (around .40), but again a larger value is obtained for the 12-year-olds. The correlations for the youngest group of subjects tend to be lower than they are for the other three age groups, which may be due to the fact that the tasks were quite difficult for the 10-year-olds. Any floor effects in the data will cause deviations from the assumption of linearity upon which the present analysis rests, so the results for this age group should be interpreted with care. These results thus show that there is a very substantial relationship between QR and Gf, and a moderate correlation between CE and Gf. What remains to be seen is how Gf and the SSSs interact with training.

Training effects and individual differences

The same set of tasks that was administered as pre-tests was also administered as post-tests, and there is little reason to believe that the training dramatically altered the measurement characteristics of the tasks. The latent variables PostQR and PostCE were, therefore, identified in the same way as the corresponding pre-test factors, and constraints of equality of the factor loadings for the pre- and post-test factors were imposed.

In a first step of the analysis, it is interesting to investigate the degree of correlation between the pre- and post-test factors. The within-treatment correlations are shown in Table 7.3. Several of the correlations are very high indeed, and particularly so for QR. Among the 14-year-olds of the QRT group there was a perfect relationship between PreQR and PostQR. This indicates that the training did nothing to change the rank ordering of the subjects' performance. At the other three age levels the PreQR and PostQR relations in the QRT treatment are somewhat lower (around .75), so in these groups there seem to have been some changes in the rank ordering of the subjects' level of performance. The PreQR and PostQR correlations for the subjects of the control and the CET groups were also close to unity. These results thus indicate a very considerable degree of stability of individual differences in QR over a period of two weeks, even though there may be a tendency for the correlations to be somewhat lower in the groups that received training on the QR tasks.

Table 7.3 Correlations between pre- and post-test factors

Factors/	CTG				QRTG				CETG			
Treatment/Age	10	12	14	16	10	12	14	16	10	12	14	16
PreQR/PostQR	76	93	85	91	72	75	100	72	100	99	71	84
PreCE/PostCE	84	61	77	71	100	51	94	89	78	71	66	89

The correlations between PreCE and PostCE tend to be lower, with several values around .60 and .70, but it does not seem that there are any tendencies towards differences between the treatments in the amount of correlation.

These simple analyses of correlations between latent variables thus indicate that there is a rather high degree of consistency of individual differences at the pre- and post-tests, but that there are some changes as well, and particularly so for CE. These changes can be investigated more closely if all the information available is integrated into a single path model.

In this model, Gf has been taken as the only latent independent variable, which is related to PreQR and PreCE, which in turn are related to PostQR and PostCE, respectively. Within one or more of the treatment groups there may, however, also be a direct relationship between Gf and PostQR or PostCE. The presence of such relationships has been investigated through comparing the fit of models which include and which do not include such direct relationships. At no age level was a significant direct relationship found between Gf and PostQR. However, PostCE was found to be significantly related to Gf within the three highest age levels (12-year-olds: chi-square=14.60, df=3, p<.002; 14-year-olds: chi-square=15.02, df=3, p<.002; 16-year-olds: chi-square=19.93, df=3, p<.000) and for the 10-year-olds there was a borderline significance (chi-square=6.58, df=3, p<.086). Thus, the path model should include a path between Gf and PostCE as well.

The homogeneity of within-treatment regressions of PostQR on PreQR and of PostCE on Gf and PreCE has been investigated through comparing the fit of models in which these are constrained to be equal within treatments, and models in which they are free to vary. The regression proved to be homogeneous for the three highest age groups (12-year-olds: chi-square= 7.43, df=6, p<.28; 14-year-olds: chi-square=6.35, df=6, p<.39; 16-year-olds: chi-square=10.04, df=6, p<.12), but not for the 10-year-olds (chi-square= 14.47, df=6, p<.02). The interaction is rather weak, however, so in a first step it will be disregarded.

The results, in general, indicate that there is a very high relationship between PostQR and PreQR, as shown already by the analysis of correlations. For PostCE, however, it is in the three oldest groups of subjects that PreCE and Gf were found to be equally strong determinants of individual differences in performance. There is no relationship between Gf and PostCE for the 10-year-olds. It thus seems that for all groups, except the 10-year-olds who did not receive any CE training, performance on the CE post-test tasks is determined to a substantial degree by the Gf factor.

Summarizing the evidence from the analyses above, it is clear that, first, the existence of the general factor, Gf, and the specific ones, the quantitative-relational and the causal-experimental SSSs, has been established. Furthermore, Gf is highly related to the QR SSS and moderately to the CE SSS. Differences in the relationship of Gf with the SSSs at different age levels have also been found. This fact indicates that the various SSSs do not make the same demands on processing capacity, and these demands vary with age.

Second, cognitive ability change through training is possible, as hypothesized, but that change was very moderate. Training quantitative-relational abilities had a certain effect in all age groups except for the 14-year-olds. Post-test performance in the QR SSS was found to be a function of the QR pre-test specific factor only. Specific training of the causal-experimental SSS did not have the same positive effect as that of the QR SSS. However, CE abilities did change significantly in the post-test. This change was a function of both Gf and the CE pre-test specific factor. Thus, there seems to be an aptitude–treatment interaction as well as age effects in training.

Obviously these findings pinpoint the complexity of the roads through which cognitive change is effected. In the analyses that follow, the issue regarding transfer and individual differences will be pursued through the prism of cognitive level.

Transfer effects

Transfer effects were first addressed through the path analysis presented above. No transfer from one SSS to the other was found. From a developmental point of view, it might be argued that this lack of transfer is due to the fact that most of the subjects did not function at the same cognitive level in both SSSs, and thus training could not affect the skill level of the non-trained SSS, particularly if the gap between the two skill levels was sufficiently wide. Things might be different if the starting point for both SSSs were the same. In order to test transfer effects in the case of subjects functioning at the same cognitive level at both SSSs, a group of 294 subjects was selected. The subjects came from all age groups, and belonged to the three treatment groups. That is, CT group, QRT group, and CET group. Table 7.4 shows that even in this case there was no transfer from one SSS to the other. Training effects were confined within the limits of the trained SSS. A series of planned contrasts ANOVAs applied to the data showed a significant pre- vs. post-test effect ($F(1,282)=82.251$, $p=.000$), but no significant interactions with treatment groups. Therefore, Hypothesis 4 regarding the lack of transfer from one SSS to another was confirmed.

Table 7.4 Mean pre- and post-test quantitative-relational and causal-experimental SSS level scores of subjects having the same pre-test level score in the two SSSs as a function of treatment group and age

Training group	Age	Pre-test Quant.-rel.	Pre-test Causal-exper.	Post-test Quant.-rel.	Post-test Causal-exper.
CTG	10	0.294	0.294	0.529	0.647
	12	0.564	0.564	0.923	0.872
	14	0.688	0.688	1.438	1.125
	16	1.474	1.474	1.789	2.053
QRTG	10	0.419	0.419	0.968	0.806
	12	0.524	0.524	1.000	0.833
	14	0.909	0.909	1.682	1.045
	16	1.368	1.368	2.421	2.053
CETG	10	0.444	0.444	0.389	0.556
	12	0.606	0.606	0.909	1.182
	14	0.917	0.917	1.208	1.083
	16	1.143	1.143	2.000	2.286

The effectiveness of training

One of the findings of confirmatory factor analysis presented above was the limited success of training in producing cognitive change. This might be due to the limited amount of training provided or the form of the training given. In order to find out the responsiveness of subjects to the training procedure and the degree of change in the case of successful training, subjects were given a score depending on their success on the training. Specifically, the subjects who failed completely to solve the training problem or had only a minor part of the solution algorithm correct were considered to be unsuccessfully trained. Subjects who had most or all of the algorithm steps correct were considered to be successfully trained. As shown in Table 7.5, training succeeded in approximately 50 per cent of the CET group subjects and in approximately 70 per cent of QRT group subjects. The sources of failure might be located in the type of training used or the individual differences factor. In fact, inspection of Table 7.5 makes it clear that age and the initial cognitive level of the subjects are critical factors in determining training results.

Table 7.5 Frequency of subjects per age and cognitive level who succeeded in the training tasks of the causal-experimental and quantitative-relational SSS

		\multicolumn{3}{c}{Causal-experimental}			\multicolumn{3}{c}{Quantitative-relational}		
Age	Cognitive level	Trained	Successful	%	Trained	Successful	%
10	0	35	17	48.57	32	24	75.00
	1	15	8	53.33	18	13	72.22
	2	12	3	25.00	21	1	4.76
	3	2	0	0.00	–	–	–
12	0	36	23	63.88	33	28	84.85
	1	28	9	32.14	21	17	80.95
	2	21	6	28.57	32	14	43.75
	3	9	8	88.89	5	4	80.00
14	0	23	13	56.52	21	14	66.67
	1	20	9	45.00	24	18	75.00
	2	29	15	51.72	25	11	44.00
	3	14	10	71.43	11	10	90.91
16	0	20	18	90.00	9	9	100.00
	1	22	9	40.91	15	11	73.33
	2	14	4	28.57	34	20	58.82
	3	25	19	76.00	21	19	90.48

With regard to age, training was least effective at the age of 10. That was expected because children at this age are on the verge of acquiring the abilities addressed. Therefore they lacked the background and/or potential for carrying out the tasks. Though some children had intuitively solved even the level 2 problems, neither training-task nor post-test performance matched their pre-test level (see also Figure 7.1). This is probably due to the fact that metacognitive awareness of the processes applied for the solution of the problems had not yet developed and the feelings of difficulty they had experienced during the pre-test acted as negative motivation. Obviously this was not the case with 16-year-olds who had the highest rate of training success.

With regard to cognitive level, training was least effective with level 2 subjects. This was unexpected because Fischer's theory does not predict different acquisition rates for the various abstract tier skill levels. This finding could be attributed to the fact that level 2 is relational in character whereas level 3 is systemic. It seems that subjects who have acquired the simple abstraction level of the abstract tier can easily be propelled to the level of mapping. The same happens with subjects who function at the level of systems. These can easily be moved on to the level of system of systems. These results indicate that training of cognitive abilities is possible, with the provision that training takes into account the age and the cognitive level of the subjects. For this reason, it is essential to understand better the ways in which these two factors interact with training.

A set of planned contrasts ANOVAs that tested the effects of age, sex, and SES on post-test performance showed that sex had no effect. SES had a significant effect but it did not interact with treatment group. Age, on the contrary, both had a significant effect and interacted with training.

Cognitive level

In order to test Hypothesis 6, which refers to the interaction of training with cognitive level, subjects in each age and training group were first categorized according to their cognitive level in the QR SSS and then in the CE SSS. Separate analyses were performed in each case. Only subjects functioning at level 0, 1, or 2 were included in the analyses, because level 3 subjects were not represented at the younger age groups.

QR cognitive level

As shown in Figure 7.1, at the age of 10, training the QR SSS helped subjects functioning at level 0. However, the effect was not strong enough to push the subjects, as a group, up to the next level. This was made possible at the age of 12, when training did make a difference. Twelve-year-old subjects of the QRT group, functioning at level 0, skipped a level and progressed to level 1. Non-trained subjects (CT group) or those trained in the CE SSS (CET group) achieved the same progress at the age of 14, i.e. two years later. That explains why at the age of 14 years no significant difference was detected between trained and non-trained subjects in the QR SSS. Furthermore, no significant change was recorded in the case of subjects functioning at levels

1 or 2 in any of the above age groups. Cognitive change in the QR SSS emerged again at the age of 16, when QRT group subjects of level 1 progressed to level 2, whereas their non-trained peers of the same cognitive level remained within the limits of level 1. It should be noted, however, that at this age subjects of level 0 in the CET group surpassed their trained peers. This might be an indication of across-SSS transfer of training.

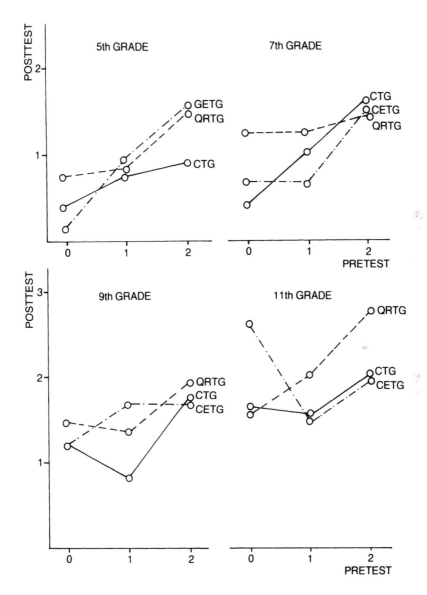

Figure 7.1 Mean post-test level scores of the quantitative-relational SSS as a function of the pre-test level score of the respective SSS, treatment group, and age

138 Inducing cognitive change

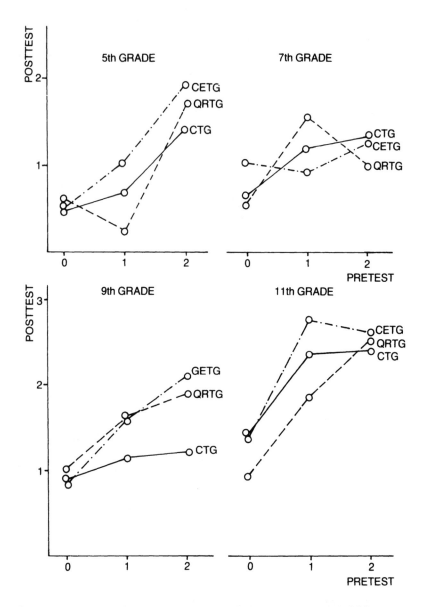

Figure 7.2 Mean post-test level scores of the causal-experimental SSS as a function of the pre-test level score of the respective SSS, treatment group, and age

CE cognitive level

Figure 7.2 shows the dynamics of cognitive change in the case of the CE SSS. At the age of 10, training serves nothing but the stabilization of the initial level of the subjects. Since experimental abilities are not trained in school, it seems that training functioned as feedback about the initial, intuitively reached solution. Training motivated change of level at the age of 12, when subjects of level 0 moved to level 1. Training did nothing to help subjects functioning at levels 1 and 2. In fact, non-trained subjects did better, within their level limits, than their trained peers. By the age of 14, all subjects of level 0, trained and non-trained, came close to level 1. Subjects of level 1 progressed within their level limits, but CT group subjects apparently fell behind their trained peers. So did the level 2 CT group subjects. CET group and QRT group subjects, on the other hand, functioned similarly at this age. At the age of 16, training made a difference for subjects of level 1 but not for subjects of level 0 or 2. That is, level 1 CET group subjects had very substantial gains and moved well above level 2. However, training the QR SSS slowed down increases in the CE abilities. This is exactly the opposite effect from that observed with CE SSS training. Training the CE abilities generalized to quantitative-relational abilities of level 0, whereas training the QR abilities did not.

The results presented are in line with Hypothesis 5. They suggest, first, that specialized training enhances the acquisition of SSS-specific abilities at certain age periods, such as 12 and 16 years of age, and for subjects of a particular cognitive level each time. This is not the case with 14-year-olds. At this age, there seems to be a general increase in processing capacity and change of level of functioning regardless of training. The opposite effect can be distinguished at the age of 10, when no cognitive change occurs because children lack the potential for processing skills of the abstract tier. Second, the two SSSs are differentially amenable to training effects, although the general finding is that training starts to have effects for both SSSs after the age of 12. However, for the CE SSS, the effects were evident only at the age of 16. At that age, there is a spurt in their development that brings CE abilities to the level of development of the QR abilities. It seems that QR abilities require long-term systematic training (such as that offered in schools) in order to progress along the developmental sequence. Conversely, CE abilities develop in spurt-like forms and the best age at which they can be trained is that of 16 years.

GENERAL DISCUSSION

As stated in the introduction, this study aimed to investigate, first, the possibility of cognitive change through training and the role of broad and narrow factors in it, and, in relation to this, the problem of the continuity of the process of change during development; second, the generalization of transfer of training, and, third, individual differences in training effects.

In brief, our results on training effects were as follows: Cognitive change is possible. There was no transfer from one SSS to the other. Age, cognitive level, and specialized and general abilities are significant determinants of training effects. With these facts as starting point, it is interesting to discuss the conditions under which cognitive change through training can occur.

Cognitive change may be approached, first, from the point of view of general and specific factors: that is, the way in which general and specialized abilities interact with training.

The analysis of within-treatment correlations indicated a weak tendency for the correlations between PreQR and PostQR to be lower in the QRT groups, but, according to the statistical tests, there was no significant heterogeneity of within-treatment regression of PostQR on PreQR. Nor was Gf found to have any direct effect on PostQR, with PreQR held constant. One reason for the lack of relationship with Gf is, of course, the very high degree of overlap between Gf and PreQR. There were, in fact, clear signs of multicollinearity in the model when Gf was allowed a direct relationship with PostQR, which provides another indication that Gf and QR are essentially the same variables.

The pattern of results was quite different for the CE than for the QR SSS: the relationship between PreCE and Gf was lower, and, in almost all groups, Gf was found to have almost as strong an effect on PostCE as PreCE had. For the 10-year-olds, however, a relationship with Gf was found only for the group of subjects that received CE training. These results might be given the following interpretation: among the older groups of subjects, those with a higher level of fluid ability profited to a greater extent from the experiences gained in taking the pre-test, as well as from the training itself, in comparison to subjects with a lower level of fluid ability. At the lowest age level, however, not even the high-Gf subjects were able to profit from the pre-test or from the CE training, but they did so from the QR training.

The fact, however, that 10-year-olds did not profit from training on CE abilities but did from QR training could indicate that the Gf factor might not be the best explanation for this finding. A closer examination of the cognitive level effects indicates that in order to have not just improvement of post-test performance but also change of level of functioning, there must be adequate processing capacity for the support of the abilities induced by training. It is important that even in the case of QR abilities, where there were training effects for the 10-year-olds, no level change was detected. This was expected, because the abilities addressed by training are normally acquired after 12 years of age according to both our theory and that of Fischer (Fischer and Pipp 1984). On the contrary, 12-year-olds, who presumably had the potential but did not possess the abilities trained, benefited from training and changed cognitive level from 0 to 1. It is of interest, though, that subjects of this age already functioning at higher levels of thinking did not move up in the developmental sequence. This is probably due to the fact that their potential could not match the demands of those levels of processing. At the age of 14, training did not have any particular effect, and all subjects changed from level 0 to level 1. Finally, at 16 years of age, training led to acquisition of level 1 and 2 abilities, but not higher. These results indicate that higher levels of thinking cannot be induced if there is lack of potential. Of course, the concept of potential needs to be redefined in terms of basic features of cognitive processing rather than fluid intelligence.

These findings suggest two general conclusions. On the one hand, general intelligence is correlated with positive transfer in such a way that high-ability subjects profit more from practice on an intellectual task and show greater improvement on a related task than do low-ability subjects. This interpretation is in line with the theory of transfer proposed by Ferguson (1954, 1956). On the other hand, having a certain general potential does not guarantee manifestation of the specialized abilities that characterize each SSS. Experience with a particular knowledge domain and, particularly, specialized training do that. More precisely, specialized training enables the individual to actualize his potential into SSS-specific abilities.

It is also of interest that spurt-like changes, that is, abrupt changes of level of functioning, occurred at 12 and 16 years of age for levels 0 and 1 respectively in the trained groups and for the trained abilities, and at 14 years of age for non-trained groups of level 0 abilities. This indicates that cognitive change is a discontinuous process. Specialized training makes use of the change of potential at its early emergence by transforming it into functional skill structures. This is its contribution to cognitive development. Thus, training gives a lead of two years, which remains essentially constant in the course of development, because non-specifically trained individuals catch up with their peers in two years time. The very fact that at 14 years no level change occurred that was higher for trained groups than for non-trained groups and that only moderate improvement of pre-test performance was obtained suggests that training effects may be purely cumulative at the interim of phases of major reorganizations. Therefore, growth of knowledge alone does not seem to suffice for attainment of higher modes of thinking. Structural reorganizations make the system receptive to *new* ways of looking at and processing the world.

Coming now to the transfer of training issue, our results from both path analysis and analysis of the groups with matched pre-test level score on both SSSs show that there is no generalization from QR SSS to CE SSS. However, in the general population, as represented by the whole sample, in which the development of abilities is uneven, training seems to have generalization effects. As shown in Figure 7.1, training either of the SSSs gave better results for both SSSs than no training at all, as represented by the control group subjects. This might indicate that training creates a learning set that facilitates performance even in non-trained skills.

The spontaneous change of cognitive level at the age of 14 should not be considered a true generalization of training either. It indicates an 'optimal level synchrony, where new capacities emerge across domains as a new developmental level emerges' (Fischer and Farrar 1988: 137). Therefore our results show that there is both specificity of transfer and generalization effects in cognitive development, but they cannot be reduced to the same mechanisms.

Finally, as far as individual differences are concerned, it seems that the major factors differentiating our results were age and cognitive level. As hypothesized, there is age momentum that propels cognitive change at certain age periods, namely 12 and 16. If SSS-specific experiences are provided at those periods, change of cognitive level is enhanced. However, change of level was a function of the previous level of the subject. Levels 0, 1, and 3 were easier to change than level 2. This is probably due to the fact that a transition from the relational to the systemic mode of thinking is required and this transition usually occurs, according to Fischer (Fischer 1980), at the age of 18. If for some reason an individual entered the systemic level at a younger age, as had happened with a number of our 16-year-old subjects, then progress to the level of system of systems was made possible.

It is clear that the results of this study have been shaped by both the structure of the abilities studied and their SSS affiliation. These two concepts, in conjunction with age-related hardware changes, are essential for understanding both cognitive developmental phenomena and individual differences. Of course, more research is needed if the exact interactions among the various SSSs during training are to be fully understood.

ACKNOWLEDGEMENT

The research reported in this chapter was supported financially by the Swedish Council for Research in the Social Sciences and Humanities.

REFERENCES

Case, R. (1985) *Intellectual Development: Birth to Adulthood*, New York: Academic Press.
Cormier, S. M. and Hagman, J. D. (1987) *Transfer of Learning: Contemporary Research and Applications*, San Diego: Academic.
De Corte, E. (1987) 'Acquisition and transfer of knowledge and cognitive skills', *International Journal of Educational Research* 11 (whole issue).
Demetriou, A. and Efklides, A. (1979) 'Formal operational thinking in young adults as a function of education and sex', *International Journal of Psychology* 14: 241–53.
—— (1986) 'Dynamic patterns of intra- and inter-individual change in the acquisition of complex thinking abilities from 10 to 17 years of age: a longitudinal study', paper presented at the AERA Annual Meeting, San Francisco, California, April.
—— (1987) 'Towards a determination of the dimensions and domains of individual differences in cognitive development', in E. de Corte, H. Lodewijks, R. Parmentier, and P. Span (eds) *Learning and Instruction*, Oxford: Pergamon, pp. 41–52.

—— (1988) 'Experiential structuralism and neo-Piagetian theories: toward an integrated model', in A. Demetriou (ed.) *The Neo-Piagetian Theories of Cognitive Development: Toward an Integration*, Amsterdam: North-Holland, pp. 173–222.

Demetriou, A., Efklides, A., and Platsidou, M. (1991) *Experiential Structuralism: A Frame for Unifying Cognitive Developmental Theories*, monograph submitted for publication.

Ekstrom, R. B., French, J. W., and Harman, H. H. (1976) *Manual for Kit of Factor-Referenced Cognitive Tests*, Princeton, NJ: Educational Testing Service.

Ferguson, G. A. (1954) 'On learning and human ability', *Canadian Journal of Psychology* 8: 95–112.

—— (1956) 'On transfer and the abilities of man', *Canadian Journal of Psychology* 10: 121–31.

Fischer, K. W. (1980) 'A theory of cognitive development: the control and construction of hierarchies of skills', *Psychological Review* 87: 477–531.

Fischer, K. W. and Farrar, M. J. (1988) 'Generalizations about generalization: how a theory of skill development explains both generality and specificity', in A. Demetriou (ed.) *The Neo-Piagetian Theories of Cognitive Development: Toward an Integration*, Amsterdam: North-Holland, pp. 137–71.

Fischer, K. W. and Pipp, S. L. (1984) 'Development of the structures of unconscious thought', in K. S. Bowers and D. Meichenbaum (eds) *The Unconscious Reconsidered*, New York: Wiley, pp. 88–148.

Fleishman, E. A. (1987) 'Foreword', in S. M. Cormier and J. D. Hagman (eds) *Transfer of Learning: Contemporary Research and Applications*, San Diego: Academic, pp. xi–xvii.

Gray, W. D. and Orasanu, J. M. (1987) 'Transfer of cognitive skills', in S. M. Cormier and J. D. Hagman (eds) *Transfer of Learning: Contemporary Research and Applications*, San Diego: Academic, pp. 183–215.

Gustafsson, J.-E. (1984) 'A unifying model for the structure of intellectual abilities', *Intelligence* 8: 179–203.

—— (1988) 'Hierarchical models of individual differences in cognitive abilities', in R. S. Sternberg (ed.) *Advances in the Psychology of Human Intelligence*, Vol. 4, Hillsdale, NJ: Erlbaum, pp. 35–71.

Gustafsson, J.-E., Lindstrom, B., and Bjorck-Akesson, E. (1981) 'A general model for the organization of cognitive abilities', report from the Department of Education, University of Göteborg.

Halford, G. S. (1988) 'A structure-mapping approach to cognitive development', in A. Demetriou (ed.) *The Neo-Piagetian Theories of Cognitive Development: Toward an Integration*, Amsterdam: North-Holland, pp. 103–36.

Jöreskog, K. G. and Sörbom, D. (1986) *LISREL VI: Analysis of Linear Structural Relationships by Maximum Likelihood and Least Square Methods*, Mooresville, IN: Scientific Software.

Pascual-Leone, J. (1988) 'Organismic processes for neo-Piagetian theories: a dialectical causal account of cognitive development', in A. Demetriou (ed.) *The Neo-Piagetian Theories of Cognitive Development: Toward an Integration*, Amsterdam: North-Holland, pp. 25–64.

Shayer, M. (1988) 'Neo-Piagetian theories and educational practice', in A. Demetriou (ed.) *The Neo-Piagetian Theories of Cognitive Development: Toward an Integration*, Amsterdam: North-Holland, pp. 245–66.

Chapter 8

Improving operational abilities in children
Results of a large-scale experiment
Benö Csapó

One of the main aims of the present project is to find methods of designing teaching material that stimulates the development of thinking abilities more effectively. In the closing phase of this work, an experiment was carried out in two age groups in regular Hungarian schools to examine the effectiveness of the modified teaching material devised previously. The main principles of this work were that only the contents of the regular teaching material could be used to form structured tasks and exercises and that all the developmental effects should be integrated into the teaching material itself. The developmental activities should not be applied outside the regular framework of the curriculum and extra time should be devoted to the developmental work.

In traditional education, chiefly mathematics and some formal grammar exercises were regarded as the best ways to form the thinking. The early Piagetian framework supported these tendencies by postulating general stages and structures and universal developmental patterns. The most remarkable shift in thinking about cognitive development is the growing importance of specific structures, content domains, and contexts. Two of the recent theories are especially close to our view: Fischer's skill theory (Fischer 1980; Bidell and Fischer, Chapter 1 of this volume) and experiential structuralism (Demetriou and Efklides 1988; Demetriou, Gustafsson, Efklides, and Platsidou, Chapter 5 of this volume). While we cannot expect that the structures acquired in a certain content domain are generalized to every other content, we aim to point out the most general operational structures that are relevant to the most important content domains of school learning. On the other hand, we presume that any school subject can provide several developmental effects if its content is reorganized and enriched with special structured tasks. As a consequence of this view, we have devised different training materials for specific parts of operational thinking and organized separate training groups to test these materials.

Many studies have dealt with the development of operational thinking in the framework of the Piagetian tradition, and many examine the structures that are at the centre of our experiment.

Studies that involve training in the binary operations of propositional logic or combinatorial reasoning, or operational thinking in the context of school subjects, are closer to the scope of this chapter. Fishbein, Pampu, and Minzat (1970) showed that even 10-year-old students were able to produce the appropriate permutations and arrangements after they had been taught to use tree diagrams. Siegler, Liebert, and Liebert (1973) trained 10-year-olds to solve the Piagetian pendulum problem. Case (1974) proved that 8-year-olds can be taught to use the control of variables strategy. Collis (1980) describes the role of mathematics teaching in the development of operational thinking, while Jurd (1978) analyses history-type material from the same aspects. These studies lead to the question of the utilization of the teaching material to improve students' operational thinking.

Our experiment shows many similarities with the CASE project (Cognitive Acceleration through Science Education: Shayer 1987; Shayer and Adey 1988). We consider the most important characteristics of the CASE project to be (1) it uses a much longer intervention period than is common, (2) the experiments take place in regular school classes, and (3) they are based on school-related tasks. Over a period of two years, up to thirty intervention lessons were presented to students aged 11 and 12 at the beginning of the intervention. The results of these studies indicated that boys gained more than girls from the interventions, and the method worked better in classes where the lessons were given by experienced researchers.

In the present experiment the original Piagetian system of formal operations was re-formulated and three groups of operations were identified: the group of *logical operations* contains the binary operations of propositional logic; the system of *combinative operations* is enhanced by taking into account further combinatorial structures not studied by the Geneva school; and the group of *systematizing operations* contains the operations of ordering (binary relations), class inclusion, classification, and multiple classification. On the basis of these systems, paper and pencil test-batteries were devised and comprehensive assessments were carried out into the structure and development of these operational abilities. The results of this phase of the research have been communicated at several conferences (Csapó 1985) and have been published in three volumes in Hungarian (Nagy 1988; Csapó 1988; Csirikné 1989).

On the basis of this earlier work the teaching material of some school subjects was analysed and methods were devised for the improvement of the children's operational abilities. The present one-year experiment was designed to study the changes caused in the student's cognition by these methods. Of course, it is to be stressed that experiments carried out in the regular school context face many problems which are not important for laboratory experiments. These problems may lead to negative findings and it is important to be aware of them. Specifically, excluding the trivial cases of experimental errors, some of the main possible causes of negative findings may be classified as follows:

1 The particular operational scheme was not modifiable at all.
2 The operational scheme has been modified, but the change could not be detected either (a) because the instrument was not sensitive enough to capture this kind of change or (b) because the effect was delayed, and could be detected only a long time after the intervention.
3 The operational scheme was not modified because the treatment applied was ineffective, ill-conceived, or misapplied.

Taking into account the methodological problems mentioned above, our strategy in this work was to organize the experiment in an ecologically valid environment in as standard a way as the practical limits allow, but at the same time to control these limits and problems in as many ways as possible. We have to adapt the design to these limits, and we must not forget them during the interpretation of the results either.

METHOD

Design

In order to reduce the ambiguity in the interpretation of the findings, we applied a complex experimental design where ages and interventions were systematically varied though the same overall concept of treatment was used. The three basic dimensions of the experimental design were the operational abilities to be improved, the age of the students, and the developmental influences (modified teaching material) on the students. We chose grammar and science in the fourth grade (10-year-olds) and chemistry and physics in the seventh grade (13-year-olds) for the purposes of experimental instruction (Table 8.1). For every combination of the four groups of subjects and the three abilities, a particular developmental task-system was devised. This gives twelve different ways of experimental instruction. In some experimental groups, the interventions were applied in both school subjects (science and grammar or chemistry and physics). This enables one to study the interaction between the different kinds of interventions. At both ages, a control group was also involved. There were three classes in the experimental groups and six classes in the control groups.

Subjects

Urban, suburban, and rural areas were represented in the twenty-eight schools taking part in the experiment. The experimental classes within these schools were selected in co-operation with the school principals and class teachers. Specifically, the principals were asked to suggest 'average' classes

Table 8.1 The system of the experimental groups

School subjects involving experimental instruction		Abilities		
		Combinative	Logical	Systematizing
4th grade	Grammar	XXX	XXX	XXX
	Science	XXX	XXX	XXX
	Grammar and science	XXX	XXX	XXX
4th grade control		XXXXXX		
7th grade	Chemistry	XXX	XXX	XXX
	Physics	XXX	XXX	XXX
	Chemistry and physics	XXX	XXX	XXX
7th grade control		XXXXXX		

X = 1 class

for both the experimental and the control groups. We opted to exclude classes regarded as 'excellent' or 'very poor', because, according to our pilot work, the effect of intervention may be influenced significantly by the starting level of the students. The control classes were selected from the same schools, preferably seventh-grade controls from the schools where the experiment took place in the fourth grade, and vice versa. As the results showed later, despite our intentions, in some of the schools principals and teachers preferred to offer the 'better' classes for the experimental instruction.

At the time of the first measurement (September 1987), the mean age for all the fourth graders (experimental + control, n=930) was 9.68 years (SD=.49). The mean age of the seventh graders (n=890) was 12.59 years (SD=.44).

No classes dropped out during the experimental year: all fifty-four intervention classes were considered, as they completed the experimental instruction. Although examination of the documentation made by the teachers in some cases led to the suspicion that they had not done exactly what they had been expected to do, these classes were not dropped either. In three experimental classes the teachers changed during the course of the year and the new teachers had to go on with the intervention procedure. This may have disturbed the experimental work, too. These effects were also considered as an integral part of the usability of the experimental methods.

A data sheet and nine tests were administered before the beginning of the interventions and five tests after the interventions. In some cases, several unexpected events made it impossible to organize a proper testing session. These cases are handled as missing data. Specifically, out of a total of 990 testings (66 classes x 10 pre- and 5 post-testings), nineteen were lost.

Measurement instruments

A variety of evidence was collected before and after the interventions. Only the characteristics of the tests used to measure the developmental levels of the abilities dealt with will be presented here. The system of variables can be summarized as follows:

1 Dependent (experimental) variables
    1.1 Logical Operations Test
    1.2 Combinative Operations Test
    1.3 Systematizing Operations Test
2 Mental background
    2.1 Cognitive domain
        2.1.1 Intelligence: Raven's Matrices
        2.1.2 School achievements: school marks in the main school subjects
    2.2 Affective domain
        2.2.1 Motivation (Kozéki and Entwistle 1984)
        2.2.2 Self-concept: effectiveness and talent (Jerusalem 1984)
        2.2.3 Test anxiety ('TAI H/C', Sipos, Sipos, and Spielberger 1985)
3 Social background/environment
    3.1 Family
        3.1.1 Social economic status
        3.1.2 Family structure
    3.2 Characteristics of living area

For the measurement of developmental levels of operational abilities, special test batteries were devised based on our earlier research. In this way, the present findings can be compared with those obtained before.

The Systematizing Operations Test was developed and validated by Nagy (1988). A short version of this test was used in the present research. It consists of nineteen dichotomously scored tasks (e.g., seriations, class inclusions, classifications, and multiple and hierarchical classifications). Achievement of a score in this test requires three to twelve consistent decisions, depending on the type of task.

The Combinative Operations Test (Csapó 1988) involves twelve tasks based on combinatorial structures (variations with repetitions, variations without repetitions, variations with different numbers of elements, combinations, all subsets of a set, Cartesian product of two sets). Performance on the tasks is quantified using a formula that takes into account both the number of the properly constructed combinations (variations, etc.) and the number of errors. Attainment of the score requires two to five consistent decisions; the maximum test score is 170.

In the Logical Operations Test the underlying structures were provided by ten binary operations of propositional logic, where the truth-value of the complex proposition is a function of both propositions. By using these operations, two equivalent tests were devised. Both tests begin with a short story that introduces a situation (e.g., children sitting around a table and waiting for breakfast), and the ten tasks then examine the subject's decisions about the truth-value of the complex propositions (which are statements in the given situation) containing a particular logical operation. Attaining a score requires four consistent decisions. Though the two versions are considered to be equivalent, to increase the reliability of the measurement both versions were administered to every child at both measurement points in two different testing sessions. In this way they can be used as mutual controls, and, where one of them was missing, its result was replaced by the other one. Their means were very close to each other: e.g., 35.28 for version A (n=923) and 34.19 for version B (n=919) for the pre-measurement of the fourth graders. During the course of data analysis, the twenty tasks in the two parallel tests are treated as tasks in a single test and their scores are summed (see Csapó 1987; Vidákovich and Csapó 1988).

The Raven's Matrices test was also administered at both measurement points. All other tests and the data sheet were administered at the beginning of the school year before the beginning of the interventions. The test data presented in this paper are always percentages of the maximum test score.

Training materials

For each combination of the operational abilities to be developed, a collection of structured tasks was devised in co-operation with practising teachers. Specifically, this team-work resulted in collections of exercises that were edited and mimeographed in booklet form. Each of the twelve (grammar-combinative, grammar-logical . . . physics-systematizing) collections contained about fifty-three of these structured tasks. The fourth grade tasks for the systematizing ability were exceptions. These tasks were devised by using the analogy and experience of the other work and were not tried out and refined before their use in the main experiment. A detailed description of the tasks and some examples can be found in Csapó (1987).

Interventions

The phenomena of 'the zone of proximal development' may exist in any educational system: there are some possibilities for improvement, but there are also some barriers that cannot be stepped over. In designing an experiment to try out methods that might improve the existing practice, we have to take these barriers into consideration. We have to consider not only what can be changed in the course of the experiment, but what can be changed in teaching practice as well.

In this experiment, the limited vocabulary of a possible metalanguage and the teachers' modest knowledge of psychology reduce the range of application of the metacognitive effects. However, the fact that during their study academic training outweighs the psychological and educational preparation offers only one, albeit stable way, to communicate everything the teachers are expected to do in the terms and categories of the specific subject they teach. The teachers of the intervention classes had not received any special training. After being provided with the intervention material, they were given a brief explanation of the aims of the research and the activity they were expected to do.

During the interventions, the use of mathematical concepts or terms was avoided. This method does not wish to assume part of the role of mathematics teaching or to be disguised maths training. No direct rules were taught (in contrast with many intervention studies, where a specific performance or skill was probably learnt, e.g. in the study by Fishbein *et al.* 1970). The training was exclusively limited to combining, classifying, etc., the concepts of teaching material in a meaningful way in the particular context or discussing why the complex propositions of the texts are true or false.

The structured tasks could be applied in several ways: in individual, in group, or in whole-class work. During the pilot studies teachers retained the right to choose their methods of working, the only requirement being that each child in the experimental classes should deal with the given fifty exercises during the school year. Decisions concerning the form and materials of the interventions of the main study were made in co-operation with teachers on the basis of reports of the pilot studies. While teaching stereotypes limited the possibilities of using the structured tasks, usually one experimental lesson per week and two tasks per lesson (one at the beginning of the lesson as whole-class work and one at the end of the lesson as individual work) should be considered as a rule. As extra time could not be devoted to the interventions, the structured experimental tasks were alternative versions rather than additions to school subjects. The school year begins on 1 September, and this month was chosen for the pre-measurements. Thus, the interventions lasted practically eight months (October to May), and the post-tests were administered within the last two weeks.

Teachers submitted written reports after each experimental lesson. These documents were gathered and could also be analysed. They are important sources for the reshaping of the task-systems and the design of further applications.

RESULTS AND DISCUSSION

Before presenting the results of training, it is worth summarizing the students' characteristics concerning operational thinking as measured in the ability tests at the beginning of the experiment. Table 8.2 presents the means and standard deviations for the two ages, involving all experimental and control groups. The ratios of the achievements in the fourth and seventh grades are also given to compare the pace of development within this age range.

Table 8.2 Results of ability tests at the beginning of the experiment (% of the maximum test score)

	Combinative Mean	SD	Logical Mean	SD	Systematizing Mean	SD	Raven Mean	SD
4th grade (n>900)	51.6	21.2	39.4	14.7	33.5	16.9	62.5	17.0
7th grade (n>950)	63.6	19.7	45.1	14.3	47.6	18.0	75.2	11.6
7th/4th grade ratio	1.23		1.14		1.42		1.21	

The systematizing ability shows the greatest change between the ages of 10 and 13, and the development of logical ability is very slow. As the starting mean score for Raven's Matrices is over 75 per cent for the seventh graders, the ceiling effect may influence the test results and part of the change cannot be detected at this age. The effects of interventions can be evaluated by comparison of the groups.

While the change during the intervention period is a function of the starting level, for a reliable comparison particular attention must be paid to the equal initial levels of the samples compared. For example, in the fourth-grade control a correlation of $r=-0.35$ was found between the starting value and the change score. While children with a lower developmental level benefit more from the treatment, this relationship is even stronger in the experimental groups. As mentioned before, the required similarity of the groups could not be reached by selecting the classes. Thus the groups to be compared were matched in the course of the data analysis. The computer program compared the frequency distributions of the two groups and chose equal numbers of subjects from each achievement interval for inclusion in the matched groups. The data presented here are results of comparisons based on 10 per cent intervals. In this way, the difference between the pre-test means is always less than 1 per cent, and also the shapes of the frequency distributions of the compared groups were very similar.

The effects of training on the abilities in question

During the data procedure, a change score was defined as the difference between the results of post- and pre-tests. A series of t-tests was carried out in order to test the significance of the difference between the means of change scores. First, we summarize the overall results of the experimental groups in a way that allows us to compare the effects of the various trainings with each other and with results published elsewhere. The effect size that is often used in meta-analysis literature is the most appropriate for this purpose (see Chapters 6 and 9).

Table 8.3 The effects of training on the operational abilities: the size and significance of the effects

		Combinative	Logical	Systematizing
Teaching material		*Targeted structures in the training*		
4th grade	Grammar	$\sigma=0.91$ $p<0.001$	$\sigma=0.40$ $p<0.05$	$\sigma=-0.48$ $p<0.01$
	Science	$\sigma=0.80$ $p<0.001$	$\sigma=0.64$ $p<0.001$	$\sigma=-0.29$ n.s.
	Grammar and science	$\sigma=0.39$ $p<0.05$	$\sigma=0.48$ $p<0.01$	$\sigma=0.08$ n.s.
7th grade	Chemistry	$\sigma=0.40$ $p<0.01$	$\sigma=0.00$ n.s.	$\sigma=-0.16$ n.s.
	Physics	$\sigma=0.32$ $p<0.05$	$\sigma=-0.05$ n.s.	$\sigma=0.09$ n.s.
	Chemistry and physics	$\sigma=0.09$ n.s.	$\sigma=-0.01$ n.s.	$\sigma=-0.10$ n.s.

Table 8.3 presents the size and significance of the effect of training on the students' targeted operational abilities. These data can be compared with the near-near effect sizes reported by Goossens (Chapter 9, this volume). In the fifty-nine training studies he examined, Goossens found an average effect size equal to .74. The effect size for the nineteen long-term interventions was equal to .51.

Although there are large differences in the sizes of the various effects, our results are systematic in the sense that they demonstrate significant effects in almost every combinative experimental group, and only at the fourth grade in the logic experimental groups. No significant positive effect was found in the systematizing training groups. These results suggest that the three operational abilities are not equally sensitive to training. It is also evident that there is an interaction between age and abilities.

In order to have a look into the background of these characteristics, we have to place our data in other contexts. Shayer (Chapter 6, this volume) suggests that we should compare the changes caused by the intervention with a baseline of normative data which describes the development of the child population. Although we do not have as sophisticated a body of data to draw a baseline as in the medical studies cited by Shayer, we do have measurements for two ages with relatively large samples (Table 8.2). These measurements allow us to draw a draft estimation of development in the range examined here. Figure 8.1 presents the results of training in this context (only for groups with one kind of training).

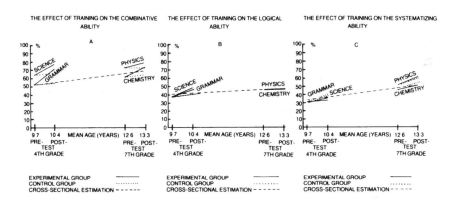

Figure 8.1 The effect of training on the combinative ability, the logical ability, and the systematizing ability

The developmental lines of *combinative* experimental groups and matched control groups are displayed in Figure 8.1a together with the baseline estimated from the cross-sectional measurements. The developmental lines of the matched control groups are almost parallel with the baseline. The development is faster and the effects are larger in those groups where the developmental level was lower at the beginning of the experiment. The differences in change are significant in all three fourth-grade groups. In both experimental groups, the size of the effect is greater when the training took place only in one school subject (Table 8.3). In the seventh grade, the only group not to show a significant gain was the one in which the children were trained in two subjects. When the gains of the experimental groups at the two ages are compared, the results consistently show that the training applied in combinative reasoning is more effective at the younger age.

At both ages it was found that training with fifty exercises during eight months has a greater (measured) effect than the use of a hundred tasks. While it is not probable that an ability that is improved by a certain kind of training will be destroyed by further training of the same kind, we presume that too many exercises in the same type of activity becomes boring, attention is reduced, and this negative attitude influences the results of the testing too. An exercise with combinative structures required about twice the time needed for an exercise concerning propositions. Thus, the smaller measured gain here is understandable.

Figure 8.1b shows the results of the propositional training on the 10- and 13-year-old children's *logical* ability. In every fourth-grade experimental group significant gains were found, and almost zero effect sizes at seventh grade. As the figure indicates, at seventh grade the development of all groups falls into the same line, which is identical with the baseline. It is not possible to re-open here the discussion about the appropriateness of the framework of propositional logic in investigations of cognitive development. Some leading theorists argue against it (e.g., Johnson-Laird 1983), while many others use it (e.g., Seggie 1978). Our view is close to the conclusion drawn by Lawson after his review of a large amount of research into the development of formal reasoning: 'Propositional logic is not isomorphic with advanced reasoning, thus without modification it serves as an unsatisfactory model of the thought processes of the advanced formal thinker' (Lawson 1985: 609).

The results of the experimental groups related to *systematizing* ability are displayed in Figure 8.1c. No significant gains for the experimental groups were found in these cases (except for a negative one, which is probably due to testing errors). The developmental lines of the matched control groups run parallel with each other and, unlike the other abilities, indicate greater changes in these groups than would be expected with regard to the cross-sectional estimation. This may indicate that the testing procedure itself improves to some degree the children's performance. The operations classified in this group appear in the pre-formal stages in the Piagetian model. However, earlier measurements (Nagy 1988) indicate that a considerable proportion of children did not master these structures by the age of 14. Therefore, it seemed promising to try to accelerate their development.

As mentioned before, the systematizing operations develop quickly in the age range examined. The changes displayed in Figure 8.1c suggest that large changes can be found in all groups from pre- to post-tests. When the development of the three operational abilities in the control groups is taken into account, the changes in the systematizing ability are much greater than those observed in the other two abilities. Two different factors may contribute to these findings. On the one hand, systematizing operations are very sensitive to training. On the other hand, the standard way of teaching covers a wide range of activities that stimulate the development of the systematizing operations.

When interpreting the results of the interventions, we have to take into consideration the argumentation of Shayer and Beasley (1987). In their study on instrumental enrichment, they concluded that the results of the interventions should be evaluated rather on the fresh learning embarked on after the intervention had ended. We share this view, but it must be mentioned that the delayed effect is greater if the training is aimed at affecting the learning potential. In the present experiment, long-term effects are also considered to be more important than the effects measured at the end of the interventions. Therefore, further investigations are planned. The aim is to study how the learning potential can be influenced and what the effects of the training are over a longer period of time. The range of effects can in part be estimated by studying their transfer on to other variables.

The effects of training on other abilities

As we administered the same set of tests to all groups, it is possible to study how the training affected the other operational abilities. These effect sizes can be compared with the 0.38 mean near-far effect size reported by Goossens (Chapter 9) for long-term interventions.

The greatest transfers were found in the logic experimental group. In the fourth-grade grammar ($\sigma=0.57$, $p<0.01$) and grammar+science ($\sigma=0.39$, $p<0.05$) groups, and in all the three seventh-grade groups (chemistry: $\sigma=0.58$, $p<0.01$; physics: $\sigma=0.70$, $p<0.001$; chemistry+physics: $\sigma=0.59$, $p<0.001$), significant gains were found in the combinative tests. The systematizing ability was significantly affected by the propositional training in only one group (seventh-grade chemistry+physics: $\sigma=0.32$, $p<0.05$). The combinative training significantly affected the systematizing ability only in the fourth-grade grammar intervention group ($\sigma=0.45$, $p<0.01$).

The training devised to accelerate the development of systematizing operations significantly affected the development of combinative operations in the seventh-grade physics group ($\sigma=0.36$, $p<0.05$). There was also one seventh-grade group (chemistry+physics: $\sigma=0.33$, $p<0.05$) where logical ability was significantly influenced by the training in systematizing abilities.

These findings do not offer a consistent view of the transfer effects. However, the transfers found clarify the picture: they show that some training procedures affected other operational structures more significantly than the targeted ones. As a significant effect was found in two of the six groups trained with systematizing material, we can drop the hypothesis that these materials are devoid of any effect. It was also shown that the seventh-grade logic training material did improve the thinking, even if its effect was not detected in the logic test; this effect was indicated by the combinative tests in all three groups.

The effects of training on intelligence

Significantly greater changes in the intelligence test were found in some of the fourth-grade intervention groups than in the control groups. Two-thirds of the combinative and logical training groups showed meaningful gains (the mean $\sigma=0.27$ for these six groups), while none of the systematizing training material influenced significantly the achievements in the intelligence test.

In the seventh-grade experimental groups, no significant gains were found compared to the controls in the Raven test. At the age of 13, the starting achievements in Raven's Matrices were over 75 per cent, so at this age the test is not sensitive enough to detect the changes in fluid intelligence. Thus, on the basis of these results it cannot be determined whether intelligence was affected by the training at the age of 13.

Improving intelligence significantly cannot be a realistic aim for an intervention within eight months. However, the changes detected in the fourth grade suggest that the enrichment of the learning material with combinative and logical structures around the age of 10, and the use of this material over a period of years, might accelerate the development of intelligence.

GENERAL DISCUSSION

From a comparison of the three groups of operations, it was found that the systematizing ability shows the fastest development in the age range studied. The development of this ability was not accelerated by the means applied in the experiment. The structured task systems devised to improve these abilities had weak effects on the other abilities. Of course, it might be argued that the testing method of treatment applied was not the proper one, or that an effect could be detected only after a considerable period of time. However, we prefer to adopt the view that this group of operations receives the strongest developmental influences from the standard teaching context. Therefore, there is no room for their acceleration by the methods tested by the present study.

Logical operations develop slowly, and they can be improved at a young age. The intervention applied has a significant effect on the other abilities at the older age, too. Thus, the intervention did improve thinking, but this change was not detected by the measurement applied. This fact supports the view that the improvement in advanced formal thinking cannot be characterized in terms of formal logic.

On their own, combinative operations develop at an intermediate pace. Because of the application of our structured exercises, a significant acceleration can be achieved at both ages. The standard teaching material does not contain enough stimulation for their development, and while children do not reach the end-stage by the age of 13, an enrichment of the teaching material with these structures seems to be worthwhile.

While the effects of the comparable interventions were very different on the examined three abilities, the training study indicates that the differences between these abilities are more than their similarities. The lower near-far transfers also support the view of domain-specific operational structures rather than the concept of universal thinking structures.

In most of the fourth-grade experimental groups (fluid) intelligence measured on Raven's Matrices was significantly improved by the interventions in combinative and logical operations. Although a direct improvement in intelligence cannot be the aim of the exercises in some specific structures, better operational thinking facilitates subsequent learning. Thus, rather a long-term effect on intelligence can be expected.

From the point of view of the training material, an enrichment with combinative and logical structures seems to be effective. The systematizing structures have much weaker effects, though in some cases they are detectable. This poor influence is not only a question of quantity (twice the number of interventions did not have a greater effect); it must have structural causes.

Although the present mathematics curriculum includes the rudiments of set theory, mathematical logics, and combinatorics, and such exercise can be found in mathematics work-books, experiences with these structures in a wide range of the context areas does facilitate the development of operational thinking. The new mathematics teaching is faced with the problem of finding real contents from everyday life that children are familiar with to exercise its specific structures. On the other hand, other school subjects, primarily in the first grades, search for ways to exercise their specific concepts, propositions, facts, and relationships. Enriching the teaching material with structured tasks might be one step towards bridging the gap between abstract mathematical structures and everyday activity with concrete contents in other school subjects. In this way, a better share of the work could be reached between mathematics and other subjects in the development of operational thinking.

The acceleration attainable within a school year is limited. After an acceptable number of the exercises, they no longer result in further development. Too much activity with the same kind of structure may even have a negative influence. In regular school practice, ten to twenty exercises in the same group of operations might be enough per school year, and their total number must not exceed thirty. Consequent enrichment of the teaching material with this activity in several school subjects over subsequent years may rather be the best way to apply these exercises in educational practice.

The results suggest that students with less mature operational thought benefit more from the training chosen than do the more mature children.

Training might be more economic if these less mature students were targeted, but this requires more complicated classroom procedures.

ACKNOWLEDGEMENTS

The research presented here was supported by the Research Council of Public Education in Hungary. I would like to thank Tibor Vidákovich and Erzsébet Csirikné for their valuable help in organizing this experiment.

The data analysis was made and this chapter was drafted while the author was a Humboldt Research Fellow at the University of Bremen, West Germany.

REFERENCES

Case, R. (1974) 'Structures and strictures: some functional limitations on the course of cognitive growth', *Cognitive Psychology* 6: 554–73.

Collis, K. F. (1980) 'School mathematics and stages of development', in S. Modgil and C. Modgil (eds) *Toward a Theory of Psychological Development*, Slough: NFER, pp. 635–71.

Csapó, B. (1985) 'Development of combinatoric operations from 10 to 17 years of age', Eighth Biennial Meetings of ISSBD, Tours, France, *Cahiers de Psychologie Cognitive* 5 (3/4): 439.

—— (1987) 'Representing the qualitative characteristics of reasoning by qualitative data', *Bremer Beiträge zur Psychologie* 67.

—— (1988) *A kombinatív képesség struktúrája es fejlödése* (Structure and development of combinative ability), Budapest: Akadémiai Kiadó.

—— (1989) 'Integration of the development of the operational abilities of thinking and the transmission of knowledge', in H. Mandl, E. De Corte, N. Bennett, and H. E. Friedrich (eds) *Learning and Instruction: European Research in an International Context*, Vol. 2.2, Oxford: Pergamon, pp. 85–94.

Csirikné, E. (1989) *A nyelvi-logikai müveletrendszer struktúrája és fejlödése* (Structure and development of propositional logic in children), CSc dissertation, Budapest Hungarian Academy of Sciences.

Demetriou, A. and Efklides, A. (1988) 'Experiential structuralism and neo-Piagetian theories: toward an integrated model', in A. Demetriou (ed.) *The Neo-Piagetian Theories of Cognitive Development: Toward an Integration*, Amsterdam: North-Holland, pp. 173–222.

Fishbein, E., Pampu, I., and Minzat, I. (1970) 'Effects of age and instruction on combinatory ability in children', *British Journal of Educational Psychology* 40: 261–70.

Fischer, K. W. (1980) 'A theory of cognitive development: the control and construction of hierarchies of skills', *Psychological Review* 87: 477–531.

Jerusalem, M. (1984) *Selbstbezogene Kognitionen in schulischen Bezugsgruppen*, Berlin: Freie Universität.

Johnson-Laird, P. N. (1983) *Mental Models: Towards a Cognitive Science of Language, Inference and Consciousness*, Cambridge, MA: Harvard University Press.

Jurd, M. (1978) 'An empirical study of operational thinking in history type material', in J. A. Keats, K. F. Collis, and G. S. Halford (eds) *Cognitive Development: Research Based on a Neo-Piagetian Approach*, Chichester: Wiley, pp. 315–48.

Kozéki, B. and Entwistle, N. J. (1984) 'Identifying dimensions of school motivation in Britain and Hungary', *British Journal of Educational Psychology* 54: 303–9.

Lawson, A. (1985) 'A review of research on formal reasoning and science teaching', *Journal of Research in Science Teaching* 22: 569–617.

Nagy, J. (1988) *A rendszerezési képesség kialakulása: Gondolkodási műveletek* (The evolution of systematizing ability: thought operations), Budapest: Akadémiai Kiadó.

Seggie, J. L. (1978) 'Concept learning and the formal operational model', in J. A. Keats, K. F. Collis, and G. S. Halford (eds) *Cognitive Development: Research Based on a Neo-Piagetian Approach*, Chichester: Wiley.

Shayer, M. (1987) 'Neo-Piagetian theories and educational practice', *International Journal of Psychology* 22: 711–22.

Shayer, M. and Adey, P. (1988) *Cognitive Acceleration through Science Education: An Introduction*, mimeographed, King's College, London.

Shayer, M. and Beasley, F. (1987) 'Does Instrumental Enrichment work?', *British Educational Research Journal* 13: 101–19.

Siegler, R. S. and Liebert, R. M. (1975) 'Acquisition of formal scientific reasoning by 10- and 13-year-olds: designing a factorial experiment', *Developmental Psychology* 11: 401–2.

Siegler, R. S., Liebert, D., and Liebert, R. (1973) 'Inhelder and Piaget's pendulum problem: teaching preadolescents to act as scientists', *Developmental Psychology* 9: 97–101.

Sipos, K., Sipos, M., and Spielberger, D. (1985) 'The development and validation of the Hungarian form of the Test Anxiety Inventory', *Advances in Test Anxiety Research* 4: 221–57.

Vidákovich, T. and Csapó, B. (1988) 'Changes in the students' logical structures after ten months training', *Development, European Perspectives*. Third European Conference, Budapest, June.

Chapter 9

Training scientific reasoning in children and adolescents
A critical commentary and quantitative integration
Luc Goossens

INTRODUCTION

The contributions to the present volume fall into two distinct categories. One group of authors discusses the potential relevance of neo-Piagetian theories for educational practice, whereas another group presents the results of intervention studies intended to improve children's thinking. The studies by Efklides, Demetriou, and Gustafsson and Csapó are examples of the latter category. Shayer's comments on intervention studies are derived from his extensive experience with similar projects and with the Cognitive Acceleration through Science Education (CASE) study in particular (Adey 1988; Adey and Shayer 1990). The two groups of studies are obviously related to one another, because intervention studies may be inspired by a given theory of cognitive development (see Shayer 1987).

The present chapter sets out to comment critically on cognitive acceleration research and takes the Efklides *et al.* study on the improvement of scientific reasoning as a point of departure. Some problems inherent in this type of research are briefly reviewed, the results of an ongoing research project at the University of Louvain are presented, and the implications of the results of this study for intervention research are discussed at length.

The remainder of this introduction discusses three general problems that confront researchers involved in intervention studies, presents a brief overview of earlier research on the training of scientific reasoning, and introduces a new statistical approach, known as meta-analysis, to this particular body of literature. Each of these three points will be addressed in turn.

Problems of intervention research

A researcher involved in intervention projects finds himself continually struggling with three problems. While the first problem may be thought of as a purely practical one, the other two clearly have to do with the interventionist's reliance on a particular model of cognitive development.

The first of these problems may be referred to as the '*magnitude-of-effect*' problem. The Efklides *et al.* study clearly illustrates this problem. Interested readers would like to know the statistical and practical importance of the training effect reported in that chapter. The authors' sole reliance on statistical significance testing leaves much to be desired in this regard. The reader is simply informed that the difference between the experimental and control groups reached a commonly accepted level of significance for certain measures (the trained abilities) and failed to do so for other abilities (the non-trained ones). Detailed comparison of the training effect obtained in this study with the results of other intervention projects, which are typically expressed in the same language of significance testing, is virtually impossible.

A second problem in training research has to do with the experimenter's conception of the general organization of knowledge or the *cognitive structures* underlying subjects' performance on a variety of tasks. The conceptualization of these structures has important implications for the design and interpretation of intervention research and seems to have changed dramatically over the years. Piaget's theory, which strongly influenced cognitive developmental research in the 1960s and 1970s, posited a single, unified structure that could account for all of the more specific changes in intellectual functioning that occur over relatively broad periods of time (Kuhn 1988). Adolescents' use of the procedures of controlled scientific experimentation were thought to emerge at roughly the same point in development as did proportional reasoning. Both scientific and proportional reasoning were manifestations of the same underlying structure, known as the 'structure-of-the-whole' that characterized formal operational thinking.

Case (1988) points out that the neo-Piagetian theories have retained some of the basic postulates of Piaget's theory. Many authors, including Halford (this volume) and Case himself (this volume), maintain a strong belief in the role of general cognitive abilities, such as cognitive capacity. At the same time, however, the neo-Piagetian theories agree that specific cognitive abilities play a non-negligible role in cognitive functioning, albeit to different degrees. Some of these theories place a particularly strong emphasis on more 'local', more content- and context-specific structures as opposed to global structures that operate across a variety of content domains and contexts of application.

The theory of experiential structuralism that underlies the Efklides *et al.* effort is a clear example of this recent trend. Scientific reasoning and proportional reasoning, referred to in the theory as the causal-experimental sphere and the quantitative-relational sphere, respectively, are thought to constitute specialized structural systems (SSS), each with its own mode of functioning and symbolic bias, that are both objectively (in factor-analytic studies) and subjectively (in subjects' experience) different from one another. Fischer's theory provides another case in point. In this theory (Bidell and Fischer this volume) it is claimed that cognitive skills first emerge in a particular context and continue to function preferentially in that specific environment. However, Fischer takes care to distinguish a whole series of 'transformation rules' (such as substitution, focusing, and compounding) that allow for the acquisition of new skills and their generalization to different environments. As a result, somewhat broader forms of cognitive organization are found to develop that are aptly called 'local' structures. In all, the theory clearly takes issue with Piaget's idea of an all-encompassing, unitary structure, while carefully avoiding the other extreme, which is represented by a set of discrete competencies that develop entirely independently from one another in completely asynchronous fashion.

This particular conceptualization of cognitive structures as found in Demetriou's and Fischer's theory has one important implication for training research. Efklides *et al.* (this volume), who adhere to the notion of 'local' structures, no longer expect to find significant transfer on non-trained cognitive abilities or skills. The situation was completely different only a decade ago, when researchers were hoping to obtain transfer on other abilities, because a common general structure was thought to underlie both trained and non-trained abilities. The results of the Efklides *et al.* study clearly confirm their predictions and seem to support the new concept of structures in cognitive developmental psychology. But, once more, the reader would like to know whether comparable training studies on scientific reasoning have yielded similar results and thus have lent support to the model of 'local' cognitive structures.

A third problem in intervention research is researchers' conceptions of the *mechanisms of change* in cognitive development. The situation is somewhat analogous to experimenters' views on cognitive structures and the influence of these on their conduct of inquiry (second problem) and at the same time more complex. Scholars of cognitive development do not share a common core of beliefs on mechanisms of cognitive development, as they do on the nature of cognitive structures. Moreover, most of them are particularly vague on this subject.

Efklides *et al.* (this volume) are not very clear either. The authors claim that experience is fundamental to the organization and development of cognitive structures. Training, which is one particular form of learning experience, is expected to affect the rate of development of subjects' cognitive organization. This argument expresses the authors' belief in the trainability of cognitive structures, but fails to offer a description of a particular mechanism of cognitive development. The authors' implicit view on cognitive change, however, may be inferred from the particular training technique they used. Exposure to more advanced forms of reasoning (one level above subjects' own level) is thought to provoke changes in cognitive organization and to promote intellectual development. The overall significant effect of this particular training study seems to corroborate this view. But the critical reader rightly points out that other forms of training, inspired by different conceptions of mechanisms of development, may yield comparable results and lend support to alternative conceptualizations.

All of the three problems mentioned earlier derive in some part from researchers' reliance on the results of a single intervention study. Review articles compare the results of a number of training studies with differing results and contrasting views on the nature of cognitive structures and the mechanisms of cognitive development. The next section, therefore, presents a brief overview of training research on scientific reasoning and attempts to place the problems encountered in intervention research in a somewhat broader perspective.

Training research on scientific reasoning

Training research intended to improve scientific thinking has concentrated on two analytic questions. The first of these questions may be related to the first two problems in intervention research, whereas the second question clearly relates to the third problem mentioned earlier on.

It should be noted here that the present review limits itself to those studies that have defined scientific reasoning as subjects' ability to disentangle causal relations in a systematic way, as did Efklides *et al*. Most of the tasks used to measure this type of scientific reasoning probe for subjects' use of the control-of-variables strategy ('all other things being equal'). Our review of training research on scientific reasoning will further be confined to review articles based on controlled studies. Only studies that have contrasted an experimental group, which received some form of training, and a group of untreated control subjects were thus included in the review.

The first analytic question concerns the *overall effectiveness of training efforts*. Earlier reviews have used the box-score or vote-counting method to answer this question. In this approach, the outcome of a test of statistical significance in a series of related studies is used to draw inferences about the effect of a particular treatment. The available studies are sorted into three categories: significantly positive (the mean difference favours the experimental group), significantly negative (favouring the control group), and non-significant results. The treatment is then assumed to have an effect greater than zero if a plurality or majority of the studies (in whatever way defined) shows statistically significant results in the positive direction (Hedges and Olkin 1985).

It will be evident from this brief description that the box-score method can provide a somewhat more balanced answer to the first problem in intervention research. Modifications of the technique that distinguish between subjects' improvements on trained and non-trained abilities may further yield insight into the pattern of transfer and into the nature of the organizational systems that underlie cognitive functioning.

Several reviews concluded that trained subjects outperformed control subjects on tasks explicitly trained (Sneider et al. 1984), but transfer to scientific reasoning tasks that were not included in the training programme and durability of the training effect had not been demonstrated in a convincing way (De Carcer, Gabel, and Staver 1978; Nagy and Griffiths 1982). Transfer to other non-trained abilities, such as proportional reasoning, was observed rarely if at all (Larivée, Longeot, and Normandeau 1989).

The box-score method has also been used in previous research to answer a second analytic question and explore *differences between training programmes*. Lawson (1985) concluded that the nature of the training did in fact make a difference in the results obtained. Interventions that were longer term, used a variety of training materials, and allowed subjects to be in control of their own actions were claimed to be more successful. More specifically, some improvement in scientific reasoning was found to occur in short-term, experimenter-directed training programmes that used a limited number of training tasks. But this positive effect was limited to trained tasks or very similar ones. The author pointed out that this finding was not at all surprising, because favourable training conditions – long, rich programmes in which subjects are actively involved – more closely resemble the environment that the developing child is exposed to in the course of natural development.

It may be added here that certain learning theorists would anticipate similar results, albeit on different grounds. Based on her research on principle-based mathematics learning and the concept of 'cognitive apprenticeship', Resnick (Chapter 11, this volume) would probably expect that subjects in self-directed, long-term, and diverse programmes score consistently higher on scientific reasoning tasks as compared to controls than the children who are enrolled in other types of training programmes. The children in the former programmes were introduced to a socially valued activity in our society, controlled experimentation, and were given the opportunity to practise this activity over an extended period of time and across a variety of domains. More positive results would be expected to ensue from this kind of intervention, particularly as regards performance on non-trained scientific reasoning tasks and retention of the training effect.

Application of the box-score method to groups of related studies has thus provided a partial answer to the two analytic questions in reviews of training research on scientific reasoning. These answers in turn constitute provisional conclusions regarding the three problems of intervention research. One may conclude that scientific reasoning can be trained with some success (Problem 1) and that the global pattern of results – lack of transfer to non-trained abilities – supports the idea of 'local' structures (Problem 2). Finally, the greater effectiveness of particular types of training programmes seems to suggest possible mechanisms of change or learning principles that are related to Piaget's notion of equilibration or to processes of self-discovery. The next section, however, moves beyond crude methods such as the box-score approach and their obvious limitations.

Meta-analysis

During the last decade, meta-analysis (or quantitative integration) has been developed as an alternative method to address the two analytic questions in reviews of training efforts. Application of this method provides a more precise answer to the three problems that have plagued intervention studies in cognitive developmental research.

At the most general level, meta-analysis has been defined as 'the statistical integration of the results of independent studies' (Mullen 1989: ix). The analysis typically comprises three phases. (a) The results of individual training studies are expressed on a common metric in order to make them comparable across studies. In intervention research, the difference between the experimental and the control group is expressed in standard deviation units. The statistic that results from this transformation thus represents a standardized mean difference and is referred to as an effect size. Important features of the different training programmes, generally referred to as moderator variables, are also coded in objective fashion in this initial phase. (b) The meta-analyst can then explore questions of central tendency and variability. The typical result of training efforts in a given domain is represented in terms of a mean or median effect size for the given sample of studies (central tendency) and the typical difference from the typical result is represented by means of indices like standard deviation or range (variability). (c) Finally, the meta-analyst moves on to the problem of prediction and tries to explain and account for the variability around the typical result in terms of the moderator variables. In so-called conventional meta-analysis, differences in mean effect size between different sub-groups of training programmes are tested for statistical significance during this final phase, using traditional statistical methods such as t-tests or F-tests as employed in the analysis of variance.

This brief and admittedly oversimplified description does not do justice to the complexities of meta-analysis. Yet, it will be evident from these general remarks that this relatively new statistical technique offers a precise, quantitative answer to the two analytic questions in reviews of training research (overall effectiveness and differences between training programmes) in phases (b) and (c), respectively. The three problems in intervention research can also be approached in a new way through the application of meta-analytic techniques. Calculation of mean effect sizes and standard deviations offers a clear-cut answer to the 'magnitude-of-effect' problem (first problem). The debate over global versus 'local' cognitive structures (second problem) can meaningfully be informed by meta-analytic results, if the relevant statistics are computed separately for trained and non-trained abilities. Finally, an analysis of the variability of training results in terms of a well-selected set of moderator variables can give hints as to the nature of the mechanisms of cognitive change (third problem).

In the remainder of this chapter, then, we will present the results of a meta-analytic integration of the training literature on scientific reasoning that forms part of the ongoing research project at the University of Louvain mentioned earlier on. Possible implications with regard to the three problems in intervention research will be outlined in the discussion.

METHOD

The present section comprises a brief description of the sample of studies on which the meta-analysis is based, of the different types of training effectiveness that have been distinguished (first analytic question), and of the category system used in coding the moderator variables (second analytic question). Finally, some remarks are in order on the particular type of statistical analysis employed in the present chapter.

The sample of studies and effect sizes

Potentially relevant studies were identified through computer-assisted search of the main data bases in psychology and education (Psychological Abstracts, Educational Resources Information Center (ERIC), Dissertation Abstracts International). The search profile included such terms as 'scientific reasoning' and 'control-of-variables (strategy)'. Additional studies were found in the reference lists of the papers thus identified. In all, thirty-eight studies could be retrieved that (a) focused on scientific reasoning and (b) compared experimental subjects to a group of untreated control subjects to evaluate the effectiveness of a training programme.

The results of ten of these studies were described in unpublished reports (mainly PhD theses), another twenty-seven studies were published as (peer-reviewed) journal articles, and only one study was published in a book. All of the studies used either children or adolescents (ages 6 to 22) as subjects. The majority of the studies were conducted in North America (United States and Canada) and Australia and the results were published or the theses submitted between 1972 and 1986. (A list of the studies used in the meta-analysis is available on request.)

The total number of effect sizes for a given type of training effectiveness may at times exceed the total number of studies. Our main interest is in fact with effect sizes or hypothesis tests (i.e., experimental–control group contrasts) rather than studies *per se* and, in the present sample of studies, several effect sizes could occasionally be derived from the same study. Groups of experimental and control subjects may be compared at different age, grade, or ability levels for example, thus providing several independent estimates of the hypothesis test under study. The number of effect sizes for each type of training effectiveness will be indicated below.

Types of training effectiveness

Four types of training effects will be distinguished. Near-near transfer (fifty-nine effect sizes) is found to occur when the group of experimental subjects outperforms the control subjects on tasks that closely resemble the task materials used in the training programmes. Near-far transfer (forty-seven effect sizes) implies that experimental subjects do better than controls on scientific reasoning tasks that do not resemble the materials used in the intervention sessions. Retention (twenty-three effect sizes) is defined as durability of experimental subjects' superiority over a certain period of time. The retention period ranged from one week to a year, with a median value of ten weeks. Finally, far-far transfer (alternatively referred to as non-specific transfer) is observed when generalization is found to occur to truly novel tasks. Experimental subjects are then superior in reasoning skills different from scientific reasoning. In the present chapter, only the results for proportional reasoning tasks (ten effect sizes) will be reported for this particular type of training effectiveness.

Coding of the moderator variables

Three different categories were distinguished for each of the three moderator variables: low (or short), medium, and high (or long). A brief description of these three categories for all three moderators (self-directedness, duration, and diversity) may clarify the precise nature of the moderator variables.

With regard to *self-directedness*, the 'low' category comprised both demonstration and correction techniques. Demonstration refers to the traditional lecture format in which the experimenter explains the principle of controlled experimentation to the subjects who are supposed to assume a passive role (see, for example, Howe and Mierzwa 1977). This particular subcategory was also used as some sort of a 'default option' for all kinds of highly directive training programmes. Bob Siegler's early work on training scientific thinking (see, for example, Siegler, Liebert and Liebert 1973) provides a nice example of such a programme. Correction techniques are employed when the experimenter first invites subjects to design experiments, which are poorly controlled, then points out alternative explanations and eventually explains the use of the control-of-variables strategy. A training study conducted by Robbie Case (1974) as part of his PhD work is the classical prototype of this type of training.

The 'medium' category included cognitive conflict techniques as well as perceptual readiness techniques. In the first of these training sub-types, subjects are presented with cognitive conflicts, such as incompatible results of different experiments, each of which is poorly designed. They are then invited to solve the contradiction and construct the adequate strategy all by themselves. The work of Jack Rowell, inspired by his particular views on scientific reasoning and on the role of cognitive conflict in intellectual development (see, for example, Rowell 1983, 1984), falls into this subcategory. Perceptual readiness techniques help subjects discriminate between different variables and variable levels. Again, as in cognitive conflict training, no formal teaching of reasoning strategies takes place. The 'dimension' training developed by Doreen Rosenthal (1979) is probably the clearest example of this type of training.

Finally, the 'high' category comprised all training programmes that made use of self-discovery techniques. This approach is completely non-directive. Subjects are expected to develop adequate reasoning skills through physical interaction with a variety of materials. A series of studies by Marcia Linn and her associates (see Linn 1980, for a review) and by Deanna Kuhn (see, for example, Kuhn and Ho 1980) form the bulk of the studies in this particular category of training efforts. It will be clear from this brief description that the training programmes were classified on a scale that ranged from extremely experimenter-directed to extremely subject-directed.

The training studies were further grouped into three categories of *training duration*. Studies in the 'short' category involved only one or two training sessions, the 'medium' category comprised all studies that had three to seven sessions, whereas the 'long' category included the remainder of the studies (eight or more training sessions).

Finally, three different categories of *diversity* in training materials were distinguished. These groupings were designated as 'low' (one or two types of training materials), 'medium' (three to five different types of materials), and 'high' (six or more types of training materials), respectively. Admittedly, the distinctions made above are rather crude and somewhat subjective, particularly in the case of diversity of materials. Yet the distribution of the training studies across the three categories of the moderator variables was rather well balanced for each of the different types of training effectiveness, as can be seen in Table 9.1. The only exception was the diversity of training materials for retention, where no studies could be found in the 'high' category.

Statistical analysis

The meta-analytic method used in the present chapter was inspired by the techniques developed by James Kulik and widely used in educational research (see Kulik and Kulik 1989, for a review). This approach is sometimes referred to as 'study effect meta-analysis' (SEM: Bangert-Drowns 1986). The analysis proceeded in three phases as described in the introduction.

(a) The effects of individual training studies were converted into effect sizes. The effect-size statistic used was d, defined as the experimental group mean minus the control group mean, divided by the pooled within-group standard deviation. The formula indicates that this particular statistic can readily be computed from summary statistics (means and standard

Table 9.1 Number of studies in each of the three categories of three moderator variables for different types of training effectiveness

Moderator	Low/short	Medium	High/long
		Category	
	Near-near transfer		
Self-directedness	31	19	9
Duration	22	18	19
Diversity	30	14	15
	Near-far transfer		
Self-directedness	18	19	10
Duration	13	16	18
Diversity	20	17	10
	Retention		
Self-directedness	5	12	6
Duration	7	12	4
Diversity	6	17	0

deviations), but it can also be inferred from standard inferential statistics (t and F values) using a series of conversion rules (see, for example, Glass, McGaw, and Smith 1981; Smith, Glass, and Miller 1980). Hedges' correction for small sample bias was applied to the d values obtained (Hedges and Olkin 1985). The moderator variables were also coded during this first phase according to the category system described earlier on. (b) An average effect size and standard error were then computed for each of the different types of training effectiveness. These statistics provide an estimate of the mean effectiveness of training efforts and of the typical variability around the mean. Assuming that effect sizes are normally distributed, this effect size can also be expressed in terms of percentage points under the normal distribution (Glass *et al.* 1981). Alternatively, the importance of an average effect size can be gauged using a set of rules-of-thumb (Cohen 1988). (c) The variability in effect sizes as a function of the three moderator variables (self-directedness, duration, and diversity) was explored through a series of univariate analyses of variance (ANOVAs).

It may be added here that the final estimates of training effectiveness (the average effect sizes) are based on a large number of subjects. Some overlap occurred because several groups that were administered different training programmes were compared to a common control group in a small number of studies. Taking this overlap into account, the average effect size for near-near transfer, for example, is based on the testing of 2760 subjects.

RESULTS

Two different sets of results will be presented that pertain to the first and second analytic question in reviews of training research, respectively.

Overall effectiveness of training

A summary of the main findings regarding overall effectiveness of training may be found in Table 9.2. In this table n refers to the number of effect sizes. For near-near transfer, an average effect size of nine-tenths of a standard deviation is obtained. This finding implies that the average (or 50th percentile) subject in the experimental group scores above 81 per cent of the subjects in the control group. Near-far transfer provides a much more stringent test of training effectiveness but yields a comparable estimate (about 0.80 of a standard deviation). The average subject, who would score at the 50th percentile, can expect to rise to the 79th percentile after receiving training. The estimate for retention of the training effect is based on a much smaller number of effect sizes, but is still substantial. The average effect size for this type of training effect implies that the average person in the experimental group scores above 74 per cent of the subjects in the control group. Using Cohen's (1988) benchmarks of 0.20, 0.50, and 0.80 for small, medium, and large effect sizes, it can be concluded that a large effect size was obtained for both types of transfer and a medium one for retention. All of these three mean effect sizes are significantly different from zero at p<.001 or beyond.

Table 9.2 Summary of effect-size statistics

Type of effect	n	Mean effect size	Standard error
Scientific reasoning			
Near-near transfer	59	0.88	0.09
Near-far transfer	47	0.82	0.11
Retention	23	0.64	0.17
Proportional reasoning			
Far-far transfer	10	0.18	0.10

The results for far-far transfer, here restricted to proportional reasoning tasks (Table 9.2 above), are completely different. The average effect size is small and not significantly different from zero. However, some caution is in order when interpreting this result because of the small number of effect sizes involved. It may be added here that the average effect sizes for other types of reasoning (combinatorial, logical, and correlational reasoning), which are based on even smaller numbers of comparisons, were equally low.

In conclusion, then, substantial effects of training were found on scientific reasoning tasks. But significant transfer to non-trained abilities and to subjects' performance on proportional reasoning tasks in particular failed to occur.

Differences in effectiveness between training programmes

The results of the ANOVAs on the effect of the three moderator variables are presented in Table 9.3. Only one significant effect emerged for the effect of training duration on near-far transfer. A posteriori comparisons (Tukey HSD tests) revealed that short- and medium-duration programmes yielded significantly larger effects than long-term training. One may object here that the striking absence of differences between different types of training can be attributed to the admittedly broad categories used in the present analyses. This particular choice of categories may have obscured important differences between training programmes. Additional analyses using the five-fold classification for self-directedness of the training programme (as described in the Method section) rather than the three-fold category system failed to support this particular criticism. A single marginally significant difference ($p<.10$) was found for near-far transfer. This result, which seemed to indicate that perceptual readiness techniques yield a larger effect size (average $d = 1.65$) than cognitive conflict techniques (average $d = 0.26$), is to be regarded with extreme caution because of the small numbers of effect sizes involved ($n = 5$ and 3, respectively).

Table 9.3 Mean effect sizes as a function of three moderator variables

Moderator	Low/short	Medium	High/long	F
		Near-near transfer		
Self-directedness	1.01	0.77	0.66	1.13
Duration	0.92	1.09	0.64	2.01
Diversity	0.86	1.05	0.77	0.58
		Near-far transfer		
Self-directedness	0.84	0.90	0.60	0.48
Duration	1.08	1.08	0.39	5.18**
Diversity	0.89	0.94	0.46	1.38
		Retention		
Self-directedness	0.36	0.91	0.35	1.38
Duration	0.23	0.98	0.36	2.37
Diversity	0.18	0.81	–*	2.85

* There were no experimental–control group comparisons in this category.
** $p < .01$.

172 Inducing cognitive change

In sum, the different types of training techniques failed to yield different effects, with the exception of short- and medium-duration training, which proved superior to long-term training in one particular instance.

DISCUSSION

The results of the present chapter clearly illustrate the potential usefulness of meta-analytic methods for cognitive acceleration research. All of the three problems in intervention research, to which we now turn in succession, may be addressed in novel ways through the application of these methods.

The 'magnitude-of-effect' problem

The quantitative integration methods used in the present review have indicated that training studies intended to improve scientific reasoning have a large effect on this particular type of thinking. The average effect size and its expression in terms of percentage points under the normal distribution in particular illustrates the statistical importance of this finding. Yet, the reader may wonder what the typical child is capable of doing before the intervention and at the end of the typical training programme, when it is found to score at the 50th and 81st percentile, respectively. An answer to this question may readily be provided, because researchers typically describe subjects' performance on scientific reasoning tasks in terms of Piagetian stages of thinking, each of which is characterized by a set of typical behaviours. A rich behavioural description would therefore be available for subjects scoring at the middle, or towards the lower or upper end of the distribution, if the distribution of these stages of scientific thinking in the general population or sample estimates thereof were known.

In order to further illustrate the practical importance of the meta-analytic findings, an attempt will be made to relate the percentage points mentioned above to the distribution of stages of scientific thinking in large, representative samples of schoolchildren. Research on British children that used a variety of tasks has arrived at somewhat divergent although not incompatible distributions. The actual distribution does in fact depend on the subjects' age and ability level as well as the scientific reasoning task employed. Two different estimates are available for the upper ability range of the 14-year-olds that are based on subjects' scores on the pendulum task.

In this particular task, subjects have to find out whether the length of a pendulum, the weight attached to it, and the impetus of the swing determine its period of oscillation. Only length has an effect, but younger children in particular have serious problems with the exclusion of the other variables. Both the content of children's reasoning (i.e., their conclusions about the effectiveness or ineffectiveness of each of the variables) and their method of experimentation are taken into account when scoring children's performance. These two aspects of subjects' behaviour are strongly intercorrelated, because incorrect conclusions about the role of the factors typically have their origin in subjects' reliance on inadequate procedures of experimentation.

A first estimate of the distribution of stages is based on the upper 40 per cent of the 14-year-olds. In this particular group, the 50th percentile subject is found to score at the transitional level between late concrete and early formal thinking, whereas the subject at the 81st percentile scores at the early formal operational level (Shayer 1979). In terms of the behavioural descriptions that characterize the different developmental levels (see also Somerville 1974), this means that subjects' conclusions about the effect of the different variables are initially incorrect and that their method is also deficient in that there is no attempt to control all of the other variables (initial transitional level). Upon completion of the training programme, however, conclusions about the length of the pendulum are basically correct, though subjects' reasoning shows certain inadequacies regarding the exclusion of the other variables and the control-of-variables strategy is not applied in a truly systematic fashion. A second estimate is based on a sub-sample of children from selective schools that comprises the upper 20 per cent of the 14-year-olds. The 50th percentile subject scores at the early formal operational level, while the subject at the 81st percentile scores at the late formal operational level (Shayer, Küchemann, and Wylam 1976). In terms of behavioural descriptions this means that the average subject moves from the inadequacies just described (early formal level) to a situation in which her conclusions are correct, including the exclusion of irrelevant factors, and in which the variables are investigated in a rigorous manner, varying only one of them at the time.

It should be stressed that caution is in order with these results, which must not be generalized to different age or ability levels nor to the other measures of scientific reasoning. Assessing the practical importance of an intervention effort, moreover, is much more complicated than described in the preceding paragraphs, because a given effect size may have a different meaning for subjects at different initial levels of ability (say the 25th and 75th percentile), as Shayer (this volume) rightly notes. But there is at least the suggestion that subjects' behaviour is qualitatively different prior to and after the training and that important transitions or shifts may be achieved by the typical subject in the experimental (or trained) group.

One practical conclusion, then, can be derived from the present review: that the results of intervention studies be routinely expressed as standardized mean differences (or effect sizes) to help potential readers grasp their practical importance (rather than their statistical significance). Benö Csapó (Chapter 8, this volume) has already taken this recommendation to heart and has expressed the results of his intervention study on combinative reasoning in standard deviation units.

The results of the present meta-analysis can also be used as a general background to gauge the effect of a given training study that was not included in the original review. By way of an example, which is presented here for purely illllustrative purposes, the meta-analytic procedures used in the present chapter will be applied to the results of the Efklides *et al.* study (Chapter 7, this volume) and compared to the overall results of the quantitative integration.

The training results for the causal-experimental sphere will first be concentrated upon. The twelve experimental–control group comparisons (at the different age and socioeconomic status (SES) levels) yield a mean effect size of 0.29 (standard error is 0.10). This result represents a relatively small effect and means that the average subject (50th percentile) can expect to rise to the 61st percentile after receiving training. Univariate ANOVAs further revealed that subjects' age did not have any effect on their trainability ($F(3,11) < 1$), which sheds some doubt on the authors' conclusion that older subjects benefit more from the intervention than do younger groups of subjects. The effects of subjects' SES, however, was clearly confirmed ($F(2,11) = 8.01, p < .01$), with a larger effect size in high SES urban groups ($M = 0.67$) as compared to both urban and rural low SES groups ($M = 0.13$ and 0.08, respectively).

The effect of causal-experimental training on quantitative-relational reasoning is much smaller (average effect size is 0.10; standard error is 0.09), but a larger effect was probably not to be expected in view of the results of the quantitative integration. The non-specific transfer effects on proportional reasoning – an ability that is comparable to quantitative-relational thinking – were equally small. The overall similarity between these two results is perhaps most apparent when they are both expressed in terms of percentage points under the normal distribution. The average subject in the experimental group could expect to rise from the 50th percentile to the 57th percentile on proportional reasoning in the meta-analytic review, and from the 50th to the 54th percentile on quantitative-relational reasoning in the Efklides *et al.* study. Neither age nor SES had a significant effect on the training result obtained for the quantitative-relational sphere ($F(3,11) < 1$ in both cases). Again, extreme cautiousness is advised in interpreting these results, because of the small numbers of effect sizes involved. But the potential usefulness of meta-analytic results as a 'yardstick' for the findings of other intervention studies seems to be particularly well illustrated in this example.

Cognitive structures

The implications of the present meta-analysis with regard to current conceptions of cognitive structures are relatively straightforward. The lack of significant transfer to non-trained abilities (and to proportional reasoning in particular) offers clear support for the notion of 'local' or specialized cognitive structures as opposed to a unified cognitive structure such as Piaget's 'structure-of-the-whole'. However, additional meta-analytic research is needed to explore the generalizability of this result. A first step in this process would be to check whether training in proportional reasoning results in significant improvements in scientific reasoning.

The present conclusions regarding the nature of cognitive structures would be strengthened if this failed to be the case, as the findings of the Efklides et al. study in fact suggest. Full application of the meta-analytic procedures outlined in this chapter to the training literature on proportional reasoning would have additional advantages as well. A comparative study of the overall effectiveness of proportional reasoning training would allow an empirical test of Efklides et al.'s claim that the specific structural systems, scientific reasoning and quantitative-relational reasoning, are differentially amenable to training.

Generally speaking, however, the results of quantitative reviews yield only indirect evidence on the topic under study. At the very best, a meta-analytic study can indicate what general type of cognitive organization is compatible or not with the results obtained. But it does not give indications as to the precise nature of these cognitive structures.

Mechanisms of cognitive development

The results of the meta-analytic study presented in this chapter are truly disappointing with regard to the third problem in intervention research. Virtually no differences in mean effectiveness have been found between different groups of training programmes. The evidence, therefore, does not support the popular notion of cognitive growth as guided by the developing subject's own actions, with a concomitant belief in mechanisms such as equilibration or self-discovery, that underlies one particular type of training efforts. Nor does it corroborate an alternative view on development as strongly influenced by the environment that underlies the group of studies at the other extreme of the scale. There are, however, serious problems with this general conclusion, both at a purely statistical and at a more conceptual level.

From a statistical point of view, a null result such as the one just reported is open to a wide variety of interpretations. One may question, for example, the appropriateness of the statistical technique used. The use of traditional statistical methods and F-tests in particular with meta-analytic data (i.e., effect sizes) has been challenged, because the homogeneity-of-variance assumption will generally not be met in this particular application (see Hedges and Olkin 1985: 11–12, for a discussion). Instead, statistical techniques specifically designed for the analysis of effect-size data have been suggested as an alternative. These analytic methods are sometimes referred to as 'modern statistical methods for meta-analysis' (Kulik and Kulik 1989).

Hedges and Olkin (1985) have suggested a particular version of these newer methods that is known as 'approximate data pooling with tests of homogeneity' (Bangert-Drowns 1986). Significant between-group differences are obtained somewhat more easily within this analytic framework. This approach, however, has been criticized in turn as being inappropriate and too liberal (Kulik and Kulik 1989, 1990). In view of the continuing discussion about the appropriateness of traditional versus modern methods of meta-analysis, it was decided to use the more conservative method (i.e., traditional F-tests) for the present analysis. The reader should bear in mind that significant differences between treatment categories might have been obtained had other meta-analytic procedures been adopted.

The analyst's choice of a particular meta-analytic technique may be dictated by other features of the technique as well. A researcher using the Hedges and Olkin method, for example, typically calculates weighted average effect sizes so that results based on larger numbers of subjects are given greater weight and uses special techniques for detection and deletion of outliers (i.e., conspicuously large effect sizes). Both of these features of the method may result in somewhat smaller estimates of overall training effectiveness. Ultimately, however, the two varieties of meta-analytic methods have somewhat different purposes. Study effect meta-analysis (SEM: Kulik) attempts to review what a given body of literature has to say about a treatment's effectiveness, whereas approximate data pooling with tests of homogeneity (Hedges and Olkin) tries to estimate population effect sizes (Bangert-Drowns 1986). The advantages and drawbacks of these methods are currently being explored in the ongoing research project at the University of Louvain, of which the present chapter presents but the first, preliminary results.

A set of statistical problems thus surrounds the application of meta-analytic methods. The problems at the conceptual level, however, are far more serious. The lack of significant differences between widely divergent training programmes or the implied suggestion that different mechanisms of cognitive change may yield comparable outcomes is not in itself problematic. The question of mechanisms in cognitive development, which has recently attracted renewed interest after years of neglect, is generally considered to be a most difficult one (Kuhn 1988) and one that is not likely to be answered in an unequivocal way (Flavell 1984). What seems to be most problematic and in fact highly questionable is the interventionist's willingness to draw inferences on the mechanisms of mental development on the basis of findings obtained in training research.

It has cogently been argued that one cannot infer the nature of the mechanisms of change in the natural course of development from the results of training studies. Many researchers have engaged in what has been called the 'intervention fallacy' (or the 'training study fallacy'). Somewhat oversimplified, these researchers reason as follows. 'Treatment A, based on a particular mechanism of development (say equilibration), is more successful than other treatments. Hence, this particular mechanism also plays a role in the natural course of development of the trained concept (or ability)' (Kuhn and Phelps 1982). In reality, however, the researcher always remains unsure about the extent to which the emergence of the specific type of cognitive performance in real life is contingent upon the mechanism supposed to be operative in his or her training study.

Alternative methods have been proposed for the study of mechanisms of cognitive change, that all involve observation of children's behaviour in natural contexts rather than experimental–control group comparisons. One of these methodological innovations, which has recently enjoyed some popularity, is the microgenetic method. This approach involves a careful observation of subjects' repeated attempts to solve a particular type of problems. Application of this method to children's performance on scientific reasoning tasks has revealed that the abandonment of old, inadequate strategies plays a more important role in the consolidation of adequate behaviours than does the development of new strategies (Kuhn and Phelps 1982; Schauble 1990).

This finding may have a wide generalizability. In a review of recent trends in cognitive development, Siegler (1989) identified competition between different strategies as one of the most general mechanisms of cognitive development, that has been found in a variety of research domains and using a wide array of complementary methods. The author's own work on children's strategy choice in elementary addition and subtraction (Siegler 1988) is just one research programme that illustrates this recent trend.

One implication of these recent developments, however, seems to be that training research, with its strong emphasis on the overall result, i.e., experimental subjects' superiority over controls following a given type of intervention, is not particularly suited for the study of mechanisms of change in development. Intervention studies do not detail how subjects come to relinquish a particular unadaptive strategy and adopt a more adequate one.

By way of a general conclusion, one may state that meta-analytic methods hold considerable promise for the future of intervention research. As the methods used in the present chapter and alternative techniques are applied to a growing number of research domains, it will ultimately be possible to create a context for intervention studies in cognitive development. The first problem in intervention research, referred to as the 'magnitude-of-effect' problem will then have been answered in a truly satisfying way. The results of these quantitative integration efforts may further shed light on a second problem in the field of intervention, the nature of cognitive structures, albeit in an indirect way. Pending further research, the evidence seems to be in favour of specialized cognitive structures rather than the traditional 'structures-of-the-whole'.

Mechanisms of development, finally, constitute a third problem in intervention research. Meta-analysis of training research is unlikely to provide clear-cut answers to this particular research question as it is presently defined, for reasons intrinsic to the design of intervention studies. Training research in its present form and orientation seems particularly ill suited for the study of this problem and has to be complemented if not superseded by a variety of alternative methods such as microgenetic analysis. Judicious choice of complementary methods seems to be a major task for all scholars of cognitive development and in fact their only hope to tackle successfully this most challenging and most difficult problem in their field, that is, the quest for mechanisms of change.

REFERENCES

Adey, P. (1988) 'Cognitive acceleration: review and prospects', *International Journal of Science Education* 10: 121–34.

Adey, P. and Shayer, M. (1990) 'Accelerating the development of formal thinking in middle and high school students', *Journal of Research in Science Teaching* 27: 267–85.

Bangert-Drowns, R. L. (1986) 'Review of recent developments in meta-analytic method', *Psychological Bulletin* 99: 388–99.

Case, R. (1974) 'Structures and strictures: some functional limitations on the course of cognitive growth', *Cognitive Psychology* 6: 544–73.

—— (1988) 'Neo-Piagetian theory: retrospect and prospect', in A. Demetriou (ed.) *The Neo-Piagetian Theories of Cognitive Development: Toward an Integration*, Amsterdam: North-Holland, pp. 267–85.

Cohen, J. (1988) *Statistical Power Analysis for the Behavioral Sciences*, 2nd edition, Hillsdale, NJ: Erlbaum.

De Carcer, I. A., Gabel, D. L., and Staver, J. R. (1978) 'Implications of Piagetian research for high school science teaching: a review of the literature', *Science Education* 62: 571–83.

Flavell, J. H. (1984) 'Discussion', in R. J. Sternberg (ed.) *Mechanisms of Cognitive Development*, New York: Freeman, pp. 188–209.

Glass, G. V., McGaw, B., and Smith, M. L. (1981) *Meta-analysis in Social Research*, Beverly Hills, CA: Sage.

Hedges, L. V. and Olkin, I. (1985) *Statistical Methods for Meta-analysis*, Orlando, FL: Academic Press.

Howe, A. C. and Mierzwa, J. (1977) 'Promoting the development of logical thinking in the classroom', *Journal of Research in Science Teaching* 14: 467–72.

Kuhn, D. (1988) 'Cognitive development', in M. H. Bornstein and M. E. Lamb (eds) *Developmental Psychology: An Advanced Textbook*, 2nd edition, Hillsdale, NJ: Erlbaum, pp. 205–60.

Kuhn, D. and Ho, V. (1980) 'Self-directed activity and cognitive development', *Journal of Applied Developmental Psychology* 1: 119–33.

Kuhn, D. and Phelps, E. (1982) 'The development of problem-solving strategies', in H. W. Reese (ed.) *Advances in Child Development and Behaviour*, Vol. 17, New York: Academic Press, pp. 1–44.

Kulik, J. A. and Kulik, C.-L. C. (1989) 'Meta-analysis in education', *International Journal of Educational Research* (Special issue), 13 (3).

—— (1990) 'Conventional and newer statistical methods in meta-analysis', paper presented at the Annual Meeting of the American Educational Research Association, Boston, MA.

Larivée, S., Longeot, F., and Normandeau, S. (1989) 'Apprentissage des opérations formelles: une recension des recherches' (The training of formal operations: a critical review), *L'Année Psychologique* 89: 553–84.

Lawson, A. E. (1985) 'A review of research on formal reasoning and science teaching', *Journal of Research in Science Teaching* 22: 569–617.

Linn, M. C. (1980) 'Teaching students to control variables: some investigations using free-choice experiences', in S. Modgil and C. Modgil (eds) *Toward a Theory of Psychological Development*, Windsor: NFER, pp. 673–97.

Mullen, B. (1989) *Advanced BASIC Meta-analysis*, Hillsdale, NJ: Erlbaum.

Nagy, P. and Griffiths, A. K. (1982) 'Limitations of recent research relating Piaget's theory to adolescent thought', *Review of Educational Research* 52: 513–56.

Rosenthal, D. A. (1979) 'Acquisition of formal operations: the effects of two training procedures', *Journal of Genetic Psychology* 134: 125–40.

Rowell, J. (1983) 'Equilibration: developing the hard core of the Piagetian research program', *Human Development* 26: 61–71.

—— (1984) 'Towards controlling variables: a theoretical appraisal and a teachable result', *European Journal of Science Education* 6: 115–30.

Schauble, L. (1990) 'Belief revision in children: the role of prior knowledge and strategies for generating evidence', *Journal of Experimental Child Psychology* 49: 31–57.

Shayer, M. (1979) 'Has Piaget's construct of formal operational thinking any utility?', *British Journal of Educational Psychology* 49: 265–76.

—— (1987) 'Neo-Piagetian theories and educational practice', *International Journal of Psychology* 22: 751–72.

Shayer, M., Küchemann, D. E., and Wylam, H. (1976) 'The distribution of Piagetian stages of thinking in British middle and secondary school children', *British Journal of Educational Psychology* 46: 164–73.

Siegler, R. S. (1988) 'Some general conclusions about children's strategy choice procedures', in A. Demetriou (ed.) *The Neo-Piagetian Theories of Cognitive Development: Toward an Integration*, Amsterdam: North-Holland, pp. 223–43.

—— (1989) 'Mechanisms of cognitive development', *Annual Review of Psychology* 40: 353–79.

Siegler, R. S., Liebert, D. E., and Liebert, R. M. (1973) 'Inhelder and Piaget's pendulum problem: teaching preadolescents to reason as scientists', *Developmental Psychology* 9: 97–101.

Smith, M. L., Glass, G. V., and Miller, T. I. (1980) *The Benefits of Psychotherapy*, Baltimore, MD: Johns Hopkins University Press.

Sneider, C., Kurlich, K., Pulos, S., and Friedman, A. (1984) 'Learning to control variables with model rockets: a neo-Piagetian study of learning in field settings', *Science Education* 68: 465–86.

Somerville, S. C. (1974) 'The pendulum problem: patterns of performance defining developmental stages', *British Journal of Educational Psychology* 44: 266–81.

Part III

Applications in specific domains

Chapter 10

Value and limitations of analogues in teaching mathematics

Graeme S. Halford and Gillian M. Boulton-Lewis

Young children are confronted regularly by mathematical representations. Some of these are concrete analogues specifically designed for teaching purposes, such as the Cuisenaire rods or the multibase arithmetic blocks, while others are representations inherent in the discipline of mathematics, such as number lines and symbols. The purpose of this paper is to consider some of the psychological processes entailed in using mathematical representations, in order to explore their role in the development of new concepts.

The theory we will use for this purpose is part of a general account of cognitive development that is outlined more fully elsewhere (Halford in press). It argues that there are two basic types of mechanisms in cognitive development. The first are essentially learning mechanisms, which lead to the gradual adjustment of mental models of the world through experience. These mechanisms are not fundamentally different from those that operate in other species. These mechanisms entail strengthening through experience, which applies to both declarative knowledge (mental models) and procedural knowledge. When applied to declarative knowledge it means that when a mental model correctly predicts the environment it is strengthened, and when it does not it is weakened. A similar principle applies to acquisition of procedural knowledge; it is strengthened when successful, and weakened when unsuccessful. These general principles can be expanded into a number of specific principles that give a detailed account of numerous learning phenomena (Halford in press; Holyoak, Koh, and Nisbett in press; Holland *et al.* 1986).

The second type of mechanism is concerned with recognition of correspondence between structures. It is involved in such processes as recognition of analogies, and with the selection and use of representations. It is argued that human beings have limited capacity to see correspondence between structures, but have much greater capacity to learn. It is suggested that this explains many cognitive developmental anomalies, such as ability to perform a task in one context but not in another. In this chapter we are primarily concerned with ability to see correspondence between structures, and the effect that our limited ability to do this has on acquisition of mathematics.

The argument is presented by reference to a few illustrative examples, but it can be applied to a wide range of subject matter (Halford in press).

Analogical reasoning, which is increasingly being seen as fundamentally important to human cognition, entails recognition of correspondence between one structure and another. Therefore we will begin by considering the theory of analogies, then we will broaden the issue to consider representations in general. According to Gentner (1983) an analogy consists of a mapping from one structure, called the source or base, to another structure, called the target. In the simple analogy 'Man is to house as dog is to kennel' (see Figure 10.1), 'Man is to house' is the source and 'dog is to kennel' is the target. Man is mapped into dog and house into kennel, and the relation 'lives in' between man and house corresponds to the relation 'lives in' between dog and kennel.

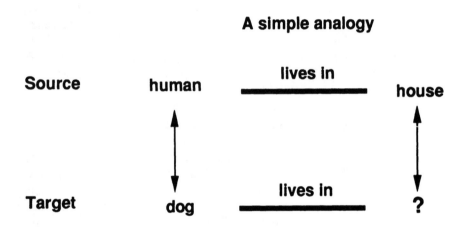

Figure 10.1 A structure-mapping analysis of a simple analogy

An important property of the structure-mapping process in analogies is that it is selective. Attributes are not normally mapped at all, so that, for example, the attribute 'wears clothes' associated with man is not mapped into, or attributed to, dog. Relations are also mapped selectively. In the present example, only one relation, 'lives in', is mapped, and other relations in the source such as 'has mortgage on' or 'repairs at weekends' are not mapped into the target. This means the mapping process selects those features of each structure that it shares with the other structure. As we will see, this has important implications for the formation of abstractions, because it means that structure mapping selects the features that are general to a particular class of structures and eliminates the features that are specific to individual structures.

The theory of analogies is very close to the theory of representations. A cognitive representation consists of a mental model that is in correspondence to the segment of the environment that is represented (Halford and Wilson 1980; Palmer 1978). A cognitive representation is a mapping from a cognitive structure to an environmental structure. An analogy is a mapping from one mental structure to another (Holland *et al.* 1986). Thus structure-mapping theory can handle both analogies and representations.

Applying Gentner's structure-mapping theory to mathematics, the concrete representation is the source and the concept to be taught is the target. The value of the concrete representation is that it mirrors the structure of the concept and the child can use the structure of the representation to construct a mental model of the concept.

It has been noted increasingly in recent literature in mathematics education that concrete representations often fail to produce the expected positive outcomes. Lesh, Behr, and Post note that 'concrete problems often produce lower success rates than comparable word problems' (1987: 56). Dufour-Janvier, Bednarz, and Belanger also note the 'negative consequences that can be caused by the use of representations prematurely or in an inappropriate context. In fact this leads the child to develop erroneous conceptions that will subsequently become obstacles to learning' (1987: 118).

There seems to be some mystification as to why concrete analogues sometimes aid and sometimes hinder acquisition of mathematics. We wish to propose that one reason why concrete analogues sometimes fail to live up to expectations is because of the processing load entailed in mapping a concept into an analogue. Previous research by Halford and his collaborators (Halford, Maybery, and Bain 1986; Maybery, Bain, and Halford 1986) has shown that structure mapping imposes a processing load, the size of which depends on the structural complexity of the concepts.

Halford (1987, in press) has defined four structure mapping levels as illustrated in Figure 10.2, the processing demands of which are known.

Element mappings. An element in one structure is mapped into an element in the other, on the basis of similarity or convention: e.g., an image or word representing an object or event.

Relational mappings entail mapping two elements with a relation between them: e.g., two sticks of different lengths to represent the fact that a man is larger than a boy. The mapping is validated by the similarity of the relation between the sticks to the relation between man and boy, and is independent of element similarity or convention. The man–house/dog–kennel analogy is a relational mapping, because it is validated by a similar relation in source and target.

System mappings are validated by structural correspondence, independent of similarity or convention. An example would be the representation of Tom > Dick > Harry by ordering the elements from left to right. Tom, Dick, Harry are mapped to left, middle, right respectively, and the relation '>' is

186 Applications in specific domains

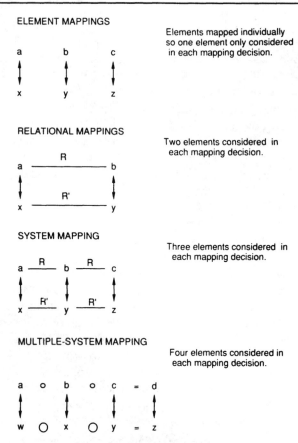

Figure 10.2 Four levels of structure mapping

mapped to 'left-of'. Mappings must be unique, and if a relation R in structure 1 is mapped into a relation R' in structure 2, the arguments of R must be mapped into the arguments of R'.

Multiple system mappings are similar to system mappings except that they depend on a composition of structures that have three elements as arguments.

PROCESSING LOADS

The load imposed by structure mapping depends on the level of structure being mapped, and can be quantified by the information required to define that structure. Elements can be defined by one item of information (e.g., label), binary relations by two items, systems of binary relations by three items, and multiple systems by four items (Halford 1987; Halford and Wilson 1980). The mental process which checks validity of mappings must transmit sets of items no smaller than these values from the representation of one structure to the representation of another. The metric is similar to that used by Leeuwenberg (1969) and Simon (1972); the complexity of a pattern or structure is equivalent to its dimensionality, i.e. the number of independent signals that define it. This means that the level of a mapping depends on the amount of information that must be processed in parallel to validate a mapping, not on the total amount of information in a structure.

The four mapping rules increase in abstractness, but at the cost of higher processing loads. This effect has been empirically confirmed using dual-task load indicators (Halford, Maybery, and Bain 1986; Maybery, Bain, and Halford 1986). Also, our research has shown that children become capable of using progressively higher rules with age (Halford 1982, 1987, in press; Halford and Wilson 1980).

This implies that the level of structure mapping that children can use will be a function of processing capacity. The view that there is a maturationally determined upper limit to cognitive processes has been a very unpopular one, at least partly because it is seen as having gloomy consequences for education (Carey 1985). This is not a valid reason for rejecting the hypothesis however, for two reasons. First, our desire to accelerate cognitive development should not bias our acceptance of the scientific evidence. One consequence of such a bias would be that studies indicating children's inability to perform a given task would be subjected to much more rigorous scrutiny than studies indicating successful performance. There are in fact some well-known studies in the literature where authors have been permitted to report chance-level results as positive results (McGarrigle, Grieve, and Hughes 1978; Siegel *et al.* 1978), apparently in pursuit of the aim of showing that children can succeed on certain tasks. This question is discussed in more detail elsewhere (Halford 1989). Second, the maturation hypothesis does not have uniformly gloomy implications, because most children are performing below their theoretical limit on some tasks, and more refined task analysis can result in very substantial improvements. Thus the maturation hypothesis is in no way incompatible with the goal of accelerating cognitive development. It simply implies that performance will be a function of processing capacity as well as experience. Therefore we will examine the capacity question next.

CAPACITY

The information required to validate structure-mapping rules raises the question of the amount of information that can be processed in parallel. Our theory links work on chunking originating with Miller (1956) to current parallel distributed processing models (Rumelhart and McClelland 1986). In the latter, information is represented as a set of activation values over a large set of units. Each pattern of activations (module) can represent a large amount of information, but its output is restricted to one concept at a time. When this limitation is combined with a restriction on the number of patterns of activations that can be transmitted from one set of modules to another (Schneider and Detweiler 1987) it provides an interesting theoretical basis for the observation that chunks can be of any size, yet only about four can be active simultaneously (Broadbent 1975; Fisher 1984; Halford, Maybery, and Bain 1988). A pattern of activations in one module can represent a chunk (information unit of arbitrary size) and since each pattern of activations can assume a range of values independent of other patterns, each pattern of activations represents a different dimension.

Schneider and Detweiler (1987) propose a multi-capacity module in which there are a number of regions, representing separate functions such as speech, vision, motor processing, etc. Each region contains up to four modules. They propose that working memory capacity can be increased by utilizing more than one region for difficult tasks. However, as mentioned above, only four patterns of activation can be transmitted from one region to another. This implies that only four patterns of activation can be processed in parallel. This in turn means that four-dimensional structures are the most complex that can be processed in parallel. This theory has been discussed in more detail by Halford (in press).

There is a link between the amount of information that can be processed in parallel and the level of structure mapping that can be achieved. Research indicating that adults process four chunks or dimensions in parallel implies that structures equivalent to multiple system mappings would be the most complex that can be processed in parallel. If children can process fewer dimensions in parallel, they would be restricted to lower-level mappings, which would explain the difficulty they have with certain concepts (Halford 1987).

Previous research (Halford 1987) has shown that children can master element mappings at one year, relational mappings at 2 years, system mappings at 5 years, and multiple system mappings at 11 years (median ages). This has been used to explain the typical age of attainment of a variety of concepts. Table 10.1 shows representative concepts belonging to each level.

SEGMENTATION AND CONCEPTUAL CHUNKING

There are of course many concepts that contain more than four dimensions, but the empirical work discussed above suggests that only four dimensions are processed in parallel, even by adults. How then are more complex problems processed? The model proposes that problems too complex to be processed in parallel are handled by either segmentation or chunking. Segmentation entails decomposing the problem into components or segments, and processing these serially. Thus there is parallel processing within segments, but serial processing between segments. There is a limit on segmentation because some problems cannot be decomposed. For example, the minimum information in an addition problem is two addends. The answer to the sum 'add 3' cannot be defined; we must know to what number

Table 10.1 Examples of concepts at each level of structure mapping

Concepts that require element mappings
Simple categories (dog, house)

Concepts that require relational mappings
Concepts based on simple binary relations (more than, bigger than)
Simple oddity
Simple analogies

Concepts that require system mappings
Transitivity and ordering
Class inclusion
Multiple classification
Dimension-abstracted oddity
Systematicity in analogies
Hypothesis testing in affirmation concepts (dimension checking and more sophisticated strategies)
Hypothesis testing in the attribute identification paradigm, with conjunctive, disjunctive, and conditional rules
Interpretation of simple algebraic expressions containing arithmetic operations

Concepts requiring multiple system mappings
Hypothesis testing in the attribute identification paradigm, with the biconditional rule
Hypothesis testing in the rule identification paradigm, for all rules other than affirmation
Interpretation of algebraic operations containing compositions of arithmetic operations

---

3 is added. The minimum information required to define arithmetic addition is a structure of the form 'a,b→c' (e.g., 2,3→5). Binary operations cannot be defined on sets of less than three elements, and therefore are irreducibly three-dimensional concepts.

Conceptual chunking reduces processing loads by recoding multiple dimensions into a single dimension, or at least into fewer dimensions than the original. Conceptual chunks are similar to mnemonic chunks in that a number of formerly separate items of information are recoded as a single item, but there is more emphasis on structure. A good example of a conceptual chunk would be speed, defined by the dimensions distance and time, but it can be recoded as a single dimension, e.g. position of a pointer on a dial.

Once multiple dimensions are recoded as a single dimension, that dimension occupies only one chunk or module, and it can be combined with up to three other chunks. This does not mean that processing limitations can be eliminated by recoding all concepts as a single chunk because a single-dimensional representation includes only one combination. Alternative combinations become inaccessible, unless a return is made to the original dimensions, which entails the original processing load. Thus, there tends to be a trade-off between efficiency and flexibility. The other limitation is that conceptual chunking, like mnemonic chunking, is possible only with constant mappings of components into chunks. Nevertheless, conceptual chunking is very useful in reducing processing loads, and permits us to master progressively more complex concepts. In a later section we will develop this argument further with reference to coding numbers in different bases.

The fact that processing loads can be reduced by segmentation and conceptual chunking does not make predictions about processing loads at each level of structural complexity untestable. It does mean, however, that hypotheses about the information that can be processed in parallel must be tested using tasks that preclude segmentation or conceptual chunking. Segmentation can be precluded by devising tasks in which the dimensions that define the structure interact, so they cannot be processed serially. Conceptual chunking can be precluded by using tasks that require new structures to be generated, because conceptual structures can exist only if there has been previous experience with that structure. These methods have been used in our previous research on this topic (Halford and Wilson 1980; Halford, Maybery, and Bain 1986; Maybery, Bain, and Halford 1986).

ANALOGUES IN MATHEMATICS

Concrete analogues have been especially popular in teaching mathematics, as the multitude of commercially available mathematical games attests. In fact the construction of concrete analogues for mathematical concepts has reached great heights of ingenuity, as is evidenced in the work of Dienes (1964). Some of the reasons why analogues are useful in learning are:

1 They reduce the amount of learning effort, and serve as memory aids.
2 They can provide a means of verifying the truth of what is learned.
3 They can increase flexibility of thinking.
4 They can facilitate retrieval of information from memory.
5 They can mediate transfer between tasks and situations.
6 They can indirectly (and, perhaps, paradoxically) facilitate transition to higher levels of abstraction.
7 They can be used generatively to predict unknown facts.

On the other hand, there are some potential disadvantages, including:

1 Structure mapping imposes a processing load (discussed above), and this load can actually make it more difficult to understand a concept.

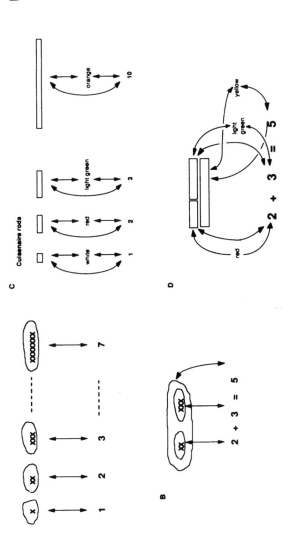

Figure 10.3 Structure-mapping analysis of some concrete aids

2 A poor analogue can generate incorrect information.
3 If an analogue is not fully integrated, and is not well mapped into the material to be learned or remembered, it can actually increase the learning or memory load.

We will explain these points by first using as an example the simple mathematical analogues in Figure 10.3. A popular way to teach simple addition facts is by using small sets of objects, as in Dienes multibase arithmetic blocks, or simply crosses on paper, to represent small numbers. Figure 10.3A shows such an analogue in structure-mapping format, with a set of one object mapped into the numeral 1, a set of two objects mapped into the numeral 2, and so on. The use of the same analogue to represent a simple arithmetical relationship, 2 + 3 = 5, is shown in Figure 10.3B. Collis (1978) has shown how this analogue can be used to represent some quite sophisticated mathematical notions, including addition and multiplication, commutativity, operations on ratios, and proportion. We will apply structure-mapping theory to assessing this analogue.

First, notice that in Figure 10.3A the mapping from sets to numerals is clear and easily verified. It is easy to recognize, by subitizing or counting, how many elements each set contains. In Figure 10.3B, the mapping of the numerals 2, 3, 5 into their respective sets is also clear and easily verified. The relation between the two addend sets and the sum set is also clear – the sum set includes all elements of the two addend sets, which have no common elements (are disjoint). This means that the structure of the base is clear and readily accessible (high base specificity in Gentner's terms). If we arrange sets in order of increasing magnitude as shown in Figure 10.3A, it is easy to see that each set contains one more element than its predecessor. This is one of many useful relationships that are contained in the analogue, and which are readily available for mapping into the target.

Contrast this with another analogue of elementary number facts, the Cuisenaire rods. In this case it is not so clear which rod should be mapped into each numeral. The longer rods are mapped into the larger numerals, but it is difficult to be sure precisely which numeral is represented by a rod of a given length. The rods are distinctive colours, to facilitate this differentiation, but, as Figure 10.3C shows, the colours complicate the mapping process. There is a two-stage map from rod to colour to numeral. The colours are arbitrary to some extent, so the mapping from rod to colour, and the mapping from colour to numeral, must be rote learned. Learning this arbitrary double mapping greatly increases the load on the children. The relationships in the base are not as clear as in the sets analogue. For example, it is not as clear that each rod represents one more unit than its predecessor.

The use of the Cuisenaire analogue to represent 2 + 3 = 5 is shown in Figure 10.3D. Because of the two-stage mapping rod–colour–numeral, which parallels the rod–numeral mapping, we can see that the structure mapping is much more complex than the corresponding mapping in Figure 10.3B, based on sets. A structure-mapping analysis therefore predicts that the set analogue would be more efficient than the coloured rods analogue. This analysis is intended to illustrate the application of structure-mapping theory to mental models of mathematics.

The sets analogue also exemplifies the second advantage listed above, because it permits verification of the truth of what is learned. As Figure 10.3B shows, the sets analogue provides a concrete model verifying that 2 + 3 = 5. Furthermore, it is a model which a child can learn to construct at any time so as to verify this relationship. The third advantage, facilitation of memory retrieval, occurs because an analogue can provide an additional retrieval cue. Siegler and Shrager (1984) have shown how this can occur with another popular small number analogue, use of fingers. Even when children are able to retrieve number facts from memory, they might use fingers as an 'elaborated representation', not to determine the answer by counting fingers, but as an additional retrieval cue.

The sets analogue illustrates how flexibility of thinking can be increased. The analogue in Figure 10.3B was constructed to show that 2 + 3 = 5, but it can be used equally well to verify that 3 + 2 = 5 (the commutativity property), and even that 5 – 3 = 2 and 5 – 2 = 3. Many good analogues can be accessed in several different ways, which makes it easy to examine a concept from a number of angles.

One reason why analogues facilitate transition to higher levels of abstraction is that they promote learning of integrated structures. For example, the analogue in Figure 10.3A would facilitate the learning of numbers as an ordered set, whereas analogues such as that in Figure 10.3B would facilitate the learning of integrated sets of relationships such as 1 + 1 = 2, 1 + 2 = 3, 1 + 3 = 4 ... 3 + 4 = 7, 3 + 5 = 8, etc. Structure mappings can be made best when the base structure is well learned (the property which Gentner (1982) calls 'base specificity'). When learning arithmetic using a concrete analogue, the concrete material is the source or base and the arithmetic facts are the target. When the transition is made to a higher level of abstraction, the arithmetic becomes the base and the algebraic relationships which mirror the arithmetic the target. This is discussed by Halford (in press), and is also developed later in this chapter. The better the arithmetic facts are learned, the better will be the base, and the better will be the structure mapping used to learn algebra.

COMPLEXITY OF CONCRETE ANALOGUES

In this section we will analyse the complexity of some concrete analogues in terms of levels of structure mapping outlined earlier. Recognition of relations between numbers (or sets) would be a relational mapping, and recognition of binary operations (addition, multiplication, and their inverses, subtraction and division) would be system mappings. Laws relating to single operations, such as that of commutativity, also entail system mappings. Concepts based on compositions of binary operations such as the distributive property a(b+c) = ab+ac entail multiple system mappings.

Simple analogues for the addition operation, 2 + 3 = 5, and for the relation 7 < 8 are shown as structure mappings in Figures 10.3B and 10.3C respectively. According to Halford's theory of levels, the mapping in Figure 10.3B is a system mapping and that in Figure 10.3C is a relational mapping. The addition operation should impose a higher processing load than recognition of relations.

For young children the verification of arithmetic facts probably depends on reference to a concrete example, based on small sets as in Figure 10.3 (fingers make admirable sets up to 10) or on a number line. If the structure mapping is too difficult they will be unable to make this verification, and to that extent their understanding will be impaired. Because arithmetic operations entail system mappings whereas understanding relations between integers or sets entails a relational mapping, it follows that, other things being equal, the former should be more difficult and should be understood later.

We will now apply structure-mapping theory to some more complex arithmetical concepts taught in schools. The basic idea of base-10 multibase arithmetic blocks (Dienes) is shown in Figure 10.4. With base-10 blocks, units are represented by small square blocks, tens are represented with

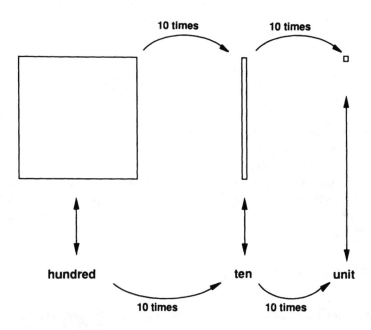

Figure 10.4 Structure-mapping analysis of a place-value analogue

blocks that are as long as 10 unit blocks (longs), and hundreds are represented by square blocks equal in area to 10 tens blocks (flats). The area relations between the blocks reflect the magnitude relations between quantities represented.

Resnick and Omanson (1984) found that the children could write numerals to represent numbers, correctly using the place-value notations, and could construct valid representations using the concrete analogues, Dienes blocks, or coins. They could also validly represent recompositions, such as changing 34 from 3 tens and 4 units to 2 tens and 14 units. However, they were not able relate this understanding to the decomposition procedures in addition and subtraction. Furthermore, an attempt to train the children to map their concrete representations into the arithmetic procedures was not particularly successful. We can begin to understand why children would have difficulty mapping these concrete representations into decomposition procedures, and why relatively brief mapping training might not remedy the problem, if we define the mappings involved more completely.

Figure 10.5 shows the structure mapping for a simple trade operation, where 324 is changed to 200 plus 110 plus 14. In the concrete representation, 324 is represented as 300 hundred blocks, two ten blocks and four unit blocks. The first point to notice about this mental model is that it really entails a two-stage vertical mapping. The three hundreds blocks are first mapped into the quantity 300, but this in turn has to be mapped into the 3 digit in the hundreds column in accordance with the place-value notation. That is we have mappings from concrete analogue to quantity to notation.

Moving horizontally we have a quantity conserving change in which the original representation is replaced by two hundreds blocks, 11 tens blocks, and 14 units blocks. To appreciate the value of the concrete representation, the child must recognize that this is a quantity conserving change. This is not easy to see because we have to sum 300 + 20 + 4 and recognize that it is equal to 200 + 110 + 14.

On the right-hand side we again have a two-stage mapping from concrete analogue to quantity to place-value notation. The value of the concrete analogue is lost unless it is realized that there is a quantity conserving change at all three levels. All in all, this is a very complex structure mapping, but it is only part of the mapping that is required to understand the decomposition procedure in subtraction, as we will soon see.

The structure mapping required to demonstrate how 324 minus 179 can be understood in terms of a concrete analogue is shown in Figure 10.6. The decomposition procedure is illustrated on the left side of the figure, as in Figure 10.5. The subtrahend, 179, is shown as concrete analogue, as quantities 100 plus 70 plus 9, and in place-value notation, 179. The resulting quantity, 145, is shown in the same way.

Note that the structure-mapping diagram is designed to show relations between elements of the representation, corresponding relations between

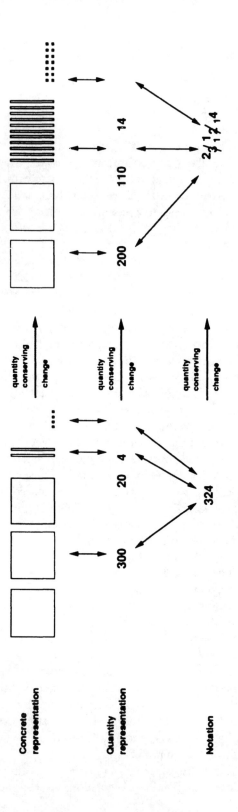

Figure 10.5 Structure-mapping analysis of a decomposition analogue

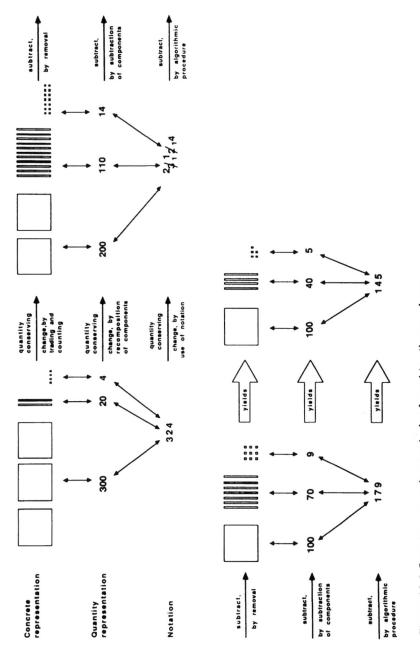

Figure 10.6 Structure-mapping analysis of a subtraction analogue

the things represented, and the mapping from one to the other. It is not designed to show the sequence of steps in the subtraction procedure. Consequently, the decomposition procedure is shown to the left of subtraction, but this is not intended to convey that one occurs before the other. Structure mapping is a way of analysing the relations that are inherent in the structure of a concept and revealing their complexity. It is not a substitute for a process model.

To realize how the concrete analogue justifies the subtraction procedure the child must recognize several sets of relationships:

1 The vertical mappings from each concrete display to the quantity represented, and then to the place-value notation.
2 There is a quantity conserving change at all three levels from the initial representation, 324, to the representation with decomposition, 200 plus 110 plus 14.
3 The subtraction process yields the same relationships at all three levels. For example, at the top level, when we remove a hundreds block from a set of 2 hundreds blocks, the result is 1 hundreds block. Similarly, at the next level, when we subtract 100 from 200, the result is 100. Similarly again, at the lowest level, subtracting a 1 in the hundreds column from a 2 in the hundreds column yields a 1 in the hundreds column. Thus the same relationships obtain at each of the three levels. This is also true for tens and units. It is the fact that the same set of relations holds at all three levels that provides the justification for the arithmetical procedure. The problem is that children will not recognize the justification unless they can see this complex set of relationships. If the justification is not understood, the concrete analogues may be worse than useless, because they are extra things to learn, they take time to manipulate, and cause distraction.

Taken over all, there is a very complex set of relationships. It is really a composite of numerous lower-level mappings. It entails more information than even an adult could process in parallel if the capacity theory outlined above is correct, so no adults could make the complete mapping in a single step. For both adults and children it would have to be learned, component by component. When we see the complexity of the mapping task, it becomes obvious why processing loads entailed in making the mapping could be impossibly high. The already complex mapping is further complicated by the fact that in this structure mapping there are two levels of representation, the concrete level and the quantity level. There is also a mapping from one to the other so that, for instance, 3 hundreds blocks represents the quantity 300, which is then mapped into the numeral 3 in the hundreds columns. As we have seen, structure mapping imposes a processing load, and if this load is excessive it will constitute a barrier to understanding. Some way must therefore be found to reduce the processing load so the concrete analogue can be useful.

There are at least two ways that the processing load can be reduced. One is by pre-learning the mappings. For example, children can be taught that a hundreds block (flat) represents hundreds, and relates to the hundreds column. Knowing this so it can be retrieved automatically from memory removes the processing load entailed in making the mapping. Much practice is required, however, to make this retrieval automatic. The other way to reduce processing loads is to recode the relationships into more abstract form. As Biggs (1968) has noted, the multibase arithmetic blocks were intended to teach abstract concepts such as power and place value. The problem, however, is that abstraction is not a process that can be taken for granted, but must itself be explained. Therefore we will consider how abstractions might arise from experience with concrete analogues in the next section, and we can assess the processing loads this entails.

STRUCTURE MAPPING AND ABSTRACTION

The processes by which abstractions are developed out of experience form a major problem at the very cutting edge of our discipline. For example, Holland *et al*. (1986) present a sophisticated model of induction, the process by which general rules are acquired through experience with specific instances. Another major problem is to explain how people progress from representing constants to representing variables. This, and the recoding issue generally, are discussed by Clark (1989), Karmiloff-Smith (1987), and Smolensky (1988). We will not summarize this issue here, except to say that the problem of how abstractions develop is far from solved. However, we will try to indicate how mapping from one structure to another might contribute to the development of abstraction.

We will develop the argument by reference to the distributive law of multiplication with respect to addition: $a(b + c) = (a \times b) + (a \times c)$. We would propose that children, and most adults, understand this rule primarily in terms of specific examples. That is, they do not understand the rationale that is provided by pure mathematicians, but have a more pragmatic, experience-based rationale. This hypothesis is consistent with the virtually ubiquitous finding that natural human reasoning is not based on formal principles of general validity, but on pragmatic schemas that have some degree of generality, but are not universal (Cheng and Holyoak 1985; Halford in press; Shaklee 1979).

A child, or for that matter an adult, might recognize the validity of the distributive law by testing it against a specific example. They might note that, for instance, $3(2 + 1) = (3 \times 2) + (3 \times 1)$. Understanding the validity of the law means recognizing the correspondence between the law and one or more specific examples. This is tantamount to recognition of structural correspondence: that is, it amounts to recognizing the structural correspondence between the example and the law.

Structure-mapping analyses are a conceptual tool for expressing structural correspondences. The process of recognizing the correspondence between the law and an example can be expressed by the structure-mapping diagram in Figure 10.7G. In terms of analogy theory, the example becomes the source (shown in the top line of the mapping) and the law is the target (in the bottom line of the mapping). The fact that the law can be mapped into a number of examples, and corresponds to those examples, is the major reason for regarding the rule as justified. It is therefore understood by analogy, but it is an analogy between a general rule and one or more examples of that rule. This might not be a conventional way to use the term analogy, but the structure-mapping processes are those of analogies.

The only additional step that is likely to be made is to check for counter-examples; the rule is accepted as valid if no example can be retrieved that does not fit it. To illustrate, we might recognize that commutativity of subtraction, $(a - b) = (b - a)$, is not valid because $(3 - 2) \neq (2 - 3)$. That is, we can produce a counter-example, or a case that cannot be mapped into the rule. As Johnson-Laird (1983) has pointed out, seeking counter-examples is one of the more sophisticated aspects of natural reasoning processes.

The process of learning the general algebraic rule is partly a matter of replacing constants by variables. That is, the specific example $3(2 + 1) = (3 \times 2) + (3 \times 1)$ is replaced by $a(b + c) = (a \times b) + (a \times c)$, in which each constant is replaced by a variable. But, as we said before, this has proved to be one of the most difficult processes for cognitive psychologists to explain, and we cannot take it for granted. We suggest, however, that structure mapping can play a role in this process. This can be demonstrated in a very general sense, and also in terms of specific examples.

At the general level, structure mapping means that specific examples of structures can be mapped into one another. This is illustrated in Figure 10.7E, where two specific instances of the distributive law are mapped into one another. The mapping is valid because the two structures are isomorphic, and mapped in such a way that they correspond. Correspondence is defined by consistency; two structures correspond if each element in one structure is mapped into one and only one element in the other structure, and if relations between elements in one structure correspond to relations between the image elements in the other structure. More generally, a predicate P in structure A corresponds to a predicate P' in structure B if and only if the arguments P are mapped into the arguments of P' and vice versa (Halford in press).

When two structures are mapped into one another, the structure itself remains constant, but the elements vary. As we see in Figure 10.7E, there are two identical structures, but the specific elements are different. Therefore structure mappings can simulate variables, because they permit a structure to be maintained while the instantiation of each part of it changes. A mapping such as Figure 10.7E does not literally contain variables, but it can

Value and limitations of analogues in teaching mathematics 201

certainly simulate the use of variables in at least some contexts, and can be a step towards the acquisition of variables, as we will see. Furthermore, structure-mapping processes are understood at quite a deep level. Holyoak and Thagard (1987) have produced a computer simulation of structure mapping based on parallel constraint-satisfaction mechanisms which explains structure mapping in terms of the very basic processes of excitation and inhibition. Whereas abstraction per se remains something of a mystery to cognitive science, and is therefore a poor basis for explanation, structure mapping is much better understood, and provides a much more solid foundation on which to build explanations.

Another reason why structure mappings aid the abstraction process is that only the common aspects of the structures tend to be mapped, and surplus attributes and relations are deleted. When discussing analogy theory earlier

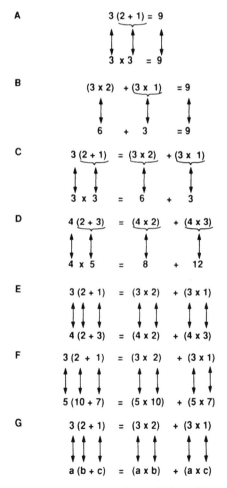

Figure 10.7 Structure-mapping analysis of acquisition of the distributive law

we pointed out that in the man–house:dog–kennel analogy attributes of man are not mapped into dog, and only certain relations between man and house are mapped into dog–kennel. Thus structure mapping is inherently selective in a way which is useful in creation of abstractions.

Now let us trace through a possible sequence of steps that might be entailed in acquiring the distributive law through structure mapping. Some hypothetical steps are shown in Figure 10.7. As mentioned earlier, we propose that the law is understood by recognizing the correspondence that it has to some specific examples. But there are knowledge prerequisites for this understanding, and these are briefly sketched in Figure 10.7.

In Figure 10.7A, we represent the child's knowledge that $3(2 + 1) = 9$. This knowledge must be acquired through calculation, and the child must learn to interpret and manipulate parentheses and operation symbols in arithmetic expressions. There is therefore procedural knowledge that must be acquired. Our concern here, however, is primarily to express the conceptual knowledge that underlies the procedural knowledge. We can express this conceptual knowledge that $3(2 + 1) = 9$ corresponds to $3 \times 3 = 9$: that is, process the operation in parentheses, which yields 3, then process the operation represented by the numeral which precedes the parentheses. This knowledge that $3(2 + 1) = 9$ corresponds to $3 \times 3 = 9$ can, like other structural correspondences, be represented as a structure mapping, as shown in Figure 10.7A. Note that, once again, structure mapping is a conceptual tool for analysing structural correspondences, and does not represent a process model as such.

The next step is for the child to recognize that $(3 \times 2) + (3 \times 1) = 9$ corresponds to $6 + 3 = 9$. This is represented as a structure mapping in Figure 10.7B. This is essentially similar to the process in Figure 10.7B. It is a major step from there however to recognize that $3(2 + 1) = (3 \times 2) + (3 \times 1)$. Understanding this depends on recognizing that it corresponds to $3 \times 3 = 6 + 3$, which is shown as a structure mapping in Figure 10.7C. The child already knows that $3 \times 3 = 9 = 6 + 3$, because of previous experiences of this kind shown in Figure 10.7A and 10.7B. Therefore the known relationship, $3 \times 3 = 6 + 3$, can serve as a mental model that enables the child to understand $3(2 + 1) = (3 \times 2) + (3 \times 1)$. For this understanding to occur, the child must recognize the structural correspondence between the kinds of expressions, as shown in Figure 10.7C.

The next step is probably to acquire further examples of this correspondence. Another example is shown in Figure 10.7D. Furthermore, Figure 10.7E expresses the correspondence between a new example and the original example. The idea here is that a child might adopt one prototypical example and compare it with other examples, recognizing the correspondence between the prototype and numerous other examples. The prototype then becomes a kind of template for the general rule. A further example of this process is shown in Figure 10.7F.

The final step occurs when the child recognizes the correspondence between the prototype arithmetic example and the general rule. An additional process is required here, because the child must know that letters can be used to represent unknown numbers. This fact would normally be taught in other ways, such as showing children how to draw a container representing an unknown number of objects, then teaching them how to write a letter to represent the unknown number of objects. Assuming the child has already learned to represent unknown numbers by letters, the step in Figure 10.7G can be taken once the correspondence between the algebraic law and the arithmetical example can be recognized.

The fact that letters can represent unknown numbers is a component of the domain knowledge that is required to learn the algebraic law, but it does not explain how the algebraic rule is understood. The point that we have wanted to illustrate through this extended example is that understanding depends on recognition of the correspondence between the algebraic rule and one or more reference examples. Structure-mapping analyses of this correspondence show that it depends on a series of multiple system mappings. The processing loads are therefore quite high, and that is the next subject we must consider.

ABSTRACTION, STRUCTURE MAPPING, AND PROCESSING LOADS

If our analysis is correct, acquisition of an abstraction entails quite high processing loads, because it entails recognizing the correspondence structures that exemplify that abstraction. In our example based on the distributive law, it is necessary to see the correspondence between different instantiations of the law, and also between one prototypical instantiation and the algebraic expression of the law. Evidence mentioned earlier indicates that humans have limited capacity to recognize correspondence between structures, and adults can probably process in parallel only correspondences between four-dimensional structures, equivalent to one quaternary operation. Children of one year can probably process structures based on only one dimension in parallel, children of 2 years on two dimensions, children of 5 years on three dimensions. This subject has been discussed in detail elsewhere (Halford in press).

Because we can recognize correspondence between structures of only limited complexity, we have other ways of processing structures. One way, as noted above, is to learn correspondences: that is, we learn which component of one structure maps into which component of another structure. Once these mappings are learned they no longer impose a processing load. The other way is to recode the correspondences in a more abstract form. This reduces the processing load once the abstraction is achieved but, as we have seen, the processing loads can be high during acquisition because of the correspondences that must be recognized.

204 Applications in specific domains

In order to reduce this load it is critically important that each correspondence is learned before progressing to the next. That is, the correspondence in Figure 10.7A must be learned before progressing to the one in Figure 10.7B, which must be learned before progressing to the correspondence in Figure 10.7C, and so on. Furthermore, the learning must be such that retrieval is automatic, so that no load is imposed. The load imposed by one structure mapping must be reduced to zero before the next structure mapping is undertaken, otherwise the cumulative load will become excessive.

Conceptual chunking can also be used to reduce processing loads. What we call an abstraction is often better conceptualized as a conceptual chunk. For example, the complex relationships in Figure 10.6 can be recoded as a conceptual chunk. The chunk consists of the idea of a number, to which decomposition can be applied, resulting in an equal number but differently configured, then subtraction is applied yielding a new number. This is a very simple set of relationships, and in itself it imposes quite a low processing load. It is equivalent to two successive relational mappings. It produces great gains in processing load by constraining more complex mappings. For example, number is mapped, or can be decomposed, into hundreds, tens, and units. The decomposition relation between two numbers at the abstract level constrains the operations that are performed on the hundreds, tens, and units; if the tens are reduced by 1, the units must be incremented by 10, and so on. The fact that the abstract concept of decomposition constrains us to adjust tens and units in this way can be learned, and when it is learned the conceptual chunk greatly reduces the processing load. This reduction does not come about automatically however, but only by learning some complex relationships. Once acquired it produces massive gains in efficiency.

ABSTRACTION OF PLACE VALUE

The multibase arithmetic blocks were designed partly to facilitate understanding of power and place value, and therefore different bases were used. Figure 10.8 shows the correspondence between base-10 and base-2 blocks. In each case the relation between a unit and a long is an increase from the zero to the first power. The relation between a long and a flat is an increase from the first to the second power. The same relationship occurs in base-10 and base-2 blocks. Notice that this correspondence is easily expressed as a structure-mapping diagram, and doing so shows that it is much simpler than the correspondence involved in the subtraction algorithm. Recognition of correspondence between the structure of base-10 and the structure of base-2 (or other bases) is an important component of abstraction. 'Raising to the next power' is the relation that is common to both structures, and this concept can be extracted by seeing the correspondence between the structures. This is another illustration of the point made earlier that analogies are

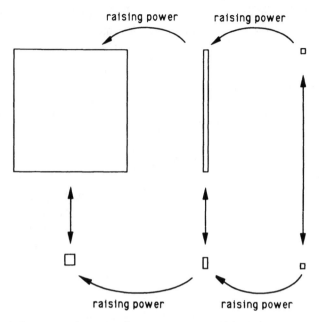

Figure 10.8 Correspondence between base-10 and base-2

useful for promoting abstractions, because they entail selectively mapping those relations that are common to both structures.

MULTIPLE EMBODIMENT

One principle which Dienes (1964) has advocated is multiple embodiment. The general idea is that the same principle is instantiated in different materials. This helps abstraction because it leads to focusing on the common features of the instantiations, to the exclusion of idiosyncratic features. A structure-mapping analysis can help to explain this process, and also leads to some insights as to how it should be employed.

A technique which has been observed in schools is to replace multibase arithmetic blocks by paddle-pop sticks. Units are represented by individual sticks, and tens by bundles of ten sticks bound together. A stick then corresponds to a unit block, and a bundle of sticks to a long. In both cases the representations are raised from the zero to the first power. A structure-mapping analysis shows that such multiple embodiments are useful only if the child sees the correspondence between the two structures. Putting it another way, the child must recognize the analogy. If the analogy is not recognized then the extra embodiment is worse than useless, because it is actually a distraction. Thus play, or the use of manipulative materials, may not achieve the desired acquisition. Analogy theory, particularly as applied

206 Applications in specific domains

to children (see Halford in press, for a review), can be used to predict the conditions under which recognition of the analogy is most likely to be achieved.

STRUCTURE-MAPPING THEORY AND PEDAGOGY

We have presented a number of examples designed to show how structure-mapping theory can be a useful way of analysing what needs to be understood, the loads imposed in such understanding, and ways of reducing those loads. Although this paper is not primarily about teaching methods we will consider briefly how the correspondence in Figure 10.7A might be taught. The idea would be to show children how to compute the number inside the parentheses, then multiply it by the number outside the parentheses, i.e., '2 + 1 = 3, 3 × 3 = 9', then point out that 3(2 + 1) = 9 is the same as 3 × 3 = 9. Children would need multiple exercises with this relationship until they could retrieve it automatically.

Correspondence between abstractions

Structure mapping can be used to represent correspondence between abstractions. For example, recognition of correspondence between equations can be represented as a structure mapping. The equation $AX = b$ corresponds to the equation $A(X + b) = c$, if the following mappings are made:

A in equation 1 is mapped to A in equation 2;
X in equation 1 is mapped to (X + b) in equation 2;
b in equation 1 is mapped to c in equation 2.

This correspondence can help a child understand the more complex equation by recognizing its relation to a simpler equation.

This illustrates the general point that structure mapping is not used only to represent correspondences between concrete analogues and arithmetic. It can be used to represent correspondences between any two isomorphic structures. The type of structure depends on the domain. When teaching arithmetical relations, concrete analogues are useful models. When teaching elementary algebra, previously learned arithmetical relations are useful models. With more advanced algebra, previously learned algebraic concepts are useful models. The appropriate mapping is between a previously learned model, treated as source, and the new concept, treated as target. Thus we are proposing an inductive concept of mathematics learning, in which previously learned concepts are used as mental models of new, higher-level concepts. This induction process depends heavily on recognition of correspondence between the mental model and the new concept. We use structure mapping to analyse the correspondences that are required and to provide estimates of their complexity.

CONCLUSIONS

We have used analogy theory and the theory of cognitive representations to analyse some problems in mathematics education. We have shown that concrete aids that exemplify mathematical concepts are technically analogues, and they can be analysed by specifying the structure mapping from external analogue to mental representation of the concept. This does not imply that children should be taught to draw structure-mapping diagrams. It means that pedagogy should be adjusted to take account of the insights gained from structure-mapping analyses. Such analyses help us to understand why some analogues are likely to be more efficient than others. Furthermore, they make it possible to analyse the processing loads that use of such analogues can impose. Perhaps most important of all, they emphasize that analogues of any kind are useless unless children see the correspondence between the analogue and the concept.

Research into structure mapping shows that humans have limited capacity to recognize correspondence between two structures. Adults can probably process only four-dimensional structures in parallel, and children can process structures of less dimensionality than adults. Our research indicates that the dimensionality of structures that children can process in parallel increases from one at age one year, two at age 2 years, three at age 5 years, and the adult ability to process four-dimensional structures is acquired at 11 years. The wider implications of this for cognitive development are considered elsewhere (Halford in press). In most contexts this limitation is overcome by using pre-learned correspondences between structures, by recoding structures so they are defined over fewer dimensions, or by segmenting problems and using a mixture of serial and parallel processing. The limitation affects performance only where one of these strategies cannot be used. This occurs where at least one of the structures is new and cannot be decomposed.

Much of mathematics learning entails acquisition of progressively more abstract concepts. Abstraction reduces processing loads, but we propose that abstractions are acquired by induction from examples. For this to occur, children must be able to see the correspondence between different examples of the same abstraction, and also between an example and the abstract rule. Unless this correspondence is recognized the rule is not really understood. Structure mapping can be used to analyse these correspondences. In general, structure mapping is important in acquisition of abstractions because it simulates the use of variables and leads to selection of attributes and relations that are common to different examples of the same concept.

We propose that mathematics is learned by using previously acquired concepts as mental models for later, more abstract concepts. Elementary number concepts are probably learned using concrete external experiences with sets as mental models. Elementary algebraic concepts are acquired by using previously learned number concepts based on constants as mental models. Some higher-level algebraic concepts are acquired using previously learned algebraic concepts as mental models. This progression from concrete experiences to increasingly abstract concepts depends, at each step, on recognition of correspondences between earlier concepts and later ones. Therefore recognition of correspondences between structures, which we analyse in terms of structure-mapping theory, is central to mathematics learning at all levels.

ACKNOWLEDGEMENT

This work was supported by a grant from the Australian Research Grants Scheme.

REFERENCES

Biggs, J. B. (1968) *Information and Human Learning*, Melbourne: Cassell.
Broadbent, D. E. (1975) 'The magic number seven after fifteen years', in A. Kennedy and A. Wilkes (eds) *Studies in Long Term Memory*, London: Wiley, pp. 3–18.
Carey, S. (1985) *Conceptual Change in Childhood*, Cambridge, MA: MIT Press.
Cheng, P. W. and Holyoak, K. J. (1985) 'Pragmatic reasoning schemas', *Cognitive Psychology* 17: 391–416.
Clark, A. (1989) 'Connectionism, non-conceptual content and representational redescription', unpublished paper, University of Sussex, Brighton.
Collis, K. F. (1978) 'Implications of the Piagetian model for mathematics teaching', in J. A. Keats, K. F. Collis, and G. S. Halford (eds) *Cognitive Development: Research Based on a Neo-Piagetian Approach*, London: Wiley, pp. 249–83.
Dienes, Z. P. (1964) *Mathematics in the Primary School*, Melbourne: Macmillan.
Dufour-Janvier, B., Bednarz, N., and Belanger, M. (1987) 'Pedagogical considerations concerning the problem of representation', in C. Janvier (ed.) *Problems of Representation in the Teaching and Learning of Mathematics*, Hillsdale, NJ: Erlbaum, pp. 109–22.
Fisher, D. L. (1984) 'Central capacity limits in consistent mapping, visual search tasks: four channels or more?', *Cognitive Psychology* 16 (4): 449–84.
Gentner, D. (1982) 'Are scientific analogies metaphors?', in D. S. Miall (ed.) *Metaphor: Problems and Perspectives*, Brighton: Harvester Press, pp. 106–32.
—— (1983) 'Structure-mapping: a theoretical framework for analogy', *Cognitive Science* 7: 155–70.
Halford, G. S. (1982) *The Development of Thought*, Hillsdale, NJ: Erlbaum.
—— (1987) 'A structure-mapping approach to cognitive development', *International Journal of Psychology* 22: 609–42.
—— (1989) 'Reflections on 25 years of Piagetian cognitive developmental psychology, 1963–1989', *Human Development*, 32: 325–57.
—— (in press) *Children's Understanding: The Development of Mental Models*, Hillsdale, NJ: Erlbaum.
Halford, G. S. and Wilson, W. H. (1980) 'A category theory approach to cognitive development', *Cognitive Psychology* 12: 346–411.
Halford, G. S., Maybery, M. T., and Bain, J. D. (1986) 'Capacity limitations in children's reasoning: a dual task approach', *Child Development* 57: 616–27.

—— (1988) 'Set-size effects in primary memory: an age-related capacity limitation?', *Memory and Cognition* 16 (5): 480–7.
Holland, J. H., Holyoak, K. J., Nisbett, R. E. and Thagard, P. R. (1986) *Induction: Processes of Inference, Learning and Discovery*, Cambridge, MA: Bradford Books/ MIT Press.
Holyoak, K. J. and Thagard, P. (1987) 'Analogical mapping by constraint satisfactions', unpublished manuscript, University of California, Los Angeles, CA.
Holyoak, K. J., Koh, K., and Nisbett, R. E. (in press) 'A theory of conditioning: inductive learning within rule-based default hierarchies', *Psychological Review*.
Johnson-Laird, P. N. (1983) *Mental Models*, Cambridge: Cambridge University Press.
Karmiloff-Smith, A. (1987) 'Beyond modularity: a developmental perspective on human consciousness', paper presented at the Annual Meeting of the British Psychological Society, Sussex, April.
Leeuwenberg, E. L. L. (1969) 'Quantitative specification of information in sequential patterns', *Psychological Review* 76: 216–20.
Lesh, R., Behr, M., and Post, T. (1987) 'Rational number relations and proportions', in C. Janvier (ed.) *Problems of Representation in the Teaching and Learning of Mathematics*, Hillsdale, NJ: Erlbaum, pp. 41–58.
McGarrigle, J., Grieve, R., and Hughes, M. (1978) 'Interpreting inclusion: a contribution to the study of the child's cognitive and linguistic development', *Journal of Experimental Child Psychology* 26: 528–50.
Maybery, M. T., Bain, J. D., and Halford, G. S. (1986) 'Information processing demands of transitive inference', *Journal of Experimental Psychology: Learning, Memory and Cognition* 12: 600–13.
Miller, G. A. (1956) 'The magical number seven, plus or minus two: some limits on our capacity for processing information', *Psychological Review* 63: 81–97.
Palmer, S. E. (1978) 'Fundamental aspects of cognitive representation', in E. Rosch and B. B. Lloyd (eds) *Cognition and Categorization*, Hillsdale, NJ: Erlbaum, pp. 259–303.
Resnick, L. B. and Omanson, S. F. (1984) 'Learning to understand arithmetic', in R. Glasser (ed.) *Advances in Instructional Psychology*, Vol. 3, Hillsdale, NJ: Erlbaum.
Rumelhart, D. E. and McClelland, J. L. (eds) (1986) *Parallel Distributed Processing: Explorations in the Microstructure of Cognition*, Boston, MA: MIT Press.
Schneider, W. and Detweiler, M. (1987) 'A connectionist/control architecture for working memory', *The Psychology of Learning and Motivation* 21: 53–119.
Shaklee, H. (1979) 'Bounded rationality and cognitive development: upper limits on growth', *Cognitive Psychology* 11: 327–45.
Siegel, L. S., McCabe, A. E., Brand, J., and Matthews, J. (1978) 'Evidence for the understanding of class inclusion in preschool children: linguistic factors and training effects', *Child Development* 49: 688–93.
Siegler, R. S. and Shrager, J. (1984) 'Strategy choices in addition and subtraction: how do children know what to do?', in C. Sophian (ed.) *Origins of Cognitive Skills*, Hillsdale, NJ: Erlbaum, pp. 229–93.
Simon, H. A. (1972) 'Complexity and the representation of patterned sequences of symbols', *Psychological Review* 79: 369–82.
Smolensky, P. (1988) 'On the proper treatment of connectionism', *Behavioral and Brain Sciences* 11 (1): 1–74.

Chapter 11

Developing thinking abilities in arithmetic class

Lauren B. Resnick, Victoria Bill, and Sharon Lesgold

This chapter reports on an intervention study that began as an effort to apply theory and data from two long-standing lines of research in developmental and learning psychology: how reasoning and thinking abilities develop and might be cultivated in school; and how particular mathematical concepts, such as number, develop. During our intervention work, we realized that a new theoretical direction was increasingly dominating our thinking about the nature of development, learning, and schooling. This is the view, shared by a growing minority of thinkers in the various disciplines comprised in cognitive science, that human mental functioning must be understood as fundamentally situation-specific and context-dependent, rather than as a collection of abstracted-from-use abilities and knowledge. This apparently simple shift in perspective in fact turns out to entail reconsideration of a number of long-held assumptions in psychology and education. We will point to several of these in the course of this chapter, even as we focus most directly on a school intervention programme and its early effects.

Virtually all psychologists of cognition, whether they come from an individual difference, a developmental, or an information-processing perspective, share the view that it is essential to try to identify individuals' thinking and reasoning *competencies* independently of their *performances* on any particular occasion. Individual difference theorists (e.g., Demetriou, Efklides, and Gustafsson in this volume) aim to define competence in terms of clusters of abilities, some specific to particular domains of knowledge or modes of representation, some more general and thought to play a role in managing and monitoring the cognitive system. Individuals' ability structures are understood to change as a result of experience, including study at school. However, it is assumed that abilities can be sensibly described without reference to the particular situations in which they were acquired or might be used. In this view it makes sense to describe people as *having* a particular set of abilities at a given time – a set that can be inferred from the individual's pattern of performances on a set of tests designed to tap indirectly the different clusters of abilities. The predictive capacity of the tests with respect to subsequent school or work performance is taken as evidence that they are measuring abilities that are real attributes of individuals.

Information-processing psychology has shared the view that thinking abilities are mental capacities that are owned by the individual, without reference to conditions of use. Early seminal work on the cognitive processes entailed in problem solving (Newell and Simon 1972) aimed to uncover the exact processes used in solving particular problems. Originally, puzzle-like problems requiring little knowledge of a domain were preferred, because these were thought to reveal in a relatively pure form the processes involved in all human thought. In an effort to link information processing with individual difference research, the tools and concepts of information-processing psychology were extended during the 1970s and early 1980s to cognitive analyses of performance on ability and aptitude tests (e.g., Pellegrino and Glaser 1982; Sternberg 1977). Processes identified in these analyses subsequently became the target of direct instruction in courses of generalized problem-solving skills and higher-order thinking (e.g., Sternberg 1986). However, as Resnick (1987a) pointed out in an analysis of the prospects for teaching higher-order thinking skills, although there have been successes in raising ability test scores as a result of such training, there is no evidence that people then apply the taught abilities to real-world or school-learning situations. Recent advances in research on thinking and problem solving in various domains of subject-matter learning and technical performance show interactive connections between acquired structures of knowledge and cognitive processes (see Glaser 1984; Klahr and Kotovsky 1989). The results of this newer work have suggested the need for close consideration of the teaching of thinking in the context of specific domains.

In developmental psychology, under the long-term influence of Piaget and other structural theorists, the attribution of generic abilities to individuals has taken a somewhat different form. Here the argument had long been that intelligence can be described as the development of certain basic logical capacities – the 'structures of thought' in the classic Piagetian formulation. According to Piaget, the logical stage (preoperational, concrete operational, formal operational) that a child has achieved defines the kind of mental processes available to the child and, thus, basically controls what kinds of specific problems he or she will be able to solve. The particular content of the problems is not central or defining of the child's ability. Application of the structural model of the development of thinking to education initially led to efforts to teach children to think operationally, sometimes by training them directly on the tasks used to estimate the level of logical development in Piagetian research. These efforts were largely abandoned as it became increasingly clear that evidence would not support a strict stage theory, because performance on different tasks presumably within the same stage of competence could be extremely variable. The strict stage theory position has been substantially modified in a number of neo-Piagetian theories, several of which are represented in this volume (e.g., Bidell and Fischer; Biggs; Case). Most developmental psychologists now recognize that specific knowledge *in addition* to logical competence and/or general mental capacity is required. Considerable effort on the part of some neo-Piagetians (see Case, Chapter 3, this volume) is now directed towards uncovering powerful guiding knowledge schemata that are thought to organize thinking and learning in a particular domain of knowledge.

All three strands of psychological theory, then – the differential, the information processing, and the developmental/structuralist – have come to recognize that both specific knowledge and general competencies are needed to account for the varied performances of individuals. All three, however, continue to assume that abilities and knowledge are both encapsulated within individuals and can successfully be defined without reference to the conditions of their use. Although some admit that variations in motivation and context may account for whether or not a designated ability or piece of knowledge is applied on a given occasion (e.g., Bidell and Fischer, Chapter 1, this volume), few question the fundamental distinction between performance and competence. They continue to view the task of cognitive psychology as building improved accounts of the structure of competence so that, eventually, we will become able to predict performance far better than we do now, as a function of defined competencies interacting with specific motives and contexts.

Our work is premised on a shift in focus that denies a fundamental distinction between competence and performance and seeks to understand cognition not as sets of competencies-in-the-head but as forms of cultural practice. We were first led in this direction by Resnick's (1987a) review of research and practical efforts to teach higher-order thinking skills, which concluded that shaping a disposition to critical thought is as important in developing higher-order cognitive abilities in students as is teaching particular skills of reasoning and thinking. Acquiring such dispositions, it was proposed, requires regular participation in activities that exercise reasoning skills, within social environments that value thinking and judgement and that communicate to children a sense of their own competence in reasoning and thinking. This, in turn, seemed to call for educational programmes suffused with thinking and reasoning, programmes in which basic subject-matter instruction served as the daily occasion for exercising and extending cognitive abilities.

It quickly became clear that to apply this line of reasoning to school mathematics we had to design a new set of cultural practices for the mathematics classroom. We found ourselves less and less asking what constitutes mathematics *competence* or *ability* for young schoolchildren, and more and more analysing the situations for performance afforded by the mathematics classroom. This focus on mathematics as a form of cultural practice does not deny that children engaging in mathematical activity must be knowledgeable and skilful in many ways; indeed, a key prerequisite for beginning our work was to learn a good deal about what mathematical knowledge we could count on as we attempted to draw children into new forms of mathematical behaviour. However, our perspective led us to focus far less on the design of a curriculum and lessons than on the development of an environment for the practice of mathematics.

What we wanted to create was an environment in which children would practise mathematics as a field in which there are open questions and arguments, in which interpretation, reasoning, and debate – all key components of critical thought – play a legitimate and expected role. To do this we needed to revise mathematics teaching in the direction of treating mathematics as if it were an ill-structured discipline (Resnick 1989b). That is, we needed to take seriously, with and for young learners, the propositions that mathematical statements can have more than one interpretation, that interpretation is the responsibility of every individual using mathematical expressions, and that argument and debate about interpretations and their implications are a normal part of mathematical activity. Participating in such an environment would, we thought, develop capabilities and dispositions for finding relationships among mathematical entities and between mathematical statements and problem situations. It would develop skill not only in applying mathematics but also in thinking mathematically. In short, it would socialize children into a developmentally appropriate form of the cultural practice of mathematics as a mode of thought, reasoning, and problem solving.

This theoretically driven venture led to a number of very practical questions to which our work was also addressed. Among these were: How early can such a programme begin? Is it necessary, as many would argue, to first teach 'basic knowledge' (e.g., basic number combinations and arithmetic procedures) before children will have anything to reason *about*? Can an interpretation- and discussion-orientated programme serve as the basic curriculum in arithmetic, or must we view it as only an adjunct to a more traditional knowledge and skills curriculum? Is an interpretation-oriented mathematics programme suitable for all children or only for the educationally able and socially favoured?

We begin our account by sketching the theory of the intuitive origins of mathematical thinking that provided initial grounds for our belief that children entering school already know enough to begin to participate in a reasoning-based mathematics programme. Next we describe the programme itself, followed by evidence on its effects. We conclude with some broad considerations about the design and functioning of cognitive apprenticeship environments in school.

THE INTUITIVE BASIS FOR EARLY MATHEMATICAL REASONING

A substantial body of research accumulated over the past decade has suggested that almost all children come to school with a substantial body of knowledge about quantity relations and that children are capable of using this knowledge as a foundation for understanding numbers and arithmetic (see Resnick 1989a; Resnick and Greeno 1990, for interpretative views). Knowledge developed prior to school includes understanding of some basic relations involving quantitative properties of objects, along with knowledge of the rules for counting sets of objects.

Protoquantitative schemata

During the preschool years, children develop a large store of knowledge about how quantities of physical material behave in the world. This knowledge, acquired from manipulating and talking about physical material, allows children to make judgements about comparative amounts and sizes and to reason about changes in amounts and quantities. Because this early reasoning about quantity is done without measurement or exact numerical quantification, we refer to it as *proto*quantitative reasoning. We can document development, during the preschool years, of three sets of protoquantitative schemata: *compare, increase/decrease,* and *part/whole* (see Figure 11.1).

The *protoquantitative compare* schema makes greater–smaller comparative judgements of amounts of material. Before they are 2 years old, children express quantity judgements in the form of absolute size labels such as *big, small, lots,* and *little.* Only a little later, they begin to put linguistic labels on the comparisons of sizes they made as infants (Clark 1983). Thus, they can look at two circles and declare one bigger than the other, see two trees and declare one taller than the other, examine two glasses of milk and declare that one contains more than the other. These comparisons are initially based on direct perceptual judgements without any measurement process. However, they form a basis for eventual numerical comparisons of quantity.

The *protoquantitative increase/decrease* schema interprets changes as increases or decreases in quantities. This schema allows children as young as 3 or 4 years of age to reason about the effects of adding or taking away an amount from a starting amount. Children know, for example, that, if they have a certain amount of something, and they get another amount of the same thing (perhaps mother adds another cookie to the two already on the child's plate), they have more than before. Or, if some of the original quantity is taken away, they have less than before. Equally important, children know that, if nothing has been added or taken away, they have the same amount as before. For example, children show surprise and label as 'magic' any change in the number of objects on a plate that occurs out of

Developing thinking abilities in arithmetic class 215

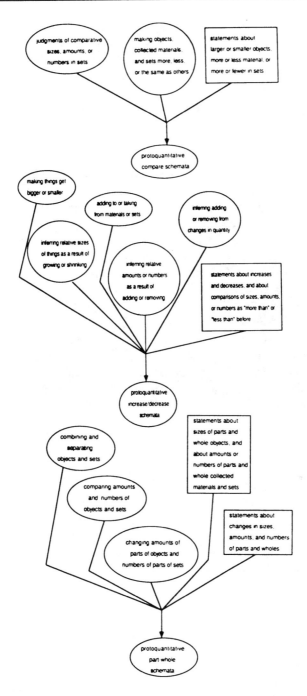

Figure 11.1 The protoquantitative schemas
Source: Adapted from Resnick and Greeno 1990

their sight (Gelman 1972). This shows that children have the underpinnings of number conservation well before they can pass the standard Piagetian tests. They can be fooled by perceptual cues or language that distracts them from quantity, but they possess a basic understanding of addition, subtraction, and conservation. The protoquantitative increase/decrease schema is also the foundation for eventual understanding of unary addition and subtraction.

The *protoquantitative part-whole* schema is really a set of schemata that organize children's knowledge about the ways in which material around them comes apart and goes together. The schemata specify that material is *additive*. That is, one can cut a quantity into pieces that, taken together, equal the original quantity. One can also put two quantities together to make a bigger quantity and then join that bigger quantity with yet another in a form of hierarchical additivity. Implicitly children know about this additive property of quantities. This protoquantitative knowledge allows them to make judgements about the relations between parts and wholes, including class inclusion (Fuson *et al.* 1988; Markman and Siebert 1976) and the effects of changes in the size of parts on the size of the whole (Irwin 1990). The protoquantitative part/whole schema is the foundation for later understanding of binary addition and subtraction and for several fundamental mathematical principles such as the commutativity and associativity of addition and the complementary of addition and subtraction. It also provides the framework for a concept of additive composition of number that underlies the place-value system (Resnick and Omanson 1987).

Counting

Counting, a culturally transmitted formal system, is the first step in making quantitative judgements exact. It is a measurement system for sets. Gelman and her colleagues have done the seminal work analysing what it means to understand counting, showing that children as young as 3 or 4 years of age implicitly know the key principles that allow counting to serve as a vehicle of quantification (Gelman and Gallistel 1978). These principles include the knowledge that number names must be matched one-for-one with the objects in a set and that the order of the number names matters, but the order in which the objects are touched does not. Knowledge of these principles is inferred from the ways in which children solve novel counting problems. For example, if asked to make the second object in a row 'number 1', children do not neglect the first object entirely but, rather, assign it one of the higher number names in the sequence.

Other research has challenged Gelman's assessment of the ages at which children can be said to have acquired all of the counting principles. Some of the challenges are really arguments about the criteria for applying certain terms. For example, Gelman has attributed knowledge of *cardinality*, a key mathematical principle, to children as soon as they know that the last number in a counting sequence names the quantity in the whole set; others would reserve the term for a more advanced stage in which children reliably conserve quantity under perceptual transformations. A challenge that goes beyond matters of terminology comes from research showing that, although children may know all of the principles of counting and be able to use counting to quantify given sets of objects or to create sets of specified sizes, they may not, at a certain point, have fully integrated their counting knowledge with their protoquantitative knowledge. Several investigators (e.g., Michie 1984; Saxe 1977; Siegler 1981; Sophian 1987) have shown that many children who know how to count sets do not spontaneously count in order to compare sets. This means that counting and the protoquantitative schemata exist initially as separate knowledge systems, isolated from each other.

Integrating counting with the protoquantitative schemata

Such findings make it clear that, even after knowledge of counting principles is established, there is substantially more growth in number concepts still to be attained. A first major step in this growth is integration of the number-name sequence with the protoquantitative comparison schema. This seems to happen as young as about 4 years of age. At this point, children behave as if the counting word sequence constitutes a kind of 'mental number line' (Resnick 1983). They can quickly identify which of a pair of numbers is more by mentally consulting this number line, without actually stepping through the sequence to determine which number comes later.

In the child's subsequent development, counting as a means of quantifying sets is integrated with the protoquantitative part–whole and increase–decrease schemata. This integration seems to develop as a result of participating in situations in which changes and combinations of quantity are called for and there is a cultural mandate for counting exact quantification. Out of school, this can occur in various play or household activities – particularly when age segregation is not strict so that young children engage freely with older children and adults. School settings can mimic the conditions of everyday life to some extent. However, a principal resource for promoting quantification of the schemata in school is the story problem. Several researchers (e.g., Carpenter and Moser 1984; De Corte and Verschaffel 1987; Nesher 1982; Riley and Greeno 1988; Vergnaud 1982) have shown that children entering school can solve many simple story problems by applying their counting skills to sets they create as they build physical models of the story situations. Because the stories involve the same basic relationships among quantities as the protoquantitative schemata, extensive practice in solving problems via counting should help children quantify their original schemata. Such practice should not only develop children's ability to solve problems using exact numerical measures, but also lead them to interpret numbers themselves in terms of the relations specified by the protoquantitative schemata (Resnick and Greeno 1990). Eventually, according to our theory, children will construct an enriched meaning for numbers – treating numbers (rather than measured quantities of material) as the entities that are mentally compared, increased and decreased, or organized into parts and wholes by the schemata.

PRINCIPLES FOR A REASONING-BASED ARITHMETIC PROGRAMME

With this research base as a grounding for our efforts, we set out to develop a primary arithmetic programme (for grades one through three) that would engage children from the outset in invention, reasoning, verbal justification of mathematical ideas. The school in which we worked served a mainly minority, low-achieving population of children. Our goal was to use as little traditional school drill material as possible in order to provide for children a consistent environment in which they would be socialized to think of themselves as mathematical reasoners and to behave accordingly. This meant that we needed a programme in which children would successfully learn the traditional 'basics' of arithmetic calculation as well as more complex forms of reasoning and argumentation. The programme evolved gradually over a period of months. We describe it here in somewhat schematized form as the instantiation of a set of six principles that guided our thinking and experimentation.

1. Draw children's informal knowledge, developed outside school, into the classroom. An important early goal of the programme is to stimulate the use of counting in the context of the compare, increase/decrease, and part/whole schemata in order to promote children's construction of the quantified versions of those schemata. This is done through extensive problem-solving practice, using both story problems and acted-out situations. Counting (including counting on one's fingers) is actively encouraged.

2. Develop children's trust in their own knowledge. Traditional instruction, by focusing on specific procedures and on special mathematical notations and vocabulary, tends to teach children that what they already know is not legitimately mathematics. To develop children's trust in their own knowledge *qua* mathematics, our programme stresses the possibility of multiple procedures for solving any problem, invites children's invention of these multiple procedures, and asks that children explain and justify their procedures using everyday language. In addition, the use of manipulatives and finger counting ensures that children have a way of establishing for themselves the truth or falsity of their proposed solutions.

3. Use formal notations (identify sentences and equations) as a public record of discussions and conclusions. Children's intuitive knowledge must be linked to the formal language of mathematics. By using a standard mathematical notation to record conversations that are carried out in ordinary language and that are rooted in well-understood problem situations, the formalisms take on a meaning directly linked to children's mathematical intuitions. First used by the teacher as a way of displaying for the class what a child had proposed, equations quickly became common currency in the classroom. Most of the children began to write equations themselves only a few weeks into the school year.

4. *Introduce key mathematical structures as quickly as possible.* Children's protoquantitative schemata already allow them to think reasonably powerfully about how amounts of material compare, increase and decrease, come apart and go together. In other words, they already know, in non-numerically quantified form, something about properties such as commutativity, associativity, and additive inverse. A major goal of the first year or two of school mathematics is to 'mathematize' this knowledge – that is, quantify it and link it to formal expressions and operations. It was our conjecture that this could best be done by laying out the additive structures (e.g., for first grade: addition and subtraction problem situations, the composition of large numbers, regrouping as a special application of the part/whole schemata) as quickly as possible and then allowing full mastery (speed, flexibility of procedures, articulate explanations) of elements of the system to develop over an extended period of time. Guided by this principle, we found it possible to introduce addition and subtraction with regrouping in February of first grade. However, no specific procedures were taught; rather children were encouraged to invent (and explain) ways of solving multidigit addition and subtraction problems, using appropriate manipulatives and/or extended notation formats that they developed.

It is important to note that a programme built around this principle constitutes a major challenge to an idea that has been widely accepted in the past twenty or thirty years of educational research and practice. This is the notion of learning hierarchies, specifically that it is necessary for learners to master simpler components before they try to learn complex skills. According to theories of hierarchical learning and mastery learning, children should thoroughly master single digit addition and subtraction, for example, before attempting multidigit procedures, and they should be able to perform multidigit arithmetic without regrouping smoothly before they tackle the complexities of regrouping. We propose instead a *distributed* curriculum in which multiple topics are developed all year long, with increasing levels of sophistication and demand, rather than a strictly sequential curriculum. To convey the flavour of the process, Figure 11.2 shows the range of topics planned for a single month of the second-grade programme. All of the topics shown are treated at changing levels of sophistication and demand throughout the school year. This distributed curriculum discourages decontextualized teaching of components of arithmetic skill. It encourages children to draw on their existing knowledge framework (the protoquantitative schemata) to interpret advanced material, while gradually building computational fluency.

Domain	Specific Content
Reading/Writing Numerals	0-9,999
Set Counting	0-9,999
Addition	2- and 3-digit regrouping, Basic Facts 20
Subtraction	2-digit renaming, Basic Facts 20
Word Problems	Addition, Subtraction, Multiplication
Problem Solving	Work backward, Solve an easier problem, Patterns
Estimation	Quantities, Strategies, Length
Ratio/Proportion	Scaling up, Scaling down
Statistics/Probability	Scaling up, Scaling down, Spinner (1/4), Dice (1/16), 3 graphs
Multiplication	Array (2, 4 tables), Allocation, Equal groupings
Division	Oral problems involving sharing sets equally
Measurement	Arbitrary units
Decimals	Money
Fractions	Parts of whole, Parts of set, Equivalent pieces
Telling Time	To hour, To half hour
Geometry	Rectangle, square (properties)
Negative Integers	Ones, tens

Figure 11.2 Topic coverage planned for a single month in second grade

5. *Encourage everyday problem finding.* In stating this principle, we deliberately use the term *everyday* in two senses. First, it means literally doing arithmetic every day, not only in school but also at home and in other informal settings. Children need massive practice in applying arithmetical ideas, far more than the classroom itself can provide. For this reason we thought it important to encourage children to find problems for themselves that would keep them practising number facts and mathematical reasoning. Second, *everyday* means non-formal, situated in the activities of everyday life. It is important that children come to view mathematics as something that can be found everywhere, not just in school, not just in formal notations, not just in problems posed by a teacher. We wanted to get children in the habit of noticing quantitative and other pattern relationships wherever they are and of posing questions for themselves about those relationships. Two aspects of the programme represent efforts to instantiate this principle. First, the problems posed in class are drawn from things children know about and are actually involved in. Second, homework projects are designed so that they use the events and objects of children's home lives: for example, finding as many sets of four things as possible in the home; counting fingers and toes of family members; recording numbers and types of things removed from a

grocery bag after a shopping trip. From child and parent reports, there is good, although informal, evidence that this strategy works. Children in the programme are noticing numbers and relationships and setting problems for themselves in the course of their everyday activities.

6. *Talk about mathematics, don't just do arithmetic.* Discussion and argument are essential to creating a culture of critical thought. To encourage this talk, our programme uses a combination of whole-class, teacher-led discussion and structured small-group activity by the children. In a typical daily lesson, a single, relatively complex problem is presented on the blackboard. The first phase is a class discussion of what the problem means – what kind of information is given, what is to be discovered, what possible methods of solution there are, and the like. In the second phase, teams of children work together on solving the problem, using drawings, manipulatives, and role playing to support their discussions and solutions. The teams are responsible not only for developing a solution to the problem, but also for being able to explain why their solution is a mathematically and practically appropriate one. In the third phase of the lesson, teams successively present their solutions and justifications to the whole class, and the teacher records these on the blackboard. The teacher presses for explanations and challenges those that are incomplete or incorrect; other children join in the challenges or attempt to help by expanding the presented argument. By the end of the class period, multiple solutions to the problem, along with their justifications, have been considered, and there is frequently discussion of why several different solutions could all work, or why certain ones are better than others. In all these discussions, children are permitted to express themselves in ordinary language. Mathematical language and precision are deliberately not demanded in the oral discussion. However, the equation representations that the teacher and children write to summarize oral arguments provide a mathematically precise public record, thus linking everyday language to mathematical language. Figure 11.3 gives an example of a typical class problem, showing how it can generate several solutions; the notations shown are copied from a child's notebook.

RESULTS OF THE PROGRAMME

We are describing here a programme that has been under development for a little over one year. The project began not as a research project, but as an effort to help an ambitious teacher apply research findings to improve her teaching. At the outset, we did not want to impose testing programmes beyond those that the school regularly administered. We are thus limited, in this first year of the project's life, to data from the school's standardized testing programme and from clinical interviews that we were able to conduct with some of the children over the course of the year, along with some impressionistic reports of child and parent reactions to the overall programme.

> Monique told her friend TaRae that she would give her 95 barrettes. Monique had 4 bags of barrettes and each bag had 9 barrettes. Does Monique have enough barrettes?

The class first developed an estimated answer. Then they were asked, "How many more does she need?" The solutions below were generated by different class groups.

Group 1 first solved for the number of barrettes by repeated addition. Then they decomposed 4x9 into 2x9 plus 2x9. Then they set up a missing addend problem, 36+59, which they solved by a combination of estimation and correction.

Group 2 set up a subtraction equation and then developed a solution that used a negative partial result.

Group 4 began with total number of barrettes needed and subtracted out the successive bags of 9.

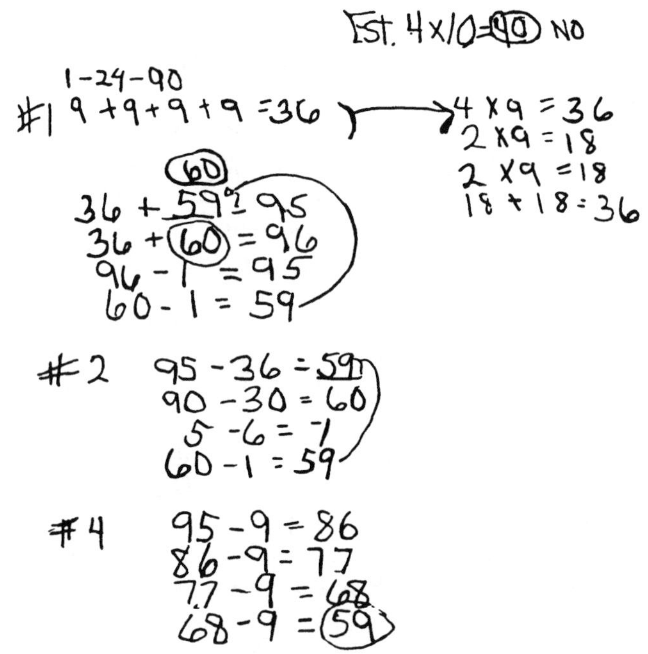

[Handwritten work:]

Est. 4×10=40 NO

1-24-90

#1 9+9+9+9 = 36
4×9 = 36
2×9 = 18
2×9 = 18
18+18 = 36

36 + 59 = 95
36 + 60 = 96
96 - 1 = 95
60 - 1 = 59

#2 95 - 36 = 59
90 - 30 = 60
5 - 6 = -1
60 - 1 = 59

#4 95 - 9 = 86
86 - 9 = 77
77 - 9 = 68
68 - 9 = 59

Figure 11.3 A second-grade problem and several solutions

Formal evaluation data consist of scores from the California Achievement Test (CAT), which is administered annually in the school each September. First graders were tested at the beginning of second grade, second graders at the beginning of third grade, and third graders at the beginning of fourth grade. Figure 11.4 compares performance of the first graders in the programme with a control group – the preceding year's first grade, taught by the same teacher. For each group, mean percentile ranks are shown for the quantitative skill area of the Metropolitan Readiness Test given in March of the kindergarten year and for the mathematics section of the CAT test given in the September following first grade. As can be seen, there was a dramatic positive effect of the programme in first grade: the mean percentile score rose from 31.3 on the kindergarten test to 84.4 on the post-first-grade test; the control group's performance remained flat over the comparable time period. The difference between the groups is highly significant statistically. (ANCOVA, using the kindergarten test as the covariate and comparing end of first grade scores. $F_{1,19}$ = 101.28; p = .000.) As important, the whole distribution shifted upward as a result of the programme: the *lowest*-scoring programme child was at the 66th percentile; the *highest*-scoring child the preceding year was at the 51st percentile. Thus, the programme appeared effective for children of all ability levels.

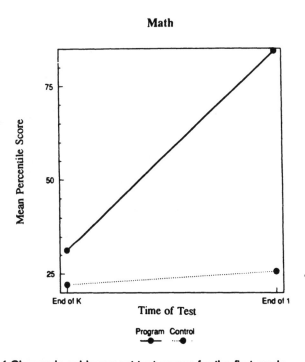

Figure 11.4 Change in achievement test scores for the first grade

Figure 11.5 compares the second-grade programme group with its control class – the previous year's second grade, taught by the same teacher. ANCOVAs showed the differences to be highly reliable for both the concepts and applications ($F_{1,29}$ = 6.63, p = .015) and the computation ($F_{1,29}$ = 8.18; p = .008) subtests. Figure 11.6 compares the third-grade programme class with its control, again the preceding year's class taught by the same teacher. ANCOVAs showed strong statistical significance for the concepts and applications subtest ($F_{1,25}$ = 12.74, p = .001), but only marginal significance

224 Applications in specific domains

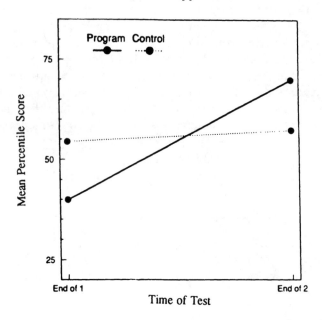

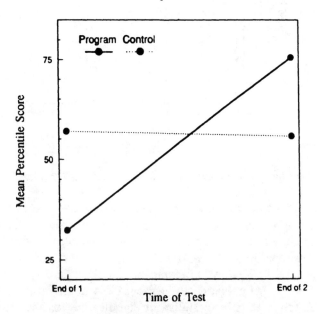

Figure 11.5 Change in achievement test scores for the second grade

Developing thinking abilities in arithmetic class 225

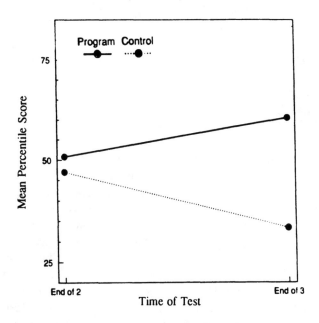

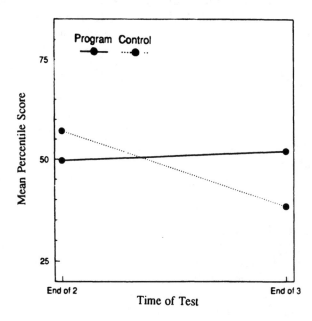

Figure 11.6 Change in achievement test scores for the third grade

for the computation subtest ($F_{1,25} = 3.34$; $p = .08$). Except for the third-grade computation, medians as well as means were higher for each group after the programme intervention than before, indicating positive effects for children at all levels of ability.

These global data tell only part of the story, of course. There is a great deal more that we would like to know about which we do not yet have systematic data. Nevertheless, we can point to some indicators based on our interviews, class observations, and reports from the school. We interviewed all first graders three times during the year, focusing on their knowledge of counting and addition and subtraction facts, along with their methods for calculating and their understanding of the principles of commutativity, compensation, and the complementarity of addition and subtraction. At the outset, these children, as might be expected given their socioeconomic status and their parents' generally low educational background, were not highly proficient. Only one-third of them could count orally to 100 or beyond, and most were unable to count reliably across decade boundaries (e.g., 29–30, 59–60). The size of the sets that they could quantify by counting ranged from 6 to 20. About a third could not solve small-number addition problems, even with manipulatives or finger counting and plenty of encouraging support from the interviewer. Only about six appeared able to perform simple subtractions using counting procedures. Thus, these children seemed very weak in entering arithmetical knowledge, especially compared with data that a number of investigators have presented for middle-class and educationally favoured populations. By December the picture was sharply different. All but a handful of children were performing both addition and subtraction problems successfully, and all of these demonstrated knowledge of the commutativity of addition. At least half were also using invented procedures such as counting on from the larger of two addends or using procedures that showed that they understood principles of complementarity of addition and subtraction. By the end of the school year, essentially all children were performing in this way, and many were successfully solving and explaining multidigit problems.

The following additional evidence indicates that the programme was having many of the desired effects. The children displayed multiple examples of confidence in doing mathematical work. Many sang to themselves as they took the standardized test. When visitors came to the classroom, they would offer to show off by solving maths problems. They frequently asked for harder problems. These displays came from children of almost all ability levels. They had not been typical of any except the most able children the preceding year. Homework was more regularly turned in than in preceding years, without nagging or pressure from the teacher. Children often asked for extra maths periods. Many parents reported that their children loved maths and wanted to do maths all the time. Parents also sent to school examples of problems that children had solved on their own in some everyday family situation. Knowing that the teacher frequently used such problems in class, parents asked that their child's problems be used. It is notable that this kind of parent engagement occurred in a population of parents that is traditionally alienated from the school and tends not to interact with teachers or school officials.

CONCLUSION

It is, of course, too early to draw major or definitive conclusions from this project's work. We need to be sure that the effects we have seen are not entirely 'Hawthorn effects' – that is, that they last over several years. We need to document better than we have exactly how classroom activities proceed, what kinds of conversations children have, what changing self-concepts they display. We need more systematic accounts of children's developing thinking performances. And, of course, we will want to study whether and how teachers other than the developer of the programme are able to use the ideas developed here.

Despite these limits, we believe that we have made a promising start. To return to our opening questions, we have shown that an interpretation- and discussion-oriented mathematics programme can begin at the outset of school, by building on the intuitive mathematical knowledge that children have as they enter school. Our standardized test score data show that this kind of thinking-based programme also succeeds in teaching the basic number facts and arithmetical procedures that are the core of the traditional primary mathematics programme. It is not necessary to teach facts and skills first and only then go on to thinking and reasoning. The two can be developed simultaneously. Assuming that we can maintain and replicate our results, this means that an interpretation- and discussion-oriented programme can serve as the basic programme in arithmetic, not just as an adjunct to a more traditional knowledge and skills curriculum.

Finally, our results so far suggest that an interpretation-oriented mathematics programme is suitable even for children who are not socially favoured or, initially, educationally able. The children with whom we have worked come disproportionately from among the least favoured of American families. Many are considered to be educationally at risk; their educational prognosis, without special interventions or changed educational programmes, is poor. Yet these children learned effectively in a type of programme that, if present in schools at all, has been reserved for children judged able and talented – most often those from favoured social groups.

What is at issue here, as we suggested at the outset, is not only an apparently successful programme, but also some fundamental challenges to dominant assumptions about learning and schooling. Both educators and researchers on education have tended to define the educational task as one of teaching specific knowledge and skills. As concern has shifted from routine to higher-order thinking abilities, psychologists and educators have developed more complex definitions of the skills to be acquired, and even introduced various concepts of *meta* skill in the search for teachable general abilities. But they have continued to think of their major concern as fundamentally one of identifying and analysing particular skills of reasoning and thinking and then finding ways to teach them, on the hopeful assumption that successful students will then be able to apply these skills in a wide range of situations. This approach has shared a fundamental assumption that has characterized most research on learning and cognition, as well as large branches of philosophy and artificial intelligence. This is the assumption that knowledge and competence can be *decontextualized*: that there is some pure or abstract form of knowing that remains intact no matter what the conditions of use; that knowledge is fully defined as something inside an individual's head, independent of the situation in which the individual acts. This decontextualization assumption underlies schooling practice as well as classical cognitive research. The conditions of learning in schools are normally far removed from the conditions of application of knowledge and skill outside school (Resnick 1987b), and it has been only a belief in the decontextualizability and transfer of knowledge and skill taught in school that validates the time and effort invested in school.

An alternative view of the function of school in society is to think of schools as providing specific contexts for knowing and acting in which children can become *apprentices* – actual participants in a process that is socially valued, even though they are not yet skilled enough to produce complicated performances without support. We are trying, in this project, to create an apprenticeship environment for mathematical thinking in which children can participate daily, thus acquiring not only the skills and knowledge that expert mathematical reasoners possess, but also a social identity as a person who is able to and expected to engage in such reasoning (see Lave 1991).

Our programme constitutes a version of the *cognitive apprenticeship* called for by Collins, Brown, and Newman (1989) in a recent influential paper. Its very success, however, calls into question some aspects of the apprenticeship metaphor as applied to early learning in a school environment. Among these is the nature of the master–apprenticeship relationship. In traditional apprenticeship, apprentices seek to become like their masters, and masters continually display all of the elements of skilled productive activity in their field of expertise. Teaching is only a secondary function of the traditional master. This simple – indeed, perhaps over-simplified – relationship does not seem applicable to the school setting, where the teacher's predominant function is not to *do* mathematics but to *teach* it. We will need to work out the particular role of the teacher in designing an environment *specifically for learning purposes*. A second issue surrounding cognitive apprenticeship in school is how to ensure that necessary particular skills will be acquired, even though the daily focus of activity is on problem solving and reasoning. Our first-year standardized test results suggest that we have not done badly on this criterion, but we need to understand better than we do now just what it is in our programme that has succeeded and what the limits of our methods might be. In short, we offer this chapter as only a very preliminary report on what we expect to be a long-term effort to revise instructional practice in ways that will bring us closer to being able to meet the goal of shaping dispositions and skills for thinking through a form of socialization into cultural environments that value and practise thinking.

REFERENCES

Carpenter, T. P. and Moser, J. M. (1984) 'The acquisition of addition and subtraction concepts', in R. Lesh and M. Landau (eds) *Acquisition of Mathematics: Concepts and Processes*, New York: Academic Press, pp. 7–44.

Clark, E. (1983) 'Meanings and concepts', in J. H. Flavell and E. M. Markman (eds), P. H. Mussen (series ed.) *Handbook of Child Psychology*, vol. 3, *Cognitive Development*, New York: Wiley, pp. 787–840.

Collins, A., Brown, J. S., and Newman, S. E. (1989) 'Cognitive apprenticeship: teaching the crafts of reading, writing, and mathematics', in L. B. Resnick (ed.) *Knowing, Learning, and Instruction: Essays in Honor of Robert Glaser*, Hillsdale, NJ: Erlbaum, pp. 453–94.

De Corte, E. and Verschaffel, L. (1987) 'The effect of semantic structure on first graders' strategies for solving addition and subtraction word problems', *Journal for Research in Mathematics Education* 18: 363–81.

Fuson, K. C., Lyons, B., Pergament, G., Hall, J., and Kwon, Y. (1988) 'Effects of collection terms on class-inclusion and on number tasks', *Cognitive Psychology* 20: 96–120.

Gelman, R. (1972) 'Logical capacity of very young children: number invariance rules', *Child Development* 43: 75–90.

Gelman, R. and Gallistel, C. R. (1978) *The Child's Understanding of Number*, Cambridge, MA: Harvard University Press.

Glaser, R. (1984) 'Education and thinking: the role of knowledge', *American Psychologist* 39: 93–100.

Irwin, K. (1990, July) *Children's Understanding of Compensation, Addition, and Subtraction*, paper presented at the 14th meeting of the International Group for the Psychology of Mathematics Education, Oaxtepec, Mexico.

Klahr, D. and Kotovsky, K. (1989) *Complex Information Processing: The Impact of Herbert A. Simon*, Hillsdale, NJ: Erlbaum.

Lave, J. (1991) 'Situating learning in communities of practice', in L. B. Resnick, J. Levine, and S. D. Behrend (eds) *Perspectives on Socially Shared Cognition*, Washington, DC: American Psychological Association, pp. 63–82.

Markman, E. M. and Siebert, J. (1976) 'Classes and collections: internal organization and resulting holistic properties', *Cognitive Psychology* 8: 516–77.

Michie, S. (1984) 'Why preschoolers are reluctant to count spontaneously', *British Journal of Developmental Psychology* 2: 347–58.

Nesher, P. (1982) 'Levels of description in the analysis of addition and subtraction word problems', in T. P. Carpenter, J. M. Moser, and T. A. Romberg (eds) *Addition and Subtraction: A Cognitive Perspective*, Hillsdale, NJ: Erlbaum, pp. 25–38.

Newell, A. and Simon, H. A. (1972) *Human Problem Solving*, Englewood Cliffs, NJ: Prentice-Hall.
Peliegrino, J. W. and Glaser, R. (1982) 'Analyzing aptitudes for learning: inductive reasoning', in R. Glaser (ed.) *Advances in Instructional Psychology*, Vol. 2, Hillsdale, NJ: Erlbaum, pp. 269–345.
Resnick, L. B. (1983) 'A developmental theory of number understanding', in H. P. Ginsburg (ed.) *The Development of Mathematical Thinking*, New York: Academic Press, pp. 109–51.
—— (1987a) 'Instruction and the cultivation of thinking', in E. De Corte, H. Lodewijks, R. P. Paramentier, and P. Span (eds) *Learning and Instruction: European Research in an International Context*, Vol. 1, Oxford: Leuven University Press/Pergamon Press, pp. 415–42.
—— (1987b) 'Learning in school and out', *Educational Researcher* 16 (9): 13–20.
—— (1989a) 'Developing mathematical knowledge', *American Psychologist* 44: 162–9.
—— (1989b) 'Treating mathematics as an ill-structured discipline', in R. I. Charles and E. A. Silver (eds) *The Teaching and Assessing of Mathematical Problem-Solving*, Hillsdale, NJ/Reston, VA: Erlbaum/National Council of Teachers of Mathematics, pp. 32–60.
Resnick, L. B. and Greeno, J. G. (1990) *Conceptual Growth of Number and Quantity*, unpublished manuscript.
Resnick, L. B. and Omanson, S. F. (1987) 'Learning to understand arithmetic', in R. Glaser (ed.) *Advances in Instructional Psychology*, Vol. 3, Hillsdale, NJ: Erlbaum, pp. 41–95.
Riley, M. S. and Greeno, J. G. (1988) 'Developmental analysis of understanding language about quantities and of solving problems', *Cognition and Instruction* 5: 49–101.
Saxe, G. (1977) 'A developmental analysis of notational counting', *Child Development* 48: 1512–20.
Siegler, R. S. (1981) 'Developmental sequences within and between concepts', *Society for Research in Child Development Monographs* 46 (2, Serial No. 189).
Sophian, C. (1987) 'Early developments in children's use of counting to solve quantitative problems', *Cognition and Instruction* 4: 61–90.
Sternberg, R. J. (1977) *Intelligence, Information Processing and Analogical Reasoning: The Componential Analysis of Human Abilities*, Hillsdale, NJ: Erlbaum.
—— (1986) *Intelligence Applied*, New York: Harcourt Brace Jovanovich.
Vergnaud, G. (1982) 'A classification of cognitive tasks and operations of thought involved in addition and subtraction', in T. P. Carpenter, J. M. Moser, and T. A. Romberg (eds) *Addition and Subtraction: A Cognitive Perspective*, Hillsdale, NJ: Erlbaum, pp. 39–59.

Chapter 12

Causal theories, reasoning strategies, and conflict resolution by experts and novices in Newtonian mechanics

J. Ignacio Pozo and Mario Carretero

The research about cognitive change and science teaching in the last two decades has been dominated by two main approaches. Piaget's theory – mainly his book about formal operations (Inhelder and Piaget 1955) – has had a strong influence during the 1960s and the 1970s. We think that the Piagetian approach is still relevant for studying both cognitive change and science teaching, but in the last fifteen years a number of important criticisms have appeared. Most of them have been based on the existence of the subjects' alternative ideas or misconceptions about scientific notions (Driver, Guesne, and Tiberghien 1985; West and Pines 1985).

This new approach has some characteristics similar to those of Piaget, although there do exist various differences. Maybe the most outstanding similarity is that they both share a constructivist point of view. Aside from this common idea, the two approaches differ regarding what it is that changes and what type of changes ought to be promoted through instruction.

According to Piaget, the changes in scientific knowledge of the subjects are *structural*. The subjects' actions and representations of scientific phenomena would be determined by a number of general logical structures, whose development would allow for more complex levels of scientific thought. These structural changes produce the appearance of different stages, characterized by qualitatively distinct cognitive operations. This structural change would be general, that is to say, independent from influences of specific contents. Thus, the Piagetian model implies, first, the use of formal operations independently of the content to which they are to be applied; second, the fostering of general scientific procedures (i.e., control of variables, combinatory, proportional reasoning, etc.) instead of emphasizing the understanding of specific contents. Therefore, the main goal of this approach would be the teaching of science by fostering structural change and facilitating acquisition of formal operations.

On the other hand, recent studies, based on subjects' misconceptions (Helm and Novak 1983), on pupils' intuitive science (Osborne and Freyberg 1985), or pupils' intuitive frameworks, adopt an essentially conceptual approach. They study specific scientific notions instead of content-free general structures. So, they have discovered that students have their own concepts, independently of the instruction to which they have been exposed. These intuitive concepts are usually very different from the scientific ones and are very resistant to change (Driver, Guesne, and Tiberghien 1985). This kind of approach emphasizes a cognitively heterogeneous subject because the relationships among the various misconceptions (i.e., of physics, history, mathematics, etc.) of the same subject are unclear. Thus, the research based on this misconceptions approach cannot even predict students' performance on different tasks belonging to the same knowledge domain. Due to this inability, such teaching models try to promote a conceptual change in specific knowledge domains rather than structural change (Hashweh 1986; West and Pines 1985).

Despite these notable theoretical differences, attempts have been made to reconcile the two traditions. There have been some attempts to apply the Piagetian structural model to describe conceptual progress in specific knowledge domains (Piaget and Garcia 1983; Shayer and Adey 1981). However, these attempts are met with the difficulty of explaining the low consistency demonstrated by the subjects across tasks which are structurally identical but whose content is diverse (i.e., the Piagetian *decalage*). At the same time, there are attempts to define conceptual structures which explain the similarities found in the ideas of the students, either as personal theories, theories-in-action (e.g., Claxton 1984), or conceptual structures with certain levels of generality. In their effort to structure the ideas of the students, a number of authors refer to the history of the specific disciplines (Strauss 1988). In this way, although through a very different approach, they recuperate Piaget's original project, namely genetic epistemology (Piaget and Garcia 1983).

From the above it can be concluded that the main differences between the two approaches have to do with the homogeneous or heterogeneous character of cognitive functioning (Flavell 1982), and the influence instruction exerts on cognitive change. Regarding the role of schooling in cognitive change, the Piagetian position is above all developmental, while the misconceptions approach emphasizes the interaction between those ideas and school learning, conjecturing the fundamental role of the educational experiences in the construction of those ideas.

These two problems are not exclusive to research in developmental and educational psychology. In fact, the general orientation of cognitive psychology has passed through a similar evolution in recent years. From the advocation of general and computational models based on memory structures and general processes, new models have been developed of increasing specificity and contextualization. A very clear example of this shift are the studies of reasoning and problem solving in which logical or general computational models of a syntactic character (e.g., the General Problem Solver by Newell and Simon 1972) have been replaced by models based on specialized knowledge, activated by semantic (e.g., mental models/schemes) (Gentner and Stevens 1983) or pragmatic processes (Holland *et al.* 1986).

This movement towards the specific has originated from studies comparing experts and novices in problem solving, situation memory tasks, and other forms of cognitive performance. It has also been evident in the substitution of general problem solvers by expert systems in the solution of rather specific tasks. As Case (Chapter 3, this volume) notes, the studies of experts and novices have been adduced in support of the models based on acquisition of specific knowledge. There is already a number of data on the differences between experts and novices and how they confront scientific tasks (Chi, Glaser, and Rees 1982). Nevertheless, one must still clarify whether the change that takes place in the transition from novice to expert is of a structural nature or simply conceptual (Carey 1985). In the same way, Brown and DeLoache (1978) suggest that changes due to cognitive development could be reinterpreted, at least in part, as changes in the content-specific knowledge of children, in the sense that they could be considered as 'universal novices'.

In the present study, we propose to analyse empirically the relationships between the three approaches described earlier (the Piagetian, misconceptions, and expert/novices approaches). Up to now each of these approaches has gathered data, which, due to their different methodologies, are not always comparable. Although we know in part the effects of cognitive development on the scientific reasoning of children and adolescents, as well as the effects of expertise on the solution of the same type of tasks by adult subjects, the differential effects of each of these variables – cognitive development and instruction – in the solution of the same task have not yet been compared. This comparison will provide more detailed knowledge of the structural and/or conceptual nature of the changes which take place in the learning of science. The results included in this chapter belong to a research project in which both history and mechanics tasks were presented to the same subjects. On this occasion, we shall present only the results concerning the mechanics tasks.

METHOD

Objectives

In this chapter, we shall describe the results of research that compares the performance of two groups of university adults, one of experts and one of novices, and of various adolescent groups in the solution of different problems in Newtonian mechanics. The tasks were presented both in the form of manipulation and in a paper-and-pencil form. We shall analyse the solution of these problems in terms of causal thinking, referring to two different aspects of it previously identified in our research (Carretero 1984, Carretero and Pozo 1991): namely, the reasoning strategies used by the subjects in the solution of the task and the concepts or specific ideas used to interpret this same task. While the reasoning strategies have a general character and can be analysed independently of the contents to which they are applied, the concepts have to do with a specific knowledge domain. In our study, beside the developmental differences sought, we will also analyse the subjects' expertise in these two components of thinking. Finally, we will present an analysis of the contradictions made by the subject when they solve the tasks. This is deemed necessary because cognitive conflict has been postulated as a necessary prerequisite for cognitive change by the authors favouring structural change (Piaget 1975) and those favouring conceptual change (Hashweh 1986; West and Pines 1985). Thus, it is interesting to know how the subjects solve the conflicts between their ideas and the data with which they are confronted.

The specific knowledge domain that we have chosen to carry out this research is Newtonian mechanics, since it is a content which has been tackled by all three approaches already described: the Piagetian research (e.g., Inhelder and Piaget 1955; Piaget and Garcia 1983), as well as the studies about misconceptions (e.g., Gunstone and Watts 1985; McCloskey 1983, McCloskey and Kargon 1988; McDermott 1984) and the studies about experts and novices (e.g., Chi, Glaser, and Rees 1982). In this way the comparison between causal ideas, reasoning strategies, and the solution of cognitive conflicts of each of our groups of subjects, when confronted with the mechanics tasks proposed, will permit us to establish the influence of the structural and conceptual aspects of knowledge in each of the analysed components.

Subjects

The sample was composed of forty-eight subjects, who were divided into four groups of twelve. Three of the groups involved adolescents of different school levels, equivalent to seventh, ninth, and eleventh grades. (Mean ages were 12.1, 14.9, and 17.1 respectively.) The fourth group was formed from young adults who had recently graduated from the university or had registered in the last year of the university. This university group was divided equally into history experts and physics experts. Their age ranged from 21.6 to 23.0, mean age of 22.1 for the history experts and from 22.9 to 24.9, mean age of 24.2, for the physics experts.

Procedure and tasks

Task I: the course of inert mobiles

This first task was in written form. It consisted of two similar parts, one administered at the beginning of the session and the other after the completion of tasks II and III. Each part consisted of three problems; it also included a written text as well as a picture. The problems used were adaptations from tasks designed by McCloskey (1983). The subject was asked to draw the course of the inert mobile, that is, the mobile upon which no unbalanced force is operating. When the subjects had concluded the two series of problems, they were asked to provide an explanation of the course drawn.

The problems, in the exact way they were presented to the subjects, are shown in Figure 12.1. It can be seen that the problems A, B, and C of both tasks are the same from a physics point of view. Problem A in both situations consists of predicting the course of a given object in an initial curvilinear movement when a force is no longer exerted upon it. The correct answer (Figure 12.2) is that the object will follow a rectilinear movement until it stops.

The introduction to problem B was the same for both parts of the test, the only difference being the variation of the position of the ball in the pictures. In this problem, the subject had to establish a relationship between his/her notion of inert movement and the continuous force of gravity. In this situation, the movement has a parabolic form, due to the simultaneous action of the two velocities – a constant horizontal velocity, in the absence of friction, due to inertia, and a vertical velocity, which increases (acceleration) as a consequence of the continuous action of gravity. But, whereas the force of gravity is the same in the four situations presented, the horizontal velocity depends on the place in the course where the cord breaks. This produces different courses in each case (Figure 12.2). Upon completion of the task, in order to ensure that the subjects were aware of the different horizontal velocities, we asked whether the velocity was the same at the moment of breaking the velocity. If it were not, the subjects had to indicate the relative velocity in each case.

Problem C was similar to the previous one. It required drawing the parabolic fall of two mobiles which maintain a horizontal velocity which is composed by a gravitory acceleration. Although the two situations, from a physics point of view, are identical, they do not create distinct conceptual problems. While problem 1C deals with a ball which displaces itself, in 2C, the object which falls is dropped by another object. Just the same, in this second problem the subject was asked to draw where the airplane would be when the ball reached the ground.

Putting aside the force of friction, the airplane will be exactly over the ball when the ball touches the ground (Figure 12.2). This is to say that, in agreement with Newton's principle of inertia, the ball will conserve its horizontal velocity, which is independent of the vertical movement being

236 Applications in specific domains

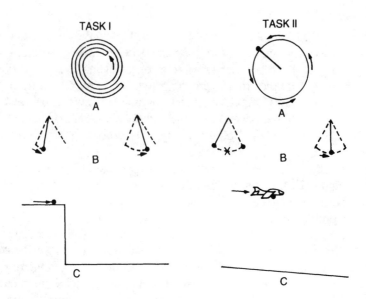

Figure 12.1 Tasks
Note: The subjects were instructed to draw the course that a ball, which moves at high speed, would follow when coming out of a tube (1A), when leaving its speeding orbit (2A), when the pendulum breaks at the point indicated by the arrow (1B and 2B), when it goes over a high step (1C), or when it is released by an aeroplane (2C)

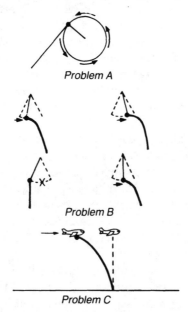

Figure 12.2 Correct answers to the problems involved in task II

followed due to the effect of gravity. Any reference to friction was deliberately omitted from the statement of the problem since we were interested in knowing to what extent the subjects resorted to using 'invisible' forces. Therefore, during the final interview, special care was taken to check whether or not the subject had this variable in mind. It was equally interesting to compare the answers to problems 1C and 2C.

Task II: inclined plane and impact of the balls

Tasks II and III were of a manipulative nature. The apparatus used was similar in both cases. Task II required the releasing of a ball on an adjustable inclined plane. The ball then struck another resting ball forcing it to ascend on a second inclined plane (Figure 12.3A). The variables in this task were: the height from which the ball was released (H), the inclination of the plane (I), the distance covered by the ball on the plane (D), the released ball (B1), and the resting ball (B2).

The subject was presented with the apparatus already set up, with an intermediate height and inclination. An explanation was given including the opportunity of possible variation. The subject was also shown the changes one could make in the apparatus. No mention was made at any time of the existing variables or of any physics concepts or terms.

Finally, a demonstration of the ball falling and hitting the other one, forcing it to rise up to the middle of the scale, followed. Once the demonstration was finished, the first part of the interview began, focusing on the exposition of the subjects' ideas on the functioning of the apparatus. In this phase, the subject was not allowed to handle the apparatus. The subject had to predict which were the influencing factors in this task. In each case, when the subject named a variable (i.e, the slope, the length of it, or what the ball is made of), s/he was asked to define it ('what do you call a slope?') as well as explain the prediction ('why does it go further when there is a sharper slope?'). No suggestions were made to the subject regarding variables not mentioned.

Finally, to conclude the first phase, the subject was asked to summarize the explanations previously given about the influencing factors. At this time, the second phase began and the subject was asked to demonstrate their ideas with the available apparatus. The subject was reminded that they could do as many tests as desired using any material necessary. The experimenter asked, each time a new test began, what it was they were going to demonstrate, and, at the end, if they had demonstrated all they had intended to. At no time was the subject reminded of a forgotten variable or provided with any information about their tests. Only when the test was clearly contrary to the predictions of the subject did the experimenter insist that s/he explain this disconfirmation. When the subject mentioned that s/he had completed all the necessary tests, the tasks were concluded. At this time the subject was asked again to summarize the intervening variables.

238   Applications in specific domains

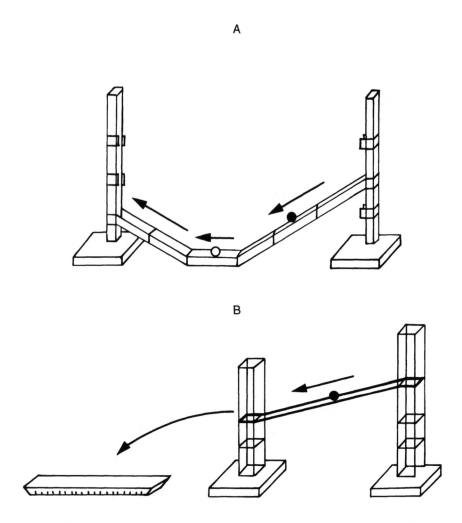

Figure 12.3 The arrangements used in tasks II and III

Task III: the descent of the balls on an inclined plane

Although the apparatus used in this task was the same as in the previous one, there were a number of modifications made to the arrangement. These modifications considerably altered the mechanical nature of the problem (Figure 12.3B). In this case, the ball was released on an inclined plane which had been elevated from the floor. Underneath the end of the inclined plane a graduated receptacle had been placed and the ball was allowed to fall freely. The problem required the identification of the factors which determine whether the balls fall closely or far away. The possible variables were the height from which the ball was released (H), the point on the plane from which the ball was released (D), the inclination of the plane (I), the height with respect to the floor at which the inferior extreme of the plane was situated, that is, the height of the fall of the ball (F), and the ball which was released (B). The procedure did not differ from the previous task. After reviewing the variations that could be applied to the apparatus, the experimenter asked the subject to point out the factors that would influence the ball to fall closer or farther away. Special care was taken to clarify the explanation that the subject offered about the influence or lack of influence on the height of the fall (F). If necessary, the subject was asked to draw the course of the ball in its fall from above and from below. The causes of this course were emphasized. The second phase was identical to the second phase of task II. Again, the contradictions of the subjects were stressed, which in this case were more abundant. To some degree, the higher frequency of contradictions can be attributed to the actual succession of the tasks. In spite of the superficial similarity, the two tasks actually imply two different physics concepts: while the first case deals with a problem of conservation of the quantity of movement or the conservation of energy, the second deals with a composition of two movements (horizontal velocity and vertical acceleration). The relevant variables in the first case are height (H) and the mass of the two balls (B1 and B2). On the other hand, in the second case, the mass of the ball is irrelevant since the only two factors which can have an influence are the velocity at which it arrives at the extreme of the ramp, which depends on the height (H), and the time that it can be subject to this horizontal movement, which is a function of the heights from which it falls (F). In this way, the actual nature of the tasks allows us to analyse the theories of the subjects more deeply than the usual descriptive predictions in other works. In particular, the role played by the weight or mass of the ball in both tasks appears fundamental in the subjects' contradictions. In the first case, an erroneous theory ('the heavier balls fall more quickly') leads to correct predictions. In the second, the ideas and predictions are incorrect.

Analysis criteria

Due to the complexity and diversity of the criteria used for the analysis of the responses, the criteria used in each task will be described in conjunction with the results obtained. The analysis involved causal ideas, reasoning strategies, and reactions to cognitive conflict.

Causal ideas

Based on earlier works on the misconceptions or alternative conceptions about Newtonian mechanics (e.g., Gunstone and Watts 1985; McCloskey 1983; Piaget and Garcia 1983), we established various levels of response qualitatively distinct for each of the concepts analysed. The concepts analysed are:

a Inertia
b Free fall
c Gravity
d Velocity and acceleration
e Conservation of energy.

Reasoning strategies

We studied the use of the control of variables schema in tasks II and III. In order to do this, we considered the number of factors which the subject varied in each of the manipulations carried out. In order to distinguish the inferential deficiencies from the conceptual ones, we differentiated the variables defined by the subject in the first phase of each task from the variables not defined by the subject but controlled by the experimenter.

Reactions to cognitive conflict

In the last formulation of his theory of equilibration, Piaget (1975) established various types of responses (*alpha, beta,* and *gamma*) to cognitive conflict, which produced various types of change in the schemes of the subject. In our opinion, this Piagetian analysis is substantially coincidental with the position of Lakatos (1978), who maintains the existence of a firm centre in the theories or programmes of investigation that becomes very difficult to modify when confronted with conflict (restructuralization, similar to the Piagetian gamma response). On the other hand, scientists usually respond to conflict by denying its relevance (Piagetian alpha response) or by modifying the protective belt (beta response).

From these theoretical positions we developed a system of analysis of five levels which reflect increasing levels of conceptual change. These range from absence of awareness of conflict to restructuralization. Each of the situations of cognitive conflict observed in tasks II and III was classified in accordance with these levels.

RESULTS

Causal ideas about mechanics

Regarding the contents of the causal ideas in mechanics, we distinguished five sets of criteria which correspond to the five concepts studied: inertia, free fall, gravity, velocity/acceleration, and energy conservation.

Inertia

The concept of inertia that the subjects had was evaluated from responses to questions 1A and 2A in the first task. The established levels of responses are the following:

1 Completely circular course (similar to the initial direction of the object)
2 Curvilinear course (something in between the curvilinear direction and the correct rectilinear)
3 Rectilinear course (not tangential to the original circular direction)
4 Rectilinear and tangential course.

In accordance with these criteria, the results obtained are shown in Table 12.1. It can be observed that only 27 per cent of the subjects have a Newtonian concept of inertia. It seems significant that, by applying the Kruskall-Wallis analysis test of variance by ranks to the total set of data, there do exist global differences between our subject with respect to the concept of inertia (df=4, p<.05).

After an analysis of the differences between the groups, through the Mann-Whitney U-test, it was found that 16-year-olds maintained a superior performance to the rest of the groups, except for the physics experts. This superior performance is reflected in the fact that 50 per cent of the subjects of this group reached the highest response level. On the other hand, it is surprising that the physics experts did not perform significantly better on this task than the rest of the groups.

Free fall

The ideas subjects have with respect to the fall of objects of inertial horizontal movement were obtained from the questions 2A, 2B, 3A, and 3B of task II. In the same way in task III, the students offered an explanation of the path followed by the ball in its fall. The established levels were the following (see also Figure 12.4B):

1 The object falls in one vertical movement or in two successive movements, the first horizontal and the second vertical (Aristotelian concept).
2 The object during the fall has two movements composing only one rectilinear diagonal movement: that is to say, of two single movements (incomprehension of the fact that gravity is a constant force and therefore produces an acceleration or constant increase of vertical velocity).
3 The falling object has two movements which become composed in the form of a curvilinear but not parabolic movement. (The two movements are conceived as dependent. In other words, it is not accepted that horizontal velocity is constant.)
4 The falling object has two independent velocities – a horizontal constant and a vertical with uniform acceleration, which gives rise to a movement which is parabolic in composition.
5 The idea just described can also be applied to the objects which move in a horizontal direction suspended by a mobile (question 3B). Before this level, relativity of the notions of rest and movement is not understood.

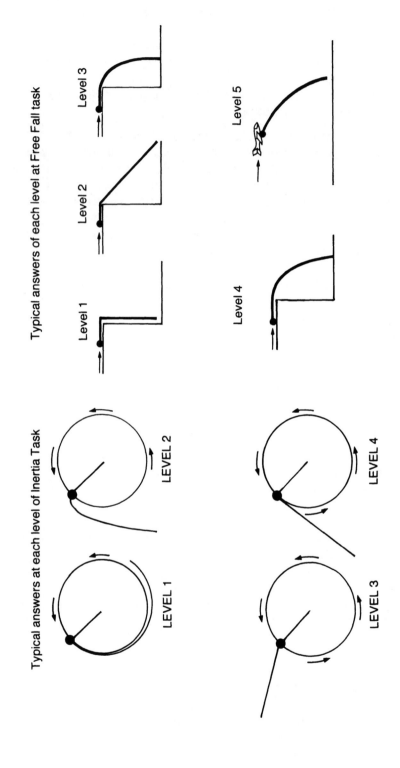

Figure 12.4 Typical answers at each level of the inertia and the free fall tasks

Causal theories, reasoning strategies, and conflict resolution   243

The results obtained are given in Table 12.1. It can be observed that half of the subjects are in the first two levels which are clearly simplistic. Only 12 per cent of the subjects, almost all of them in the physics experts group, conceive the movement as parabolic; furthermore, only 6 per cent of them apply it to the suspended objects.

Table 12.1 Frequency of subjects per response category in the case of the five concepts investigated

Age	N	Concept	1	2	3	4	5
12	12	Inertia	3	4	2	3	–
		Free fall	4	5	3	0	0
		Gravity	8	3	1	–	–
		Velocity & acceleration	6	6	0	0	0
		Conservation of energy	6	6	0	0	–
14	12	Inertia	3	8	0	1	–
		Free fall	1	4	7	0	0
		Gravity	10	1	1	–	–
		Velocity & acceleration	4	8	0	0	0
		Conservation of energy	4	8	0	0	–
16	12	Inertia	0	3	3	6	–
		Free fall	6	1	4	1	0
		Gravity	9	3	0	–	–
		Velocity & acceleration	0	8	2	1	1
		Conservation of energy	6	4	2	0	–
History experts	6	Inertia	2	3	0	1	–
		Free fall	2	1	3	0	0
		Gravity	5	0	1	–	–
		Velocity & acceleration	2	3	1	0	0
		Conservation of energy	3	3	0	0	–
Physics experts	6	Inertia	1	2	1	2	–
		Free fall	0	0	1	2	3
		Gravity	1	1	4	–	–
		Velocity & acceleration	0	0	0	3	3
		Conservation of energy	0	0	3	3	–

Given what we can affirm, by applying the Kruskall-Wallis test, it does appear that significant differences do exist in the studied sample. Comparing the various groups, the only systematic and significant differences are those of the physics experts group from the other remaining groups, except for the slight differences between 12- and 14-year-old adolescents. All these groups, including history experts, demonstrated a very similar performance. According to Mann-Whitney U, we found significant differences between 12- and 16-year-olds ($p<.05$) and between physics experts and 12-year-olds ($p<.001$), 14-year-olds ($p<.001$), and history experts ($p<.01$).

Gravity

Understanding gravity was studied in the Tests II and III, although the subjects did refer to it in task I when discussing the velocity of the fall of the object in terms of its weight and mass. We found three kinds of responses:

1 The heavier balls fall more quickly because the ground attracts them with greater force.
2 An intermediate position which seems to alternate between the two ideas (1 and 3). The subject fluctuates in his/her response seemingly unable to establish a universal law.
3 The weight is always independent of the velocity at which an object falls, given that gravity is constant.

The results obtained following these criteria are shown in Table 12.1. About 15 per cent of the subjects have a correct scientific conception of this notion. Almost 70 per cent are convinced that the heavier objects fall more quickly, an idea that Galileo refuted centuries ago. Even an expert in physics could fall into this erroneous idea. Nevertheless, according to the Kruskall-Wallis test, the results show that there are differences in the total sample ($df=4$, $p<.05$). Upon comparing the groups, the only significant differences are found between the physics experts group and the rest of the groups. Actually, although some subjects in this group have erroneous ideas, it clearly distinguishes itself from the other groups who have similar ideas about gravity.

Velocity and acceleration

The differences between these two concepts were evaluated by means of a question about velocity related to the pendulum in task I, questions 2A and 2B. The responses of the subjects were classified in the following way:

1 The velocity of the pendulum is the same at all points. This indicates a total incomprehension of these concepts of positive and negative acceleration.
2 As the mobile covers more space and time, the velocity is greater.
3 The velocity is greater when the object reaches the lowest point and slower at the highest point, but it is not the same at the two intermediary points. It is greater at the point when the ball is descending. The acceleration is confused, which is effectively different in A and B, with the velocity, which is the same.

4 Velocities are conceived in the correct order. Nevertheless, it is not understood that at point C the velocity is zero. Difficulties do exist upon calculating the instant velocity of the mobile and, as a consequence, an incomprehension of the functioning of the pendulum results.
5 There is a correct differentiation between the concepts of velocity and acceleration. The object will go more rapidly at the lower points and more slowly at the higher.

Table 12.1 summarizes the obtained results. As can be observed, 77 per cent of the total number of subjects were in the first levels, which are clearly simplistic. Only the physics experts clearly achieved the higher categories. When applying the Kruskall-Wallis test, one can see a clear difference between the subjects included in our sample (df=4, p<.001). At the same time, detailing the differences between the groups the physics experts have ideas which are clearly distinct from those of the other groups with respect to velocity and acceleration. At the same time, 16-year-old subjects are clearly differentiated from the other adolescent groups but not from the group of historians.

Conservation of energy

In this section we refer to the content of the explanations given by the subjects in tasks II and III. As we commented earlier, despite the apparent similarity of the situations presented in both tasks, the explanatory physics concepts are clearly different in both cases. Task II ought to be explained by referring to the concepts of potential and kinetic energy or to the conservation of the quantity of movement. On the other hand, task III can be explained by the horizontal velocity acquired by the ball. Therefore, keeping in mind the capacity of the subjects to realize the conceptual differences between both tasks and the quality of the explanation proposed in each task, we have established the following levels of responses:

1 The subjects explain both tasks by concepts of force and velocity.
2 The subjects explain task II using the concepts of force and task III of velocity.
3 The subjects explain both tasks using the concept of energy.
4 Task II is explained by the conservation of energy and task III by the composition of movement (velocity).

Table 12.1 shows the results of this task. As can be seen, only 16 per cent of the subjects refer to the concept of energy in their explanation, and only 6 per cent apply it correctly. The Kruskall-Wallis test shows that not all subjects belong to the same population (df=4, p<.01). As for the differences between the groups, the only significant ones are those of physics experts from the other groups. According to Mann-Whitney U, we found significant differences between physics experts and every other group: 12-year-olds (p<.001), 14-year-olds (p<.001), 16-year-olds (p<.001), and history experts (p<.001). Therefore, while the subjects offer similar explanations, the physics experts resort to different concepts in their understanding of the problems.

Relationship between the analysed ideas

Among the objectives of this research was the recording of the consistency of causal ideas of subjects in mechanics. We have already observed that not all causal ideas pose the same amount of difficulty. Nevertheless, in all of them, global success was minimal (between 6 per cent and 27 per cent) and was usually restricted to the physics experts group. These data show that the majority of the subjects (non-experts) have incorrect ideas of the scientific models accepted in mechanics. Even among the experts, not one subject attained the maximum number of points in the five analyses, demonstrating that, although their knowledge is clearly superior to that of the other groups, it is not what would be expected of these subjects. The question remains – do these ideas consist of just one or of various different theories?

The correlations between the different concepts provide a preliminary answer. The correlations between inertia and the rest of the concepts were very low (mean $r=.17$, $sd=.15$). However, the correlations between all other four concepts (ie., conservation of energy, velocity and acceleration, gravity, and free fall) were quite satisfactory (mean $r=.46$, $sd=.15$).

These correlations indicate a close relationship among all of the concepts analysed, with the exception of inertia, precisely the only task in which the physics experts did not demonstrate a clearly superior performance. The common explained variance was close to 50 per cent. The correlations are especially high between velocity/acceleration and free fall (.69) or conservation of energy (.59), indicating that these three situations have a common conceptual core. On the other hand, the low correlations of inertia show that this concept, just as it was measured, is only slightly connected to the other concepts of mechanics. This is confirmed by the appearance of the distinct differential patterns from those of the rest of the concepts.

It does not seem risky then to affirm, based on the common variance found, that the ideas analysed form part of the same implicit theory, one in which nevertheless notable variability exists from one subject to another.

Reasoning strategies

We have observed that the physics experts possess a clearly different causal knowledge of mechanics than the rest of the subjects, yet at the same time the rest of the subjects have ideas which are extremely similar. Is this difference also found in the reasoning strategies used by the subjects? In relation to this, we have analysed the demonstrations carried out by the subjects in tasks II and III, focusing on the use made of the 'control of variables' scheme. With respect to this scheme, we have established the following levels of response.

1 'Control of variables' does not exist. Systematically, more than one factor at any time was modified in the demonstrations.
2 An incorrect 'control of variables' scheme exists. This is to say that, in the tasks carried out, only one factor is modified while the rest are maintained constant. Nevertheless, the varied factor is not the one the subject is attempting to test but rather it is another distinct factor.
3 There is a correct 'control of variables' scheme in which the subjects, from one task to another, maintain constant all of the factors except the one whose effect they are trying to test.

When analysing subjects' performance according to these criteria, the first thing that needs to be mentioned is the difficulty in situating each subject with respect to these criteria. Although all of the subjects carried out correctly at least once the scheme of 'control of variables', almost 40 per cent of the subjects also carried out reasoning strategies of a lower level, as in type 1 or 2. In relation to this, we used as a complementary criterion, the dominant form of performance, i.e., the performance present in a whole array of the tasks solved (III). Then we placed the subject in the highest level at which s/he had performed. In case of doubt, we resorted to the performance carried out in task II.

Based on these criteria, it was found that none of the subjects systematically solved the problem varying more than one factor at a time. Only two of the youngest subjects repeatedly performed according to level 2. The rest of the subjects, forty-six in total, systematically used the control of variables scheme. Logically, there exist no significant differences in these data between different ages. We can therefore infer, from our sample, that the scheme of 'control of variables' is present in a general sense among the adolescents, at least between 12 and 13 years old. To what can we attribute the difference between this information and that obtained in many other studies? In our opinion, the difference is due to the different criteria utilized. In other studies it was considered that the subject controlled variables if s/he maintained all other variables constant, except the one being tested. In our case, we have evaluated subjects' performance only in terms of the variables that, according to their own theory, intervened.

The difference between the two analyses is clear. When we evaluate the control-of-variables ability only in terms of the subjects' variables, the percentage of correct performance of all subjects rises to 80 per cent. When we make the same analysis considering the experimenters' variables the correct application of the control of variables falls to 50 per cent. This is also the percentage usually found in the replication of the research of Inhelder and Piaget (1955) in the age range used in our research. Actually, it is very possible that in these earlier studies, where no analysis of the ideas of subjects took place, researchers attributed to inferential errors what are actually conceptual deficiencies. According to our data, the adolescents almost universally are able to use the inference rules of multiple causality, although they do not always use them correctly.

In regard to this we have two other types of data. It seems that the nature of the variables that are being tested influences the type of inferences that are drawn. Thus, if we compare in task II the total inferences made with respect to the variables situated on the ramp or in the balls, there does exist a significant chi-square of 7.95 ($p<.05$), in favour of the inferences regarding the ramp. Just as other studies show, subjects seem to have problems separating the effects of the two balls. This seems to hinder the rules of inference used with this material significantly.

A second effect of task content is the following. To demonstrate the effect of the three variables in the inclined plane (height, length, and distance), it is not possible to apply a strict control of variables since the three are already integrated in such a form that it is not possible to vary one while maintaining the other two constant. In fact, the only way to test the possible influence of any of them is the opposite: to maintain constant the variable to be analysed and vary the other two. Only four subjects in the 16-year-old group and two physics experts were able to make this type of demonstration. Adding this performance, as a fourth category in the earlier analysis, there do exist significant differences (Mann-Whitney U) of 12- vs. 16-year-old ($p<.001$), 14- vs. 16-year-old ($p<.05$), 12-year-old vs. physics experts ($p<.05$) and 14-year-old vs. physics experts ($p<.05$). The difference always favoured the group mentioned in second place.

In this way, we can see that the 'control-of-variables' strategy is present in all of the subjects, but its use is subject to dramatic differences in terms of the contents to which the rules are applied. This leads us directly to the relationship between causal theories and reasoning strategies.

Reactions to cognitive conflict

It should be remembered here that the order established between tasks II and III purported to provoke in the subject contradictions between his/her expectations and the observed facts. Specifically, the theory that the heavier objects fall with greater acceleration was apparently proved in task II. Nevertheless, this idea was obviously refuted by task III. In the same way, other contradictions appeared between ideas and inferences in relation to the height of the fall since many subjects were not capable of correctly predicting its effect in task III. In task II, the contradictions were less frequent, even though they did occasionally occur.

In order to classify the reactions of the subjects in these situations of cognitive conflict, we relied upon the positions of Piaget and Lakatos regarding the change of theories. The following levels have been established.

1 No awareness of contradiction exists. The subjects do not realize that their expectations and their observations clearly differ and, therefore, they make no attempt to resolve the conflict.
2 The subject is aware of the contradiction but does not resolve it. S/he does not provide an explanation for the disagreement, limiting him/herself to verifying its existence and describing the conflict. The subjects maintain their theory as invariable, denying the relevance of the data and being incapable of finding an alternative explanation.
3 The subjects resolve the contradiction through an 'ad hoc' explanation which protects their theory against the contrary strength of the data. This explanation is only a complementary argument, generally referring to certain situational restrictions in relation to the initially defended explanations.
4 The subject resolves the conflict by resorting to a concept already existing in his/her knowledge structure. In contrast to the previous levels, the subject reassumes a denial of the theory maintained earlier. That is to say, an actual change in theory is produced ('from within') without the incorporation of new ideas or concepts. The reorganization produced does not imply the appearance of new ideas.
5 The subject resolves the conflict through the formulation of a new idea or concept, which does not exist beforehand, and which clearly denies the earlier explanation. In this case, the cognitive reorganization gives rise to an authentic theoretical progress in which the subject agrees to a new theory.

As can be observed, these levels of response have a close correspondence with the positions of Piaget and Lakatos. In the same way one can see that the transition from one level to another is generally gradual and at times difficult to establish. For example, it is difficult to determine, based on just one experimental session, whether the idea the subject resorts to in order to resolve the conflict is or is not new in his/her system of ideas. In a broader sense, one might think that all theoretical change implies restructuration of both levels 3 and 4. Nevertheless, it does seem convenient to us to maintain this distinction, since, in our opinion, it in itself discriminates two different forms of performance. In fact, we observed that some subjects performed the task with two opposing ideas and, when confronted with the data, they were able to reject one. This type of situation does not imply in any sense the type of 'conceptual revolution' normally suggested in the level 5 performance.

With these criteria established, we proceeded to analyse those situations in which the ideas previously held by the subject were refuted by the conclusions of their inferences. The first interesting result found, just as in the use of the reasoning strategies, was the systematic utilization by the same subject of more than one type of reaction to the contradiction. Given that the major part of the subjects fell into at least one or two contradictions, it was impossible to assign each subject to a typical performance category of the solution of the contradiction. In other words, the diverse forms of resolving a contradiction do not only respond to cognitive characteristics of the subjects but, above all, they are a product of the interaction between those subjects and the contents with which they are confronted. This is to say that they are a product of interaction between the knowledge of the subject and the new information.

Table 12.2 Cognitive conflict resolution

Groups	n	1	2	3	4	5
12-year-olds	17	1	7	4	5	–
14-year-olds	21	4	7	6	4	–
16-year-olds	21	1	3	5	8	4
History experts	9	–	4	2	3	–
Physics experts	5	–	2	–	3	–
Total	73	6	23	17	23	4

n = the total number of contradictions produced in each group

Faced with the difficulty of assigning one level score to each subject, we entered in the analysis responses belonging to each level by each group of subjects. The totals of these answers are shown in Table 12.2. Differently from in earlier tables, 'n' on this occasion does not represent the number of subjects in each group, but rather the total number of contradictions each group had in tasks II and III. It can be seen that, with the exception of the physics experts group, the number of contradictions is, in proportion to the number of subjects, very similar in all the groups.

It can be seen that the responses are distributed evenly in the three central levels, while the two extremes appear infrequent. By applying the Kruskall-Wallis analysis of rank, a global difference appears with a significance level very close to the limit (df=4, p<.05). When comparing the groups, the only significant differences are those between 16-year-olds and the other adolescent groups. On the other hand, the physics experts do not demonstrate a difference from any of the other groups. In this sense one must point out that the contradictions are produced in a greater amount when the theories of the subjects are incorrect. In this manner, the physics experts commit fewer contradictions, which in more than half of the cases can be resolved by means of resorting to concepts already present in the theoretical system. On the other hand, the adolescents and the history experts group show a higher amount of contradictions which they resolve in one of three ways: non-explanation of the conflict, an 'ad hoc' explanation, and resorting to pre-existing concepts. Only the 16-year-old subjects, who do not follow this norm, tend to offer solutions which imply greater cognitive restructuring of the situation. Only in this group do radical conceptual changes appear which are completed with a higher relative frequency of internal reorganizations of knowledge. This difference, more notable with respect to the other adolescent groups, is very interesting since it could indicate that, while the reasoning strategies did not vary from some adolescents to others, the efficiency of these strategies does change. Possibly this change in the effectiveness of the strategies is due to the higher grade of elaboration or 'awareness' of the theories and therefore would be related more to causal knowledge than to actual reasoning strategies.

DISCUSSION

In this final part, we will first summarize the main conclusions drawn from the results obtained with respect to each of the three aspects previously analysed (causal ideas about mechanics, reasoning strategies, and reactions to cognitive conflict). Then we will place these results in the theoretical framework described in the introduction in relation to the generality or specificity of the cognitive processes implied in the comprehension of science.

As far as causal ideas are concerned, we have observed that the major part of the novice subjects in physics – the adolescents as well as the historians – maintain ideas regarding the movement of objects far away from those of Newtonian physics yet very close to those of Aristotelian or medieval concepts. Even though this historical parallelism is limited (McCloskey and Kargon 1988), this result coincides with those obtained in other studies with adolescent samples (e.g., McCloskey 1983; McDermott 1984; Gunstone and Watts 1985). Nevertheless, our results show that these same ideas are shared by the adults who are experts in other areas, in this case history. History experts' comprehension of mechanics is very similar, if not inferior, to that of the adolescents. Thus, age, which is supposedly related to general cognitive development, does not produce differences in the comprehension of such notions as force, movement, and gravity. The critical variable seems to be expertise, connected to the acquisition of specific knowledge and its later reorganization (Carey 1985). Contrary to certain interpretations which attribute 'pre-Newtonian cosmology' to the cognitive immaturity of the adolescents, our results show that the history experts – capable of using very elaborate conceptual systems to interpret social phenomena (Pozo and Carretero 1989; Carretero and Pozo 1991) – have a comprehension of mechanics as limited as the adolescents'.

Another interesting result derived from our study is the grade of consistency of the ideas maintained by the subjects, scarcely investigated until now. The results obtained – with those subjects in which the relationship between the ideas would account for almost 50 per cent of the variance in the performance of the subjects – indicate that the subjects do not possess isolated ideas but, rather, these form part of a certain common structural concept. Even though there is not maximum consistency among the various concepts, possibly due to the effects of context on the activation of the ideas (Bidell and Fischer, Chapter 1, this volume), one can speak about the existence of certain 'implicit causal theories' about the movement of objects. The degree of consistency of these 'implicit theories' as well as the conceptual organization and the variables that influence their activation are aspects that deserve more research if we wish to have a more detailed understanding of the scientific knowledge which the students possess.

There is, nevertheless, an exception in the consistency found within the ideas of each student. We are referring to the task of inertia that shows a low correlation with the rest of the ideas and thus appears not to form part of the implicit theory. This interpretation is supported by the data that show that the inertia task gave a pattern of results different from that of the others: it is the only task in which the experts do not perform superiorly to the rest of the groups. A recent study by Yates *et al.* (1988) has shown that in the solution of the problems designed by McCloskey (1983) about inert movement, subjects could be using inactive representations, based on the activation of prototypical concrete situations, instead of resorting to their implicit or – in the case of the experts – explicit theories about movement.

Regarding the use of inference rules, we can conclude that all of the subjects showed their capability of controlling the variables which they had previously defined, although they did not always do it correctly. In this way, our results show a more general use of the schema of control of variables than those which generally appear in other studies. Nevertheless, when one keeps in mind not only the variables previously defined by the subject, but rather all those present from 'the experimenter's point of view', the percentage of answers based on the control of variables falls to the usual percentage, around 50 per cent. Therefore the difficulties might be derived from a lack of adequate knowledge, which impedes a correct conceptual differentiation, rather than from a lack of logical competence to use the rule of inference. The only relevant variable is again the level of previous knowledge or the expertise of each subject. These results are in accordance with those obtained by the same sample in the solution of history tasks (Pozo and Carretero 1989; Carretero and Pozo 1991). Given that in social problems the differentiation and separation of variables is more difficult than in physics tasks, the same subjects used the control-of-variables rule of inference with less frequency and efficiency in the history task than in the mechanics task. In addition to that, the difference in the use of the rules of inference between experts and novices was greater in the case of the history task.

Finally, we have analysed the results obtained regarding the reactions to cognitive conflict between inferences and previous knowledge. First of all, no characteristic response type exists for each subject; rather, the reaction varied from one context to another. The consequences of cognitive conflict are therefore variable and complex. The analyses indicated that there are few situations in which cognitive conflict generates a conceptual change; furthermore, cognitive conflict does not appear to be a sufficient condition, or perhaps even a necessary one. Possibly it would be necessary to design situations of microgenesis, those in which students were repeatedly submitted to the same conflicts, in order to observe the effects of theories activated by the subjects. The consequences of cognitive conflict seem to depend a great deal on the previous knowledge of the subject and on the type of conflict created. The subjects with an intermediate level of knowledge, that is, the older adolescents, are the ones who benefited most from the conflict. In their case, conflict led in some cases to restructuralization of their ideas. On the one hand, the empirical nature of the conflicts presented in this investigation facilitates an awareness, even though this rarely leads to restructuralization. On the other hand, in social tasks, the conflicts between data and theories are more difficult to detect but easier to resolve (Pozo and Carretero 1989; Carretero and Pozo 1991), given that their nature is more conceptual than empirical.

Actually, returning to the theoretical framework described in the introduction, the results of our investigation can be interpreted more easily in terms of previous knowledge and of conceptual change rather than in terms of the general cognitive level of the subjects and of the possible structural changes which take place. It is expertise, not age, which serves as the best explanatory variable. Adult experts in history show in the mechanics tasks a similar, if not inferior, performance to that of the adolescents.

As far as the models of general development, in contrast to those of acquisition of specific knowledge, are concerned, our results, by showing the importance of expertise in the solution of scientific problems, seem to support more clearly the positions based on the existence of specific models. Nevertheless, we think that in the results of this field there are some data that suggest that this interpretation ought to be made with caution. Although they do show the importance of the expertise, they also reveal the necessity of analysing in more depth its theoretical significance. Based on the idea that expertise rests in the accumulation of specific knowledge, the experts seem to differ from the novices in the personal theories they use to interpret the analysed phenomena. The alternative conceptions could be not just isolated ideas but rather parts of more general theories or conceptual structures about which we still know little. As Case (this volume) maintains, it is potentially useful to establish a level of analysis intermediary to general homogeneous structures and specific heterogeneous knowledge: the level of the central conceptual structures, that could explain the consistency found in the ideas of the subjects. The change from novice to expert would imply, therefore, a true restructuralization (Carey 1985), but it would be a structural change tied to a specific area or domain and not a general structural change *à la Piaget*.

This line of investigation, whose empirical support is far from being firm, requires a deeper understanding of the studies about experts and novices. We need to analyse in greater detail the differences not only of explicit and implicit causal theories but also the manner in which they activate their knowledge by converting it into useful procedures (Bidell and Fischer this volume). Finally, we need to know the mechanisms of change that allow the passage from one theory to another. After all, every expert was once a novice.

ACKNOWLEDGEMENTS

This chapter is based on the doctoral dissertation of the first author carried out under the supervision of the second. We are grateful for the grant received from CAICYT (number 2716/83), supervised by Mario Carretero and Juan Antonio Garcia Madruga. We would also like to thank Jeannine Bogaard very much for her invaluable assistance in making the English version of this paper possible.

REFERENCES

Brown, A. L. and DeLoache, J. S. (1978) 'Skills, plans and self regulation', in R. Siegler (ed.) *Children's Thinking: What Develops?*, Hillsdale, NJ: Erlbaum.
Carey, S. (1985) *Conceptual Change in Childhood*, Cambridge, MA: MIT Press.
Carretero, M. (1984) 'De la larga distancia que separa la suposición de la certeza' (The great distance between supposition and certainty), in M. Carretero and J. A. Garcia Madruga (eds) *Lectura de psicologia del pensamiento* (Psychology of thinking), Madrid: Alianza.
Carretero, M. and Pozo, J. I. (1991) *Novices and Experts: Causal Explanations in History*, paper presented at the 4th EARLI Conference, Turku, Finland.
Chi, M. T. H., Feltovich, P. J., and Glaser, R. (1981) 'Categorization and representation of physics problems by experts and novices', *Cognitive Science* 5: 121–51.
Chi, M. T. H., Glaser, R., and Rees, E. (1982) 'Expertise in problem solving', in R. J. Sternberg (ed.) *Advances in the Psychology of Human Intelligence*, Hillsdale, NJ: Erlbaum.
Claxton, G. (1984) *Live and Learn*, London: Harper & Row.
Driver, R., Guesne, E., and Tiberghien, A. (eds) (1985) *Children's Ideas in Science*, Milton Keynes: Open University Press.
Flavell, J. H. (1982) 'On cognitive development', *Child Development* 53: 1–10.
Gentner, D. and Stevens, A. L. (eds) (1983) *Mental Models*, Hillsdale, NJ: Erlbaum.
Gunstone, R.F. and Watts, M. (1985) 'Force and motion', in R. Driver, E. Guesne, and A. Tiberghien (eds) *Children's Ideas in Science*, Milton Keynes: Open University Press.
Hashweh, M. Z. (1986) 'Toward an explanation of conceptual change', *European Journal of Science Education* 8 (3): 229–49.
Helm, H. and Novak, J. D. (eds) (1983) *Proceedings of the International Seminar: Misconceptions on Science and Mathematics*, Ithaca, NY: Cornell University Press.
Holland, J. M., Holyoak, K. J., Nisbett, R. E., and Thagard, P. R. (1986) *Induction, Process of Inference, Learning and Discovery*, Cambridge, MA: MIT Press.

Inhelder, B. and Piaget, J. (1955) *De la logique de l'enfant à la logique de l'adolescent*, Paris: PUF.
Karmiloff-Smith, A. and Inhelder, B. (1975) 'If you want to get ahead, get a theory', *Cognition* 3: 195–212.
Kuhn, D., Amsel, E., and O'Laughling, H. (1988) *The Development of Scientific Thinking Skills*, New York: Academy Press.
Lakatos, I. (1978) *The Methodology of Scientific Research Programmes: Philosophical Papers*, ed. J. Worall and G. Currie, Cambridge: Cambridge University Press.
McCloskey, M. (1983) 'Naive theories of motion', in D. Gentner and A. L. Stevens (eds) *Mental Modes*, Hillsdale, NJ: Erlbaum.
McCloskey, M. and Kargon, R. (1988) 'The meaning and use of historical models in the study of intuitive physics', in S. Strauss (ed.) *Ontogeny, Phylogeny and Historical Development*, Norwood, NJ: Ablex.
McDermott, L. C. (1984) 'An overview of research on conceptual understanding in mechanics', *Physics Today* 37: 7–24.
Newell, A. and Simon, H. A. (1972) *Human Problem Solving*, Englewood Cliffs, NJ: Prentice-Hall.
Osborne, R. J. and Freyberg, P. (1985) *Learning and Science: The Implications of 'Children's Science'*, New Zealand: Heinemann Educational.
Piaget, J. (1975) *L'equilibration des structures cognitives: Problème central du développement*, Paris: PUF.
Piaget, J. and Garcia, R. (1983) *Psychogenèse et histoire des sciences*, Paris: PUF.
Pozo, J. I. (1987) *Aprendizaje de la ciencia y pensamiento causal* (Science learning and causal thinking), Madrid: Visor.
Pozo, J. I. and Carretero, M. (1989) 'Las explicaciones causales de expertos y novatos en historia' (Causal explanations in history experts and novices), in M. Carretero, J. I. Pozo, and M. Asensio (eds) *La enseñanza de las ciencias sociales* (Social sciences teaching), Madrid: Visor.
Shayer, M. and Adey, P. (1981) *Towards a Science of Science Teaching*, London: Heinemann.
Strauss, S. (ed.) (1988) *Ontogeny, Phylogeny and Historical Development*, Norwood, NJ: Ablex.
West, L. H. T. and Pines, A. L. (eds) (1985) *Cognitive Structure and Conceptual Chance*, Orlando: Academic Press.
Yates, J. T., Bessman, M., Dunne, M., Jertson, D., Sly, K., and Wendelboe, B. (1988) 'Are conceptions of motion based on a naive theory or on prototypes?', *Cognition* 29: 251–75.

Chapter 13

Cognitive prerequisites of reading and spelling
A longitudinal approach

Wolfgang Schneider and Jan Carol Näslund

Longitudinal research on the preschool prediction of academic achievement has accumulated over the last three decades. This research has been fuelled by the concern about high rates of school children with learning problems. As a consequence, there has been an increasing interest in the early identification and treatment of learning problems in order to facilitate school learning and prevent or minimize learning problems (see Bryant and Bradley 1985).

Horn and Packard (1985) presented one of the first meta-analyses (i.e., a quantitative review and statistical synthesis of the published literature; see Hedges and Olkin 1982) based on fifty-eight correlational longitudinal studies conducted mainly between 1960 and 1980. The studies summarized and analysed by Horn and Packard all dealt with the relation of measures administered in kindergarten or first grade and reading achievement later in elementary school. Overall, behavioural measures, language measures, and intelligence appeared to be the best single predictors of reading achievement in grades one to three.

A more concise quantitative review of the research in this area was undertaken by Tramontana, Hooper, and Selzer (1988). In the meta-analysis by Tramontana *et al.*, a total of seventy-four studies published from 1973 to 1986 were included, the majority of these studies focusing on reading skills as the criterion variable. Major differences between the Horn and Packard (1985) and Tramontana *et al.* (1988) meta-analyses concerned the inclusion criteria relevant to the type of predictor relationship among criterion measures and the timing of predictor assessment. That is, the focus in the Horn and Packard review was on univariate prediction, whereas Tramontana *et al.* also considered approaches where various measures were combined in order to maximize predictive accuracy. Further, unlike the Horn and Packard review, Tramontana *et al.* selected only those studies in which predictor measures were assessed *prior* to first grade. Despite these differences in design, the findings obtained by Tramontana *et al.* (1988) very much resembled those reported by Horn and Packard in that measures of general cognitive abilities, language, and visual-motor skills, along with measures of letter naming, were identified as good predictors of reading in the early elementary school years.

In our view, there are at least two general problems with the numerous longitudinal studies summarized by Horn and Packard and Tramontana et al. and dealing with the early prediction of reading skills: (1) The selection of predictor measures was not guided by and derived from theoretical considerations concerning reading, in particular. It is obvious from the review by Tramontana et al. (1988) that a vast array of (mostly psychometric) measures were used that, in most cases, were not proximal to reading processes (e.g., motor skills, behavioural-emotional functioning, general cognitive ability). Interestingly enough, many of these measures predicted later reading performance surprisingly well, particularly when the focus was on univariate prediction. Needless to say, such an outcome does not facilitate the task of researchers trying to come up with a diagnostic screening instrument consisting of a few, effective predictor variables.

(2) Another, related problem concerns the fact that discriminant or differential validity of predictor variables was either not assessed at all or found to be low. In the latter case, measures important for the prediction of reading were equally powerful in predicting maths achievement in elementary school. In general, most attempts to identify a differential pattern of predictors for later achievement in reading versus maths were relatively unsuccessful.

Given these problems, approaches that derive predictor measures from theoretical assumptions concerning possible prerequisites of reading seem preferable to the basically a-theoretical approach dominating longitudinal research on this issue in the 1960s and 1970s. Such studies have indeed been successfully carried out within the last decade and will be summarized in the subsequent section.

PHONOLOGICAL PROCESSING ABILITIES AND READING

Most longitudinal studies on causal relations between the early development of phonological processing abilities and the acquisition of reading skills are based on assumptions derived from the information-processing paradigm. The term phonological processing refers to the use of phonological information (i.e., the sounds of one's language) in processing written and oral language (cf. Wagner 1988; Wagner and Torgesen 1987). Although a generally accepted taxonomy of phonological processing abilities does not exist, the following components are frequently distinguished (cf. also Torgesen et al. 1989): (1) *Phonological awareness*, that is, the awareness of and access to the phonology or sound structure of one's language. This ability includes aspects of analysis (i.e., segmenting a word into units) as well as aspects of synthesis (i.e., combining the constituent segments of a word into a whole word, as realized in the common sound-blending task). The relation of these phonological awareness components to early reading seems evident: processes of analysis are involved when the beginning reader is confronted with a new word and tries to break apart the string of visually presented letters, and processes of synthesis are activated when it comes to putting the sounds of the letters together to form a word.

(2) *Phonological recoding in lexical access*, that is, accessing the referent of a word in a semantic lexicon or internal dictionary. This component implies the retrieval of the phonological codes associated with an object from long-term memory. As noted by Wagner (1988), the objects for which phonological codes are retrieved in actual reading are letters or letter pairs. Tasks typically used to assess this ability involve the rapid naming of colours or objects and deciding whether a string of letters represents a word or a non-word.

(3) *Phonetic recoding to maintain information in working memory*, that is, recoding information into a sound-based representational system that enables it to be maintained in working memory during ongoing processing (Baddeley 1986; Wagner and Torgesen 1987). Examples of tasks assessing this ability include memory-span tasks which include both storage and processing components for stimuli that can be coded with verbal labels, such as numbers, letters, words, or sentences. Efficient recoding in working memory seems important for early reading because beginning readers have to accomplish several tasks when confronted with a new word. First, they have to retrieve the sounds of the letters. Next, the initial sounds must be stored while subsequent sounds are being retrieved, and all of the sounds must be kept in working memory for subsequent processing. Third, the entire set of sounds in working memory has to be blended together to form a word (cf. Wagner 1988).

Research on the relevance of these three components of phonological processing for the acquisition of subsequent reading skill generally yielded impressive results. As indicated by a meta-analysis conducted by Wagner (1988) based on nine correlational longitudinal studies and seven training studies, reliable causal relations between phonological processing abilities and subsequent reading skills were obtained for both types of studies, with median correlations of .38 and .70 for the correlational and training studies, respectively. A path analysis carried out on the correlations aggregated across the two types of studies revealed that about 75 per cent of the variance in the dependent variable (i.e., word analysis) was explained by the three phonological processing abilities described above.

All in all, these findings indicate that metalinguistic abilities assessed during the preschool and kindergarten years strongly influence subsequent reading skills (cf. also Maclean, Bryant, and Bradley 1987; Vellutino and Scanlon 1987, for similar results; these more recent studies were not included in Wagner's meta-analysis). Moreover, it was repeatedly shown that the close relationship between metalinguistic predictors and reading skills did not generalize to theoretically unrelated domains like arithmetic (cf. Bryant and Bradley 1985; Maclean *et al.* 1987).

Given these impressive findings, it is no longer sufficient to ask whether phonological skills play a causal role in the acquisition of reading skills. The question now is which aspects of phonological processing skills (e.g., phonological awareness, recoding in lexical access, recoding in working memory) are most important for the prediction of which aspects of reading (e.g., word recognition, word analysis, sentence comprehension). It was the major goal of the present study to explore this issue in more detail.

MAJOR GOALS OF THE PRESENT STUDY

One basic characteristic of many longitudinal studies exploring the relationship between early phonological processing skills and subsequent reading skill was that only a few components of phonological skills were simultaneously considered as predictors of reading (e.g., Bryant and Bradley 1985; Maclean *et al.* 1987; Perfetti *et al.* 1987; Tunmer, Herriman, and Nesdale 1988). From these studies, it is difficult to tell how and to what extent the inclusion of additional components would have changed the overall pattern of results. Other studies including comprehensive batteries of phonological predictor variables were not longitudinal in nature (e.g., Wagner *et al.* 1987). While such models are informative concerning the factorial structure of preschoolers' phonological processing abilities, they do not allow any conclusions regarding the relative importance of the various components for subsequent reading acquisition. Even those few studies based on both large sample sizes and multiple preschool predictors of reading achievement (e.g., Butler *et al.* 1985; Share *et al.* 1984; Vellutino and Scanlon 1987) were not without problems when estimating predictor qualities via traditional regression analyses or path analysis techniques based on observed variables. Due to the usually large number of predictors and the significant interrelationships among these predictors, the problem of multicollinearity could not be adequately dealt with in these studies, probably resulting in biased parameter estimates and overestimation of 'true' explained criterion variance.

To cope with these problems, a latent variable causal modelling approach (LISREL; cf. Jöreskog and Sörbom 1984) was chosen in our study. In short, the major advantage of this approach is that it distinguishes between a measurement model representing the relationships among observed variables and latent, theoretical constructs, on the one hand, and a structural model representing the interrelations among the latent constructs, on the other hand. As structural/causal relationships are estimated at the level of theoretical constructs and not at the level of fallible observed variables, the number of variables included in the path model is comparably small. The distinction between a measurement model and a structural model also allows for a separate estimation of measurement errors in the observed variables and specification errors in the structural part of the model: large specification errors usually indicate that the causal model was not completely specified, that is, that important predictors were obviously missing. Another advantage of this causal modelling approach is that several so-called goodness-of-fit tests exist that detect the degree of fit between the causal model and the data set to which it is applied. Causal models are said to be 'confirmed' when the goodness-of-fit parameter indicates better-than-chance fit between the model and the data.

Based on this methodological approach, we explored the following questions: (1) How do the three components of phonological processing assessed during the kindergarten years affect reading skill as measured in second grade? (2) What is the relative impact of verbal intelligence and early literacy on the prediction of reading comprehension in second grade, and (3) how specific are the structural patterns, that is, does the causal model specified to explain reading comprehension also generalize to the prediction of spelling in second grade?

The data used in the present study were taken from part of the Munich Longitudinal Study of the Genesis of Individual Competencies (LOGIC; see Weinert and Schneider 1987, for a more detailed description of the longitudinal study). In the LOGIC study, children's intellectual and social competencies were first assessed in 1984 when they were about 4 years old, and have been followed up annually since then.

DESCRIPTION OF SAMPLE AND TEST INSTRUMENTS

The models predicting reading comprehension and spelling were based on different sample sizes. Complete data sets from 185 children were available for the analyses focusing on spelling. As only a subsample of children participated in the reading comprehension tests, the analyses concentrating on this variable were based on only 121 subjects.

All tests, except for the reading comprehension measures, were taken individually. Reading comprehension measures were administered to all children in the classrooms in which they attended. Most measures included in this analysis can be easily linked to the three components of phonological processing described above.

Phonological awareness

Four different measures were used to represent phonological awareness. First, a German version of Bryant and Bradley's (1985) phonological oddity task was used to assess children's understanding of *rhyming*. In this task, children were instructed that they would hear four words from a tape recorder, and that one of the four words would not sound like the others. In the middle sound oddity condition, the target word always shared the last phone with the other three words but differed regarding the middle sound. In the end sound oddity condition, the target word always shared the same middle phone as the other three words but differed concerning the end sound. Finally, in the first sound condition, children had to detect the one out of four words with a first sound differing from that of the three other words. Correct answers were given one point. There was a total of twenty-seven trials, yielding a maximum score of 27.

The second subtest assessing children's phonological awareness was adapted from the Bielefeld Longitudinal Study on Early Risk Identification (Skowronek and Marx 1989). This test consisted of ten word pairs. For each pair, children had to indicate whether the items sounded alike. Again, correct responses were given one point, yielding a maximum score of 10.

A *syllable segmentation task* was also adapted from the Bielefeld Longitudinal Study (Skowronek and Marx 1989). In this task, children were instructed that they would participate in a word repetition game. When presenting the practice items, the experimenters segmented the words into syllables and clapped their hands. Children were instructed to clap their hands when repeating the words. The number of correct word segmentations was used as the dependent variable in this task (max. = 10).

The *sound-to-word-matching task* was also taken from the Bielefeld study (cf. Skowronek and Marx 1989). Children were told that they would hear a number of words, and that they had to listen very carefully. They first would have to repeat each word and then to indicate if a specific sound pronounced by the experimenter was in that particular word. As an example, the experimenter presented the word 'Auge' (eye) and asked subjects if they could hear an 'au' in it. The number of correct responses was recorded (max. = 10).

Phonological recoding in lexical access

Two rapid naming tasks were used to represent phonological recoding in lexical assess. The two rapid naming tasks were also taken from the Bielefeld study. In the first, *rapid colour naming of non-coloured objects*, eight sets of black-and-white drawings of four different objects were presented and labelled by the experimenter. The children were asked to name the correct colours of these objects as quickly as possible.

In the second rapid colour-naming task (*rapid colour naming of objects with incongruent colours*), the same stimulus materials were used. The only difference was that all objects had wrong colours in this task. The children were instructed to give the correct colours of the objects as quickly as possible. Total time needed to complete the tasks and the number of errors were taken as dependent measures in both rapid naming tasks.

Phonetic recoding in working memory

Two verbal memory-span tests were used to assess phonetic recoding in working memory. A German version of the Case, Kurland, and Goldberg (1982) word-span task tapped children's word span. The set sizes varied between three and seven one-syllable words. Beginning with sets of three words, two trials were given for each set size. Children were instructed to first listen to the entire set, then repeat the words they heard. Scores were taken from the maximum number of words repeated in the correct order. This scoring procedure was not in accordance with Case *et al.*'s suggestion of ignoring order because developmental differences in memory span should not be confounded with differences in encoding and preserving information about order. We decided to use the serial word span as dependent variable because it generally showed more predictive quality than the unconstrained word-span measure recommended by Case *et al.* (1982).

A *sentence-span* or *listening-span measure* was adapted from Daneman and Blennerhassett (1984). Seventy-five sentences (at maximum), ranging in length from three to seven words, were read to each child. Sentences were grouped in five sets each of one, two, three, four, and five sentences. Children were presented the one-sentence sets first, followed by the two-sentence sets, etc. With the exception of the one-sentence sets, sentences within each set were read in quick succession. Children were asked to repeat the sentences in each set verbatim. Testing terminated when the child failed to recall all five sentences at a particular level. The total number of sentences recalled correctly was chosen as the dependent variable.

Additional measures

In addition to the three components of phonological processing, two further constructs which had been referred to as important predictors of reading skill in the literature were also included in our battery of predictors. For example, as emphasized by Lomax and McGee (1987) and Share *et al.* (1984), signs of *early literacy* or young children's concepts about print seem to qualify as relevant predictors of reading skill. We thus decided to include three variables tapping this construct in our collection of predictor measures. A *letter-naming task* assessed children's grapheme–phoneme correspondence knowledge. Here, the number of letters correctly identified was chosen as the dependent variable.

The second task (*sign knowledge* or *Logo task*) was originally developed by Brügelmann (1986) and later modified by the Bielefeld group (Skowronek and Marx 1989). The Logo task tapped children's knowledge of letters and words that are hidden in familiar settings. Typical examples are traffic signs (e.g., the STOP sign) and trade marks. In some trials, only the original letters were given without any graphic context. In others, only the graphic context was given and the letters were omitted. We used the number of correct responses in trials focusing on the letters (without graphic context) as the dependent variable in the present analysis.

Finally, *name writing* was chosen as another variable tapping early literacy. Children were asked to write down a word they already knew on a sheet of paper. Those children who were able to write down at least one word were told that the experimenter wanted them to write down another twelve words. The number of words correctly spelled was used as the dependent variable.

The list of predictor variables was completed by tests of *verbal intelligence*. Three verbal sub-tests (i.e., general knowledge, vocabulary, general understanding) from the Hannover-Wechsler Intelligence Test for Preschool Children (HAWIVA; Eggert 1978) were chosen to represent the verbal intelligence construct. The HAWIVA was administered twice, when children were 4 and 5 years old. Combined scores of the three verbal sub-tests were computed on both occasions and used to represent verbal intelligence in the present study.

With the exception of the verbal intelligence measures and the indicator of reading speed, all predictor variables were assessed during the last kindergarten year.

The *criterion measures*, that is, indicators of *reading comprehension* and *spelling*, were taken around the end of second grade. A thirty-item test developed by Näslund (1987) was used to measure reading comprehension and word knowledge within the context of single sentences and longer text (short stories). A total of eighteen multiple-choice items tapped *word knowledge*. They included finding synonyms and antonyms within the context of a sentence. The *text comprehension* part consisted of five short stories followed by two or three multiple choice questions. This task was designed to test children's understanding of the text, deducing answers from inferences based only on information in the stories.

Finally, the *spelling test* consisted of two partially overlapping versions, one presented at the beginning of second grade and the other shortly before the end of second grade. Each test included about twenty target words which were taken from different sources and seemed particularly suited to assess spelling competence in second grade. For all criterion measures, the number of correct items was chosen as the dependent variable.

RESULTS

The means, standard deviations, and ranges obtained for the various predictor and criterion measures are given in Table 13.1. Except for the Bielefeld rhyming task which turned out to be rather easy for most children, the measures were moderately difficult and approximately normally distributed. There were neither ceiling nor floor effects.

Table 13.1 Means, standard deviations, and range for the predictors and criterion variables included in the analyses

Construct/Variable	Mean	SD	Minimum	Maximum
1) *Verbal intelligence*				
HAWIVA 1	34.30	9.42	5.00	58.00
HAWIVA 2	46.08	9.10	8.00	64.00
2) *Phonological awareness*				
Sound oddity	22.91	1.74	18.67	27.00
Bielefeld rhyming	8.13	1.35	3.00	10.00
Sound-to-word match	6.85	2.20	0.00	10.00
3) *Phonological recoding in lexical access*				
Rapid colour naming 1	51.83	18.20	22.00	142.00
Rapid colour naming 2	84.36	29.51	32.00	220.00
4) *Recoding in working memory*				
Word span	3.47	0.97	1.00	6.00
Sentence span	14.04	6.63	2.00	38.00
5) *Early literacy*				
Letter knowledge 1	6.75	7.44	0.00	26.00
Letter knowledge 2	8.31	8.13	0.00	26.00
Sign knowledge	1.00	1.47	0.00	5.00
Written words	2.01	1.92	0.00	12.00
6) *Reading comprehension*				
Word usage in text	14.44	3.62	3.00	18.00
Text comprehension	7.42	3.31	1.00	12.00
7) *Spelling*				
Words correct 1	10.21	2.18	4.00	17.00
Words correct 2	11.03	3.99	1.00	18.00

In a second step of analysis, we calculated the intercorrelations among predictor variables and criterion measures. These are given in Table 13.2, with the reading comprehension measure and the second spelling test serving as criterion variables. As can be seen from Table 13.2, zero-order correlations among most predictors and the two criterion variables were moderately high, ranging between .15 (syllable segmentation task and reading comprehension) and .42 (sound oddity task and reading comprehension). To assess the impact of verbal intelligence on the relations among predictor and criterion variables, we additionally calculated partial correlations controlling for verbal intelligence. The partial correlations are also listed in Table 13.2. A comparison of the zero-order and partial correlations reveals that controlling for verbal intelligence generally led to a drop in correlations. The effects of verbal intelligence on the predictor–criterion relationships seem larger in the case of spelling than for the reading comprehension measures, and they affect the phonological awareness measures more than they influence recoding in lexical access and early literacy. It seems interesting to note that most relationships remained significant even after influences of verbal intelligence had been partialled out.

Table 13.2 Zero-order and partial correlations of predictor variables with reading and spelling measures

Predictor	Reading comprehension correlations Zero order	Partial	Spelling correlations Zero order	Partial
Verbal intelligence	.33		.32	
Word span	.30	.29	.28	.22
Sentence span	.32	.23	.36	.20
Sound oddity task	.42	.36	.39	.27
Bielefeld rhyming	.30	.21	.38	.25
Syllable segmentation	.15	.04	.25	.10
Sound-to-word match	.28	.17	.27	.11
Rapid colour naming 1	−.29	−.29	−.35	−.25
Rapid colour naming 2	−.24	−.24	−.34	−.17
Letter knowledge 1	.37	.31	.39	.29
Letter knowledge 2	.36	.27	.39	.29
Sign knowledge	.29	.28	.25	.13
Written words	.21	.18	.25	.13

Note: Correlations larger than .15 are statistically significant at the p = .05 level.

STRUCTURAL EQUATION MODELLING VIA LISREL

As noted above, the computer program LISREL VI (Jöreskog and Sörbom 1984) was used to analyse the influence of the three phonological processing components, early literacy, and verbal intelligence on later reading related measures and spelling. The measurement model indicated in Table 13.1 was used for all models to be described below.

Three different structural models were specified. The first structural model represented a traditional multiple regression model based on latent variables.

By using such a model, relative direct effects of the predictor variables on the criterion can be assessed. However, nothing is known about possible indirect predictor effects because all predictor measures serve as exogenous, independent variables that are not further explained in the model.

The second structural model was specified as a path model and based on both theoretical assumptions drawn from the relevant literature and the temporal structure of data collection. In this model, verbal intelligence assessed at age 5 was considered the only independent, exogenous variable not further explained in the model. The assumption was that verbal IQ should directly influence other predictor domains but show minor direct effects on the criterion measures (i.e., reading comprehension and spelling). On the other hand, working memory (assessed about half a year later than IQ and about three months earlier than the remaining predictor measures) was assumed to have significant direct impacts on both the other predictor domains as well as the criterion measures. Furthermore, the expectation was that the working-memory construct would also have indirect effects on the criterion measures, mediated by its influence on the remaining predictors which all were assumed to show direct effects on reading comprehension or spelling. Given that the role of working memory for reading acquisition has been demonstrated in numerous studies (e.g., Daneman and Blennerhassett 1984; Mann 1984), a dominant position was reserved for this construct in our Model 2.

A third, alternative model neglected the temporal structure of the data collection process. Instead, the emphasis was solely on theoretical considerations derived from the relevant literature. In this model, verbal intelligence, phonological awareness, and working memory were considered the central explanatory constructs in the model which would influence both early literacy and phonological recoding in lexical access.

Finally, in order to assess the estimability of our causal model, given the structure of our data, we tested a model which theoretically should not fit our data; namely, the assumption that reading comprehension (or spelling) measured at age 7 should predict verbal intelligence two years earlier. From a structural point of view, this model was almost equivalent to Model 2 described above. The only exception was that the positions of the exogenous and criterion variables were exchanged. Our expectation was that such a model should not fit the data. The inclusion of such a 'nonsense' model is useful in order to justify that theoretically based models can be specified given the indicator variables included. If one can show that alternative models, which counter theoretical expectation, do not fit the data, one is in a better position to justify the significance of the causal models proposed.

PREDICTION OF READING COMPREHENSION

In a first step of analysis, a multiple regression model based on latent variables was specified and estimated via LISREL. The maximum likelihood estimates of structural (regression) parameters obtained for this model are depicted in Figure 13.1. According to this LISREL solution, reading comprehension measured at the end of second grade was best predicted by the phonological awareness variable, followed by the phonological recoding in lexical access and working memory constructs. Our regression model fitted the data (chi-square = 108.63, df = 89, p > .05).

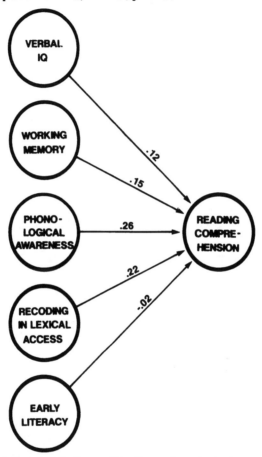

Figure 13.1 Relative contributions of the three phonological processing components, verbal intelligence, and early literacy to the prediction of reading comprehension in second grade

One obvious shortcoming of such a traditional regression approach is that the covariance among the predictor variables is not accounted for by the model. As can be seen from Table 13.3, the intercorrelations among the various predictor variables in our model were indeed considerable. The causal modelling approaches specified above all have in common that they make use of this information. Both causal models specified above yielded chi-square values indicating acceptable data fit (chi-square = 110.49, df = 94 for Model 2, chi-square = 89.39, df = 93 for Model 3, all p's > .05). To determine the best-fitting model, the differences in chi-square values can be compared. These differences form again chi-square statistics that can be used to evaluate the importance of the parameters that differentiate between competing models. A comparison of the two models revealed that significantly better data fit was obtained for Model 3 which was basically derived from theoretical considerations and did not follow the temporal structure of data collection. The LISREL solution for Model 3 is given in Figure 13.2. Only the causal links (i.e., structural coefficients) among the six latent variables are included for the sake of clarity.

Table 13.3 Intercorrelations among latent variables

Variables	(2)	(3)	(4)	(5)	(6)	(7)
1) Verbal IQ	.40	.53	.25	.38	.38	.36
2) Working memory		.60	.46	.28	.36	.41
3) Phonological awareness			.45	.42	.47	.50
4) Recoding in lexical access				.43	.60	.51
5) Early literacy					.39	.49
6) Reading comprehension						.41
7) Spelling						

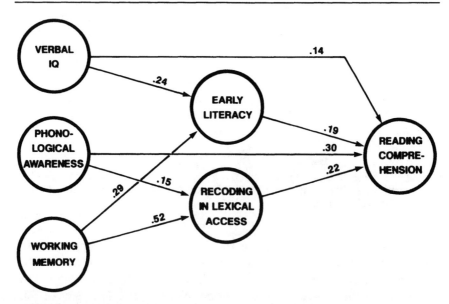

Figure 13.2 Best-fitting structural equation model for the reading comprehension construct

As can be seen from Figure 13.2, only the phonological awareness and phonological recoding in lexical access constructs showed a significant direct impact on reading comprehension. The effect of early literacy was not reliable, and the direct effect of verbal intelligence was very small. The working-memory construct had a strong direct influence on phonological recoding in lexical access, thereby indirectly affecting reading comprehension. Similarly, verbal intelligence and phonological awareness had an additional indirect impact on reading comprehension via their direct influence on the phonological recoding in lexical access and early literacy variables. However, these indirect effects were almost negligible. In total, about 47 per cent of the variance in reading comprehension was explained by Model 3.

In a final step of analysis, the 'nonsense' model described above was estimated and tested. As expected, no acceptable data fit was obtained for this model (chi-square = 155.10, df = 94, p < .001). It was good to see that this model fitted the data significantly worse than the regression model which also yielded an unacceptable fit.

PREDICTION OF SPELLING

The procedure used to determine the best-fitting model predicting spelling performance in second grade was identical to that used for the prediction of reading comprehension. In a first step, a regression model based on latent predictors was estimated and tested. The regression model did not fit the data (chi-square = 198.96, df = 94, p < .001). Given the extremely poor data fit, this model will not be discussed further.

In a second step, the two path models specified above were estimated and tested. Interestingly, Model 3 did not fit the spelling data very well (chi-square = 116.17, df = 95, p = .06). On the contrary, Model 2 representing the temporal sequence of data collection yielded an acceptable data fit (chi-square = 103.04, df = 94, p = .25). As the data fit for this model was significantly better than that for Model 3 the LISREL solution (structural coefficients only) for Model 2 is given in Figure 13.3.

As can be seen from Figure 13.3, the structural pattern describing and explaining spelling performance differs considerably from that describing and explaining the reading-comprehension variable. A certain advantage of Model 2 over Model 3 is that working memory and phonological awareness serve as dependent variables and can be explained in the model. Obviously, verbal intelligence does not only have a strong direct effect on working memory but also directly influences the phonological recoding in lexical access variable. Thus, while verbal intelligence does not directly affect spelling, its indirect impact on the criterion variable is essential. There is little doubt that the total effect of verbal intelligence on spelling is at least comparable to that of verbal intelligence on reading comprehension.

270   Applications in specific domains

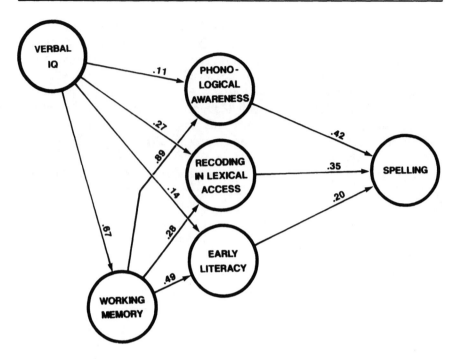

Figure 13.3 Best-fitting structural equation model for the spelling construct

Similarly, the working-memory construct plays an important role in that it strongly affects phonological awareness and early literacy. Moreover, working memory directly influences phonological recoding in lexical access. Again, no direct effect of working memory on the criterion variable was observed. Compared to the reading-comprehension model, the direct effects of phonological recoding in lexical access on spelling are larger, and the direct impacts of early literacy and phonological awareness on spelling are more pronounced. Taken together, the various predictor measures explained about 62 per cent of the variance in the criterion variable.

Last not least, it should be noted that the 'nonsense' model specified for the spelling data was far away from fitting the data (chi-square = 176.87, df = 95, $p < .001$). Again, we were glad to see that the data fit obtained was significantly worse than that of all other competing models.

DISCUSSION

The major aim of the present study was to explore the relative impacts of three phonological processing components (i.e., phonological awareness, phonological recoding in lexical access, and phonetic recoding in working memory) assessed during the kindergarten years on reading comprehension and spelling as measured at the end of second grade. Further questions of main interest were whether individual differences in verbal intelligence and early literacy would contribute significantly to the prediction of both reading comprehension and spelling, and whether different causal (structural) patterns have to be specified in order to explain reading comprehension versus spelling outcomes.

Taken together, the results of the LISREL models seem straightforward in that (1) significant effects of the three phonological processing skills described above on both reading comprehension and spelling could be demonstrated; (2) both verbal intelligence and early literacy significantly contributed to the prediction of both outcome variables; and (3) the causal models showing the best data fit differed for the reading comprehension and spelling criterion measures.

Our findings seem to square well with the existing literature in several regards. First, they demonstrate that the direct effect of intelligence on reading comprehension or spelling is moderate at best when more specific indicators of metalinguistic skills are simultaneously considered (cf. also Bryant and Bradley 1985; Stanovich, Cunningham, and Feeman 1984). This does not mean, however, that the role of verbal intelligence can be neglected, as the visual inspection of the regression model depicted in Figure 13.1 would lead one to suggest. On the contrary, the LISREL solutions shown in Figures 13.2 and 13.3 demonstrate that, by influencing various phonological skills, verbal intelligence does have an indirect effect on both reading comprehension and – even more pronounced – on spelling performance.

Second, and related to this, the strong impact of working memory or memory capacity on the acquisition of literacy emphasized in many recent publications (e.g., Mann 1984; Swanson, Cochran, and Ewers 1989; Yuill, Oakhill, and Parkin 1989) was also confirmed in our study. Again, the multiple regression estimates for this variable were less impressive than the solutions obtained for the causal modelling approach which point to the importance of indirect influences of memory capacity on related phonological processing skills.

We should note here that our memory-span tasks are essentially measures of capacity. As indicated by Swanson *et al.* (1989), the sentence-span task does not separate the storage and processing components of working memory and therefore makes interpretations of performance differences between reading groups difficult. However, we agree with Swanson *et al.* in that the task is appropriate for determining the contribution of information stored in long-term memory to working-memory performance, which seemed to be essential for our theoretical frame of reference.

A comparison of data fit obtained for the traditional multiple regression model and the two theoretically plausible path models reveals that the regression model did not fit the data very well, regardless of whether the reading comprehension or spelling model was concerned. It is obvious that the basic theoretical assumption of the regression model, namely independence of predictor variables, was not met in our study. There is reason to assume that this assumption does not hold for most research in this field, and that the problem of multicollinearity may have been underestimated in many studies. As a consequence of such a bias, overestimations of explained variance in the criterion variables may result. This is at least what we found when we compared the results of multiple regression analyses based on observed variables with analyses based on the latent variable approach. While more than 70 per cent of the criterion variance could be explained in the analyses based on observed variable, not more than 45 per cent of the variance in the criterion variable was accounted for by the predictors included in our LISREL analyses. It appears to us that the latter represents a more accurate estimate of the true relationship.

Still, a few caveats regarding the status of causal modelling analyses seem in order. First, the few LISREL analyses available in the literature share the problem of small sample sizes (cf. Lomax and McGee 1987; Torneus 1984). Our study does not provide an exception, at least not with regard to the reading comprehension data. Replication studies based on independent, larger samples are therefore badly needed to validate the findings presented in this chapter.

Moreover, the question of appropriate alternative models is not trivial. In our case, this means that a number of additional conceptualizations seem intuitively plausible and can be principally tested via causal modelling procedures. For example, we could assume a causal path from phonological awareness to early literacy or reverse the relationship and postulate that the familiarity with print predicts the quality of phonological awareness (see Valtin 1984, for a detailed discussion of this point). We actually did so and estimated such models, which yielded unacceptable data fit.

To summarize, the major outcome of the present study was that components of phonological processing skills represent important prerequisites for the development of subsequent reading and spelling skills. While the strength of the interrelationship seems to vary as a function of the skill under consideration, all of these components function as reliable predictors of reading and spelling skills developed early in the schooling process. It would be premature, however, to generalize this finding across the whole period of elementary school. Recent findings by Butler *et al.* (1985) and Juel (1988) indicate that, while phonological processing skills measured in kindergarten influence reading in early primary grades, early reading achievement seems to be the major determinant of later reading performance.

ACKNOWLEDGEMENTS

We would like to thank Hans Brügelmann and Werner Zielinski for their helpful comments on an earlier version of this chapter.

REFERENCES

Baddeley, A. (1986) *Working Memory*, New York: Oxford University Press.
Brügelmann, H. (1986) *Lese- und Schreibaufgaben für Schulanfänger*, Universität Bremen: Studiengang Primarstufe.
Bryant, L. and Bradley, P. (1985) *Rhyme and Reason in Reading and Spelling*, Ann Arbor, MI: University of Michigan Press.
Butler, S. R., Marsh, H. W., Sheppard, M. J., and Sheppard, J. L. (1985) 'Seven-year longitudinal study of the early prediction of reading achievement', *Journal of Educational Psychology* 77: 349–61.
Case, R., Kurland, D. M., and Goldberg, J. (1982) 'Operational efficiency and the growth of short-term memory span', *Journal of Experimental Child Psychology* 33: 386–404.
Daneman, M. and Blennerhassett, A. (1984) 'How to assess the listening skills of prereaders', *Journal of Educational Psychology* 76: 1272–381.
Eggert, D. (1978) *Hannover Wechsler Intelligenztest für das Vorschulalter (HAWIVA)*, Bern: Huber.
Hedges, L. V. and Olkin, I. (1982) 'Analyses, reanalyses, and meta-analyses', *Contemporary Educational Review* 1: 157–65.
Hogaboam, T. W. and Perfetti, C. A. (1978) 'Reading skill and the role of verbal experience in decoding', *Journal of Educational Psychology* 70: 717–29.
Horn, W. and Packard, T. (1985) 'Early identification of learning problems: a meta-analysis', *Journal of Educational Psychology* 77: 597–607.
Jansen, H., Knorn, P., Mannhaupt, G., Marx, H., Beck, M., and Skowronek, H. (1986) *Bielefelder Screening zur Vorhersage von Lese-Rechtschreibschwierigkeiten*, Universität Bielefeld, SBF 227, W. Germany.
Jöreskog, K. G. and Sörbom, D. (1984) *LISREL IV: Analysis of Structural Relationships by the Method of Maximum Likelihood*, Mooresville, IN: Scientific Software.
Juel, C. (1988) 'Learning to read and write: a longitudinal study of 54 children from first through fourth grades', *Journal of Educational Psychology* 80: 437–47.
Lomax, R. G. and McGee, L. M. (1987) 'Young children's concepts about print and reading: toward a model of word reading acquisition', *Reading Research Quarterly* 22: 237–56.
Maclean, M., Bryant, P., and Bradley, L. (1987) 'Rhymes, nursery rhymes, and reading in early childhood', *Merrill-Palmer Quarterly* 33: 255–81.
Mann, V. (1984) 'Reading skill and language skill', *Developmental Review* 4: 1–15.
Näslund, J. C. (1987) *Leseaufgabe* (Reading Comprehension Test for German Second Graders), Munich: Max-Planck-Institute for Psychological Research.
Perfetti, C. A., Beck, I., Bell, L. C., and Hughes, C. (1987) 'Phonemic knowledge and learning to read are reciprocal: a longitudinal study of first grade children', *Merrill-Palmer Quarterly* 33: 283–319.
Rott, C. and Zielinski, W. (1986) 'Entwicklung der Lesefertigkeit in der Grundschule', *Zeitschrift für Entwicklungspsychologie und Pädagogische Psychologie* 18: 165–75.
Share, D. L., Jorm, A. F., Maclean, R., and Matthews, R. (1984) 'Sources of individual differences in reading acquisition', *Journal of Educational Psychology* 76: 1309–24.
Skowronek, H. and Marx, H. (1989) 'The Bielefeld longitudinal study on early identification of risks in learning to read and write: theoretical background and first results', in M. Brambring, F. Lösel, and H. Skowronek (eds) *Children at Risk: Assessment, Longitudinal Research, and Intervention*, Berlin: Walter de Gruyter.
Stanovich, K., Cunningham, A. E., and Feeman, D. J. (1984) 'Intelligence, cognitive skills, and early reading progress', *Reading Research Quarterly* 19: 278–303.

Swanson, H. L., Cochran, K. F., and Ewers, C. A. (1989) 'Working memory in skilled and less skilled readers', *Journal of Abnormal Psychology* 17: 145–56.

Torgesen, J. K., Wagner, R. K., Balthazor, M., Davis, C., Morgan, S., Simmons, K., Stage, S., and Zirps, F. (1989) 'Developmental and individual differences in performance on phonological synthesis tasks', *Journal of Experimental Child Psychology* 47: 491–505.

Torneus, M. (1984) 'Phonological awareness and reading: a chicken and egg problem?', *Journal of Educational Psychology* 76: 1246–358.

Tramontana, M. G., Hooper, S. R., and Selzer, S. C. (1988) 'Research on the preschool prediction of later academic achievement: a review', *Developmental Review* 8: 89–146.

Tunmer, W. E., Harriman, M. L., and Nesdale, A. R. (1988) 'Metalinguistic abilities and beginning reading', *Reading Research Quarterly* 23: 134–58.

Valtin, R. (1984) 'Awareness of features and functions of language', in J. Downing and R. Valtin (eds) *Language Awareness and Learning to Read*, New York: Springer-Verlag, pp. 227–60.

Vellutino, F. R. and Scanlon, D. M. (1987) 'Phonological coding, phonological awareness, and reading ability: evidence from a longitudinal and experimental study', *Merrill-Palmer Quarterly* 33: 321–63.

Wagner, R. K. (1988) 'Causal relations between the development of phonological processing abilities and the acquisition of reading skills: a meta-analysis', *Merrill-Palmer Quarterly* 34: 261–79.

Wagner, R. K. and Torgesen, J. K. (1987) 'The nature of phonological processing and its causal role in the acquisition of reading skills', *Psychological Bulletin* 101: 192–212.

Wagner, R. K., Balthazor, M., Hurley, S., Morgan, S., Raskotte, C., Shaner, R., Simmons, K., and Stage, S. (1987) 'The nature of prereaders' phonological processing abilities', *Cognitive Development* 2: 355–75.

Weinert, F. E. and Schneider, W. (1987) *The Munich Longitudinal Study on the Genesis of Individual Competencies: Report Number 3: Results of Wave One*, Munich: Max-Planck-Institute for Psychological Research.

Yuill, N., Oakhill, J., and Parkin, A. (1989) 'Working memory, comprehension ability, and the resolution of text anomaly', *British Journal of Psychology* 80: 351–61.

Concluding chapter

Chapter 14

Returning to school
Review and discussion
John B. Biggs

EVERYDAY AND SCHOOLED LEARNING

It is not intended in this chapter to explore how far neo-Piagetians have been able to reach consensus on theoretical issues, but how far they have come along the road towards viable educational applications. The first question has been well explored in the collection edited by Demetriou (1988), which includes chapters written by many of the present contributors.

To ask if modern cognitive developmental theories can profitably go to school is to ask what school learning involves; and what, then, the theories and experimental studies reported here might have to offer. As several contributors have indicated (Bidell and Fischer; Biggs; Case; Resnick, Bill, and Lesgold; Valsiner), school learning differs from everyday learning in certain ways that developmental psychology must recognise (see also Resnick 1987; Sternberg and Wagner 1986). Two such ways are outstanding: content and context.

The content and context of schooling

Whereas everyday learning is concerned with personally valued content, experienced firsthand, and dealt with in context, the content learned in school is mostly declarative knowledge, an abstraction of what others have discovered. The coming generation has not had firsthand experience in constructing that knowledge nor will they be putting it to use in the context of their own felt needs. Learning codified abstractions causes motivational and consequent problems. Most children simply don't like it.

Schools assume 'a separation between knowing and doing, treating knowledge as an integral, self-sufficient substance, theoretically independent of the situations in which it is learned and used. The primary concern of schools often seems to be the transfer of this substance' (Brown, Collins, and Duguid 1989: 32). Brown *et al.* argue that cognition is *situated*; situations co-produce knowledge through activity, and, by ignoring this, 'education defeats its own goal of providing usable robust knowledge' (ibid.). These authors do not consider declarative knowledge to be 'robust', so that in continuing to focus on the transfer of such knowledge, the school culture becomes 'inauthentic', providing students with *ersatz* activities. Schools should instead provide students with a context and activities that lead to the construction of knowledge as it used (ibid.).

The link between this view and the present concern is made clear by Bidell and Fischer (Chapter 1): that without theoretical descriptions of cognitive development that adequately capture the role of context in the production and organization of knowledge, there will continue to be a gap between cognitive developmental theory and educational practice'.

But can we in fact separate content and context? Are knowing and doing inseparable? There could be a problem in accounting for civilization if they were not; to know only through doing involves multiple reinventions of the wheel. On the other hand, there is no doubt that context-based learning is very much more powerful than learning disembedded content. Perhaps we are talking about two different things: the status of different kinds of knowledge and the most efficient means of learning any kind of knowledge.

The problem with a fully blown situated view of cognition, then, is that it fails to recognize that there are different kinds of knowledge: tacit, procedural, declarative, theoretical, to name but some of those mentioned by Biggs. These forms of knowledge both implicate cognitive development and differentiate targets for schooling. Professional preparation, for example, is to make espoused theory drive theory-in-practice (Argyris 1976), thereby putting declarative knowledge to work, both procedurally and conditionally. Declarative knowledge may be hard to learn, and harder to apply, but that does not mean it is *ersatz* knowledge. Knowledge, like a word-processing document, once constructed needs to be saved; the document can be retrieved and printed, or added to, cut-and-pasted, and edited at any time, and thus reconstructed to be saved again. The skills both of knowledge processing and of knowledge reconstruction need to be widely available; compulsory education is there to see to that, at least in the latter case.

That somewhat laboured simile is meant to define a function for schooling that helps students ultimately to beat the undoubted situatedness of cognition, not to succumb to it. Shayer, Efklides *et al.*, Csapó, and Goossens explicitly, and all other contributors implicitly, are concerned with transfer. Learning by 'just plain folks' in the here-and-now is one thing (Brown *et al.* 1989); transferring that learning to cope with the there-and-then is quite another. The school is the place designed to be where all folks, not just the plain ones, acquire the tools for best effecting that transfer. Whether schools do that adequately is a very different question. I would argue that they do not; they make learning harder than it should be, and actually turn some people off learning.

The iatrogeny of school is not so much due to its content, then, but to its *context*, which, when compared to the conditions in everyday life, provides us with a paradox (Resnick 1987; Sternberg and Wagner 1986).

Mentoring relations. In everyday life, people tend to work with the same colleagues, and their mentor works in a one-to-one, generally supportive, way. In almost all secondary schools, teachers are shuffled across classes according to their content specialism, inhibiting the formation of strong mentor relationships.

Motivation. Much everyday learning springs from a felt need to learn; the reasons for engaging currently important learning are simple and direct. Most male adolescents don't have to be 'motivated' to learn to drive, but most do need to be 'motivated' to learn mathematics. Codified knowledge does not provide its own motivation for learning; students are required to learn content that rarely creates a fierce need to know.

Individual versus social learning. The context of everyday practice is most frequently social, in which problem solving is shared and roles are complementary. School learning emphasizes the solitary role of the individual in learning and problem solving. Shared problem solving is rarely encouraged, but is mostly punished as 'cheating'.

Accreditation and assessment. Emphasis on the individual working solo is a necessary consequence of the accrediting function of school; the 'purity' of cognitive processing cannot be guaranteed unless it is taught and tested individually. The existence of assessment in whatever form, but in some forms more than in others, drastically affects the context of learning (Crooks 1988). Being assessed, publicly, is one of the most frequent, and potentially most damaging, things experienced in schools (Bloom 1971). Yet the charter of schools prescribes assessment. Not to assess would be to abrogate the school's responsibilities to society.

Formal structure. Schools have an elaborate superstructure involving the design, delivery, and evaluation of course content: the length and timing of classes, the design of the curriculum, the allocation of human and material resources, the need for assessment, and the like. This superstructure exists mainly for administrative, collegial, and social reasons, not for educational ones, and it frequently undermines the educational functions it is supposed to serve (Reid 1987). Everyday learning is largely free of this superstructure.

It is therefore inevitable that school learning should differ from learning in everyday life. Schools exist precisely because there are socially and culturally important things to learn that would not be learned if left to the fortuities of everyday experience. Schools are deliberately set to sail against the winds of existential needs. But need they be so *aggressive* about it?

Paradoxes of schooling

This picture of school learning is not only discouraging, it involves a double paradox. First, school work is unnatural, difficult, unpleasant, and at variance, in its insistence on solo performance and generality of process, with the very world for which it is intended to be preparatory. This inconsistency must place a barrier between knowledge acquisition and its deployment in the non-school environment. For example, students use 'alternative frameworks' to interpret their world, when their science education is supposed to provide the framework for so doing (Driver 1983). While Pozo and Carretero (this volume) show that most such frameworks – not all, inertia for example – gradually give way to the momentum acquired by declarative expertise, probably most students strike a multistructural coalition between the declarative knowledge endorsed by examination and the cognate procedural knowledge developed in the context that they use to interpret their world.

There is yet a second paradox. Despite the emphasis in school on learning general processes in solitary contexts, the most successful programmes for developing higher cognitive skills have a content-specific focus and feature characteristics of out-of-school contexts such as collaborative and socially shared intellectual work (Resnick 1987).

Other studies come up with similar results. Successful learning has been particularly noticed when:

1 Students teach other students: 'There is a wealth of evidence that peer teaching is extremely effective for a wide range of goals, content, and students of different levels and personalities' (McKeachie *et al.* 1986: 63).
2 One-to-one interaction occurs between tutor and tutee, involving 'scaffolded' instruction (Fischer and Bullock 1984; Wood, Bruner, and Ross 1976).
3 Formal content is learned in the context of solving actual professional problems. Problem-based learning has become hugely successful in professional education (Boud 1985; Newble and Clarke 1986).
4 Abstract, conceptual learning is built on lower-level learning, particularly where a variety of hands-on experiences are used (Bruner 1964; Dienes 1963).
5 Formally taught knowledge is specifically linked to sensory and enactive experiences (McKenzie and White 1982).

The content taught by these apparently 'non-academic' methods includes academic subjects like mathematics, and at university, secondary, and primary levels.

We return, then, to the point of separating content and context. Successful methods of teaching abstract, depersonalized content appear *not* to be those that treat content in an abstract, depersonalized way. If the content of teaching is 'cold' (Brown *et al.* 1983), then its methods of delivery seem best to be 'hot'. And when they are, Resnick concludes, schools might not only deliver content more effectively, but teach those affective, social, and value-laden contents and processes that permit 'a population to function as a true society can be developed' (1987: 19).

If we are asking for ways in which developmental theory might go to school, here's not a bad start. As psychologists, we are not querying what schools set out to do so much as the funny way they insist on doing it.

PREPARING FOR SCHOOL

How can theory cope with the content and context of schooling? Some crucial issues need to be resolved; all are variously addressed by the present contributors.

Theory building

Although Piaget originally started out in the 1920s to explore more than the logico-mathematical domain, he later became entrenched in it, and only very late in his career did he begin to move again on a broader, softer, front. As far as application is concerned, this has led to many problems, as Bidell and Fischer have already pointed out. First, education is about more than science and mathematics learning, or even than thinking in terms of formal logic: as Bidell and Fischer indicate (p. 18), education is a broad social process involving, among others, factors of cognition, emotion, culture, class, race, and gender.

Second, Piagetian theory, along with psychometric theory, proposes context-neutral conceptions of cognitive abilities, which in the case of developmental psychology implies a general stage structure. Education, on the other hand, takes place in and is inextricably tied to specific contexts (Chapter 1).

If it is to go to school, then, developmental theory needs to address areas other than those of logico-mathematical reasoning, and all contributors would agree with this (the particular subject-matter foci of the great majority notwithstanding). Certainly, Bidell and Fischer, Case, and Valsiner emphasize the social domain and, with Biggs, the affective domain.

The second point, on the specificity of context, is not so readily resolved, although there has been considerable development since the Genevan heyday, which followed the prevailing model of the 'One Grand Theory', be it behaviourism, cognitivism, or whatever. In that hypothetico-deductive mode of theory building, the attempt was made to construct a theory for all seasons, based on impeccable data obtained under controlled, noise-free conditions. However, if we try to enumerate the practical applications that have been derived from such theories, there are few.

If, on the other hand, the conceptual framework for education is derived bottom-up, from a study of educational contexts, the game changes (Biggs 1976; Desforges and McNamara 1977; Snow 1974). Generalizing across contexts ceases to be the issue, but developing what works within each context certainly is, Resnick, Bill, and Gold's chapter being a special case in point. What data do we accept for purposes of theory building? All contributors accepted at least some input from classroom data (some considerably more than did others), and, while Halford and Boulton-Lewis used a general operation, structure mapping, they were concerned to apply it to a classroom issue, the teaching of number through blocks and other analogues.

The generality of stages

Does development proceed across a broad front, or is it context-specific? The Genevan response saw development as proceeding across as broad a front as may be conceived. That theme now reappears in a transposed key, with a full range of variations. At the most general end are Case's 'central conceptual structure' and Halford's mappings; then Demetriou et al.'s 'specialized structural systems', the contents of which are isomorphic to the traditional academic subject disciplines; Biggs's topic-specific realizations of general structures within and across different modes of representation; and, more towards the specific extreme, Bidell and Fischer's highly context-dependent skill structures, and, finally, Valsiner's indeterministic constraints model. There's something for everyone here.

While all writers who address the issue abjure a classical *structure d'ensemble*, Case's 'neo-structuralist' CCS is suspiciously like one. The domain specificity of the CCS would extend broadly across most curricula, covering such diverse areas as number handling, music sight reading, and social empathy (Case and Griffin 1990); the CCSs are not, in other words, specific to particular problems. Efklides, Demetriou, and Gustafsson report that this evenness breaks down when tested *across* different SSSs, which seemingly are equivalent to Case's CCSs, but, despite their seeming heterogeneity, Case's tasks are all within the same SSS. How far this challenges Case's fundamental position has yet to be resolved.

Case thinks his CCSs differ from a *structure d'ensemble* in the following ways: they are semantic in nature, not syntactic; are specific in form and to a domain; may be acquired socially; and are directly teachable. The last point, if demonstrable, has important implications for curriculum, both for what to teach, in what order, and how to teach it. Case thus appears to be treading a very narrow path between reconciling domain and context specificity with the hitherto irreconcilables, teachability and generality of transfer. If his findings are replicated widely, the implications for application are exciting.

Halford and Boulton-Lewis's ubiquity of mappings suggests an operational generality redolent of Genevan operations, with working memory also as a general structural feature (Case, Demetriou *et al.*, Halford and Boulton-Lewis, and Schneider and Näslund also specifically use working memory in their models). Halford and Boulton-Lewis are, however, not concerned so much with the aspect of generality as with the question of teaching mathematics by analogy, and certainly within that well-structured domain they make an excellent case for showing how abstraction can be explained in terms of structure mapping, but whether maths should be *taught* using a mapping paradigm is, they admit, a separate question. Their approach, and Resnick *et al.*'s, seem to address the same area, the learning of number, from opposite corners: the one general, the other highly contextual. We return to that issue later.

Context specificity

The related matter of context also is unresolved. Two contributors in particular recognize that the context affects the nature both of what is learned and of learning itself: Valsiner speaks of the 'pupils' co-constructivist role in their cognitive development in the school setting' (p. 76) and Bidell and Fischer emphasize that 'skill theory starts with the actions of the person-in-a-context, examining the process of development as it occurs in everyday settings' (p. 18). Such a view implicates school (*inter alia*) at the heart of the process of cognitive development. This is quite different from the view that cognitive development occurs, and then school has to contend with the result: the classical view, vestiges of which remain in some of the present contributions.

Context specificity depends crucially on the next issue, the nature of the stages, or levels within stages.

The nature of what is represented at various stages

As to the nature of the basic structural unit, or what is represented by a stage, disagreement is rife (see also Case 1988). Bidell and Fischer refer to skills throughout all stages; Case to semantic nodes and relations within the CCS, and problem, goal, and strategies for reaching the goal, within stages; Biggs to the mode in which the element is represented across stages, and structures within stages; and Halford and Boulton-Lewis to symbols and mapping, different stage levels being distinguished by the nature of the mapping, whether elemental, relational, or system.

There is thus a distinction between the nature of stages themselves and the nature of what occurs within stages. 'Structure' is used at both levels: Halford's mapping structures across stages and Biggs's SOLO structures within stages. Fischer's original 'skills' (1980) seem to do service at all levels, his present contribution taking the original on board, but concentrating on macro matters of context and application.

There seem to be several questions here: what is represented (the content of the task); how it is represented (the medium in which the contents are displayed); how the contents are structured; how the contents get to be structured (the mechanism of learning); how change in representation occurs (the mechanisms of development); and many more. Not only has nobody addressed all the questions, but some would argue that some of them shouldn't be asked. Bidell and Fischer would deny any distinction between the last one, while Valsiner would, I think, argue in terms of a process that would bypass all of the above.

A related question is the developmental pathway through stages. Bidell and Fischer offer two models: linear, through which all individuals must pass; or the developmental web, offering alternative pathways, depending on the task, the culture, the gender, or other affective or social factors. Most writers would not subscribe to the single ladder, but there is clearly plenty of divergence between a view implying few such ladders – and it seems that Case, Halford, and Demetriou would be doing so – and the full web treatment, espoused certainly by Bidell and Fischer, Valsiner, and Resnick *et al*. An implication for instruction would be that those holding a modified ladder position would opt for strong direct instruction, scaffolding from rung to rung as it were (possible examples being Case, and Halford and Boulton-Lewis), while those seeing relativity and alternative pathways would propose bottom-up instruction (such as Resnick *et al*.).

Inducing cognitive change

One of the important features of neo-Piagetian theories is that they focus on the interface between stages, and what happens within a stage, as much as or more than upon differences between stages. Thus, instead of global strategies for instructing, or for withholding instruction, based on notions of readiness or of optimal mismatch, more task-oriented strategies of learning and instruction can be devised on the basis of what actually happens between developmental changes.

Part of what happens may be biological, which Case and Fischer acknowledge, but other mechanisms are posited that suggest strategies for instruction. It is quickly becoming an empirical matter to see which of these are viable in the classroom. Case and Halford and Boulton-Lewis emphasize the importance of working-memory limitations: Case with the representation of the problem, the goal, and the strategies for reaching the goal; and Halford with the four levels of mapping and the space required for each. For both, deriving strategies of instruction then becomes a matter of maximizing the availability of working memory so that higher-level mappings or other processes are possible, which can be done by automatizing lower-level processes and contents of knowledge or teaching in a way that is parsimonious in the use of working memory. Case however goes further and postulates generic structures, a sequence, and possibly a process for teaching them.

Bidell and Fischer use the term 'skill' precisely as a context-defined unit of development, and hierarchical skill sequencing as what happens in development. They put strong emphasis on social support and scaffolding as means of hastening the development and 'constructive' generalization of skill sequences; and on different routes of sequencing for different students in different contexts.

Metacognitive mechanisms have had considerably more mileage in the general than in the developmental literature, but they are given prominence here by Demetriou *et al*. as part of their overall system. They show that in humanities subjects, metacognition may be more significant for performance than the specific knowledge base. Their provision for integration between developmental and gender theories of learning, and for individual differences – a matter not dealt with by any other theorist – is of great significance with regard to educational applications.

What, then, of deliberate intervention to induce cognitive change? We might follow Shayer, and ask what we are trying to achieve through intervention: to improve instruction or to accelerate development? The answer is not as simple as it looks; if school is in fact an important agent in development, we might find problems in distinguishing where one began and the other ended. Another tack would be to take Shayer's reference to Perkins and Salomon's (1989) 'high' and 'low' roads to transfer. The high road involves far transfer, which implies metacognition, the use of higher-order principles, and, in so far as that involves a modal shift, development. The low road involves near transfer, within the given context, and is based on the lower-level processes of familiarity and practice.

The present contributors take the high road, focusing on a high-level construct, presumably mediating school performance, as the target for change. Depending on one's theory of that meta-level target – whether it be a CCS, or an SSS, or a set of logical operations – so one will predict enhanced performance in those school subjects participating in that meta-target, and not in others. The target is near-near or near-far transfer, depending on how close the training task is to the set task. No one here is aiming for far-far transfer (see Goossens).

Efklides *et al.*'s results were complex, not to say 'phenomenally contradictory' as they report, but provide some evidence for the sought-for high road. The causal-experimental SSS showed evidence for training effects, but not the quantitative-relational, although CE gains were less than QR gains; and, as expected, there was no transfer across SSSs. Greater effects were found with 16-year-old than with younger students, possibly because of more sophisticated metacognitive behaviour in older children; however, it is not clear in the training and tasks if correct responses could be given simply by modelling the supplied algorithm or if higher-order metacognitive processes indeed needed to be involved.

Csapó's even larger-scale study also produces a complex mix of results. The targets of intervention were three groups of formal operations: logical, combinative, and systematizing. Enhancement of each was predicted to have differential effects on different school subjects. In outline, the model could be conceptualized in terms of Demetriou *et al.*'s SSSs, except the latter are content based, not logically based. Again, the results were mixed. Using Shayer's suggested method of comparing intervention effects against expected normative trends over time, some results stood out: effects due to combinative ability training affected all school subjects at both fourth- and seventh-grade levels; effects due to logical-ability training affected the younger group only, again on both science and grammar, while systematizing training appeared to have no effect, perhaps because of this ability showed strong spontaneous development. As opposed to Efklides *et al.*, then, Csapó achieved best results with younger, not with the oldest, students.

Goossens helps put these and other findings into focus with his meta-analysis of transfer findings. His overall figures are astonishing. Depending on the particular comparison, the results of thirty-eight studies, involving nearly 3,000 subjects, give near-near and near-far transfer an average effect size of .88 and .82 sigma scores respectively. Thus, an average student in an experimental group would rise from the 50th to the 80th percentile and from the 50th to the 74th percentile on retention over an average of ten weeks. Effects of far-far transfer were, not so astonishingly, zero.

Looking at the type of training, it was found, again surprisingly, that short-term and medium-term programmes achieved larger effects than long-term programmes (eight or more training sessions). Training was coded according to high direction vs self-direction but no differences between training methods were found.

Such data should have implications for the present debate on the generality of cognitive structures, but Goossens is cautious, simply suggesting that the lack of far-far transfer seems counter to a *structures d'ensemble* interpretation. Goossens echoes everyone's disappointment at the lack of differential for qualitatively different training techniques; this would not be expected given the current emphasis on metacognitively mediated transfer. He himself attributes this to methodological problems in meta-analysis. I hope he is right.

Again, we have the uncomfortable feeling of interpreting a very accommodating ink-blot. The very thing we want to focus on – to what can we attribute these impressive effect sizes following intervention – becomes a fuzzy set. In particular, it is not very clear what we are really trying to influence:

1 logical operations, distilled from Piaget, certainly appeared to be Csapó's target, and possibly form a Caseian CCS;
2 content areas, which might then be a Demetriouian SSS;
3 modes, or higher order ways of representing the data;
4 metacognitive control.

Pozo and Carretero's work on alternative frameworks or naive theories is relevant at this point. They asked if misconceptions of scientific concepts become corrected by cognitive development or by instruction. The answer seems to be that it depends on the topic: in most of the mechanics problems, physics experts, fortunately for our faith in schooling, showed fewer misconceptions than history experts or high-school students, but sometimes the history experts showed fewer misconceptions than 16-year-olds, sometimes the science taught in school gave the 16-year-olds the edge. Basically, they conclude that (with the exception of the concept of inertia) expertise, not age, is the most important factor in determining the quality of scientific thinking.

Three topics, velocity/acceleration, free fall, and conservation of energy, showed strong intercorrelation, suggesting 'a common conceptual core'.

Thus, the training studies did seem to induce change in a way that affected more than the task under training. It seems likely that some content-specific common conceptual core would account for this, but the nature, and the breadth, of such a core is as yet unclear.

Social interaction

Nobody denies the importance of social interaction in cognitive development, but it is specifically mentioned by Case, Bidell and Fischer, and Valsiner. The last three would argue that any applications to school would have to be encased in a social context, school being itself an essentially social experience. Yet that is part of the paradox: school might be social, but schooling emphasizes the asocial, accrediting the individual's competence, not the group's (Goodnow 1991; Resnick 1987). In fact, it could be argued that it was the heavy legacy from both cognitive and individual difference psychology that set schooling in that individualistic, norm-referenced direction, but to do so would be to give too much credit to psychology's influence. Rather, let us say that other factors, such as society's demand for assessment and accreditation, gave schooling that character, and that educators were only too glad to take on board Binet, Spearman, Thurstone on one deck, and Piaget on another, to help navigate a course already determined.

This being so, then the thrust from latter-day developmentalists is welcome, to add both affect and people to the process of education. The interesting thing is that to do so would enhance rather than weaken academic outcomes.

GOING TO SCHOOL

The previous section has concentrated more on the metatheoretical aspects of applying psychology to education; here we consider the basics. These are usually taken under the headings of curriculum, instructional method, and assessment. Here, however, instructional method has been addressed more than the other areas, except in Biggs's chapter, which reversed that emphasis, saying more about assessment and curriculum objectives than about method, so what has been said there will not be repeated here. Very little was otherwise said about assessment, so in this section we deal with curriculum and instructional method.

Curriculum

On curriculum, Case makes an important distinction between logical sequencing of materials in the curriculum and psychological, a theme also taken up by Bidell and Fischer. Case suggests that his own work, and that on children's 'naive theories' for construing science, could be used to suggest more psychologically appropriate sequences, but this point is not developed. These naive theories, or 'alternative frameworks' (Driver 1983), should not be regarded simply as pathologies of thinking arising from inappropriate curriculum development and teaching, but as arising out of the nature of development itself.

Resnick et al.'s 'protoquantitative schemata' (PQSs) are a case in point. These seem awfully like mathematical alternative frameworks, represented in the ikonic mode. She uses them as the basis for further development through bottom-up instructional procedures. As Pozo and Carretero also show in physics, the naive theories held by their (often highly educated) students would not have been considered naive by scientists of another age; the ontogeny of these theories follows their phylogeny. Newtonian or even Aristotelean physics are hardly pathologies so much as developments along the way to modern expert thinking. Would scientists have reached relativity without Aristotle, and then Newton, as precursors to their thinking? Would modern students reach relativity without alternative frameworks as precursors to theirs?

The suggestion by both Case and by Bidell and Fischer for curriculum design could be one way to go: to plot skill sequences for different populations within topics and subject matters. Although this might seem reminiscent of learning hierarchies (Gagne 1968), it is not; it is buying the point made by Case that the way children best develop ideas may not be the way expert adults see it. Further, the notions of social support and non-cognitive educational goals go well beyond learning hierarchies themselves.

The *modes x levels* model of Biggs might be helpful in providing the macro framework, if not the topic detail in such an exercise. An implication of this model is that the adult expert conception of a topic is couched in concrete-symbolic or formal modes, but it has a sensori-motor and an ikonic history that ought not to be ignored; naive theories are simply cast in a mode and/or level that is lower than that targeted. Bidell and Fischer add to this by saying that there are alternative routes to the target conception, depending on the specific context of the learner, and their analysis seems a way of operationalizing optimal routes. This is clearly an aspect that needs developing in detail.

Instructional method

Implications for instructions do not exactly leap from the work reported in Part II on inducing cognitive change, not even when considering methods of inducing change; as noted, they all seemed equally effective. Is the picture any clearer when we focus on specific subject domains?

Halford and Boulton-Lewis concentrate on a particular and highly significant task in the context of primary-school number teaching. The problem is one that has disappointed teachers and progressive educators generally: blocks seem intuitively an excellent way to teach number, but they don't work reliably. The results are inconsistent and non-replicable rather than consistently negative. Why?

Their discussion of structure mapping the task required of the Dienes blocks is illuminating; the processing load is excessive, and likely to be a barrier to understanding. The point that the extra load imposed by the analogue itself might interfere with higher-order coding – that unless the students see that a base-2 representation is in fact a representation of a concept, and not another set of blocks to manipulate – is well taken, and seems self-evident. However, a study carried out when the Dienes blocks were originally used in Leicestershire (Biggs 1967) suggested, on the contrary, that children were using the materials very effectively, leading them both to understand the concept of place value (which is what the blocks were designed to teach) and also to calculate speedily and accurately, which was unexpected. Also unexpected was finding a strong *ability × treatment* interaction: the lower-ability children gained most in understanding, not the brightest. This particular finding was quite the opposite when evaluating the structurally simpler Cuisenaire rods: this time, it was the brightest students who benefited, normal and below average children being no different from controls.

Possibly a distinction can be drawn between analogical material, such as the Cuisenaire rods, and abstractive materials such as the MAB when used appropriately. The first materials map directly, the second are intended to be mediated by higher-order constructs. Another difference, which is the complement of the first and is probably even more crucial, is that the Cuisenaire rods mimic the symbolic number system fairly directly; it was even originally suggested that 6-year-olds were doing 'algebra' when modelling '1 + 2 = 3' as 'white plus red becomes green', and writing the 'equation' as '$w + r = g$' (Cuisenaire and Gattegno 1957)! Dienes blocks, on the other hand, require a great deal of preliminary hands-on activity, using not only the blocks, but beans and cups, tree diagrams, and other enactive and ikonic materials: very much a bottom-up approach in fact.

However, Halford and Boulton-Lewis say they are more interested in showing how structure mapping can improve our understanding of how children form mathematical (and possibly other) abstractions and generalizations than in prescribing instructional methods. In this they are successful, but I would make two points:

1 the mapping model provides a neat top-down construction of the process, but, in the nature of the case, misses the bottom-up component;

2 what is needed is an intervention study to test instructional derivations from the theory, in particular to discover when mapping by analogy does work and when it does not. As they say, the evidence is conflicting here.

Resnick, Bill, and Lesgold provide an illuminating foil to Halford and Boulton-Lewis, in that theirs is a bottom-up approach to much the same problem, the early teaching of number. Their theoretical starting point is in sharp contrast to almost all other contributors except Valsiner, and possibly Bidell and Fischer: no general processes or abilities or other competencies-in-the-head, so that children can learn through cultural exchange in a rich context. This is evidently the embodiment of a situated theory. Children in their everyday context form, in the case of maths, protoquantitative schemata (PQSs), which it is the task of school to massage into the concrete-symbolic mode. Six principles underlie their work:

1 Children's out-of-school maths-related activities and knowledge are used in class.
2 Children are encouraged to trust their own knowledge. Naive theories are not to be treated as pathologies.
3 Concrete-symbolic conventions and notation are to be used from scratch.
4 PQSs are to be regularized by linking with accepted schemata, as opportunity dictates, not as logical sequencing would suggest.
5 Encourage children to find problems out there.
6 Talk mathematics, don't do algorithms.

The results of this programme are hugely encouraging, especially given what many would regard as unpromising, unmotivated students. I would, however, hesitate to call this a victory for situated cognition as such. Clearly the context is crucial, but so too are the other elements: the PQSs-in-the-student's-head and the accepted or regular schemata-in-the-teacher's-head. In other words, there is a marriage here between top-down and bottom-up, and between in-school and out-of-school. Their technique seems to me to illustrate very clearly both a theory of schooling and a theory of development, each of which contains general and specific components. Thus, learning in school is best done in a situated context, but the targets of learning are the different forms of knowledge, including declarative. You simply just don't start with the latter. Problem-based learning, used highly successfully in professional preparation (Boud 1985), is an adult version of the same technique.

Development, for its part, is realized in content-specific tasks, but using ways of representing those tasks that are both age-typical and cumulate over age. You don't fight those ways of representing a task or a problem that are typical of an age earlier than you as a teacher would like them to be; you go with the flow.

Another study, from a totally different conceptual stable, that addresses getting over the ikonic/concrete-symbolic hump, is that by Schneider and

Näslund of reading, the concrete-symbolic activity *par excellence*. Despite the centrality of a competencies-in-the-head theory, their analysis and conclusions are both similar to and different from Resnick *et al.*'s. They are similar in that they take what might be regarded as 'protosymbolic schemata' such as sign knowledge and name writing; they are different in also taking in conventional measures of intelligence, phonological awareness, and recoding, to predict later spelling and comprehension performance. They are also different from Resnick in that they did not focus on instructional processes that might lead to more efficient acquisition of reading skill; indeed, their methodology is to hold the instructional environment constant, and see what individual difference factors might help us understand the acquisition of reading, thereby implicating a central role for working memory, along with Case and Halford. Resnick *et al.*, on the other hand, hold individual factors constant (as it were: I doubt they would see it this way) and see what instructional factors help us understand the acquisition of mathematical skill.

REMAINING ISSUES AND CONCLUSIONS

There are obvious unresolved issues here, both theoretical and practical:

1 Does competent performance develop on a broad or a narrow, topic-specific front?
2 Should we be looking at context-dependent or context-general theories of learning and knowing?
3 Should instruction be driven top-down by 'correct' formulations of what is to be learned (direct) or driven bottom-up by learners' misconceptions (indirect)?

The three questions oversimplify and overlap, as do their answers. (1) and (2) imply each other, but are distinct in the literature. Divergence exists here on (1); it depends on how broad is 'broad'. Our broadest is Case's CCS, or possibly a Halford mapping; our narrowest, the individual 'semiotically coded forms of internal senses' suggested by Valsiner. If I were to referee a fight on this, I think I would have to award most points, both in terms of evidence and of seeming consensus, to a narrowish front, conscious that in so doing I'd be refusing to be intimidated by a creaking *structure d'ensemble*. But fortunately there isn't a fight, and I'm not refereeing it.

The intervention studies in Part II should have contributed to this more than, in the event, they did. Again, the question became how near is 'near' and how far is 'far' when we talk about transfer. Certainly Efklides *et al.*, Csapó, and Pozo and Carretero's central conceptual core in some mechanics topics suggest something more than a totally task-specific position would advocate. The trouble is, of course, that each of us works within our own framework, with our methodology, and with different tasks, so that, when

Goossens meta-analyses the answer, what he comes up with is 'fruit': yes, we do get nice overall effect sizes, but no, we can't discriminate the apples of direct instruction from the oranges of self-directed learning.

On the question of curriculum, what to teach and how to organize the content into psychologically appropriate sequences, there seemed a lot of promise and some delivery. Case, Bidell and Fischer, and Biggs referred to the need for structuring curriculum objectives in terms of theory, and Efklides, Demetriou, and Gustafsson actually went further, using Fischer's analysis for their intervention. Clearly much more work is needed here.

Contextuality appears to be a source of divergence, but I wonder if it is. The evidence now seems overwhelming that people learn what is in their casually experienced context much more easily than disembedded content. Accordingly, it is socially redundant to teach such content; what you do need to teach is socially valued content that students don't learn spontaneously. But that does not mean, as so many educators seem to have concluded, that you teach disembedded content in depersonalized ways. The lesson from Resnick *et al.*'s study is that you take the embedded content the students already know and, over the long haul, sensitively disembed that with the tools of the discipline in a highly personal, co-operative culture. What we don't know is how this approach would work in other schools, with other students, other teachers, and in other subjects.

A final issue is very practical: the mode of instruction. Traditionally, instruction has been direct and top-down. The teacher sets the content and the students have to assimilate that as accurately as possible. Everyone here who has addressed that issue comes out on the side of determining the curriculum in terms of how the students might best encode it. Nevertheless, there is a discernible difference between those who would advocate a direct instructional paradigm and those who favour a student-led, indirect approach to instruction. The dichotomy is expressed by several, perhaps most forcibly by Valsiner and Resnick, and is itself a child of questions (1) and (2) above. Do we accept that there is (essentially) one or few paths of development, followed by all, or do we situate development in a context of relativities?

Thus, at the one end Halford and Boulton-Lewis take a powerful paradigm, structure mapping, and use that to explore mathematics learning, and to take instruction from there. At the other end, Resnick *et al.* take some messy PQSs their students thought they had smuggled into the classroom, and use them to explore mathematics learning, and to take instruction from there.

A multistructural solution is to have it both ways. The imposition of higher-order modes of representing learning can be helpful to the teacher and researcher, and ultimately represents the target for the learner. But that is down the track. Recognizing that students will have encoded their experience in lower-order, including presymbolic, modes is important if they are to be met and taken further along the trail. It seems likely to me that the problems of schooling have arisen out of failing to make that recognition; instead, they have used pure concrete-symbolic confrontation.

That contextuality, context specificity, and constructivity of learning are what, to me, emerge from neo-Piagetian theory to be taken to school. Developmental psychology no longer prescribes *structures d'ensemble* for all. It is not only different stages at different ages, which it always was: it may well be different rules in different schools; and, according to the developmental web, you get there using different modes on different roads. A significant difference from the old days.

REFERENCES

Argyris, C. (1976) 'Theories of action that inhibit individual learning', *American Psychologist* 31: 638–54.

Biggs, J. B. (1967) *Mathematics and the Conditions of Learning*, London: National Foundation for Educational Research.

—— (1976) 'Educology: the theory of educational practice', *Contemporary Educational Psychology* 1: 274–88.

Bloom, B. S. (1971) 'Affective consequences', in J. H. Block (ed.) *Mastery Learning*, New York: Holt, Rinehart & Winston.

Boud, D. (ed.) (1985) *Problem-Based Learning in Education for the Professions*, Sydney: Higher Education Research and Development Society for Australasia.

Brown, A., Bransford, S., Ferrara, R., and Campione, J. (1983) 'Learning, remembering and understanding', in P. H. Mussen (ed.) *Handbook of Child Psychology* (4th edition), Vol. 3, *Cognitive Development*, New York: Wiley.

Brown, J. S., Collins, A., and Duguid, P. (1989) 'Situated cognition and the culture of learning', *Educational Researcher* 18 (1): 32–41.

Bruner, J. S. (1964) 'Some theorems on instruction illustrated with reference to mathematics', in E. R. Hilgard (ed.) *Theories of Learning and Instruction*, 63rd Yearbook of the National Society for the Study of Education, Chicago: University of Chicago Press.

Case, R. (1988) 'Neo-Piagetian theories and educational practice', in A. Demetriou (ed.) *The Neo-Piagetian Theories of Cognitive Development: Toward an Integration*, Amsterdam: Elsevier, pp. 267–86.

Case, R. and Griffin, S. (1990) 'Child cognitive development: the role of central conceptual structure in the development of scientific and social thought', in C. Hauert (ed.) *Advances in Psychology: Developmental Psychology*, North Holland: Elsevier.

Crooks, T. J. (1988) 'The impact of classroom evaluation practices on students', *Review of Educational Research* 58: 438–81.

Cuisenaire, G. and Gattegno, C. (1957) *Numbers in Colour*, London: Heinemann.

Demetriou, A. (ed.) (1988) *The Neo-Piagetian Theories of Cognitive Development: Toward an Integration*, North Holland: Elsevier.

Desforges, C. and McNamara, D. (1977) 'One man's heuristic is another man's blindfold: some comments applying social science to educational practice', *British Journal of Teacher Education* 3: 27–39.

Dienes, Z. P. (1963) *An Experimental Study of Mathematics Learning*, London: Hutchinson.

Driver, R. (1983) *The Pupil as Scientist*, Milton Keynes: Open University Press.
Fischer, K. (1980) 'A theory of cognitive development: the control and construction of hierarchies of skills', *Psychological Review* 57: 477–531.
Fischer, K. and Bullock, D. (1984) 'Cognitive development in school-age children: conclusions and new directions', in W. Collins (ed.) *Development during Middle Childhood: The Years from Six to Twelve*, Washington, DC: National Academy of Sciences Press.
Gagne, R. M. (1968) 'Contributions of learning to human development', *Psychological Review* 75: 177–91.
Goodnow, J. J. (1991) 'Cognitive values and educational practice', in J. Biggs (ed.) *Teaching for Learning*, Hawthorn, Vic.: Australian Council for Educational Research.
McKeachie, W. J., Pintrich, P., Lin, Y-G., and Smith, D. (1986) *Teaching and Learning in the College Classroom*, University of Michigan: NCRIPTAL.
McKenzie, A. and White, R. T. (1982) 'Fieldwork in geography and long-term memory structures', *American Educational Research Journal* 19: 623–32.
Newble, D. and Clarke, R. M. (1986) 'The approaches to learning of students in a traditional and in an innovative problem-based medical school', *Medical Education* 20: 267–73.
Perkins, D. N. and Salomon, G. (1989) 'Are cognitive skills context-bound?', *Educational Researcher* 18 (1): 16–25.
Reid, W. A. (1987) 'Institutions and practices: professional education reports and the language of reform', *Educational Researcher* 16 (8): 10–15.
Resnick, L. B. (1987) 'Learning in school and out', *Educational Researcher* 16 (9): 13–20.
Snow, R. E. (1974) 'Representative and quasi-representative designs for research on teaching', *Review of Educational Research* 44: 265–91.
Sternberg, R. J. and Wagner, R. K. (eds) (1986) *Practical Intelligence*, Cambridge: Cambridge University Press.
Wood, D., Bruner, J. S., and Ross, G. (1976) 'The role of tutoring and problem solving', *Journal of Child Psychology and Psychiatry* 17: 89–100.

Name index

Adey, P.S. 107, 111, 113, 116, 145, 160, 232
Allen, J.B. 36
Altanucci, J. 13
Argyris, C. 278

Baddeley, A. 258
Baillargeon, R. 20
Bain, J.D. 185, 187, 188, 190
Baldwin, J.M. 52, 66
Bangert-Drowns, R.L. 168, 176
Beasley, F. 118, 155
Bednarz, N. 185
Behr, M. 185
Belanger, M. 185
Bidell, T. 3, 11–29, 40, 83, 144, 161, 212, 252, 254, 277–92 passim
Biggs, J. 3, 6, 20, 31–49, 53, 199, 277–93
Bill, V. 5, 32, 210–29, 277, 281, 290
Bjorck-Akesson, E. 92, 129
Blagg, N. 113
Blennerhassett, A. 262, 266
Bloom, B.S. 279
Borke, H. 34
Boud, D. 44, 280, 290
Boulton-Lewis, G. 5, 183–208, 281, 282, 283, 284, 289, 290, 292
Bradley, P. 258, 259, 260, 271
Brainerd, C.J. 52
Broadbent, D.E. 188
Brown, A. 233, 277, 278, 280
Brown, J.S. 32, 228
Brügelmann, H. 262
Bruner, J.S. 25, 33, 35, 36, 44, 45, 46, 280
Bryant, L. 258, 259, 260, 271
Bukovsky, V. 71
Bullock, D. 18, 20, 34, 40, 280

Butler, S.R. 259, 272

Canfield, R.L. 53
Carey, S. 13, 53, 62, 187, 251, 253
Carpenter, T.P. 217
Carretero, M. 5, 231–54, 280, 286, 288, 291
Case, R. 3, 13, 20, 34, 35, 40, 52–63, 83, 122, 145, 161, 167, 233, 253, 262, 277–92 passim
Cattell, R.B. 91
Ceci, S.J. 41
Charbonneau, M.P. 12
Cheng, P.W. 199
Chi, M.T.H. 46, 53, 62, 234
Chipman, S. 40
Chomsky, N. 14, 53
Clark, A. 199
Clark, E. 214
Clarke, R.M. 280
Claxton, G. 232
Cochran, K.F. 271
Cohen, J. 169, 170
Cole, M. 24
Collings, J. 110
Collins, A. 32, 228, 277
Collis, K. 20, 34, 35, 37, 38, 42, 44, 45, 47, 53, 145, 192
Commons, M.C. 38
Cormier, S.M. 122
Craft, A. 113
Cronbach, L. 118
Crooks, T.J. 279
Csapó, B. 4–5, 144–58, 173, 278, 285, 286, 291
Csirikné, E. 145
Cuisenaire, G. 289
Cunningham, A.E. 271

Name index

Daneman, M. 262, 266
Davey, H.A. 47
De Bono, E. 113
De Carcer, I.A. 164
De Corte, E. 122, 217
DeLoache, J.S. 233
Delpit, L.D. 16
Demetriou, A. 2, 4, 14, 34, 37, 40, 61, 79–102, 117, 122–42, 144, 162, 210, 277–92 passim
Dennis, S. 55, 62
Desforges, C. 33, 281
Detweiler, M. 188
DeVries, R. 12
Dienes, Z.P. 46, 190, 194, 205, 280
Dodds, A.E. 37
Donaldson, M. 31, 34, 37
Driver, R. 41, 231, 232, 280, 288
Duckworth, E. 12, 16
Dufour-Janvier, B. 185
Duguid, P. 32, 277
Duncan, Isadora 36, 43

Edwards, C.P. 13
Efklides, A. 4, 34, 37, 79–102, 117, 122–42, 144, 160, 161, 162, 163, 174, 175, 210, 278, 282, 285, 286, 291, 292
Egan, K. 36, 45, 49
Eggert, D. 263
Ekstrom, R.B. 92, 128
Elbers, E. 67
Elkind, D. 110
Embretson, S.E. 118
Entwhistle, N.J. 148
Ericsson, K.A. 72
Erikson, E. 37
Ewers, C.A. 271

Falkner, F. 107
Farrar, M.J. 17, 18, 26, 123, 142
Feeman, D.J. 271
Feldman, D. 13
Ferguson, G.A. 141
Feuerstein, R. 114, 115, 117, 118
Fischer, K.W. 3, 11–29, 34, 35, 40, 53, 83, 122, 123, 127, 136, 140, 142, 144, 161–2, 212, 252, 254, 277–92 passim
Fishbein, E. 145, 150
Fishbein, H.D. 66
Fisher, D.L. 188
Fitts, P. 43
Flavell, J.H. 52, 176, 232

Fodor, J. 14
Ford, W. 25
French, J.W. 92
Freyberg, P. 231
Froufe, J. 117
Furby, L. 118
Furth, H.G. 1, 15
Fuson, K.C. 216

Gabel, D.L. 164
Gagne, R.M. 62, 288
Gallistel, C.R. 20, 25, 216
Garcia, R. 232, 234, 239
Gardner, H. xii, 13, 14, 36, 37, 42, 53
Gattegno, C. 289
Gelman, R. 20, 25, 52, 53, 216
Gentner, D. 184, 185, 192, 193, 233
Gilligan, C. 13
Glaser, R. 40, 46, 211, 234
Glass, G.V. 169
Goldberg, J. 262
Goldstein, K. 68
Gollin, E. 66
Good, R. 118
Goodnow, J.J. 287
Goossens, L. 5, 152, 155, 160–78, 278, 285, 286, 292
Gottlieb, G. 66
Goudena, P.P. 67
Greeno, J.G. 214, 215, 217, 218
Grieve, R. 187
Griffin, P. 24
Griffin, S. 54, 55, 282
Griffiths, A.K. 164
Guesne, E. 231, 232
Guilford, J.P. 91, 124
Gunstone, R.F. 234, 239, 251
Gustafsson, J.E. 4, 79–102, 112–42, 144, 210, 282, 292

Hagman, J.D. 122
Halford, G.S. 5, 20, 40, 53, 122, 161, 183–208, 281–92 passim
Harman, H.H. 92
Harriman, M.L. 259
Hashweh, M.Z. 232, 234
Hatch, T. xii
Haywood, H.C. 113
Hedges, L.V. 163, 169, 175, 176, 256
Heidmets, M. 72
Helm, H. 231
Ho, V. 168

Name index

Holland, J.H. 183, 199, 233
Holyoak, K.J. 183, 199, 201
Hooper, S.R. 256
Horn, J.L. 14, 91
Horn, W. 256
Howe, A.C. 167
Hughes, M. 187
Hunter-Grundin, E. 113
Hunt, J.McV. 41
Hyde, J.S. 111

Illich, I. 32
Inhelder, B. 54, 231, 234, 247
Irwin, K. 216

Jensen, A.R. 119
Jerusalem, M. 148
John-Steiner, V. 12
Johnson-Laird, P.N. 154, 200
Jöreskog, K.G. 129, 259, 265
Juel, C. 272
Jurd, M. 145

Kamii, C. 12
Kargon, R. 234, 251
Karmiloff-Smith, A. 53, 199
Keil, F.C. 53
Kenny, S.L. 21
Kitchener, K.S. 24
Klahr, D. 211
Koh, K. 183
Kohlberg, L. 15, 16
Kotovsky, K. 211
Kozéki, B. 148
Küchemann, D.E. 110, 173
Kuhn, D. 38, 161, 168, 176, 177
Kulik, C.L.C. 168, 175
Kulik, J.A. 168, 175
Kurland, D.M. 262

Lakatos, I. 240, 248, 249
Larivée, S. 164
Larkin, J. 118
Lave, J. 228
Lawrence, J.A. 37
Lawson, A.E. 154, 164
Leary, D.E. 65
Leeuwenberg, E.L.L. 187
Lesgold, S. 5, 32, 210–29, 277, 281, 290
Lesh, R. 185
Levinson, D. 37
Lewin, K. 66, 67

Liebert, D. 145, 167
Liebert, R.M. 145, 167
Liker, J. 41
Lindstrom, B. 92, 129
Linn, M.C. 168
Lipson, M. 33
Lomax, R.G. 262, 272
Longeot, F. 164
Luria, A.R. 68

McClelland, J.L. 187
McCloskey, M. 234, 235, 239, 251, 252
McDermott, L.C. 234, 251
McGarrigle, J. 187
McGaw, B. 169
McGee, L.M. 262, 272
McKeachie, W.J. 280
MacKenzie, A. 46, 280
Maclean, M. 258, 259
McNally, D.W. 46
MacNamara, D. 33, 281
Mann, V. 266, 271
Marini, Z.A. 54–5, 60
Markman, E.M. 216
Marton, F. 41
Marx, H. 261, 262
Mason, J.M. 36
Masters, G. 46, 49
Maybery, M.T. 185, 187, 188, 190
Mayer, K. 15, 16
Mehl, M. 117
Michie, S. 217
Miedema, S. 67
Mierza, J. 167
Miller, G.A. 187
Miller, T.I. 169
Minzat, I. 145
Moser, J.M. 217
Mullen, B. 165

Nagy, J. 145, 148, 154, 164
Näslund, J.C. 5–6, 256–72, 263, 282, 291
Neisser, U. 45
Nesdale, A.R. 259
Nesher, P. 217
Newble, D. 280
Newell, A. 211, 232
Newman, D. 24
Newman, S.E. 228
Nisbett, R.E. 183

Normandeau, S. 164
Novak, J.D. 231

Oakhill, J. 271
Oerter, R. 72
Olkin, I. 163, 169, 175, 176, 256
Omanson, S.F. 195, 216
Oppenheimer, L. 67
Osborne, R.J. 231

Packard, T. 256
Paivio, A. 43
Palmer, S.E. 185
Pampu, I. 145
Paris, S. 33
Parkin, A. 271
Pascual-Leone, J. 122
Paulhan, F. 74
Pellegrino, J.W. 211
Perfetti, C.A. 259
Perkins, D.M. 117, 285
Phelps, E. 177
Piaget, J. 13, 26, 35–6, 40, 52, 53, 54, 72, 211, 231, 232, 234, 239, 240, 247, 248, 249, 281
Pines, A.L. 231, 232, 234
Pipp, S. 35, 122, 140
Platsidou, M. 79–102, 124, 144
Post, T. 185
Pozo, I. 5, 231–54, 280, 286, 288, 291
Prevez, M. 81

Rainard, B. 118
Ramsden, P. 41, 46
Rand, Y. 115
Rees, E.T. 46, 53, 234
Reid, W.A. 46, 279
Renninger, K.A. 67
Resnick, L.B. 5, 25, 32, 114, 119, 164, 195, 210–29, 277–92 *passim*
Richards, F.A. 38
Riley, M.S. 217
Rogoff, B. 13, 24
Rosenthal, D.A. 168
Ross, G. 280
Rowell, J. 167–8
Rumelhart, D.E. 187
Ryle, G. 31, 32

Salomon, G. 117, 285
Sandieson, R. 55, 62
Saxe, G.B. 12, 13, 217

Scanlon, D.M. 258, 259
Schaie, K.W. 37
Schauble, L. 177
Schneider, W. 5–6, 188, 256–72, 282, 290
Segal, J. 40
Seggie, J.L. 154
Seligman, M.E.P. 31
Selzer, S.C. 256
Shaklee, H. 199
Share, D.L. 259, 262
Shayer, M. 4, 81, 107–19, 145, 153, 155, 160, 173, 232, 278, 285
Shrager, J. 193
Shuell, T.J. xii
Siebert, J. 216
Siegel, R.S. 187
Siegler, R.S. 54, 145, 167, 177, 193, 217
Silvern, L. 34, 35
Simon, D.P. 53
Simon, H. 53, 72, 187, 211, 232
Sipos, K. and M. 148
Skinner, B.F. 26
Skowronek, H. 261, 262
Smith, M. 118
Smith, M.L. 169
Smolensky, P. 199
Smollett, E. 76
Sneider, C. 164
Snow, R.E. 281
Sophian, C. 217
Sörbom, D. 129, 259
Spearman, C. 91
Spelke, E.S. 14, 53
Spielberger, D. 148
Stanovich, K. 271
Staver, J.R. 164
Sternberg, R.J. 14, 32, 211, 277, 278
Stevens, A.L. 233
Strauss, S. 232
Swanson, H.L. 271

Tanner, J.M. 107–9
Thagard, P. 201
Thurstone, L.L. 91, 124
Tiberghien, A. 231, 232
Tizard, J. 119
Torgesen, J.K. 257, 258
Torneus, M. 272
Toulmin, S. 65
Tramontana, M.G. 256
Tulving, E. 45

Tunmer, W.E. 259
Turiel, E. 16

Valsiner, J. 3–4, 40, 65–77, 277–92
 passim
Valtin, R. 272
Van der Veer, R. 67, 68
Van Oers, B. 67
Vellutino, F.R. 258, 259
Vergnaud, G. 217
Vernon, P.E. 91
Verschaffel, L. 217
Vidákovich, T. 149
Volet, S. 37
Vygotsky, L.S. 24, 40, 68, 74

Wachs, H. 15
Wagner, R.K. 32, 257, 258, 259, 277, 278
Wardekker, W. 67
Wasch, H. 1

Watts, M. 234, 239, 251
Weinert, F. xii, 260
Weller, K. 113
Werner, H. 75
West, L.H.T. 231, 232, 234
White, R.T. 46, 280
White, R.W. 41
Whiting, B.B. 13
Wilson, M. 47
Wilson, W.H. 185, 186, 187, 190
Winegar, L.T. 67
Witkin, H.A. 110
Wixson, K. 33
Wolcott, H.F. 76
Wood, D.J. 25, 280
Wylam, H. 110, 173

Yates, J.T. 252
Yuill, N. 271

Subject index

abilities: operational 144–58; primary mental 124; specialized/general 100, 101, 123, 125; structure of 84; thinking 210–29
abstract concepts 75, 99–101, 184, 199–205, 207–8, 289
abstract skills 21–3, 35, 280
academic content and cognitive structures 19–20
achievement: and cognitive structures 84–102; and fluid intelligence 90–5; prediction of 256
actions: internalization of 36; and knowledge 277–8
addition 226
age: and cognitive conflict 248–51; and combinative abilities 156, 285; and curriculum design 79, 290; and forms of thinking 124, 140; and inference 248; and logical abilities 156, 285; and mathematical thinking 95; and organismic constraints 40, 41, 53, 59; and processing loads 187, 188; and scientific thinking 172–4, 241–51, 253, 286; and specialization 100, 101; and stages of development 34, 79, 290; and systematizing abilities 156, 285; and training 122, 123, 125, 130–42, 152–8, 174, 285–6; and understanding 57, 58, 251
alienation 16, 27
alternative developmental pathways 27–8, 283–4
alternative frameworks of knowledge/naive theories 41, 62, 280, 286, 288, 290
analogues in teaching mathematics 183–208, 290
apprenticeship, cognitive 164, 228

argument and discussion 221, 227, 290
arithmetic 12, 17, 21–2, 25–62, 210–29, 282; counting 216–18, 226, 282, 290; *see also* mathematical thinking
arts 43, 83
assessment *see* evaluation
asynchrony in development 57, 60
atomism 29n

behaviourist models of transfer 26
Bielefeld Longitudinal Study on Early Risk Identification 261, 262, 264, 265
bottom up learning 44, 284, 288, 289, 290, 291, 292
bounded indeterminacy 76–7
bridging 117–18

California Achievement Test (CAT) 222–3
categorization *see* classification
causal-experimental (CE) *see* specialized structural systems (SSSs)
causal ideas 246
causal modelling 259–60
central conceptual structures (CCS) 54–63, 282, 283, 286, 291
child–school interactions 76–7
chunking 187–90, 204; *see also* decomposition of problems
class *see* sociocultural; socioeconomic
classification 75, 83, 128
classroom learning 33, 281
co-construction of knowledge 68–77, 283
cognitive abilities 11, 122, 161
cognitive acceleration 122, 187, 285
Cognitive Acceleration through Science Education (CASE) 111, 145, 160

Subject index 301

cognitive apprenticeship 164, 228
cognitive change 284–7; and
  instruction 122–42, 162–3, 232
cognitive competence 14, 79, 210, 291
cognitive conflict 167–8, 234, 240,
  248–51, 252–3
cognitive level and training 136–9
cognitive-metacognitive (COMET)
  consistency 96–7
cognitive performance 40–4
cognitive representations 183–208
cognitive skills 11
cognitive structures: and academic
  content 19–20; and achievement
  84–102; and context-embedded
  activity 28; and intervention research
  161, 162; and learning 15–16, 19–20;
  local 162, 164, 165, 174–5; of
  sciences 83; and training 174–5
collaboration 25, 280
collective cognitive constructions 99
combinative abilities 152–4, 156, 285
Combinative Operations Test 148
competence, cognitive 14, 79, 210, 291
complexity of tasks 125
conceptual change 253
conceptual chunking 187–90, 204; see
  also decomposition
conceptual knowledge 202, 280
concrete representations 18, 21, 183,
  185, 190–9, 205, 206–7
concrete-symbolic representations
  36–7, 42, 290, 291
conditional-genetic investigations 67
conditional knowledge 33, 42, 43
confidence in mathematics 226
conflict, cognitive 167–8, 234, 240,
  248–51, 252–3
constraint systems 65–77
constructive externalization 72–3
constructive generalization 18, 26–8
constructivism 11–13, 231
content: and context 277–9, 280, 283,
  290; disembedded 32, 37, 99–100,
  278, 292; encoding of 45
context: and content 277–9, 280, 283,
  290; of development 65–77, 175, 210,
  212, 232, 291, 292–3; and evaluation
  20–1, 279; of knowledge 12, 228,
  252, 283; of schooling 76–7, 277–9,
  281; see also interactions;
  sociocultural context

context-embedded skills 11–29, 284
context-neutral views of cognition
  11–17
control of variables strategy 167, 247,
  248
convergent development 27–8
correspondence: between abstractions
  207–8; between structures 183,
  199–200, 202–3, 207–8
CORT 113
counting 216–18, 226, 282, 290; see also
  arithmetic
creativity 12
criterion-referenced performance 44
cross-modal learning 38–9, 40
crystallized intelligence 124
Cuisenaire rods 183, 192–3, 289
cultural see sociocultural
curriculum 287–8; design of 45, 62, 79,
  288, 290; objectives 44–5, 292; spiral
  33

décalages 34, 57, 60, 232
declarative knowledge 32–3, 36, 42, 43,
  183, 277, 280, 290
decomposition of problems 45, 195,
  196, 204; chunking 187–90, 204
decontextualization 228
deschooling 32
Deterministic State Model (DSM) 34,
  65–6
development: curves 107–9, 111;
  linearity of 66–7
developmental ladder 27–8, 284
developmental levels 125, 194
developmental pathways 12–13, 283–4;
  alternative 27–8, 283–4
developmental range 23–6, 27
developmental relations 23
developmental sequences 20, 23
developmental web 27–8, 283–4
Dienes blocks 192, 194–5, 204–5, 289
differences, individual 122–42, 210,
  211, 212, 285, 287
discussion 221, 227, 290
disembedded content 32, 37, 99–100,
  278, 292
distributed processing 187–8
divergent development 27–8
domain-free factors 124
domain-general hardware (DGH) 82–3,
  85, 125

Subject index

domain-general software (DGS) 82–3, 95, 124
domain specificity 13–14, 59, 80, 83, 85, 101–2, 123, 253, 282
domains: of intelligence 14–15, 53, 54; of knowledge 13–14, 100, 232; of reality 80
duration of training 168–78, 227

early literacy 262, 265–71
education 281
effect sizes 110–11, 161, 165, 166, 170–8, 286, 292
effectiveness of training 134–6, 163, 167–78
element mappings 185, 188, 189
embodiment, multiple 205–6
encoding of content 45
enrichment 157
environment *see* context
equilibration 164, 240
ethnicity *see* sociocultural; socioeconomic
evaluation 46–8, 49, 279, 287; and context 20–1, 279
everyday problem finding 220–1, 226–7, 290
experiential knowledge: and abstractions 199
experiential structures 122, 123–42, 161, 162
experiment design 107–19
expert systems 233
expert/novice paradigm 53, 233, 234, 243, 244, 245, 246, 250, 251, 253, 254, 286
externalization: of constraints 65–77; constructive 72–3; of internal knowledge 72; and internalization 65–77

far-far (non-specific) transfer 167, 285, 286
Feuerstein Instrumental Enrichment 113, 117
figure classification test 128
fluid intelligence (Gf) 90–5, 100, 124, 125, 128–33, 140–1, 156, 157
formal language 31, 218
formal thinking 37, 43, 280
forms of knowledge 31–49, 278
forms of thinking 36–8, 124, 140

functional level 24–5
functionalism 61

gender and cognitive change 136, 285
general problem solvers 232–3
general problem approaches 59, 61, 68
generalizability of models 111–15, 281
generalization 18, 75, 162, 199, 259, 282, 289; constructive 18, 26–8; and prior competence 40; and training 122–3, 139, 142; *see also* transfer
genetic views of development 67
Gf *see* fluid intelligence

Hannover-Weschler Test (HAWIVA) 263
hardware of cognitive system 82–3, 85, 123, 124
Headstart Project 62–3, 110
hidden figures test 128–9
hierarchical models of intelligence 91
history teaching 145
homework 220–1, 226–7, 290
hypothesis tests 166

ikonic learning 36, 291
imaginal-spatial specialized structural systems (SSSs) 80–1, 83, 95, 98, 102
implicit theories 252
Indeterminate Constraints Model (ICM) 66–8
individual cognitive constructions 99
individual differences 122–42, 210, 211, 212, 285, 287
individual learning 12, 279, 287
inference 248, 252
informal knowledge 218
informal language 31
information processing 211; capacity 187–8, 271, 284; loads 185, 186–7, 188, 189–90, 192, 198–9, 203–4, 289; parallel 187–8, 198, 203, 207; and reading skills 257; serial 188; *see also* working memory
inheritability of intelligence 119
instruction 62, 284, 287, 288–91, 292; and cognitive change 122–42, 162–3, 232; and intervention 118–19; modes of 292–3; and structure-mapping 206, 207; and transfer 60–1; *see also* training
instrumental enrichment (IE) 113,

Subject index

115–18
intelligence: domains of 14–15, 53, 54; fluid (Gf) 90–5, 124, 125, 128–31, 141, 257; inheritability of 119; models of 91; psychometric 14–15; and training 156; verbal 263, 264, 265–71
interactions 23–6, 65–77, 287; child–school 76–7; peers 16, 280; teacher–pupil 16, 279; *see also* context
internalization: of actions 36; of constraints 65–77; and externalization 65–77
intervention 107–19, 122–42, 144–58, 160–78, 285, 291; and instruction 118–19; and normative data 107–10, 285
intervention fallacy 176–7
intra-modal learning 38, 40, 41–2, 48
intra-organismic processes 67–8
intra-personal/interpersonal processes 67–8, 79
intuitive knowledge 32–3, 214–18, 227, 231–2
IQ tests 110

knowing-how/knowing-that 31–2, 33
knowledge: acquisition of 17; and action 277–8; alternative frameworks of 41, 62, 280, 286, 288, 290; co-construction of 68–77, 283; conceptual 202, 280; conditional 33, 42, 43; construction of 12, 13, 16, 68, 278; context of 12, 228, 252, 283; declarative 32–3, 36, 42, 43, 183, 277, 280, 290; domains of *see* domain; experiential, and abstractions 199; forms of 31–49, 278; informal 218; intuitive 32–3, 214–18, 227, 231–2; metatheoretical 33; naive theories 41, 62, 280, 286, 288, 290; organisation of 12, 13–14, 15, 16; prior 40, 41, 116, 122, 214, 218, 252–3; procedural 33, 183, 202, 280; and schooling 31–2, 277; sociocultural context of 12, 13–14; tacit 32–3; theoretical 33

language 31; formal 31, 218; informal 31; written 37
latent variable causal modelling 259–60
learning: bottom-up 44, 284, 288, 289, 290, 291, 292; in classroom 33, 290; and cognitive structures 15–16, 19–20; cross-modal 38–9, 40; ikonic 36, 291; individual 12, 279, 287; intramodal 38, 40, 41–2, 48; mechanisms of 183; modes of 31–49; multimodal 38–9, 40, 42–4, 45–6, 48; optimally complex 34, 42; practice-based 43–4; and schools 38–49, 277–93; sensori-motor 35–6, 41, 42–3; sociocultural context of 62–3, 212–13, 228–9, 281; top-down 42–4, 289, 291, 292
learning cycles 38, 39–40
Learning Potential Assessment (LPA) 118
letter naming 262, 264, 265
letter sets test 128
levels, theory of 125, 194
lexical access 258, 259, 261, 264, 268, 269, 270
linearity of development 66–7
LISREL 129, 259, 265–70, 271, 272
listening span 262
literacy, early 262, 265–71
local cognitive structures 162, 164, 165, 174–5
logical abilities 152–4, 155, 156, 285
Logical Operations Test 149
logo task 262–3, 264, 265
longitudinal studies of achievement 85–90, 124, 256–72
Longitudinal Study of the Genesis of Individual Competencies (LOGIC) 260

magnitude of effect 110–11, 161, 165, 166, 170–8, 286, 292
mapping between structures 184–208, 281, 282, 283, 284, 289, 290, 291, 292
mathematical thinking 52–63, 95, 102, 145, 182–208, 213–18, 289–90; *see also* arithmetic
maturity, physical 40, 41, 53, 59; *see also* age
meaning and sense 74
mechanisms of cognitive development 175–8
memory *see* information processing; working memory
meta-analysis 160, 165–78, 256–7, 286
metacognition 38, 96–8, 123, 124, 284–5

metacognitive-metacognitive (METMET) consistency 96–7, 98
metalinguistic predictors of reading 258–9, 271
metatheoretical knowledge 33
Metropolitan Readiness Test 222
microgenic analysis 177, 178
mind, modularity of 53, 54, 61
misconceptions approach 232, 233, 234, 239, 286
models: causal 259–60; generalizability of 111–15, 281; of intelligence 91; testing of 111–19
modes: of learning 31–49; of representation 35–8
modularity of mind 53, 54, 61
motivation 279
motor learning 35–6, 41, 42–3
multibase (Dienes) arithmetic blocks 192, 194–5, 204–5, 289
multimodal learning 38–9, 40, 42–4, 45–6, 48
multiple embodiment 205–6
multiple system mappings 186, 188, 189, 194
Munich Longitudinal Study of Genesis of Individual Competencies (LOGIC) 260
mythic stage 36

naive theories 41, 62, 280, 286, 288, 290
name writing 263
near-near/near-far transfer 167, 169–78, 285, 286
neo-structuralism 61, 282
non-specific (far-far) transfer 167, 285, 286
norm-referenced data and normative data 110
normative data: and intervention 107–10, 285; and norm-referenced data 110
novelty of tasks 125, 167
novice/expert paradigm 53, 233, 234, 243, 244, 245, 246, 250, 251, 253, 254, 286
number *see* counting
number domain 54–7, 60
number series test 129

oddity *see* phonological oddity, sound oddity

open-ended internalization 68–72
open systems approaches 68
operational abilities 144–58
optimal development 40–1
optimal level 24–5, 35
optimally complex learning 34, 42
organismic constraints and age 40, 41, 53, 59

parallel processing 187–8, 198, 203, 207
pathways *see* developmental pathways
pedagogy *see* instruction
peer interactions 16, 280
performing arts 43
phenotypic analysis of development 66
phonological awareness 257–8, 259, 260–1, 264, 268, 269–70
phonological oddity 260–1, 264, 265
phonological processing 257–72
phonological recoding 258, 259, 261–2, 264, 269
physical maturity 40, 41, 53, 59; *see also* age
physics teaching 231–54
post-tests 115–17
postformal thinking 37–8
practice and theory 43
practice-based learning 43–4
pragmatism 199
pre-test/post-test design 115–17
prediction of achievement 256
predictors of reading 257–69, 270–2
primary mental abilities *see* abilities
primary effects studies 114–15
prior competence/knowledge 40, 41, 116, 122, 214, 218, 252–3; *see also* transfer
problem finding 220–1, 290
problem solving 40–1, 211, 232–3, 280, 290; shared 279
problems: decomposition of 45, 187–90, 195, 196, 204; segmentation of 188–90
procedural knowledge 33, 183, 202, 280
processing *see* information processing
professional training 43–4
professionalism 43
proportional reasoning 164, 170
propositional-verbal *see* specialized structural systems (SSSs)
protoquantitative schemata (PQS) 214–16, 217–18, 288, 290, 292

prototypical examples 202–3
prototypical representations 74, 75, 291
psychometric intelligence 14–15
psychometric testing 109–10

qualitative-analytic *see* specialized structural systems (SSSs)
quantitative reasoning 214–21
quantitative-relational (QR) specialized structural systems (SSSs) 80–1, 83, 93, 94, 95, 98, 100, 123, 126, 127–8, 129–42, 285

race *see* sociocultural; socioeconomic
readiness 15–16, 28
reading 256–72, 291
reading comprehension 263, 266–9, 270–2
reality, domains of 80
reasoning 232, 234, 240, 246–8; and age 172–4, 241–51, 253, 286; proportional 164, 170; protoquantitative 214–16, 217–18, 288, 290, 292; scientific 52–63, 83, 160–78
recoding 199; phonological 258, 259, 261–2, 268, 270
relational levels 40
relational mappings 185, 188, 189, 193
replication studies 113
representation: cognitive 183–208; concrete 18, 21, 183, 185, 190–9, 205, 206–7; concrete-symbolic 36–7, 42, 290, 291; modes of 35–8; prototypical 74, 75, 291; of variables 199, 200–1, 203
reschooling 32
retention of training effects 167–78
rhyming 260–1, 264, 265

scaffolding 16, 25–6, 27, 280, 284
schools: environment of 76–7, 277–9, 281; and knowledge 31–2, 277; and learning 38–49, 277–93; structure of 279
science: and structural systems 79–102; teaching 231–54, 280
scientific thinking 52–63, 83, 160–78; and age 172–4, 241–51, 253, 286
segmentation of problems 188–90
selective mapping 184
self-directedness/discovery 164–5, 167, 168–78, 292

self-monitoring 101
sense and meaning 74
sensori-motor learning 35–6, 41, 42–3
sentence span 262, 264, 265, 271
serial processing 188
shared problem solving 279
sign knowledge 262–3, 264, 265
signs 74–5; *see also* symbols
skill theory 17–29, 122, 282, 283
skills: acquisition of 35; context-embedded 17–29, 284
skills approaches and skill theory 28–9n
social control 68
social interactions *see* interactions
social others 68–72
social support 24–6, 40, 41, 60, 284, 288
sociocultural context: of development 15, 16–17, 21–3, 27–8, 65–77, 283–4; of knowledge 12, 13–14; of learning 62–3, 212–13, 228–9, 281; *see also* context
socioeconomic status (SES) 62–3, 136, 174, 227
SOLO taxonomy 38–49, 283
sound oddity 260–1, 264, 265
sound-to-word matching 261, 264, 265
spatial-imaginal *see* specialized structural systems (SSSs)
specialized abilities *see* abilities
specialized structural systems (SSSs) 79–102, 123–42, 161–2, 282, 285; causal-experimental (CE) 80–1, 83, 86–90, 93, 94, 95, 98, 100, 101, 123, 126, 128, 129–42, 174, 285; qualitative-analytic 80–1, 83, 86–90; quantitative-relational (QR) 80–1, 83, 93, 94, 95, 98, 100, 123, 126, 127–8, 129–42, 285; spatial-imaginal 80–1, 83, 95, 98, 102; verbal-propositional 80–1, 83, 86–90, 95, 98
spelling 263, 265–6, 269–72, 291
spiral curriculum 33
stages of development 11–13, 14, 26, 33, 34–5, 40–4, 52–4, 59, 65–6, 211–12, 231–3, 283–4; and age 34, 79, 290
statistical techniques 168–9, 175, 176
story form 45
story problems 217–18
structural correspondence 183, 199–200, 202–3, 207–8
structuralism 11–13, 52–4, 57–61, 211–12, 231–2, 233

structure mapping 184–208, 281, 282, 283, 284, 289, 290, 291, 292
structure of the whole 57–60, 175
study effect meta-analysis (SEM) 168, 176
suboptimal performance 41
subtraction 195, 197, 198, 226
support, social 24–6, 40, 41, 60, 284, 288
syllable segmentation 261, 265
symbolic systems 81
symbols 31, 32, 36–7, 183, 283; *see also* signs
system mappings 185–6, 188, 189, 194
systematizing abilities 152–4, 155, 156, 285
Systematizing Operations Test 148
systems approaches 59, 61, 68

tacit knowledge 32–3
talking about mathematics 221, 290
Tanner curves 107–9, 111
task-specificity 56–7, 60
tasks: analysis 20; complexity 125; novelty 125, 167
taxonomy *see* classification
teachers: interactions with pupils 16, 279; training 113
teaching 227–8
testing of models 111–19
text comprehension 263, 264
theoretical knowledge 33
theory and practice 43
thinking: abilities 210–29; formal 37, 43, 280; forms of 36–8, 124, 140; postformal 37–8
thinking aloud 72
Thurstone Primary Mental Abilities Test 115–16
time-dependent effects 67, 85–90, 285
top-down instruction 42–4, 289, 291, 292
training: and age 122, 123, 125, 130–42, 152–8, 174, 285–6; and cognitive change 122–42, 162–3, 232; and cognitive level 136–9; and cognitive structures 174–5; duration of 168–78, 227; effectiveness of 134–6, 163, 167–78; and generalization 122–3, 139, 142; and intelligence 156; materials 168–78; and operational abilities 152–8; professional 43–4; retention of effects 167–78; and scientific reasoning 160–78; of teachers 113; *see also* instruction
training programme differences 164
training study fallacy 176–7
transfer 122, 278, 282, 285, 286, 291; behaviourist models of 26; and bridging 117–18; far-far 167, 285, 286; and instruction 60–1; near-near/near-far 167, 169–78, 285, 286; and training 122–3, 125, 133–4, 139, 141–2, 155, 162, 164, 174; *see also* generalization; prior competence
transformation *see* internalization
trust in own knowledge 218, 290

uncertainty in developmental phenomena 66
understanding 24–5, 57; and age 57, 58, 251
unilinearity of development 66–7
unimodal *see* intramodal

variables: control of 247; representation of 199, 200–1, 203
verbal intelligence 263, 264, 265–71
verbal-propositional *see* specialized structural systems (SSSs)
visualization 124

webs, developmental 27–8, 283–4
Weschler tests 110
word knowledge 263, 264, 265
word span 262, 264, 265, 271
word-to-sound matching 261, 264–5
working memory 40, 188, 271, 284; recoding in 258, 259, 262, 264, 268, 269–70; *see also* information processing
written language 37

zone of proximal development 24, 40, 149